Remediating the 1820s

Edinburgh Critical Studies in Romanticism
Series Editors: Ian Duncan and Penny Fielding

Visit our website at: www.edinburghuniversitypress.com/series/ECSR

Remediating the 1820s

Edited by Jon Mee and
Matthew Sangster

EDINBURGH
University Press

Edinburgh University Press is one of the leading university presses in the UK. We publish academic books and journals in our selected subject areas across the humanities and social sciences, combining cutting-edge scholarship with high editorial and production values to produce academic works of lasting importance. For more information visit our website: edinburghuniversitypress.com

Edinburgh University Press Ltd
The Tun – Holyrood Road
12(2f) Jackson's Entry
Edinburgh EH8 8PJ

Typeset in 10.5/13 Sabon by
Cheshire Typesetting Ltd, Cuddington, Cheshire
and printed and bound in Great Britain

A CIP record for this book is available from the British Library

ISBN 978 1 4744 9327 7 (hardback)
ISBN 978 1 4744 9329 1 (paperback)
ISBN 978 1 4744 9330 7 (epub)

Contents

Figures

Preface

This collection addresses what seemed to us to be a major lacuna in our understanding of nineteenth-century culture. The 1820s is commonly overlooked in literary and cultural studies because it is seen as a barren interregnum between the achievements of Romanticism and the Victorian era proper, or, at best, as a time of transition bridging two major periods of literary production. However, closer examination reveals a fascinating decade of swift social transformation, massive infrastructural development, radical cultural experimentation and pervasive insecurity that triggered both intense nostalgia and anxious, future-focused productivity. Understanding the 1820s is of considerable interest in itself and vital for comprehending how Victorian and Romantic culture emerged in tandem, writing and visioning one another into being.

In order properly to explore both the general trends in 1820s culture and a range of revealing specifics, *Remediating the 1820s* mixes research essays with a series of shorter contributions or 'keywords' that highlight some of the issues that contemporaries took to be the signs of the times. Partly inspired by Raymond Williams's famous project, these keywords provide way markers to aid the reader in journeying through the volume as a whole. The co-authored introduction with which the volume opens provides a map of some major events, trends and debates, starting with Peterloo in 1819 and ending with the opening of the Liverpool to Manchester railway in 1830. The chronology provides further orientation for readers unfamiliar with the decade. Eleven chapters follow, each of which uses a particular case study or studies to explore aspects of the spirit of the age. These essays are placed in a roughly chronological order in terms of their topics, but they are also clustered in manners that provide complementary perspectives on the large-scale shifts in culture and society that occurred across the decade. The interleaved keywords home in on terms that were extensively aired in the 1820s. These actors' terms convey the decade's own sense of itself as a period of rapid expansion in terms of the projection of British power and knowledge, but also a time of tremendous uncertainty that left traditional identities and values casting around for new moorings.

The book's coherence lies in its origins in discussions supported by a formal research network, 'The Media Revolution of the 1820s', generously funded by the Royal Society of Edinburgh. The RSE's support allowed us the freedom to schedule a series of meetings to discuss broad themes, draw together a large group of interested scholars and work collaboratively to refine the arguments this collection advances. We would like to thank the RSE for facilitating these exchanges and the National Library of Scotland for its unstinting support for our research, the provision of digital resources and facilitating the public engagement events we conducted to disseminate the network's findings.

At our first network meeting, at the University of York in July 2018, a steering group comprising the editors along with Jenny Buckley, Angela Esterhammer, Porscha Fermanis, John Gardner, Kirsty McHugh, Graham Hogg, Ralph McLean, Tom Mole and David Stewart spent two days discussing our senses of the decade, exploring previous scholarship, compiling resources for our website (https://1820s.net/) and composing a Call for Papers designed to bring together a diverse range of scholars to present their ideas at an international conference.

The resulting conference, 'The 1820s: Innovation and Diffusion', was held at the University of Glasgow in April 2019. As well as the contributors to this collection, speakers included Daniel Adleman, Geoffrey Baker, John Cammish, Ernest De Clerck, Helen-Frances Dessain, Joan Garden Cooper, Katie Garner, Brecht de Groote, Katie Halsey, Tomasz Jędrzejewski, Daniel Jenkin-Smith, Ruth Kellar, Gary Kelly, Hope Läubli, Cheng Li, Charlotte May, Silvia Mergenthal, Alison O'Byrne, Jennifer Orr, Honor Rieley, Gillian Russell, Danielle Schwertner, Sammi Scott, James Thomas, Jonathan R. Topham, Josefina Tuominen-Pope, Jim Watt, Amy Wilcockson and Christine Woody. We would like to thank all these scholars for sharing their invaluable insights, as well as Brenna Lopes, Rachael Tarrant and Diego Zuniga for their assistance with organisation.

After the conference, we invited collection contributors to work with us to refine their essays over the course of two workshops, one held in York in September 2019 and one in Glasgow in January 2020. We would like to thank both universities for their help in organising these events; Tom Mole for agreeing to attend both workshops and offer his views; Jenny Buckley for her indispensable intellectual and administrative contributions; and all our contributors for taking the time to produce great work and the trouble to travel considerable distances to discuss the contents of the collection as it developed. Jon Mee would also like to thank the British Academy for the Senior Research Fellowship that gave him time to complete the project. We are very grateful to the Lewis Walpole Library, the National Science and Media Museum, the National Library of Australia and the National Archives for permission to reproduce the images this volume includes. We would also like to thank Susannah Butler, Fiona Conn, Michelle Houston, Caitlin Murphy and Caroline Richards for the exemplary care they have taken preparing this volume for the press.

It seems strange after many months of pandemic isolation to think back to intense, wide-ranging discussions conducted in small rooms in King's Manor and University Gardens – or to enjoying ice cream in Exhibition Square, pizza in the York Assembly Rooms and tapas at Café Andaluz – but these convivial exchanges enormously enriched both this collection and our broader understanding of the overarching trends and peculiar phenomena of the 1820s. Digital meetings have major advantages in terms of reach and accessibility, but their formalities can also be constricting or stifling. While one of the major themes of this collection is the scaling up of cultural participation through the affordances created by new media and new ideas, it has nevertheless benefited enormously from the willingness of those listed above to commit to being in a particular place at a particular time, engaging enthusiastically, constructively and respectfully with the work of others.

Jon Mee and Matthew Sangster

Notes on Contributors

Lara Atkin is Lecturer in Victorian Literature at the University of Kent. They have research interests in the global nineteenth century, particularly the literature and literary institutions of the British Empire and literary collaborations between settler and Indigenous writers. Their most recent monograph is *Writing the South African San: Colonial Ethnographic Discourses* (Palgrave Macmillan, 2021). They are also co-editor, with Emily Bell, of *The Curran Index*, an index revealing the authorship of over 168,000 contributions to nineteenth-century periodicals: http://curranindex.org/.

Clara Dawson is Senior Lecturer in Victorian Literature at the University of Manchester. As a specialist in poetry of the long nineteenth century, her research has developed along two pathways: print culture and environmental humanities. Her work on print culture resulted in a monograph, *Victorian Poetry and the Culture of Evaluation* (Oxford University Press, 2020). It develops new methodologies for analysing poetry and periodicals. Her two-volume edition of *Critical Heritage: Elizabeth Barrett Browning* anthologised contemporary reviews of Barrett Browning's poetry. Her new research project on avian poetics takes a more interdisciplinary approach and is based in the field of environmental humanities.

Ian Duncan is Florence Green Bixby Chair in English at the University of California, Berkeley. He is the author of *Human Forms: The Novel in the Age of Evolution* (Princeton University Press, 2019), *Scott's Shadow: The Novel in Romantic Edinburgh* (Princeton University Press, 2007) and *Modern Romance and Transformations of the Novel: The Gothic, Scott, Dickens* (Cambridge University Press, 1992). He has co-edited essay collections on Scottish Romantic-period writing, and edited works of fiction by Walter Scott, James Hogg, Robert Louis Stevenson and

Arthur Conan Doyle. He is a general editor of the *Collected Works of James Hogg* (Edinburgh University Press) and the Edinburgh Critical Studies in Romanticism series.

Angela Esterhammer, FRSC, is Professor of English and Principal of Victoria College at the University of Toronto. Her book publications include *The Romantic Performative: Language and Action in British and German Romanticism* (Stanford University Press, 2000), *Romanticism and Improvisation, 1750–1850* (Cambridge University Press, 2008) and *Print and Performance in the 1820s: Improvisation, Speculation, Identity* (Cambridge University Press, 2020). She is co-editor of *Spheres of Action: Speech and Performance in Romantic Culture* (University of Toronto Press, 2009) and *Romanticism, Rousseau, Switzerland: New Prospects* (Palgrave Macmillan, 2015). Her current research interests include late-Romantic print culture, performance, periodicals and fiction, and she is General Editor of the *Edinburgh Edition of the Works of John Galt*.

Porscha Fermanis is Professor of Romantic Literature at University College Dublin. Her latest books are *Worlding the South: Nineteenth-Century Literary Culture and the Southern Settler Colonies* (ed. with Sarah Comyn, Manchester University Press, 2021) and *Romantic Pasts: History, Fiction and Feeling in Britain, 1790–1850* (Edinburgh University Press, 2022). She is currently Principal Investigator of the European Research Council project 'SouthHem', for which she is completing a book on nineteenth-century settler fiction and southern spatial imaginaries.

Tim Fulford is a Professor at De Montfort University, Leicester. He has written many books and articles on Romantic-era literature and culture, most recently *Wordsworth's Poetry 1815–45* (University of Pennsylvania Press, 2019), which won the Robert Penn Warren/Cleanth Brooks Award for Distinguished Literary Scholarship, and *The Collected Letters of Sir Humphry Davy* (edited with Sharon Ruston, Oxford University Press, 2020), which received an Honorable Mention from the Biennial MLA Morton N. Cohen Award for a Distinguished Edition of Letters. Current projects include *The Collected Poems of Henry Kirke White* (Liverpool University Press, 2023), *The Collected Letters of Thomas Beddoes* (Cambridge University Press, 2026) and a further monograph on the later Wordsworth entitled *Dialogues with the Dead*.

John Gardner is Professor of English Literature at Anglia Ruskin University and is currently a Leverhulme Trust Research Fellow pursuing a project on Engineering Romanticism. John's recent work has been on Percy Shelley's steamship; Thomas Love Peacock's 'Iron Chickens'; Robert Wedderburn; and Samuel Beckett, Edmund Burke and the politics of the pig.

James Grande is Senior Lecturer in Eighteenth-Century Literature and Culture at King's College London. He is the author of *William Cobbett, the Press and Rural England: Radicalism and the Fourth Estate* (Palgrave Macmillan, 2014) and co-editor of *The Opinions of William Cobbett* (Routledge, 2013), *William Cobbett, Romanticism and the Enlightenment* (Routledge, 2015) and *William Hazlitt: The Spirit of Controversy and Other Essays* (Oxford University Press, 2021). He was a postdoctoral research fellow on the European Research Council project 'Music in London, 1800–1851' and is working on a monograph entitled *Articulate Sounds: Music, Dissent, and Literary Culture*. He is a trustee of Keats-Shelley House, Rome and edits *The Keats-Shelley Review*.

Sara Lodge is Senior Lecturer in English at the University of St Andrews, specialising in nineteenth-century print culture and interdisciplinary relationships between literature, visual art and music. Her books include *Thomas Hood and Nineteenth-Century Poetry: Work, Play, and Politics* (Manchester University Press, 2007), *Jane Eyre: A Reader's Guide to Essential Criticism* (Palgrave, 2008) and *Inventing Edward Lear* (Harvard University Press, 2018). She has published over forty articles and chapters on topics including John Clare, John Keats, Charles Lamb, the literary annuals, bad eaters in Victorian children's literature and Victorian physical comedy. She is currently writing a book, provisionally titled *The Victorian Female Detective: Myth and Reality*, and editing *Literature in Transition: The 1820s* for Cambridge University Press.

Gerard Lee McKeever is Research Fellow on the AHRC-funded 'Books and Borrowing 1750–1830' project at the University of Stirling, having been a British Academy Postdoctoral Fellow at the University of Glasgow between 2017 and 2020. He is the author of *Dialectics of Improvement: Scottish Romanticism, 1786–1831* (Edinburgh University Press, 2020), winner of the BARS First Book Prize 2021. He is currently finishing a book titled *Regional Romanticism: Southwest Scotland, 1770–1830* for Palgrave Macmillan and editing John Galt's autobiographies for Angela Esterhammer's *Edinburgh Edition of the Works of John Galt*.

Jon Mee is Professor of Eighteenth-Century Studies at the University of York. His most recent books are *Print, Publicity and Popular Radicalism*

(Cambridge University Press, 2016) and an edition of Hazlitt's essays, *The Spirit of Controversy*, for Oxford World's Classics (with James Grande, 2021). He is currently working on a study of the literary and intellectual culture of the Industrial Revolution in the north of England for University of Chicago Press, due for publication in 2023 under the title *Networks of Improvement*, and co-editing the collection *Institutions of Literature, 1700–1900* with Matthew Sangster for Cambridge University Press (2022).

Lindsay Middleton is a PhD researcher working at the University of Aberdeen and the University of Glasgow. Her interdisciplinary Scottish Graduate School for Arts & Humanities-funded project, 'The Technical Recipe: A Formal Analysis of Nineteenth-Century Food Writing', investigates how food writers in the nineteenth century used material food technologies to situate themselves in culinary histories. She has written and presented on food adulteration, narrative cookbooks, the ideology of food and thrift, tinned foods and Edinburgh's culinary history. Lindsay has published on tinned foods as a disruptive technology, on broiling and on the culinary imagination. Other research interests include heritage and Scottish gastronomic history.

Phillip Roberts is the Bern and Ronny Schwartz Curator of Photography at the Bodleian Libraries in Oxford. His work explores the histories of photographic and visual media from the eighteenth century to the present day.

Matthew Sangster is Professor of Romantic Studies, Fantasy and Cultural History at the University of Glasgow. He is the author of *Living as an Author in the Romantic Period* (Palgrave Macmillan, 2021) and the editor of *David Bowie and the Legacies of Romanticism* (Romantic Circles, 2022). He is currently co-editing *Institutions of Literature, 1700–1900* with Jon Mee, working on the Arts and Humanities Council-funded 'Libraries, Reading Communities and Cultural Formation in the Eighteenth-Century Atlantic World' and 'Books and Borrowing, 1750–1830' projects, and writing a new introductory book on Fantasy.

David Stewart is Associate Professor of English Literature at Northumbria University. He has published widely on periodicals, poetics, place, and print culture in the early nineteenth century. *Romantic Magazines and Metropolitan Literary Culture* (Palgrave Macmillan, 2011) explores the literary magazines of the period after Waterloo. *The Form of Poetry in the 1820s and 1830s: A Period of Doubt* (Palgrave Macmillan, 2018) presents a new account of the poetic culture in these decades, emphasising both its vitality and its fretful self-consciousness. He is currently at work on an edition of Pierce Egan's *Life in London* and a project on the 1830s.

Tom Toremans is Associate Professor of English Literature at the University of Leuven, Belgium. He has published on Romantic (pseudo) translation, Thomas Carlyle and Romantic periodical culture in a transnational context. He has also co-edited special issues for *Studies in Romanticism* (on 'Waterloo and British Romanticism', with Philip Shaw), *Studies in the Literary Imagination* (on 'Thomas Carlyle and the Totalitarian Temptation', with Tamara Gosta) and *Victoriographies* (on 'Literature and Economics in Nineteenth-Century Germany and Britain', with Ortwin de Graef). He is currently supervising two research projects on translation and cultural transfer in Romantic periodicals (1815–29).

A Chronology of the 1820s

This selective chronology places texts and issues discussed in the essays in the context of a larger range of key political, social and cultural events.

1819 'Six Acts' restricting rights of assembly and freedom of the press passed. Foundation of the Leeds Philosophical and Literary Society. Thomas Pringle's 'The Emigrant's Farewell' appears in *The Harp of Caledonia* (1819). Leigh Hunt's *Indicator* launched. Publication of Byron's *Mazeppa* and first two cantos of *Don Juan*; William Hazlitt's *Lectures on English Comic Writers*, *Political Essays* and *Letter to William Gifford*; William Hone's *Political House that Jack Built*; Washington Irving's *Sketch Book* (in New York); John William Polidori's *The Vampire*; Walter Scott's *Bride of Lammermoor* and *A Legend of Montrose* (third series of *Tales of My Landlord*); and William Wordsworth's *Peter Bell* and *The Waggoner*.

February	Stamford Raffles establishes Singapore as a British trading post.
June	Sarah Siddons makes her last appearance on stage.
August	Peterloo Massacre (16 August); Théodore Géricault's painting 'Raft of the Medusa' causes a sensation at the opening of the Paris Salon.
December	Sir Walter Scott's *Ivanhoe* published.

1820 Revolution in Spain, Portugal and the Kingdom of Naples. Trial of Queen Caroline. Robert Owen's *Report to the County of New Lanark* offers a vision of co-operative communities as a solution to the crisis in poor relief. Foundation of the Royal Society of Literature. Publication of Maria Edgeworth's *Memoirs of Richard Lovell Edgeworth*; James Hogg's *Winter Evening Tales*; Melville

Horne's *The Moral and Political Crisis of England*; John Keats's *Lamia, Isabella, the Eve of St Agnes and Other Poems*; John Clare's *Poems Descriptive of Rural Life and Scenery*; Thomas Robert Malthus's *Principles of Political Economy*; Charles Maturin's *Melmoth the Wanderer*; William Wordsworth's *The River Duddon*; Walter Scott's *The Monastery*; Percy Bysshe Shelley's *Prometheus Unbound*; and Robert Southey's *Life of John Wesley*.

January	Death of George III (29 January). First issue of the new *London Magazine*, under the editorship of John Scott. First edition of Friedrich Accum's *A Treatise on Adulterations of Food and Culinary Poisons* published.
February	Exposure of the Cato Street Conspiracy to assassinate the prime minister Lord Liverpool and his cabinet (23 February).
March	Foundation of the Royal Astronomical Society.
April	Radical War in Scotland.
August	Publication of 'Recollections of the South-Sea House' in *The London Magazine*, the first of the essays of Elia (Charles Lamb).
December	Launch of the *John Bull* newspaper (19 December) with Theodore Hook as editor.

1821 Greek War of Independence begins. The instrument maker Philip Carpenter begins selling his Improved Phantasmagoria Lantern. Publication of Pierce Egan's *Life in London* (as a single volume); James Fenimore Cooper's *The Spy*; John Galt's *Annals of the Parish*; James Mill's *Elements of Political Economy*; Robert Southey's *A Vision of Judgment*; William Cobbett's *Cottage Economy*; Byron's *Sardanapalus*, *The Two Foscari*, *Cain* and Cantos III–V of *Don Juan*; Thomas Chalmers's *The Christian and Civic Economy of Large Towns*, first volume (vol. 2 1823 and vol. 3 1826). Joanna Baillie's *Metrical Legends of Exalted Characters* published; her *De Monfort* produced at Drury Lane.

January	Henry Colburn relaunches the *New Monthly Magazine* under the editorship of Thomas Campbell; Scott's *Kenilworth: A Romance* published.
February	Duel between John Scott (*The London Magazine*) and James Christie (16 February); John Keats dies in Rome (23 February).

May	Death of Napoleon (5 May).
June	Paddle steamer *James Watt* launched to take passengers between London and Edinburgh.
July	Coronation of George IV (19 July).
August	Death of Queen Caroline (7 August).
September	The first part of Thomas De Quincey's *Confessions of an English Opium Eater* published in *The London Magazine*.
October	The School of Arts for educating mechanics opens in Edinburgh with financial support from Walter Scott.

1822 Publication of *Sketch of the Mosquito Shore, including the Territory of Poyais*; the first iteration of Rudolph Ackermann's annual *Forget Me Not, a Christmas and New Year's Present*; Jeremy Bentham's *Influence of Natural Religion upon Temporal Happiness*; Marguerite Blessington's *The Magic Lantern*; Allan Cunningham's *Traditional Tales of the English and Scottish Peasantry*; Thomas Love Peacock's *Maid Marion*; William Wordsworth's *Ecclesiastical Sonnets* and first standalone version of his *Guide to the Lakes* (to which Dorothy Wordsworth also contributed). *The Liberal* – the periodical collaboration between Byron, Shelley and John and Leigh Hunt – begins its short existence.

March	*Noctes Ambrosianae* commence in *Blackwood's Edinburgh Magazine*.
July	Percy Bysshe Shelley drowns off the coast of Italy (8 July).
August	George IV visits Scotland, choreographed by Walter Scott. Lord Castlereagh commits suicide (12 August).
September	The first emigrants set sail for Poyais, arriving 11 February 1823; survivors return to Britain in August 1823.
November	First weekly number of the *Mirror of Literature, Amusement, and Instruction* (2 November).
December	Sheffield Literary and Philosophical Society founded at a meeting in the Cutlers' Hall (12 December).

1823 War between France and Spain. Beginning of the first Anglo-Ashanti War. Members of the African Society, Thomas Clarkson, William Wilberforce and Zachary Macaulay among them, form the Anti-Slavery Society. 'Discovery doctrine' confirming dispossession of Native American peoples confirmed in the United States

Supreme Court. Publication of Thomas Campbell's 'The Last Man'; William Hazlitt's *Liber Amoris*; Charles Lamb's *Essays of Elia* (in book form); Mary Shelley's *Valperga*; and Byron's *Don Juan* Cantos VI–XIV.

January	De Quincey begins his 'Letters to a Young Man whose Education has been Neglected' in *The London Magazine*.
March	Royal Academy of Music opens.
April	Hazlitt's 'My First Acquaintance with Poets' appears in *The Liberal*.
June	Singapore Institution established (5 June).
July	Transportation Act allows convicts to be employed on public works. Gaols Act passed in response to Elizabeth Fry's campaigning. Mechanics' Institution in Glasgow opens after a dispute at Anderson's Institution.
August	Demerara uprising of 100,000 slaves led by Jack Gladstone and his father Quamina brutally repressed. The missionary John Smith dies in prison after his trial for complicity in the rising.
September	First Burmese War begins; death of David Ricardo (11 September).
October	*The Lancet* medical journal begins publication.
November	George Birkbeck chairs the inaugural meeting of the London Mechanics' Institute (11 November).
December	Mary Anning finds the first complete Plesiosaurus skeleton; Sheffield Mechanics' and Apprentices' Library inaugurated (27 December); the *South African Commercial Advertiser* commences.

1824 The National Gallery opens its doors in London. Campaign to erect a statue in commemoration of James Watt begins. Publication of John Banim's *Revelations of the Dead-Alive*; Byron's *Don Juan* Cantos XV and XVI; Thomas Carlyle's translations of Goethe's *Wilhelm Meister's Apprenticeship; The Chimney-Sweeper's Friend, and Climbing-Boy's Album* arranged by James Montgomery; *The Correspondence between John Gladstone, Esq. M. P. and James Cropper, Esq. on the Present State of Slavery*; James Hogg's *Memoirs and Confessions of a Justified Sinner*; Letitia Elizabeth Landon's *The Improvisatrice*; Walter Savage Landor's *Imaginary Conversations*; P. B. Shelley's *Posthumous Poems* (edited by Mary Shelley). Elizabeth Heyrick publishes *Immediate, not Gradual*

Abolition and sells thousands of copies in Britain and the United States. The first volume of Mary Russell Mitford's *Our Village* appears in book form.

January	First issue of the *Westminster Review*.
February	Theodore Hook, *Sayings and Doings* (first series).
April	Death of Lord Byron at Missolonghi (19 April).
June	Act for Ascertaining and Establishing Uniformity of Weights and Measures enters the statute books.
October	Mexico becomes a republic.

1825 Banking crash related to speculative investments severely affects the economy, producing a spate of bankruptcies into 1826. Publication of Thomas Campbell's *Letter to Henry Brougham on the Subject of a London University*; Samuel Taylor Coleridge's *Aids to Reflection*; Allan Cunningham's *Songs of Scotland, Ancient and Modern*; William Hazlitt's *The Spirit of the Age*; James Montgomery's *The Christian Psalmist*; Thomas Moore's *Memoirs of Sheridan*. John McDiarmid's short-lived *Dumfries Magazine* commences. Thomas Hood's print *The Progress of Cant* published.

February	Simón Bolívar takes the title of *El Libertador*. After a House vote, John Quincey Adams elected sixth President of the United States (9 February).
April	Theodore Hook's 'Bubbles of 1825' published in *John Bull*.
June	Repeal of the Bubble Companies Act (a failed attempt to avert financial crisis).
August	Scottish adventurer Gregor MacGregor issues a £300,000 loan, with 2.5% interest, for the fictitious Central American republic of Poyais.
September	The Stockton and Darlington railway opens. John Poole's farce *Paul Pry* premieres at the Haymarket Theatre, London. It was produced in New York the following year.
December	The lithographers Ingrey and Madeley produce 'Viaorama, or The Way to St Paul's'. Decembrist rising in Russia against Tsar Nicholas I.

1826 The British East India Company establishes the Straits Settlements colony. Robert Wilmot-Horton begins chairing a parliamentary committee on emigration. Publication of Edward Baines junior's *Letter to the Unemployed Workmen of Lancashire and Yorkshire*;

James Fenimore Cooper's *Last of the Mohicans*; William Hazlitt's *The Plain Speaker*; Thomas Hood's *Whims and Oddities*; and Mary Shelley's *The Last Man*. Collapse of Archibald Constable & Co. results in Scott's public unveiling as the Author of Waverley.

January   Thomas Telford's Menai Suspension Bridge is opened, linking Anglesey to the Welsh mainland.

February   University of London founded.

June   The Pan-American Congress of Panama fails in its attempt to unify the republics of the Americas.

August   Alexander Gordon Laing becomes the first European to reach Timbuktu.

1827 Publication of John Clare's *The Shepherd's Calendar*; Elizabeth Fry's *Observations on the Siting, Superintendence and Government of Female Prisoners*; Reginald Heber's *Hymns, Written and Adapted to the Weekly Church Service of the Year*; Thomas Hodgskin's *Popular Political Economy*; James Montgomery's *The Pelican Island*; Walter Scott's *Life of Napoleon Bonaparte*; and Alfred Tennyson's *Poems by Two Brothers*. *Metropolitan Improvements* by illustrator Thomas Hosmer Shepherd and writer James Elmes begins publication. *The Blunders of a Big-Wig; or Paul Pry's Peeps into the Sixpenny Sciences* performed.

March   The first African American-owned and published newspaper in the United States – *Freedom's Journal* – is founded in New York City. Death of Ludwig van Beethoven (26 March).

April   George Canning succeeds Lord Liverpool as Prime Minister (10 April). John Galt founds the town of Guelph in Canada.

June   J. R. McCulloch's influential essay on cotton manufacture appears in the *Edinburgh Review*.

August   Death of George Canning (8 August). Death of William Blake (12 August).

October   Battle of Navarino, a key conflict in Greek War of Independence, the last in which the Royal Navy fought only with sailing ships (20 October).

November   Robert Owen uses the term 'socialist' in *The Co-operative Magazine and Monthly Herald*.

1828 Zoological Society in London opens its doors to the public. Publication of Edward Bulwer Lytton's *Pelham*; John Keble's *The Christian Year*; Humphry Davy's *Salmonia*; Leigh Hunt's *Lord*

Byron and Some of his Contemporaries; Letitia Elizabeth Landon's *The Venetian Bracelet*; and Jane C. Loudon's *The Mummy!*

January	The Duke of Wellington becomes prime minister.
April	Noah Webster registers his American dictionary for copyright.
June	Death of Dugald Stewart (11 June).
May	Repeal of the Test and Corporation Acts.
December	Andrew Jackson elected seventh President of the United States.

1829 Crisis over Daniel O'Connell's exclusion from Parliament. Colosseum Panorama opens in Regent's Park. Publication of Thomas Cotterill's *A Selection of Hymns for Public and Private Use*; Robert Southey's *Sir Thomas More: or, Colloquies on the Progress and Prospects of Society*; and E. G. Wakefield's *A Letter from Sydney*. William Wordsworth publishes in the *Keepsake*. Thomas Carlyle publishes his essay 'Signs of the Times' in the *Edinburgh Review*.

April	The Roman Catholic Relief Act, also known as the Catholic Emancipation Act, receives royal assent.
June	Sir Robert Peel introduces the Metropolitan Police Act.
September	The first Metropolitan police appear in London.
October	The Rainhill Trials conducted to test George Stephenson's claim that locomotives would provide the best motive power for the nearly complete Liverpool and Manchester Railway.
December	Britain outlaws 'suttee' in India (widow burning).

1830 Wellington's ministry falls and Earl Grey becomes prime minister. Publication of William Cobbett's *Rural Rides*; Samuel Taylor Coleridge's *On the Constitution of Church and State*; Humphry Davy's *Consolations in Travel*; Charles Lyell's *Principles of Geology*; Thomas Moore's *Life of Byron*; and Alfred Tennyson's *Poems, Chiefly Lyrical*.

February	Greek Independence confirmed in Treaty of London.
June	Death of George IV (26 June). William IV accedes to the throne.
July	July Revolution in France.
September	Opening of the Liverpool–Manchester Railway and death of William Huskisson (15 September). Death of William Hazlitt (18 September).

November   *Blackwood's* publishes Edward Stanley's 'Railer' essay.

December   Death of Simón Bolívar (17 December).

1831 Publication of Ebenezer Elliott's *Corn Law Rhymes* and Thomas Love Peacock's *Crotchet Castle*.

June   Death of Sarah Siddons (8 June).

September   First meeting of the British Association for the Advancement of Science in York. Coronation of William IV and Queen Adelaide (8 September).

December   Christmas rebellion of Jamaican slaves led by the Baptist preacher Sam Sharpe begins (27 December).

1832 Representation of the People Act (Great Reform Bill) passed at the third attempt by Earl Grey's government.

Introduction

Jon Mee and Matthew Sangster

Every age, perhaps, is an age of transition, but not every age is as anxiously and exquisitely conscious of this condition as the 1820s was. Contemporaries were quick to identify the decade as marking the passing of a more stable epoch and presaging the uncertain emergence of a new era. In an 1831 essay that, like many of its contemporaries, laboured to catch 'The Spirit of the Age', John Stuart Mill contended that 'the first of the leading peculiarities of the present age is, that it is an age of transition'.[1] Shortly afterwards, Edward Bulwer Lytton, in *England and the English*, employed a more exact characterisation, describing his time as one of 'visible and violent transition'. He warmed to the theme later in the book:

> I have said that we live in an age of visible transition—an age of disquietude and doubt—of the removal of time-worn landmarks, and the breaking up of the hereditary elements of society—old opinions, feelings—ancestral customs and institutions are crumbling away, and both the spiritual and temporal worlds are darkened by the shadow of change. The commencement of one of these epochs—periodical in the history of mankind—is hailed by the sanguine as the coming of a new Millennium—a great iconoclastic reformation, by which all false gods shall be overthrown.[2]

Such foreboding characterisations were not uncommon. In 'Signs of the Times', Thomas Carlyle saw Catholic emancipation and the repeal of the Test and Corporation Acts as astonishing transformations in the order of things: 'Those things seemed fixed and immovable—deep as the foundations of the world; and lo! in a moment they have vanished, and their place knows them no more!'[3]

---

[1] A.B. [John Stuart Mill], 'The Spirit of the Age, No. 1', *The Examiner*, 1197 (9 January 1831), 20–1 (p. 20).

[2] [Edward Bulwer Lytton], *England and the English*, 2 vols (London: Richard Bentley, 1833), vol. II, p. 100.

[3] [Thomas Carlyle], 'Signs of the Times', *Edinburgh Review*, 49.98 (1829), 439–59 (p. 440).

On the more optimistic side of the equation, Mill claimed that by the end of the 1820s a great change had 'taken place in the human mind'. Looking forward to the Reform Bill of 1832, he celebrated the appearance of 'new men, who insisted upon being governed in a new way'.[4] Bulwer Lytton, on the other hand, was far from sanguine about the prospects of a reformed society:

> To me such epochs appear but as the dark passages in the appointed progress of mankind—the times of greatest unhappiness to our species—passages into which we have no reason to rejoice at our entrance, save from the hope of being sooner landed on the opposite side.[5]

Few even among the most ardent partisans of the 'march of intellect' failed to acknowledge the uncertainties that haunted their sense of progress. While innovations in print and other media were disseminating knowledge across the globe in a decade during which mass emigration was a controversial public issue, even those who contributed to or benefited from such innovations were often deeply ambivalent about their consequences.

Mill worried that the 'grand achievement of the present age is the *diffusion* of *superficial* knowledge'.[6] James Montgomery celebrated the provincial enlightenment he encouraged, but also feared the 'dislocation, in fact, of every thing' as 'one of the most striking proofs of the extraordinary diffusion of knowledge – and its corruption too, – if not a symptom of its declension by being so heterogeneously blended, till all shall be neutralised'.[7] He numbered not just Lord Byron, predictably enough, but also Sir Walter Scott, Robert Southey and William Wordsworth among those who had abandoned tried and trusted pathways to 'scale the heights by leaping from rock to rock up the most precipitous side, forcing their passage through the impenetrable forests that engirdle it, or plunging across the headlong torrents that descend in various windings from their fountains at the peak'. Montgomery, who tried to keep Scott's novels out of the Mechanics' and Apprentices' Library in Sheffield, accused such writers of straining to 'attract attention and excite astonishment'. The judgement is a striking contrast to Bulwer Lytton's

---

[4] [Mill], 'Spirit of the Age', p. 20.
[5] [Bulwer Lytton], *England and the English*, vol. II, p. 100.
[6] [Mill], 'Spirit of the Age', p. 21.
[7] James Montgomery, *Lectures on Poetry and General Literature: Delivered at the Royal Institution in 1830 and 1831* (London: Longman, 1833), pp. 373–4. Montgomery had lectured on the same topic in Sheffield and Leeds in the early 1820s. See also the discussion of Montgomery as hymn-writer by James Grande in Chapter 8 in this volume.

more familiar suggestion that Wordsworth's poetry tended to 'refine—to etherealize—to exalt; to offer the most correspondent counterpoise to the scale that inclines to earth'.[8] Both assessments also differ markedly from the positions Wordsworth himself had taken in the preface to *Lyrical Ballads* at the close of the 1790s, as Montgomery aligns the poet with the modern overstimulation he had decried and Bulwer Lytton carries him a considerable distance from being 'a man speaking to men'.[9] Such positionings reflect both the shifting and contested manners in which the Lakers were presented (by themselves and by others) and the period's conflicted sense of the roles British culture should henceforth play for its ever-expanding and increasingly unpredictable audiences.

Any account of the 1820s necessarily wrestles with myriad contrasting responses to the experience of transformation, ranging from the excited promotion of new opportunities grounded in new technologies and new media to the mournful sense that something essential was being lost. We have called this volume *Remediating the 1820s* for three reasons: first, because our aim is to recover the importance of a decade often lost between Romantic and Victorian periodisations; second, to think about the literary as part of an increasingly expansive, complex and self-reflexive media culture; and, third, to draw attention to the ways in which change was self-consciously represented across different forms, some understood as projecting a bright future, others mourned as passing away. In combination, these three approaches provide further nuance to the claims made about the self-reflexivity of Romantic historicism in James Chandler's influential study *England in 1819*, demonstrating how a decade that has hitherto been relatively neglected in cultural studies nevertheless considered itself as possessing a hot chronology in which change felt omnipresent.[10]

During the 1820s, anticipation and nostalgia were involved in distinctive forms of remediation, sometimes forming queasy combinations. Anticipations, somewhat perversely, often appeared in reconfigurations of the past, whether in the novel visualisations of history in Scott's prose, or the reinvention of the magic lantern as a supposedly new medium, or attempts to speculate on a future that was felt to be imminent but remained as yet unknown. Angela Esterhammer's compelling study of

[8] Montgomery, *Lectures*, p. 377, and [Bulwer Lytton], *England and the English*, vol. II, pp. 100–1. On Montgomery's campaign against novels, see J. W. Hudson, *The History of Adult Education* (London: Longman & Rees, 1851), p. 160.

[9] William Wordsworth [and Samuel Taylor Coleridge], *Lyrical Ballads, with Pastoral and Other Poems*, 3rd edn, 2 vols (London: Longman & Rees, 1802), vol. I, p. xxviii.

[10] James Chandler, *England in 1819: The Politics of Literary Culture and the Case of Romantic Historicism* (Chicago: University of Chicago Press, 1998), p. 3.

the decade opens with an analysis of John Banim's *Revelations of the Dead-Alive* (1824), a tale that looks back to its own time from two hundred years later.[11] Does this make Banim's text a form of science fiction, or strangely nostalgic, or a shifting hybrid, unable comfortably to settle the questions of temporal judgement with which it engages? Much the same question might be asked of Mary Shelley's plague novel *The Last Man* (1826). The sense of the 1820s as a decade of dislocation is often associated with a nostalgia for past certainties, perhaps most obviously manifested in the radical Toryism that the Lake Poets played their part in creating.[12] Nostalgia, though, is a complex phenomenon, far from simply conservative. In the 1820s, it was often focused not on times but on places, on landscapes that formed pockets of the past in the present.[13] While the love of place fostered by the Lake Poets is an obvious case in point, complex forms of nostalgia were also expressed in innovative urban art and writing, in the new localisms that sprang up across Britain, and in the testimonies of migrants across the Empire, who participated in recreating and reinventing the cultural heritages of their homelands.[14]

The 1820s has often been represented rather fuzzily in literary histories, a fuzziness that belies some very specific historical circumstances that framed the decade's transformative anxieties. Neil Ramsey has given a thoughtful account of Montgomery's lectures as a response to the decades of international war that had dominated much of the poet's adult life.[15] There is a strong case for thinking of the 1820s more generally as a post-war decade. Lord Liverpool's Tory government was eager to retrench after the strains placed on the nation by the distinctive version of the fiscal-military state developed during the Napoleonic Wars.[16] Beyond government, there were widespread hopes of a peace dividend. Joseph Hunter, writing about Sheffield, anticipated that a reanimated

---

[11] Angela Esterhammer, *Print and Performance in the 1820s: Improvisation, Speculation, Identity* (Cambridge: Cambridge University Press, 2020), p. 1.

[12] See Philip Connell's account of this process in *Romanticism, Economics, and the Question of 'Culture'* (Cambridge: Cambridge University Press, 2001).

[13] See Ruth Livesey, *Writing the Stage Coach Nation: Locality on the Move in Nineteenth-Century British Literature* (Oxford: Oxford University Press, 2016) on the interrelation of time and space in nostalgia for the 'just past' of the 1820s in the mid-Victorian novel, including an analysis of 1820s writers like Hazlitt and Scott who 'refuse to let the localities of the past fade out of view' (p. 6).

[14] See Chapters 6 and 7 in this volume by Gerard Lee McKeever and Lara Atkin respectively.

[15] Neil Ramsey, 'James Montgomery's Waterloo: War and the Poetics of History', *Studies in Romanticism*, 56 (2017), 361–78.

[16] See Boyd Hilton, *Corn, Cash, Commerce: The Economic Policies of the Tory Governments 1815–1830* (Oxford: Oxford University Press, 1977).

spirit of improvement would replace 'the painful state of disunion' that had prevailed in the war years.[17] Like William Roscoe in Liverpool, another of J. E. Cookson's 'Friends of Peace', Hunter saw his native town turning its commercial prosperity into a provincial urban renaissance.[18] Such optimism rarely survived the immediate post-war years. Debt and poor harvests triggered by the climactic events of 1816 – the Year Without a Summer – contributed to an economic depression that shaped the 1820s in less positive ways. Economic distress brought mass migration to Australia, Canada and South Africa, among other places. Emigration had its part in the Church of Scotland minister Thomas Chalmers's decade-long campaign against the idea that poor relief could be considered a right. Chalmers offered self-reliance and the iron laws of Malthus, backed up by the Bible and house-to-house visitations, as the answer to poverty.[19] While for some the 1820s was a decade of flourishing and prosperity, this prosperity was extremely unevenly distributed.

The year Hunter's book appeared – 1819 – was marked by one of the most infamously bloody episodes in British history: the Peterloo Massacre. In terms of transitions, it was a complex event. Although often regarded as a clash between factory workers and cotton manufacturers, the great majority of those who marched to St Peter's Field were weavers – part of a domestic industry that boomed to service the cotton-spinning factories that came online from the 1760s. Those who sent the yeomanry to ride them down were representatives of 'Old Corruption', clerical magistrates who wielded authority in a town without a corporation or a member of parliament.[20] The mill owner Samuel Greg, who was present as an observer, provided a witness to testify to the illegality of the magistrates' actions in the shape of the clergyman Edward Stanley, who was also present at another shocking, epoch-making event at the other end of the decade, as we shall discuss shortly.[21] It was against 'Old Corruption' – Pitt's system that seemed to reward fund-holders and large landowners with the profits

---

[17] Joseph Hunter, *Hallamshire. The History and Topography of the Parish of Sheffield* (London: Lackington et al., 1819), p. 128.

[18] J. E. Cookson, *The Friends of Peace: Anti-War Liberalism in England 1793–1815* (Oxford: Oxford University Press, 1982), p. 134 on Baines and pp. 221–2 on Roscoe as 'anti-war leader'.

[19] See Boyd Hilton, *The Age of Atonement: The Influence of Evangelicalism on Social and Economic Thought 1795–1865* (Oxford: Oxford University Press, 1991), pp. 55–63.

[20] See Robert Poole, *Peterloo: The English Uprising* (Oxford: Oxford University Press, 2019), pp. 363–4. On 'Old Corruption', see Philip Harling, *The Waning of 'Old Corruption:' The Politics of Economical Reform in Britain, 1779–1846* (Oxford: Oxford University Press, 1996).

[21] David Sekers, *A Lady of Cotton: Hannah Greg, Mistress of Quarry Bank Mill* (Stroud: History Press, 2013), p. 204.

of war – that Henry Hunt, William Cobbett and a range of reformist and radical opinion raged in the years after 1815. Things seemed to be worsening rather than improving when the government passed repressive measures like the Six Acts, which restricted political debate by introducing a new tax on knowledge that was not fully repealed until 1855.

Nothing captured 'Old Corruption' better than the bloated figure of the Prince Regent, soon to reign over the 1820s as George IV. He was lampooned again and again in satires and caricatures by William Hone and George Cruikshank that reached a crescendo in the Queen Caroline Affair of 1820. It is worth remembering, as Malcolm Chase has pointed out, that Percy Shelley's scathing sonnet 'England in 1819' was called 'England in 1820' until Mary Shelley changed its title after his death, showing how Peterloo became increasingly prominent as a totem of authoritarian malfeasance.[22] The outrage provided a powerful synecdoche for the complex assemblage of conservative systems and processes against which a wide range of political reformers sought to articulate their ideas of a potential new order. However, the shape to be taken by Shelley's 'glorious Phantom' remained contested even among the friends of change. Present at Peterloo was Edward Baines junior, the son of the editor of the *Leeds Mercury*, the reformist newspaper which had won national notice for its sensational exposure of the government spy 'Oliver'. However, the paper also consistently aimed its editorials against mass platform politics. Shortly before Peterloo, Baines senior had advised workers to petition for relief or an assisted emigration scheme rather than demand universal suffrage.[23] Baines senior was another of Cookson's 'Friends of Peace', with a long record of writing against 'Old Corruption', but he was no radical, as the 1820s made increasingly clear.[24] Baines father and son were associated with moderate reform, the celebration of the new republics in southern Europe and South America, the abolition of colonial slavery and the campaign for Catholic emancipation, but their liberalism was also committed to the doctrines of political economy as a 'science' in ways that went beyond the old-style commercial humanism of William Roscoe or even Adam Smith's sense of human beings as motivated by complex moral sentiments. Influenced by David Ricardo's work of the 1810s and early 1820s, political economy increasingly treated people as autonomous

---

[22] Malcolm Chase, *1820: Disorder and Stability in the United Kingdom* (Manchester: Manchester University Press, 2015), p. 1.

[23] Poole, *Peterloo*, p. 217.

[24] See Cookson, *Friends of Peace*, pp. 111–13.

agents governed by self-interest.[25] When campaigners like Chalmers used the authority of Malthus to dismiss the idea of a customary right to relief, Southey and Wordsworth reacted with horror, showing the profoundly vexed nature of discourses of regulation and improvement.[26]

These developments started to appear in what might seem unexpected places. Drawing on a reading of Smith's discussion of the productivity of free as against slave labour in *The Wealth of Nations*, James Cropper, a Quaker sugar merchant in Liverpool, helped reignite the cause of abolition by arguing against the support of the West Indian plantation economy by preferential tariffs. Many advocates of the abolition of the slave trade in 1807 had assumed that slavery itself would naturally cease to be a viable institution. Instead, emancipation had become mired in arguments about the international trade. Cropper set up an anti-slavery society in Liverpool – with the veteran abolitionist Roscoe as its president – and began to lobby Thomas Clarkson and William Wilberforce. The government made promising noises but did little.[27] An acrimonious newspaper war began in the burgeoning Liverpool press between Cropper and John Gladstone, father of the future prime minister, who owned a sugar plantation in Demerara. Gladstone pointed out that until recently Cropper had been an importer of American slave-grown cotton to the Manchester industry. Now that he had become an importer of East Indian sugar, he had self-interested motives for his new campaign. Gladstone presented the introduction of modern factory discipline to the plantations as a form of melioration, but he was attacked in turn by hard-line planters of the old school for his innovations. The missionaries he invited onto his estates, it was claimed, had provoked the Demerara uprising of 1823 by spreading news of Cropper's campaign.[28] News had certainly reached the slaves about the renewed agitation for abolition back in Britain, but they scarcely needed reasons to seek their freedom. Gladstone showed no qualms about supporting the brutal repression of the rising and an increased military presence on the islands. Found guilty of fomenting the rising, the London Missionary

---

[25] Mary Poovey, *Genres of the Credit Economy: Mediating Value in Eighteenth- and Nineteenth-Century Britain* (Chicago: University of Chicago Press 2008), p. 224.

[26] See Ruby Tuke, 'Gifts, Gratitude, Charity: Representing Indebtedness 1790–1834' (unpublished doctoral thesis, Queen Mary University of London, 2021).

[27] David B. Davis, 'James Cropper and the British Anti-Slavery Movement, 1821–1823', *Journal of Negro History*, 45.4 (1960), 241–58.

[28] See *The Correspondence between John Gladstone, Esq. M. P. and James Cropper, Esq. on the Present State of Slavery in the British West Indies and in the United States of America* (Liverpool: West India Association, 1824) and Trevor Burnard, 'Sir John Gladstone and the Debate over the Amelioration of Slavery in the British West Indies in the 1820s', *Journal of British Studies*, 57.4 (2018), 760–82.

Society's John Smith died in prison on the island after a trial that caused a sensation back in Britain.[29]

Cropper might seem to capture the spirit of the age in his presentation of political economy as a logic of liberty – an idea reiterated by Harriet Martineau in her 'Demerara: A Tale' (1832) – but it is arguable how far he managed to 'harness free trade to the cause of emancipation'.[30] A much more powerful driver of the popular campaign for abolition was the new civic culture associated with the evangelical movement, especially strong in the expanding manufacturing towns, that had been developing over the previous two decades with the help of Sunday schools and missionary societies. The same groups often feared settler societies would corrupt Indigenous peoples who might be brought within the Christian fold.[31] This sense of a pervasive sinfulness that required atonement gave evangelical abolitionism great urgency. Impatient with cautious leaders negotiating with governments over matters like compensation for slave owners, innovative women campaigners put themselves to the fore. One key voice was Elizabeth Heyrick, a Leicester Unitarian turned Quaker, who had grown up in a family active in the first wave of campaigning against the slave trade. Heyrick's *Immediate, not Gradual Abolition* (1824) scorned the interminable negotiations over the terms of emancipation and chastised the gradualism of Cropper and his allies as a mealy-mouthed derogation of Christian principles.[32] By the 1820s, Heyrick was already the author of radical pamphlets defending the right to strike and calling for pay rises to meet the economic distress of the working

---

[29] Michael Craton, *Testing the Chains: Resistance to Slavery in the British West Indies* (Ithaca, NY: Cornell University Press, 2009), pp. 267–90. See also the account of the rising provided by Thomas Harding, *White Debt: The Demerara Uprising and Britain's Legacy of Slavery* (London: Weidenfeld & Nicolson, 2022).

[30] Roger Anstey, 'The Pattern of British Abolitionism in the Eighteenth and Nineteenth Centuries', in *Anti-Slavery, Religion and Reform: Essays in Memory of Roger Anstey*, ed. Christine Bolt and Seymour Drescher (Folkstone: Dawson, 1980), pp. 19–42 (p. 25); and Harriet Martineau, 'No IV: Demerara: A Tale', in *Illustrations of Political Economy*, 9 vols (London, 1832), vol. II.

[31] Elizabeth Elbourne, 'The Sin of the Settler: The 1835–36 Select Committee on Aborigines and Debates over Virtue and Conquest in the Early Nineteenth-Century British White Settler Empire', *Journal of Colonialism and Colonial History*, 4.3 (2003), doi: 10.1353/cch.2004.0003.

[32] Elizabeth Heyrick, *Immediate, Not Gradual Abolition: Or, An Inquiry into the Shortest, Safest, and Most Effectual Means of Getting Rid of West Indian Slavery* (London: Hatchard et al., 1824). See Clare Midgley, 'The Dissenting Voice of Elizabeth Heyrick: An Exploration of the Links between Gender, Religious Dissent, and Anti-Slavery Radicalism', in *Women, Dissent, and Anti-Slavery in Britain and America, 1790–1865*, ed. Elizabeth J. Clapp and Julie Joy Jeffrey (Oxford: Oxford University Press, 2011), pp. 88–110.

classes.[33] *Immediate, not Gradual Abolition* offered a very different kind of economic analysis than Cropper's, advocating the boycott of West Indian produce in order to render the plantation system unsustainable.

Despite Wilberforce's reservations about women activists, Heyrick seems to have inspired a series of female associations around the country.[34] In 1827, the Sheffield Female Anti-Slavery Society, founded in 1825, was the first society to call for immediate abolition.[35] At the centre of the urban missionary movement in Sheffield were the Congregationalists Elizabeth Read and her daughter Mary Anne Rawson, both of whom sat on the committee of the Female Anti-Slavery Society from its inception. Throughout the 1820s and after, Rawson worked closely with James Montgomery on a variety of philanthropic publishing projects, including literary albums like *The Chimney Sweeper's Friend, and Climbing-Boy's Album* (1824) and *The Bow in the Cloud* (1834), to neither of which Wordsworth felt able to contribute. These albums grew naturally from the 'domestic mission' centred in the Read household, where manuscript poems and missionary narratives were circulated between members of the family and sent out into wider networks of believers.[36] The Reads innovated in other ways with the forms of female domesticity. The Female Anti-Slavery Society distributed work bags filled with tracts and engravings. Extracts on the suffering of slaves were hidden within many of them.[37] By 1831, the Anti-Slavery Society in London had accepted the case for immediate emancipation, but the Christmas Rebellion on Jamaica of 1831–2 made the case for emancipation seem inarguable. Led by the black Baptist deacon Samuel Sharpe, who drew on the example of the Demerara rising, 60,000 slaves rose against the plantation owners they believed were refusing to implement an emancipation already agreed upon by the British government. Sharpe, who probably surrendered to try and prevent the shedding of more blood, was hanged

---

[33] Elizabeth Heyrick, *Exposition of One Principal Cause of the National Distress, particularly in Manufacturing Districts* (London: for the Author, 1817).

[34] Wilberforce told Thomas Babington that 'for ladies to meet, to publish, to go from house to house stirring up petitions – these appear to me proceedings unsuited to the female character as delineated in Scripture'; *The Life of William Wilberforce*, ed. Robert and Samuel Wilberforce, 5 vols (London: John Murray, 1838), vol. V, pp. 264–5.

[35] Clare Midgley, *Women Against Slavery: The British Campaigns, 1780–1870* (London: Routledge, 1991), p. 106.

[36] See Alison Twells, 'Missionary Domesticity, Global Reform and "Woman's Sphere" in Early Nineteenth-Century England', *Gender & History*, 18.2 (2006), 266–84 (p. 269).

[37] Felicity James and Rebecca Shuttleworth, 'Susanna Watts and Elizabeth Heyrick: Collaborative Campaigning in the Midlands, 1820–34', in *Women's Literary Networks and Romanticism: "A Tribe of Authoresses"*, ed. Andrew O. Winckles and Angela Rehbein (Liverpool: Liverpool University Press, 2017), pp. 47–72 (p. 56).

at Montego Bay. The planters, for their part, received thousands of pounds in damages.[38]

Despite the murky moral compromises at the heart of the emergent middle-class power in Britain, polemicists like Baines father and son exploited every available form of print to represent liberal economics – driven forward by the factory-steam paradigm – as the fulfilment of the promise of the Reformation. The steam engine and the invention of the printing press were linked in the long narrative of Protestant liberty that lay behind Baines junior's *History of the Cotton Manufacture of Great Britain* (1835). Baines had already been a loud voice on the machinery question and attacked Luddism in his *Letter to the Unemployed Workmen of Lancashire and Yorkshire* (1826).[39] Over the course of the 1820s, this species of reform turned the Whig Party of the Yorkshire aristocracy associated with Earl Fitzwilliam and Wentworth House towards the economic liberalism of Mill and his ally Henry Brougham. The abolition movement and the struggle over the machinery question both give credence to William Hay's claim that the decade's realignments meant 'provincial opinion carried greater weight in national political discussion at Westminster'.[40] The paradoxes of emergent liberalism became very public when the Ten Hours movement contrasted the support given by Bainesocracy to the abolition of colonial slavery with their refusal to back calls to cut the hours of children working in local factories.[41] Baines and his allies assumed that if the British working classes were taught the principles of political economy, they would readily accept their place in this new order. Their advocacy for mechanics' institutes in Yorkshire was part of this drive towards the diffusion of knowledge, but these and other institutions of domestic mission were often treated with suspicion by factory operatives. Liberal reforms made in the name of political economy attracted ongoing criticism from radicals, who saw them as shabby compromises, and conservatives, who feared they would undermine traditional hierarchies. Some evangelicals raged against the exploitation of other races they believed to be at least nominally equal before a Christian God. Consensus was rhetorically conjured but remained deeply unstable in practice.

---

[38] Craton, *Testing the Chains*, chapter 22.

[39] In *The Machinery Question and the Making of Political Economy 1815–1848* (Cambridge: Cambridge University Press, 1980), Maxine Berg describes Baines junior as 'a provincial industrial ideologue' (p. 103).

[40] William Hay, *The Whig Revival 1808–1830* (Basingstoke: Palgrave Macmillan, 2005), p. 1.

[41] On the Yorkshire slavery question as a national issue, see Cecil Driver, *Tory Radical: The Life of Richard Oastler* (Oxford: Oxford University Press, 1977).

If this decade of contested and ambivalent reform might be framed by the violence of Peterloo at its outset, then a very different kind of violent event, rich with symbolic portents, marked the other end of the decade. The opening of the Liverpool to Manchester railway line in 1830 was understood by at least one observer who had been at Peterloo, the Reverend Edward Stanley, to presage 'a fresh era in the state of society; the final results of which it is impossible to contemplate'.[42] Fears about the future were crystallised around the tragic death of the Tory politician William Huskisson. Huskisson had been at the centre of the pragmatic manoeuvring of the administrations of Lord Liverpool and his successors towards the idea that Britain's future was as the workshop of the world: exporting manufactured goods and importing much of its food. The transition was an anxious one for a society whose ruling classes were still primarily drawn from an oligarchy of agricultural landowners. Huskisson's death was arguably a direct result of tensions within the ranks of the landowning classes, as he was on the tracks attempting to mend relations with the Prime Minister, the grand old Duke of Wellington. Huskisson had ignored advice to stay in the railway carriage when the train – *The Northumbrian* – stopped to take on water. He was moving down the rails to offer his hand to the Duke, when Stephenson's *Rocket* suddenly appeared on the parallel track. Possibly unable to judge the unprecedented speed of the engine, or to process distance against its rapidly increasing size, Huskisson panicked. When he tried to clamber back into the carriage, its door swung open and delivered him into the maw of the oncoming engine.[43]

Stanley's essay for *Blackwood's* keeps the bloody details of the tragedy off stage, but makes the dejection it induces the occasion for dark reflections. The pseudonym he adopted for the essay – 'A Railer' – is a locomotive pun that speaks of someone shaking his fist at an onrushing futurity: 'who could have surmised, at such a moment, that within the short-space of another hour, this all-pervading joy should be exchanged for one pervading gloom—under a solemn lesson of man's mortality, and the frail tenure upon which his existence is held' (p. 824). This sense of reaching after traditional verities that seemed to be steaming

---

[42] [Edward Stanley], 'Opening of the Liverpool and Manchester Railroad', *Blackwood's Edinburgh Magazine*, 28.173 (November 1830), 823–30 (p. 825). References to Stanley's essay are given in the main text from this point on. We are grateful to Phillip Roberts for pointing this essay out to us and to Kirsty McHugh for confirming Stanley's authorship on the basis of the Blackwood archive at the National Library of Scotland.

[43] Details of the accident can be found in Huskisson's entry in the *Oxford Dictionary of National Biography*.

out of view is a common strain in the period, but Stanley's essay is not solely defined by its nostalgia. Interestingly for our purposes here, it makes its own use of remediation as a rhetorical device: 'At times it was difficult to recognise or distinguish the countenances of the long continuous line of spectators, as they seemed to glide away, like painted figures swiftly drawn through the tubes of a magic lantern' (p. 825). The new experience of speed and the disorientation of perspective it brings – the disorientation that may have contributed to Huskisson's death – contributes to the fantastical nature of Stanley's writing as it struggles to process a new kind of sensory experience:

> In the rapid movement of these engines, there is an optical deception worth noticing. A spectator observing their approach, when at extreme speed, can scarcely divest himself of the idea, that they are not enlarging and increasing in size rather than moving. I know not how to explain my meaning better, than by referring to the enlargement of objects in a phantasmagoria. At first the image is barely discernible, but as it advances from the focal point, it seems to increase beyond all limit. Thus an engine, as it draws near, appears to become rapidly magnified, and as if it would fill up the entire space between the banks, and absorb everything within its vortex. (p. 825)

The passage calls to mind J. M. W. Turner's painting *Rain, Steam and Speed* – exhibited at the Royal Academy in 1844, but probably painted earlier – not least in the way it seems to blur the boundaries of traditional forms of representation, both excited and repelled by the coming of an astonishing newness.

Scarcely less threatening than the engine in Stanley's essay are the crowds that came to witness the event. Despite the fact he thought Peterloo was an outrage, he was no radical and had no time for the democratic reforms proposed there by Henry Hunt. The essay on the railway makes the crowds of spectators into a strange Malthusian nightmare. As his carriage brings him towards Manchester, the spectators become 'dense in a geometrical ratio'. First the objects of a Peterloo-focused paranoia – 'the very beau-ideal of that class of deputy candle-snuffers to Hunt and Cobbett' – the crowd then becomes the focus of a calculation of what it would cost to feed them and where they might be buried: 'Chatmoss would at any moment swallow the whole of such an assemblage at a meal, and digest every man, woman, and child of them in a month' (pp. 827, 828). Typically for the decade, the sense of history hurtling forward is caught by a counter-current in the image of a solitary peasant glimpsed outside the window of the locomotive, 'pursuing his daily work with as much indifference to what was going on as if he had been Robinson Crusoe on his desert island' (p. 826). When the engine startles a snipe as it races through the dreary wastes of Chat Moss, the driver finds the bird cannot be overtaken. Time seems to be running on at least two different tracks, experienced in different ways and at different speeds. The past is not simply left behind but opens onto an alternative perspective that seems to provide – temporarily at least – a kind of refuge from present anxieties about the future. In this regard, like the Lake District for Wordsworth and his friends, it seems one of those spots where the certain forward motion of time might be resisted.

The *Blackwood's* essay captures many of the themes that emerged in the discussions of the 1820s that fed into this collection. Population growth and the question of what to do with the urban poor were major issues that resulted in government-sponsored migration programmes and, eventually, the New Poor Law of 1834, brought in by Earl Grey's ministry after the Reform Bill. The fear that the hungry were a ready audience for radical agitators was a key theme in the paternalist Toryism associated with Robert Southey. These issues all fed into the panic about food adulteration, discussed in Chapter 3 by Lindsay Middleton, that crested several times in the post-war years. As Britain reoriented towards becoming a manufacturing society, a strain was placed on the idea of domestic agriculture as the traditional means of feeding the poor. The figure of the solitary peasant was activated again as a potent symbol for values that had been lost in the rush towards modernity, but in forms that were increasingly conscious of themselves as repetitions or reiterations. After Robert Bloomfield's death in 1824, John Clare wrote that he would 'readily (nay gladly) acknowledge his superiority as a Poet in my opinion he is the most original poet of the age & the greatest Pastoral Poet England ever gave birth too'. Echoing the new discourses of genius developed in the magazines for which he wrote, and eliding Bloomfield's huge success in the 1800s, Clare opined that 'neglect is the only touchstone by which true genius is proved'. By contrast, 'every day scribblers' merely produced 'nonsense ginglings called poems'.[44] Amid the sound and the fury of the modern media environment, the idea of restricting true value to those who stood outside the general flow became increasingly attractive. However, such positionings were most effectively conducted through the very media they inveighed against. Clare's own works were promoted in periodicals as technologies through which urban readers might access 'natural objects . . . just as they breathe or bloom'. Writing of *The Shepherd's Calendar*, the *Eclectic Review* opined that 'any poor wight, in cities pent, by means of this *camera lucida*, may see them as he sits with his book in his hand by the side of his hanging

---

[44] John Clare to Thomas Inskip, 10 August 1824, in *The Letters of John Clare*, ed. Mark Storey (Oxford: Oxford University Press, 1986), p. 300.

garden of flower-pots'. However, Clare's remediated and remediating status risked his being rendered passé or secondary. Reviewing the same poem, the *Ladies' Monthly Museum* asserted that 'Pastoral poetry ... must, of necessity, possess such a sameness, as will, on repetition, divest it of much of its interest.' A laudatory account in the *Literary Chronicle* noted of a line the reviewer particularly admired that 'A distinguished friend of Clare [Harry Stoe Van Dyk] has quoted it in his Gondola, and we remember being struck with its powerful originality long before we were aware of it being the property of the latter.'[45] While the sentence presumably means to assign 'powerful originality' to Clare himself, its ambiguous grammar betrays the ease with which attempts to assert authority and ownership could slip away amidst the decade's maelstrom of remediations.

Nevertheless, for those with the cultural clout to influence their own receptions, the 1820s provided new and willing listeners. Southey and his friends, who had promoted alternative visions of literary authority when their works initially failed to find the audiences they believed they deserved, were able successfully to re-evaluate their careers as the world changed around them: a process explored in Chapter 9 by Tim Fulford. The 1820s was the decade in which the Lake Poets became canonical. Expanding markets for print made them famous on a global scale, but they presented themselves increasingly in terms of a set of values associated with nature and depth of feeling. Southey was an increasingly vociferous spokesman for traditional hierarchies, railing in the *Quarterly Review* against radical printers like William Hone whom he saw as promoters of discontent. He railed equally against Thomas Malthus for wearing away the bonds that he thought properly tied together the rich and the poor. For someone like Southey, literary figures like Byron and William Hazlitt, who encouraged varieties of liberal ideas in politics, were doing the same corrosive work: privileging sensation over the rhetorical commonalities that had traditionally bound society together.

Hazlitt represents an interesting figure in this regard. Many with his background in Dissent – like Baines father and son – hastened to the liberal principles of reform in politics and economics that may seem to define the Victorian period, but Hazlitt was not of this ilk. While he was deeply sceptical of the way that the Lake School made a defence of customary values a vehicle for tracking backwards to a paternalist society, he also refused to accede to the principles of the new political economy.

---

[45] *Eclectic Review*, 27 (June 1827), 509–21 (pp. 509–10); *Ladies' Monthly Museum*, 25 (May 1827), 288–9 (p. 288); *Literary Chronicle*, 441 (27 October 1827), 674–5 (p. 675).

His lifelong hatred for Malthus – first articulated in Cobbett's *Political Register* in 1807 – matched Southey's in its venom, but he saw no reason to long for the hierarchies of the past.[46] Hazlitt thrived in the magazines that were such a distinctive feature of the print ecology of the 1820s, but he also remained sceptical of the idea of literary value as the object of mechanical reproduction. Like many other writers for magazines in the decade, as David Stewart has shown, he adhered to literary values – of genius and gusto – that seemed at odds with the diffusion of knowledge he otherwise celebrated.[47] The melancholy ending of his late great essay 'The Letter Bell', with its sense not just of time but of a way of life passing, comes with the hoped-for news of the Revolution of 1830 in France delivered by the new technology of the telegraph. Where there is nostalgia in Hazlitt, as Kevin Gilmartin has shown, it often appears as a resource for radical critique, as it did for Cobbett. It serves not as an expression of longing for a traditional past used to push away a nameless future, but as a way of calling to account the inequalities of the present.[48]

Hazlitt also had an appetite for the array of media spectacles that marked part of the difference between Londoners and country people. London was a world of exhibitions, shows and – above all, for Hazlitt – of the theatre. If the 1820s saw the rise of provincial and colonial opinion through channels like the *Leeds Mercury*, the *Dumfries and Galloway Courier* and the *South African Commercial Advertiser*, then they also saw the further rise of London as a world city. John Nash's Regent Street thrust commercial colonnades through the circuits of the old West End, but this was only the most prominent among a great drive of urban redevelopments. While earlier topographical plate series of the city tended to cap out at around a hundred images, *Metropolitan Improvements* (commenced in 1827) bloated to 158 plates as its illustrator Thomas Hosmer Shepherd and writer James Elmes rushed to sate demand for images of the new cityscape of the post-war years. From the gates and terraces of Regent's Park to the Islington canal tunnel; from George Smith's St Paul's School to Sir John Soane's New Treasury and Decimus Burton's New Government Mews; from the Hammersmith suspension bridge to the new Covent Garden market: a brash capital infrastructure was bursting out from, over, across and under the old

---

46 Hazlitt's 'On the Principle of Population' was published in *Cobbett's Weekly Political Register*, 23 May 1807, and later included in his *Reply to Malthus* (1807).

47 David Stewart, *Romantic Magazines and Metropolitan Literary Culture* (Basingstoke: Palgrave Macmillan, 2011).

48 See Kevin Gilmartin, *William Hazlitt: Political Essayist* (Oxford: Oxford University Press, 2015), especially pp. 196–222.

city. London had long been experienced as overwhelming, but the 1820s saw a sharp intensification of its sights, sounds and challenges. It rose inexorably as both a centre of production and a crucial transition point mediating the faster circuits of emerging industrialised society.

In the new media world that encompassed and was transmitted from the metropolis, there was a vast appetite not only for consuming new kinds of spectacle, but also for being seen and watching others watch. Spectacle in this pervasive sense made London its own show, perhaps nowhere more obviously than in Pierce Egan's *Life in London* (1821), a composition that actually makes a show of Hazlitt,

> lolling at his ease upon one of *Ben Medley's* elegant couches, enjoying the reviving comforts of a good *tinney*, smacking his *chaffer* over a glass of old hock, and topping his *glim* to a *classic* nicety, in order to throw a *new light* upon the elegant leaves of ROSCOE's Life of Lorenzo de' Medici, as a *composition* for a NEW LECTURE at the Surrey Institution. This is also LIFE IN LONDON.[49]

Egan's narrative is an exemplary new media artefact. Originally issued in parts, the sprees of Jerry Hawthorn, Corinthian Tom and Bob Logic were dramatised both through the wildly performative typography of Egan's text and the lavish hand-coloured caricature plates produced by George and Isaac Robert Cruikshank. *Life in London* is an unabashed celebration of the traditions and novelties of the capital. In his opening invocation, Egan calls on Henry Fielding and Tobias Smollett, whose styles he freely appropriates, but also on the great publisher of prints Rudolph Ackermann, who was in part responsible for the introduction of gaslight to London. Egan praises the Tories of *Blackwood's* alongside the Whig politician, dramatist and man-about-town Richard Brinsley Sheridan and the radical parodist Hone: all, in his view, contributed to the rich tapestry that he first sweeps across to give 'a *Camera Obscura* View' and then plunges into along with his roistering protagonists.[50] London took Egan's flash performance to its bosom, spawning prints, spin-offs, piracies and at least six different theatrical productions. However, the phenomenon's wild reproductions also reveal the growing ease with which showy representations could be manipulated for profit. Two years after *Life in London*'s publication, the busker Billy Waters, whose black, disabled body had been staged in the book's plates and playhouse adaptations, died impoverished in St Giles Workhouse. His appropriated memory lived on in commercial porcelain crafted in the

---

[49] Pierce Egan, *Life in London* (London: Sherwood, Neely, and Jones, 1821), p. 31.
[50] Egan, *Life in London*, p. 18.

potteries of Staffordshire and Derby.[51] Egan himself soured somewhat on the whirling world his work engendered; he killed off two of his central characters in the *Finish* he published at the close of the decade. That work includes a huffy three-page footnote that details unauthorised works 'which did not come under the cognisance of the Author . . . calculated not only to produce employment, but profit to the various speculators'.[52]

Typically, Hazlitt himself reserved higher praise for a London writer who 'steals off the pavement to pick his way in the contrary direction'.[53] For Charles Lamb, in Hazlitt's view, 'The streets of London are his fairy-land, teeming with wonder, with life and interest to his retrospective gaze.'[54] Lamb has often been read as a writer who takes sidelong swipes at the present before retreating to evoke a purer past. His essay 'A Complaint of the Decay of Beggars in the Metropolis' begins, with studied magnificence, 'The all-sweeping besom of societarian reformation—your only modern Alcides' club to rid the time of its abuses—is uplift with many-handed sway to extirpate the last fluttering tatters of the bugbear MENDICITY from the metropolis.'[55] However, his nostalgia was deeply aware of itself as nostalgia, and he took a very modern delight in the artifices it required. For Lamb, hidden as he was behind Elia's mask, to insist always on authenticity was to apply an impossible stricture. Concluding his 'Complaint', he urges his readers to 'Act a charity sometimes':

> When a poor creature (outwardly and visibly such) comes before thee, do not stay to inquire whether the "seven small children", in whose name he implores thy assistance, have a veritable existence. Rake not into the bowels of unwelcome truth, to save a halfpenny. It is good to believe him. . . . When they come with their counterfeit looks, and mumping tones, think them players. You pay your money to see a comedian feign these things, which, concerning these poor people, thou canst not certainly tell whether they are feigned or not.[56]

---

[51] For more on Waters, see Mary L. Shannon, 'The Multiple Lives of Billy Waters: Dangerous Theatricality and Networked Illustrations in Nineteenth-Century Popular Culture', *Nineteenth Century Theatre and Film*, 46.2 (2019), 161–89.

[52] Pierce Egan, *Finish to the Adventures of Tom, Jerry, and Logic* (London: G. Virtue, 1830), p. 9.

[53] William Hazlitt, 'Elia—Geoffrey Crayon', in *The Spirit of the Age*, 2nd edn (London: Henry Colburn, 1825), pp. 395–408 (p. 396).

[54] Hazlitt, 'Elia—Geoffrey Crayon', p. 401.

[55] Elia [Charles Lamb], 'A Complaint of the Decay of Beggars in the Metropolis', in *Elia, Essays which have appeared under that signature in the London Magazine* (London: Taylor and Hessey, 1823), pp. 262–75 (p. 262).

[56] Ibid. pp. 274–5.

Such writing has a complex relationship with the discourses of its decade, modelling kindness against the paranoia of surveillance or the systematising large-scale solutions promised by political economy, but also undermining the sense that transparent truths can be found by looking back. Elia repeatedly reveals that his objects of scrutiny were always already performative. The unstable retrospections occasioned by 1820s media reflections usually discovered that in the present, the past was no longer what it once was.

Friedrich Kittler's *Discourse Networks 1800 / 1900* draws a hard distinction between 1800 and 1900.[57] Kittler defines 1800 by the depth experience of close reading the printed word. The proliferating networks of new electronic media distinguish 1900. As this introduction and the essays that follow demonstrate, this contrast is overdrawn. The 1820s was a decade of shows, panoramas, magic lanterns, public lectures (including demonstrations of electric power), and – as we have seen – of the beginning of the craze for the railway, the medium that might seem to define the nineteenth century as a networked era. Print interacted with residual and emergent forms in ways that require a rethinking of 'the supposed asociality that surrounded the rise of silent reading and private viewing that have often been thought to characterize our period'.[58] Nevertheless, Kittler does helpfully identify print and writing as technologies, specific forms of media among others, that served to familiarise an expanding public with reading as a form of 'audio-visual hallucination'.[59] Scott's ability to render history in mental pictures was a major driver in this process, as Ina Ferris has argued, and his images were quickly remediated into stage plays and paintings.[60] Renditions of turbulent national pasts were circulated around Britain and Ireland and far beyond by the railways, canals and turnpikes that joined up the different parts of the United Kingdom, its empire and the rest the world as never before.

This feat was partly enabled by unprecedented interventions by central government in road building in the 1820s, making celebrities of the engineers Thomas Macadam and Thomas Telford.[61] The infrastructural

---

[57] Friedrich Kittler, *Discourse Networks 1800 / 1900*, trans. Michael Metteert (Stanford, CA: Stanford University Press, 1990).

[58] The Multigraph Collective, *Interacting with Print: Elements of Reading in the Era of Print Saturation* (Chicago: Chicago University Press, 2018), p. 5.

[59] See James Brooke-Smith, 'Remediating Romanticism', *Literature Compass*, 10.4 (2013), 343–52 (p. 345).

[60] Ina Ferris, '"Before Our Eyes": Romantic Historical Fiction and the Apparitions of Reading', *Representations*, 121.1 (2013), 60–84. See Chapter 2 by Ian Duncan for a full exploration of Scott's negotiations with history.

[61] See Jo Guldi, *Roads to Power: Britain Invents the Infrastructure State* (Cambridge, MA: Harvard University Press, 2012).

state made possible endless acts of remediation, even as it also enabled provinces and colonies to make their own identities both through – and through circumventing – metropolitan power, for instance (as Lara Atkin shows in Chapter 7) feeding Scottish verse into the newspapers of the Cape Colony. At the same time, the pleasure of producing new kinds of spectacle for consumption, like the sheer rate of flow of information, had a sinister side. The 1820s saw a new world of surveillance where the state and private interests encroached further and further into the lives of others. From the penitentiary system to the New Poor Law of 1834, there were more institutions of control in society than ever before. Provincial newspapers like the *Leeds Mercury* brought the news closer to home – and extended home across empire – but they also made the home into news, as was the case with the craze for Paul Pry or the thirst for local antiquarian knowledge and fabrications.[62] There was an intense desire for public-oriented privacy, fed in part by the curation of poets like L.E.L, and the ways in which published poetry albums turned domestic networks into commercial forms. For Thomas Carlyle, the age threatened to sacrifice all human feeling to the machine, but he worked out his ideas in one of the decade's most characteristic media, the literary periodical, a form turbo-charged by the steam press and increasingly transmitted via steam-powered transport. Like many others who started to write in the 1820s, including the poet laureate of the next age, Alfred Tennyson, Carlyle had to remediate his own career out of the 1820s as he positioned himself as a Victorian sage (the same could be said for Wordsworth, perhaps). Such personal remediations ultimately relied both on the technologies of transmission the decade had begun to come to terms with and on the desire for certainty its plethora of burgeoning alternatives fostered.

Perhaps literary history has tended to skip over the 1820s because it seems too full of unformed narratives, uncertain roads and empty spectacles that were looking at other times for more secure origins and more readily identifiable futures. However, perhaps as we enter the 2020s with an acceptance that identities may not be such certain things, there will be a new appetite for looking at the flickering arrays of contingent forms that lit up the 1820s. Among those forms may be the form of Romanticism itself, a conception to a large extent forged – at least in its most institutionally powerful iterations – in competition with but also out of the shock of the new in the 1820s. Kittler understood Romanticism as deep reading and textual immersion precipitated by changes in forms of communication. By looking more closely at the

---

[62] Discussed in Chapters 5 and 6 by Sara Lodge and Gerard Lee McKeever respectively.

1820s, we can see a much broader range of remediations at work in making Romanticism, some of which stuck while others fell away. Its complexity, like many other complexities, began to resolve itself out of the anxious potential of an age that perceived itself to be at once strikingly new and fearfully unmoored.

Chapter 1

Truth, Fiction and Breaking News: Theodore Hook and the Poyais Speculation

Angela Esterhammer

The decade of the 1820s abounds in literature that blends fact and fiction. With more and more writers publishing in magazines and other periodicals, current events easily make their way into fiction, and prose of the 1820s often crosses over – in one direction or the other – from immediate real-world reference to imaginative fantasy. Writers sometimes elide this distinction entirely; at other times they call attention to it by making insistent truth-claims within forms and genres that are patently fictitious. Other chapters in this volume address problematic truth-claims in the experiential environment of the 1820s: Lindsay Middleton discusses concerns over the authenticity and adulteration of food and Phillip Roberts examines the different articulations of truth made possible by visual media such as the magic lantern. In the realm of print culture, truth in the sense of fidelity to real-world experience is further complicated by authors who write imaginative fiction and poetry, but at the same time produce non-fictional media such as daily and weekly newspapers. As Gerard McKeever shows in his chapter, this convergence of roles results in newspapers with aesthetic motivations and a distinctly literary texture.

At the nexus of these developments was Theodore Hook (1788–1841), a political journalist, novelist, satirist and improviser of verses who manifested a provocative attitude towards truth in both the widely read metropolitan newspaper and the bestselling fiction that he launched in the early 1820s. During the same era, a grandiose speculation that was perpetrated around the colonial settlement of Poyais in central America highlighted issues of fact and fiction by making the truthfulness of descriptive texts into a matter of stark socio-economic reality, and even of life and death. Hook responded explicitly to the Poyais affair in his journalism; it also made its way more subtly into his fiction, which reflects the 'experience-near' quality of the era's popular literature with its rich texture of allusions to current events. In this chapter, I will examine the intersection of Hook's writing with the Poyais affair in order to show how genres of writing in the 1820s hybridised facticity and fictionality, and how the decade's media created expectations of truth out of speculation and performance.

By the time he began writing and editing a London newspaper in 1820, Theodore Hook already had a colourful background in theatre and colonial governance, as well as important connections in political and literary spheres. As the son of the composer and Vauxhall organist James Hook, he made an early acquaintance with the theatres of London. During the first decade of the nineteenth century, while still in his teens, he enjoyed considerable success at Drury Lane and the Haymarket with plays he wrote in popular genres of the day: melodramas, comic operas and one-act afterpieces. Severe attacks of stage fright kept Hook himself off the theatrical stage, yet among London's beau monde he was well known for his extraordinary skill in improvising verses that he performed at upper-class parties and at dinners attended by politicians and journalists. Hook's older brother was chaplain to the Prince Regent; in 1812 this connection, and the Regent's appreciation of Hook's talent as an entertainer, brought him a patronage appointment as treasurer of the island of Mauritius in the Indian Ocean. Although that adventure ended badly and Hook was sent back to London under arrest in 1818 after a large sum of money disappeared from the island's treasury, he remained loyal to the Regent on his accession to the throne as George IV. In 1820, Hook became the clandestine writer-editor of *John Bull*, a fiercely royalist weekly newspaper with one clear agenda: to consolidate a readership loyal to George IV by discrediting the king's estranged wife Caroline and her supporters. Hook made his living from the profits of this bestselling metropolitan paper, from the fiction-writing career he launched in 1824 with *Sayings and Doings*, and from the dinner invitations he received in the expectation that he would display his renowned wit. Thanks to this varied career, Hook self-consciously occupied a position of dependence on high society while also keeping a sharp eye on its sayings and doings. He was both guest and hired entertainer at parties, both instigator and critic of political scandal, both documentary journalist and creative writer in both his newspaper and his fiction.

In the inaugural issue of *John Bull*, Hook sets his tendentious newspaper under the banner of 'plain truth':

We commence our Paper without comment or prospectus – our object is speaking plain truth, and we will do our duty. . . . The test by which we shall try every thing, is TRUTH – Truth is the sole corrector of the mischiefs which stare us in the face, and TRUTH will eventually triumph[.] (17 December 1820, p. 4)[1]

John Bull thus begins with an abrupt first-person present-tense performative declaration – 'We commence our Paper' – and touts this unadorned announcement as evidence in itself of journalistic candour: 'our object is speaking plain truth'. But Hook goes on to underline his allegiance to 'Truth', rather oddly, by quoting a stanza of poetry:

All that mortal art hath wrought
In our cell returns to nought,
The molten gold returns to clay,
The polish'd diamond melts away:
All is altered, all is flown,
Nought stands fast but Truth alone! (17 December 1820, p. 4)

Identified in *John Bull* only as being by 'our greatest living poet', these verses are drawn from Walter Scott's novel *The Monastery*, published earlier in 1820. Hook's choice to illustrate 'plain truth' with the words spoken by Scott's magical White Lady in a scene of enchantment within a mystical cavern suggests that his notion of truth will have a distinctly literary inflection. In the same editorial opening statement, he positions *John Bull*'s truth as the 'antidote' to 'a prostituted Press', 'caricatures' and 'inflammatory speeches' (17 December 1820, p. 4) – a rather bold move that would seem to invite charges of hypocrisy, considering that caricatures and inflammatory speeches formed the main content of *John Bull* itself. As for a prostituted press, Hook was widely rumoured to be secretly in the pay of George IV for editing *John Bull* and to have been recommended for the job by Walter Scott, who periodically sent him financial support.[2] Nevertheless, *John Bull* continues to sound the drumbeat of truth throughout its early years, asserting in the year-end editorial of 31 December 1821 that 'The country, to be saved, must be told the truth, even though the laws themselves pronounce it to be a libel' (p. 4) and, two weeks later, that 'The longer we live, the more satisfied do we feel of the ultimate triumph of TRUTH and JUSTICE' (14 January 1822, p. 4).

---

[1] References to *John Bull* will be given in the text by the date of the issue and page numbers.

[2] In a letter to Daniel Terry of 22 December 1823, Scott offers to send £50 to Hook on account of his financial distress after the Mauritius affair. Scott quotes a letter of appeal from Hook, dated 17 December, in which Hook alludes to his clandestine role in supporting the royalist cause and to Scott's 'kindness' to him in the past; *The Letters of Sir Walter Scott, 1823–1825*, ed. H. J. C. Grierson (London: Constable, 1935), p. 135.

What is truth, then, in this context – or what version of truth is it that uses caricature, romance fiction, inflammatory rhetoric and libel as its vehicles? It would be easy enough to dismiss Hook's truth-claim as sarcasm, cynicism or simply a lie that flouts the dictionary definition of truth as conformity with reality or fact. But there may be more at stake, given how typical Hook's journalistic tactics are for the period. His claim that *John Bull* will contain 'plain truth' is less descriptive than it is declarative. He founds his paper on a rhetorical, performative, media-dependent notion of truth: what is printed in *John Bull* is to be taken as truth *because* it appears in a newspaper that has declared the exposure of truth to be its primary goal. While this circular logic hardly constitutes a viable alternative definition of truth, it is a significant characteristic of Hook's discursive environment that truth is asserted as a pre-eminent value closely associated with the medium of print.

Perhaps ironically, because Hook in other contexts proved himself an expert hoaxer, he pointedly sets truth in opposition to hoaxing.[3] From the outset, *John Bull* styles its prime adversary, Queen Caroline, as the 'Queen of Hoaxers' (24 December 1820, p. 4). A year and a half later, when the newspaper announces that it will refrain from its usual attacks on the Queen in view of her grave illness, Hook nevertheless takes the opportunity to reassert that '[w]e have throughout the whole of our career . . . in the execution of our self-imposed duty . . . deemed it right at all hazards to speak truths' (6 August 1821, p. 5). The subtle shift here from 'truth' to 'truths' – the latter suggesting individual pieces of information rather than a transcendent concept – is underlined by a further elaboration that makes truth appear oddly subjective: 'we have never flinched from speaking what *we thought* just, or narrating that which *we believed* authentic' (italics added). When Queen Caroline died on the following day, *John Bull* lost its original *raison d'être*, but Hook reoriented the profitable publication by reinterpreting his dedication to truth as a mission to debunk hoaxes, lies, fabrications, fallacies, misrepresentations and mistakes – everything that he habitually terms 'humbug'. If this mission often devolved into invectives against political opponents and rival papers, it also inflected Hook's responses to the speculative economy of the 1820s in general and the Poyais affair in particular.

Along with foreign, colonial and provincial news, parliamentary and court reporting, theatre reviews, editorials and letters to the editor, the

---

[3] On Hook as perpetrator of the Berners Street Hoax and other notorious schemes, see R. H. Dalton Barham, *The Life and Remains of Theodore Edward Hook*, 2 vols (London: Bentley, 1849), vol. I, pp. 47–77.

pages of *John Bull* contained Hook's satirical poetry, another vehicle for his brand of truth. On 4 April 1825, the paper printed his 'Bubbles of 1825', a caricature of the current bull market that was being fuelled by heavily hyped speculative ventures. The final stanza of this poem, especially, stretches the truth in order to parody financial speculation:

> Then a company is form'd, tho' not yet advertising,
>   To build, upon a splendid scale, a large balloon,
> And send up tools and broken stones for fresh Mac-Adamizing
>   The new discover'd turnpike roads which cross the moon.
> But the most inviting scheme of all, is one proposed for carrying
> Large furnaces to melt the ice which hems poor CAPTAIN PARRY in;
> They'll then have steam boats twice a week to all the newly-seen land,
> And call for goods and passengers at Labradore and Greenland!
>   Run, neighbours, run, you're just in time to get a share,
>   In all the famous bubbles that amuse John Bull. (4 April 1825, p. 5)

The poem alludes to actual investment schemes in steamboats, canals and railways that were being advertised daily in the newspapers and often by means of popular songs which, as in Hook's refrain, urged fellow citizens to buy shares. Hook's verses extend these ventures seamlessly into the realm of the fantastic – turnpike roads discovered on the moon, furnaces to melt sea ice, even a visionary Eurostar line: 'A tunnel underneath the sea, from Calais straight to Dover, sir, / That qualmish folks may cross by land from shore to shore'. In eliding actually existing technology such as macadamised roads, and current events such as Captain Parry's Arctic voyages, with imaginative projection, 'Bubbles of 1825' not only parodies the lure of real-world financial speculations but also mimics their modus operandi. Speculative ventures typically have a basis in material fact, but their perceived value is a fiction augmented by collective belief that balloons beyond the value of actually existing resources. Thomas Love Peacock traces a similar arc from reality to fantasy in his *Paper Money Lyrics*, also written in 1825–6. Peacock's 'Chorus of Bubble Buyers' alludes to speculative projects that begin with fairly realistic 'inspectors' offering samples of 'metals omnigenous streaked and emboss'd', but they quickly inflate into fictitious 'lakes overflowing with treasure', 'gold-dust that rolled in each torrent and stream', 'bridges to span the Atlantic' and 'gas to illumine the poles'.[4] Byron, in the contemporaneously published canto 12 of *Don Juan*, depicts the speculative economy supported by international financiers such as Rothschild and Baring – 'the true lords of Europe' – and the

[4] Thomas Love Peacock, *Paper Money Lyrics*, in *The Works of Thomas Love Peacock, Volume 7: Poems and Plays* (London: Constable, 1931), pp. 122–3.

booming investments of the moment, including loans to new republican governments in South America. 'Every loan,' he continues, 'Is not a merely speculative hit, / But seats a nation or upsets a throne. / Republics also get involved a bit; / Columbia's stock hath holders not unknown / On 'Change'.[5] While intentionally hyperbolic, the examples in all these satires just as intentionally allude to the genuine drivers of the 1820s bull market: advances in transportation technology, geographical exploration and resource development, and the economies of new republics and expanding colonies.

Byron and Hook were schoolfellows together at Harrow, and although *John Bull* savagely critiques His Lordship's behaviour during the 1820s and the vulgarity of *Don Juan*, their writing continued to share common ground. In particular, Byron's satire on English society in the late cantos of *Don Juan* forms a close parallel to Hook's silver-fork fiction. Hook's career as a popular novelist began with a three-volume collection of tales entitled *Sayings and Doings: A Series of Sketches from Life*, published in early 1824 and followed by two three-volume sequels in 1825 and 1828. A compilation of stories satirising high life and manners that draws on Hook's colonial experience as well as his political connections, this project was reportedly suggested to Hook by Edward Shackell, the publisher of *John Bull*.[6] Hook's fiction aligns itself with the *John Bull* newspaper in its strident but paradoxical claim to speak plain truth: blending sociological documentation with imaginative hyperbole, *Sayings and Doings* is therefore a prime example of the way fact and fiction transgress their boundaries in the 1820s. In an Advertisement that appeared at the beginning of the first volume and also, in shortened form, in *John Bull*, Hook avows that *Sayings and Doings* is based on eyewitness observation and simultaneously calls his book a 'speculation': 'I have watched the world, and have set down all that I have seen ... I have thought it a curious matter of speculation to compare the "DOINGS" of the moderns with the "SAYINGS" of the ancients.'[7] Hook's claim that these tales will expose truths about social relationships, financial behaviour and political injustice echoes many times throughout *Sayings and Doings*. His journalistic experience with *John Bull* comes through in the voice of a narrator obsessed with documentary truth but also hyperconscious of the way language constructs socio-economic reality.

---

[5] Lord Byron, *Don Juan*, vol. 5 of *Complete Poetical Works*, ed. Jerome J. McGann (Oxford: Clarendon, 1993), p. 496.

[6] Barham, *Life and Remains of Theodore Edward Hook*, vol. I, p. 236.

[7] Theodore Hook, *Sayings and Doings: A Series of Sketches from Life*, 3 vols (London: Colburn, 1824), vol. I, pp. iv–v. See also *John Bull*, 23 February 1824, p. 6.

The journalistic inflection of *Sayings and Doings* is especially evident in the novel-length tale 'Merton', which crosses sentimental fiction with sensational news coverage. 'Merton' is an unremitting melodrama of coincidences, chance meetings, failures to meet, missed deadlines, letters delivered a minute too late, misunderstandings caused when two characters or towns have the same name, an apoplectic fit that kills the hero's father in the moment when he is about to make a crucial revelation and so on and on. Alternately rich and bankrupt, on the point of marrying his true love and banished forever from her presence, the recipient of a comfortable patronage appointment and a condemned murderer seconds away from execution, Hook's protagonist Henry Merton seems doomed to dizzying reversals of fortune from one moment to the next. The story thus parodies both the improbable coincidences common in romance novels and the sensational news items about accidents and crimes that provided copy for metropolitan papers. Yet throughout the incredible tale the narrator protests that he is 'stating facts as they have occurred', that 'the facts I have here narrated, are in substance, *literally true*' and that readers should 'beware how they indulge in such dangerous incredulity' for '*It is truth*'.[8] Here and elsewhere, Hook's habit of pairing his most insistent, italicised truth-claims with his most fantastic narratives dares readers to dismiss his rhetoric as facetious pretence. In 'Merton', his provocative claims to documentary truth also incorporate serious passages of socio-political critique: when he charges the British legal system with failing to guarantee the right to a speedy trial, or blames the increasingly bureaucratised welfare system for failing to help the poor, the storyteller's voice is inflected by that of the political journalist. Hook draws a direct line between journalism and fiction when he claims that the quick changes of fortune and status exemplified by 'Merton' are exactly the observations that motivated him to write *Sayings and Doings*: 'These are the things, these are the changes, and such as these, which first set me upon the scheme of noting down what I see in the world.'[9] 'Merton' reveals the sociological core of Hook's writing even as its plot spirals off into hyperbole.

Elsewhere in *Sayings and Doings*, however, the notion of truth in journalism is the direct target of Hook's satire. Despite the strong truth-claims he is simultaneously making in *John Bull*, Hook seizes opportunities in *Sayings and Doings* to undermine the concept of newspaper truth entirely. The first story in the 1824 collection, entitled 'Danvers', critiques London newspaper writers who – as Hook himself did in

---

[8] Hook, *Sayings and Doings* (1824), vol. II, p. 279; vol. III, pp. 138, 232.
[9] Ibid. vol. III, p. 182.

John Bull – hide behind a distanced editorial 'WE' in order to construct authority and tell readers what to think:

> what right, what claim has a worthy gentleman, shut up in his garret, to prescribe, by the melancholy gleamings of his rushlight, rules for our observance, directions for the guidance of our taste, and hints towards forming our judgment upon facts and objects as visible and open to *us* as to *him*. His obscurity alone gives him importance, as vessels at sea seem larger in a fog; and the combination of that mysterious monosyllable WE, by which he dispenses his ordinances in the plural number, with the notorious apathy of the world at large, confers upon the hidden individual in his editorial capacity a consequence and an influence, which, if he were known, neither *he* nor his fellows could possibly obtain, and affords him the power and opportunity of dictating to his superiors in intellect, and of regulating society, into which he would not personally be suffered to intrude.[10]

The speaker of this passage, the nouveau riche Thomas Danvers, claims allegiance with a different 'we': not the writers, but the readers of newspapers. While admitting that a London newspaper 'is excessively convenient in a large city, where one has ten thousand other things to do', because 'it saves one all the pain of making up opinions', Danvers exposes the way newspaper writers impose their opinions on readers by manipulating language and by hiding, literally, in the dark.[11] The passage seems to apply pointedly to Hook himself, given his official anonymity as writer-editor of *John Bull* and his discomfort over the class distinctions that placed limits on his acceptance in 'superior' circles. Despite being Harrow-educated and patronised (in obscure ways) by the king, Hook habitually accords to himself an insider-outsider status that demands the construction of a compensatory authority in the form of the anonymous editorial voice.

If the above passage from 'Danvers' seems heavy with self-satire, the story 'Passion and Principle' in the 1825 series of *Sayings and Doings* indicts journalists more generally. Here Hook has the urbane aristocrat Lord Feversham enlighten a provincial schoolmaster about journalistic practices in London:

> 'if you knew the glorious ignorance of facts, in which newspaper-mongers in general live in this great town, and the perfect facility with which, by a dash of the pen, a plausible falsehood (always at the command of an inventive journalist) can supply the place of real information, you would not be surprised that an editor should occasionally send a cripple fox-hunting, convert an elegant and accomplished equerry into a weather-beaten veteran; burn a Countess to death in the North, before she had admitted fires into her

---

[10] Ibid. vol. I, pp. 109–10.
[11] Ibid. vol. I, p. 109.

boudoir; marry a couple who have never been introduced; or appoint a noble-
man to an office in the government which never was intended for him, and
which, I can assure you in the present instance, he would not have accepted
had it been offered.'

'Dear me!' said Tickle, 'that is very strange.'

'Not more strange than true,' said Feversham[.][12]

By the last line, what is 'true' is that newspaper writers lie; they use
language to invent facts rather than to describe reality. Hook's fictional
spokesperson in *Sayings and Doings* makes explicit what is implicit in
John Bull: a media-dependent notion of truth whereby the authority
ascribed to the public press allows and even encourages journalists to
use language performatively rather than constatively.

Another passage from 'Passion and Principle' illustrates some of the
distinctive preoccupations that Hook's journalism and his fiction have in
common, including political economy and theatrical performance. Every
issue of *John Bull* included stock market reports and reviews of the
London theatres; in *Sayings and Doings*, Hook draws out and impro-
vises upon this content, among other things by bringing his characters
into a theatre in virtually every story. 'Passion and Principle' includes
a scene that takes place in the mixed society of London's Haymarket
Theatre, where the first-person narrator takes the opportunity to super-
impose the marriage market, the stock market and the Haymarket in
order to comment on the mode of speculation that is endemic in each of
these contexts:

> I believe more has been done in the way of matrimonial speculation in the
> compact recesses of the Opera circle, than any where else in London . . . As
> for the Opera pit, it is the Royal Exchange of good society, and divided into
> *walks*, as regularly as the Exchange in the City. . . . In the Haymarket, the
> state of fashionable parties forms the current business of the night, as the
> state of foreign funds engrosses the attention of Cornhill during the day.
> Invitations to a noble gourmand's dinner stand relatively in the one, to the
> four per cents. in the other. *Blue* coteries rank with Prussian stock, and a rich
> widow's assemblies, with Spanish securities; small dances without supper, run
> parallel to Poyais bonds, and water parties in the Spring, to Chili Scrip. In
> short, the dandy and the dealer might shut up shop, were they not in their dif-
> ferent vocations regularly to visit one or other of these great national marts,
> during the hours of business.[13]

When he introduces the opera circle as a place of 'matrimonial speculation', Hook picks up a leitmotif of *Sayings and Doings*, a project he

---

[12] Theodore Hook, *Sayings and Doings: or, Sketches from Life*, second series, 3 vols
(London: Colburn, 1825), vol. III, pp. 284–5.

[13] Ibid. vol. III, pp. 93–4.

advertised to readers at the outset as 'a curious matter of speculation'.[14] In this episode, his theatre-goers engage in speculation by calibrating the relative value of one another's companions, behaviour and dress; audience members become inadvertent performers as they are evaluated on the basis of what they say, wear and consume. Hook outlines a table of equivalences between the status of social events – the subject of gossip among theatre-goers – and the value of the foreign securities traded on the Royal Exchange, thereby capturing the details of a moment when trade in foreign investments was at its height during the stock market mania of the early 1820s. His examples accurately represent a descending scale of value, from stock in the Prussian state that was increasing in economic dominance after it gained territory at the Congress of Vienna in 1815, all the way down to risky investment in Chile, whose loan failure was one of the first indicators of the incipient stock market crash of 1825–6. The global connotations of the scene are enhanced by a distant echo of Joseph Addison's article about the Royal Exchange in *The Spectator*, where Addison had developed a detailed analogy between the stock exchange and the world of international diplomatic relations: 'Factors [i.e., agents] in the Trading World are what Ambassadors are in the Politick World', according to Addison.[15] By Hook's time, the dominant parallel is not international diplomacy but social performativity. The marriage market calculates valuations as deliberately and precisely as the stock market; conversely, in a stock market caught up in speculative mania, gossip and rumour have become major influencers of economic value.

Almost hidden amidst Hook's calibration of equivalences in the Haymarket scene are 'Poyais bonds'. The subtle, seemingly casual, yet far from neutral mention of Poyais is an instance of the dynamic allusiveness of 1820s fiction: the text displays its experience-near quality by citing a name that would have jumped out at any contemporary newspaper reader. The inclusion of Poyais bonds in the list of possible investments takes the mixing of fact and fiction to another level, since Poyais was both a colonial settlement project and the most notorious of contemporary scandals, and it was promoted in a way that capitalised on the era's propensity to couch fictional content in strident truth-claims. The author of the Poyais project was Gregor MacGregor (1786–1845), an adventurer from Edinburgh who claimed to be a descendant of Rob Roy MacGregor, the Highland hero whose name was conveniently on readers' lips in the wake of Scott's 1817 novel *Rob Roy*. Having made

---

[14] Hook, *Sayings and Doings* (1824), vol. I, p. v.
[15] *The Spectator*, 69 (19 May 1711).

his name as a military leader in the Venezuelan and Colombian wars of independence, MacGregor received a nominal land grant in central America from a Native American chief in 1820. Although the grant was soon revoked (if it was ever valid at all), MacGregor capitalised on it as the basis for a nation he called Poyais, located on the Mosquito Coast of present-day Honduras and Nicaragua, an area in which Britain had pursued colonial interests earlier in the eighteenth century. MacGregor raised hundreds of thousands of pounds in investment from British speculators to colonise Poyais; in a vain attempt to secure capital from Nathan Rothschild, he also proposed a 'Hebrew Colony' of Jewish settlers to be recruited from Germany and Poland.[16] Four boatloads of emigrants, mainly from Scotland, set sail in 1822 and 1823 for what they were promised was a fully fledged settlement with a town of 15,000 to 20,000 people, a welcoming harbour, an idyllic climate, fruitful soil and natives particularly friendly to the British. Yet Poyais did not actually exist as a country or a settlement. MacGregor was able literally to put Poyais on the map of central America; the problem is that he put it only on the map, without any correspondence in geographical reality. The adventure ended tragically for nearly two hundred would-be settlers who died in the wilderness of fever and exposure, as well as for investors who were left holding worthless paper bonds.

Gregor MacGregor personally sought backing for his project from major financiers by letter-writing and networking among the fashionable circles of London that Theodore Hook frequented and that he portrayed in *Sayings and Doings*. To attract settlers to Poyais, MacGregor and his agents used a variety of vehicles including newspaper advertisements, periodical articles, handbills, poems, maps and a 355-page guide for travellers and emigrants entitled *Sketch of the Mosquito Shore, including the Territory of Poyais . . . Chiefly intended for the Use of Settlers*, published in Edinburgh by William Blackwood and by his partner Cadell in London. Like other investment ventures of the day, though on an unusually bold scale, Poyais was promoted by means of texts that blended truth and fiction. *Sketch of the Mosquito Shore*, which was published under the name 'Thomas Strangeways' but widely suspected to be the work of MacGregor himself, begins with a claim both to eyewitness evidence and to published authorities. The author avows that he has proceeded by 'combining the knowledge . . . which he acquired

[16] Letter of Gregor MacGregor to N. M. Rothschild, 30 June 1821; available at https://www.rothschildarchive.org/collections/treasure_of_the_month/october_2018_the_land_that_never_was_correspondence_between_gregor_macgregor_and_n_m_rothschild_1821 (accessed 7 February 2022). My thanks to Sara Lodge for bringing this letter to my attention.

during a portion of his life spent *in that part of the world* – with the information afforded to him by the few but authentic authors who have written any thing on the subject', and that he has 'confined himself, *as much as possible*, to such plain and positive facts, as are established beyond the shadow of doubt, by reference to the authorities alluded to' (italics added).[17] It is a prominent yet oddly qualified truth-claim, not only because of the hedging phrase 'as much as possible' but also because of the vagueness of the author's assertion that he has lived 'in that part of the world'. Nevertheless, in their form and content *Sketch of the Mosquito Shore* and other texts advertising Poyais blended seamlessly into the marketplace of the 1820s, which abounded with literature of travel and emigration. As Lara Atkin and Porscha Fermanis show in their contributions to this volume, the genres of emigrant literature that proliferated during the 1820s – emigration guidebooks, sentimental lyrics of farewell, 'booster ballads' extolling the settler colony – provided abundant opportunities to give textual presence to a new settlement venture. In advertising Poyais, MacGregor and his collaborators filled these popular genres with imaginative content supported by an admixture of fact, so that readers found it hard to disentangle real-world reference from pure speculation.

Even after the Poyais bubble burst, it proved difficult to distinguish truth from fraud. Victims of the disastrous speculation who claimed to have been misled by fallacious texts used the public press, including the pages of *John Bull*, to lay blame on MacGregor's accomplices and agents. Yet MacGregor himself came in for remarkably little criticism. He was imprisoned briefly for debt, but never convicted of fraud. Most remarkably, he continued to pursue the Poyais project well into the following decade. Even after the news became known that three-quarters of the original colonists had lost their lives, MacGregor continued to sell Poyais bonds and land, opening a 'Poyais office' in Paris in 1824. After being charged in France with 'conspiracy to defraud, selling titles, and disposing of land in Poyais' – a charge of which he was acquitted in July 1826 – he again offered Poyais bonds, convertible into land, for sale in London in 1827 and beyond.[18] The National Records of Scotland hold a handwritten stock certificate for 'Poyaisian Three per Cent. Reduced Stock', made out in English and French and signed by

---

[17] Thomas Strangeways, *Sketch of the Mosquito Shore, including the Territory of Poyais, Descriptive of the Country; with some information as to its productions, the best mode of culture, &c. Chiefly intended for the Use of Settlers* (Edinburgh: Blackwood; London: Cadell, 1822), pp. v–vi.

[18] Richard T. Gregg, *Gregor MacGregor, Cazique of Poyais 1786–1845* (London: International Bond & Share Society, 1999), p. 17.

MacGregor in London on 10 September 1831. In the same collection there is a handwritten notebook in which, probably during the early 1830s, MacGregor outlined an elaborate constitution covering civil rights, taxation, representation, form of government, property, judiciary and militia, intended for 'The Inhabitants and those persons who shall have become Settlers in the Poyaisian and the other Districts of Territory of the Indian Coast in Central America'.[19]

Historical evidence suggests that the Poyais project gained so much uptake and persisted through so many revivals because the genres used to describe and promote it were so similar to those used by legitimate emigration projects. Recent scholarship has affirmed this resemblance: while the financial crisis of 2007–8 brought renewed attention to the Poyais affair as one of the most elaborate of historical financial scandals, it also generated revisionary assessments arguing that Poyais was less an out-and-out fraud and more of a piece with the speculative economy of the 1820s than has usually been thought. Locating Gregor MacGregor in the context of Spanish-American colonial history, Matthew Brown argues that although he may have been 'errant and even error-prone on occasions', he 'cannot continue to be dismissed as a fraud and a fool who dressed up his deceptions with political rhetoric'. Rather, Brown ascribes his negative portrayal in history to the fact that 'his ambitions continually fell foul of the interests of various Caribbean elites and of the distinctive historical circumstances of the region'.[20] Kit Nicholls continues Brown's argument with a stronger literary orientation, illustrating how MacGregor's self-representation resonated with the role of Scottish Highlanders in both contemporary literature and global finance.[21] However, these viewpoints stand in stark contrast to critiques, from the 1820s to the present day, that describe Poyais as a hoax and a scandal, a project that went far beyond other ventures of the day in deluding investors with untruths.[22]

[19] 'Plan of a Constitution for the Inhabitants . . .', GD50/68, National Records of Scotland, General Register House, Edinburgh. In his article 'Inca, Sailor, Soldier, King: Gregor MacGregor and the Early Nineteenth-Century Caribbean', *Bulletin of Latin American Research*, 24.1 (2005), Matthew Brown claims that this constitution was published in 1836 (p. 55); Gregg, in *Gregor MacGregor* (p. 25), reports that it was published in 1839, though with a date of 4 July 1836.
[20] Brown, 'Inca, Sailor, Soldier, King', pp. 46, 56, 44.
[21] Kit Nicholls, '"All Abbotsford to an acre of Poyais": Highlandry and the Revolutionary Atlantic', *European Romantic Review*, 22.6 (2011), 727–44.
[22] For accounts of Poyais as a hoax, see 'Review of *Sketch of the Mosquito Shore, including the Territory of Poyais*', *Quarterly Review*, 28 (1822), 157–61; A. R. Hope Moncrieff, 'Gregor MacGregor', *Macmillan's Magazine*, 92 (1 May 1905), 339–50; Alfred Hasbrouck, 'Gregor McGregor and the Colonization of Poyais, between 1820 and 1824', *Hispanic American Historical Review*, 7.4 (1927), 438–59; Victor Allan,

Given the blending of fact and fiction in the literary and financial marketplace of the 1820s, both these interpretations are valid, and indeed interdependent. A hoax on the scale of Poyais was enabled by the speculative economy and the print culture of the decade, specifically by the existence of genres in which fact could extend seamlessly into fantasy and of media in which truth could be a matter of first-person authority or a quality ascribed by readers to the medium itself. As the failure of the Poyais speculation played itself out in newspapers, pamphlets and courtrooms during the mid-1820s, inquiries into the truth of MacGregor's claims focused, interestingly, on textual issues: that is, on questions of authorship, plagiarism, narrative perspective and the credibility of printed texts. Survivors of the disastrous emigration scheme who published their testimony in the *Edinburgh Annual Register* for 1823 emphasised the disparity between the advertised descriptions of Poyais and the geographical reality they found:

> We also feel it a duty, as much as has been blazoned to the world of the existence of Poyais seas, of Poyais cities and towns, and of Poyais people and lands, to put in your power the means of apprizing his Majesty's Government of the fallacy of these assertions. . . . We assure you there is no Poyais sea or city of Poyais in existence, or any appearance in any part of the country to warrant such an assertion; and indeed, to sum up the whole, we cannot better exemplify it than by declaring that the whole scheme of the establishment has been built 'upon the baseless fabric of a vision'.[23]

A review of *Sketch of the Mosquito Shore* in the *Quarterly Review* accused the author of never having set foot on the Mosquito Shore and instead plagiarising published histories of the Caribbean to construct a 'garbled' fantasy about an idyllic landscape that existed nowhere in the world.[24] Similarly, in the course of a lawsuit, the Court of King's Bench probed the question of whether the advertisements that lured 'deluded speculators' to Poyais were really based on eyewitness testimony or on unacknowledged quotation from sources such as Bryan Edwards's *History of the British Colonies in the West Indies* (1793; 5th edn 1819) and John Wright's *Memoir of the Mosquito Territory* (1808).[25] The court questioned the authorship – and, for that matter, the literary merit – of *Sketch of the Mosquito Shore* and of poems that were used to advertise Poyais, such as one entitled 'The Poyais Emigrant' by Scottish poet

'The Prince of Poyais', *History Today*, 2.1 (1952), 53–8; and David Sinclair, *Sir Gregor MacGregor and the Land that Never Was: The Extraordinary Story of the Most Audacious Fraud in History* (London: Headline, 2003).

23 'Poyais Settlement', *Edinburgh Annual Register* (1823), 278–83 (p. 282).
24 'Review of *Sketch of the Mosquito Shore*', p. 160.
25 'Court of King's Bench, Guildhall, Jan. 9', *Annual Register* (1824), 17–23 (pp. 20–1).

Joanna Belfrage Picken.[26] Picken's brother Andrew also wrote verses to advertise the Poyais scheme before he himself embarked as a Poyais colonist; being one of the lucky ones who returned, he testified at the King's Bench trial and later emigrated to a more realistic destination, Montreal, along with his sister. Meanwhile, Herman Hendriks, a financial backer of MacGregor's who had been attacked in the press for promoting the Poyais scheme, fought back by printing his side of the story as a pamphlet entitled *A Plain Narrative of Facts*. In it, Hendriks testifies that MacGregor persuaded him of the reality of Poyais by showing him a Poyais banknote and a '*printed* list' (Hendriks's italics) of the officials appointed to govern the colony.[27] Hendriks shows a rather pathetic faith in the truth-value of the printed page as the irresistible evidence by which he was persuaded and the medium he must now use to persuade readers of his own innocence.

One of the most vehement early critics of the Poyais affair, the duplicity with which it was advertised, the lax government oversight that made it possible and the gullibility of investors was Theodore Hook. Ironically, though, *John Bull* was initially among the newspapers that advertised the Poyais scheme. On 6 January 1823, the newspaper's listing of just-published books announces *Sketch of the Musquito [sic] Shore; including the Territory of Poyais* alongside the second edition of another book published by Blackwood and Cadell entitled *Some Account of the Mosquito Territory; contained in a Memoir, written in 1757, while that country was in possession of the British* (6 January 1823, p. 8). The simultaneous advertising of two books about the Mosquito Shore no doubt helped to draw attention and lend credibility to the dubious Poyais guidebook. The front page of the 16 March 1823 edition of *John Bull* announces that freight or passage to Poyais may be booked in 'the fine, fast-sailing, coppered Brig Alknomack' (16 March 1823, p. 1). A year later, however, the bubble had burst and Poyais became the topic of *John Bull*'s critiques and exposés. On 23 February 1824, Hook ran a first long article on 'the proceedings at POYAIS' based on a 'very voluminous report' that appeared in the *Jamaica Royal Gazette* of 10 January (23 February 1824, p. 5). Focusing on the 'heart-rending testimonies' of the surviving colonists, who in place of 'the promised large city of Saint Joseph's' found only '*three huts*', *John Bull* avows that '[w]e certainly never heard of any *hoax* upon so extensive a scale as this' and calls for the enactment of laws that would prevent such a 'shameless delusion' before it could claim more victims.

---

[26] Lara Atkin discusses this poem at greater length later in this volume (Chapter 7).
[27] Herman Hendriks, *A Plain Narrative of Facts* (London, 1824), p. 8.

This condemnation of the Poyais fraud is immediately followed by the first announcement in *John Bull* of the forthcoming publication *Sayings and Doings*, in which Hook puffs his own book as being by 'a gentleman of considerable notoriety in the political as well as literary world' (23 February 1824, p. 6). Although perhaps coincidental, the pairing of *John Bull*'s first critique of Poyais with its first advertisement of *Sayings and Doings* interestingly foreshadows the reappearance of Poyais in Hook's fiction. In 'The Sutherlands', the first story of the 1825 series, the young adventuress Emily inveigles her way into marriage with the upper-class George Sutherland. Emily's dubious background is gradually exposed with the admission that her father's 'important situation in a foreign country' is that of 'Surveyor General of Poyais'.[28] It emerges that her father is really a bankrupt innkeeper who 'got off to Edinburgh, and was appointed by somebody, Surveyor-general at Poyais, went out and found no Poyais to survey'; since his return to England, he has been serving a jail term for theft. Hook continues his satire on the scam of pretentious Poyaisian titles by making Emily's sister's lover a major in 'the Third Regiment of Poyasian Green Hussars'.[29] Here and elsewhere in Hook's fiction, Poyais becomes shorthand for fraudulent hoaxes and the gullibility of their victims. To Hook's contemporary readers, the allusion would have been a giveaway that Emily and her family are swindlers; to readers today, it is another indication of the experience-near quality of 1820s popular fiction.

In *John Bull*, Hook continued his exposure of the Poyais fraud throughout 1824. For weeks the newspaper carried reports, critiques and letters to the editor on the Poyais affair, culminating in a satirical poem entitled 'The Court of Poyais' in which Hook derided both the pretence of a Poyaisian government and his own political opponents. The heavily ironic refrain that ends each stanza mocks MacGregor's assumed authority, but hints darkly that those who – like the singer of the verses, the 'POYASIAN POET LAUREATE' – allow themselves to be duped by MacGregor are flouting the monarchy and the established order:

> Then a fig for KING GEORGE and his old-fashioned sway!
> And hey for MACGREGOR, Cacique of Poyais!! (15 March 1824, p. 5)

In mid-August 1824, the Poyais controversy returned to the pages of *John Bull* for several more weeks. Rival factions among Gregor MacGregor's agents and adherents used the newspaper to air their positions and rebut

[28] Hook, *Sayings and Doings* (1825), vol. I, p. 18.
[29] Ibid. vol. I, p. 55.

one another's attacks, while Hook used his editorial comments on their letters to express his astonishment at the extent of the Poyais 'humbug'. *John Bull*'s motive in printing the letters, he asserts, is 'that they may stand recorded as proofs of the most unqualified folly, as examples of credulity and quackery, the existence of which, without ocular proof of the facts, persons in after times could not be made to believe' (30 August 1824, p. 5).

Deflating what he called the 'Poyais humbug' and 'bubble' (16 August 1824, p. 5) was very much in line with what Hook conceived of as his dedication to truth. In the end, however, the strategies used by Hook and MacGregor to expound their worldviews seem remarkably similar. Both of them define truth rhetorically and subjectively from the perspective of the first-person observer; as Hook writes at the outset of *Sayings and Doings*, 'I have watched the world, and have set down all that I have seen.' *Sayings and Doings* claims the author's eyewitness observation as a guarantee of truth, yet situates him partly outside and partly within the society he describes, leaving the author and the notion of truth irremediably conflicted. Both Hook and MacGregor capitalise on the facticity that readers are prepared to ascribe to certain genres and media such as the newspaper, the first-person travel account and even printed matter in general. *Sketch of the Mosquito Shore*, like other advertisements for Poyais, relies on the expectations of truth associated with guidebooks for emigrants and implies a grounding in first-person experience, but ultimately lays itself open to criticism for failing to provide a true eyewitness perspective on the Mosquito Coast. Parodies of Poyais and other grandiose investment schemes expose the way speculators extrapolate from real resources and technologies into the realm of the fictional and the fantastic – yet the Poyais scheme was so effective because it was itself a 'serious' parody of colonial speculation and the media it employed, from guidebooks to popular ballads to stock offerings.

Looking back from the vantage point of a quarter century, later commentators noted how disruptive the Poyais affair had been to economic activity and public opinion during the 1820s: 'Emigration received a great shock', they remarked, and '[t]he Poyais loan was an epoch from which many dated for the remainder of their lives'.[30] With further historical distance, the conjunction of the Poyais speculation, the *John Bull* newspaper and *Sayings and Doings* serves to highlight some of the features of print culture during the 1820s. The journalistic mode of writing 'to the moment' infuses literary genres: 1820s fiction is full

---

[30] John Francis and Daniel Defoe, *Chronicles and Characters of the Stock Exchange* (London: Willoughby, 1849), p. 278.

of allusions to real-world colonial projects and speculative ventures, and questions about truth, fictionality, eyewitness observation and the role of language in constructing reality swirl and bubble around them. Truth often looks like a situated, genre-specific, performative category. Whether in a weekly newspaper, poetry, prose tales or the prospectus for a financial speculation, the awareness that all texts are hybrids of fact and fiction is never very far from the surface – a feature that may, from a vantage point two hundred years later, seem both historically odd and oddly contemporary.

Acknowledgement

This chapter expands on ideas that are discussed briefly in other contexts in my book *Print and Performance in the 1820s: Improvisation, Speculation, Identity* (Cambridge: Cambridge University Press, 2020). I thank Cambridge University Press for permission to reprint material from chapters 5 and 7 in revised form.

Chapter 2

The Surfaces of History: Scott's Turn, 1820

Ian Duncan

With the publication of *Ivanhoe* (December 1819, dated 1820), the career of 'the Author of Waverley' took a well-noted turn. The turn was topical, from the recent past of modern Scottish history, 'sixty years since' (the subtitle of Scott's first novel, *Waverley*), to the remote past of medieval England, six hundred years since. It was also technical, from a realism that modelled 'the objective dialectical framework of a particular historical crisis', according to Georg Lukács's influential account of 'the classical form of the historical novel', to an antiquarian and ecphrastic rendition of period forms – from effects of historical depth, in other words, to effects of surface.[1] In a 'succession of brilliant pictures, addressed as often to the eye as to the imagination', *Ivanhoe* transports its readers 'from the reign of nature and reality, to that of fancy and romance', wrote Francis Jeffrey; Scott's novel glitters with 'splendid descriptions of arms and dresses—moated and massive castles—tournaments of mailed champions—solemn feasts—formal courtesies, and other matters of external and visible presentment'.[2] Other reviewers concurred, some dismissively: 'The costume which the actors have borrowed from ancient times, is perceived to be the only thing which claims affinity with reality', until 'no other impression is left on the mind, than that of a pageant or a masquerade'.[3]

Recent commentary develops the theme. Writing on *Ivanhoe*, Ina Ferris links Scott's 'unprecedented mobilization of reading's powers of visualization' with a contemporary vogue for the scientific explanation of apparitions, as effects of psychosomatic disorder (hallucinations)

---

[1] Georg Lukács, *The Historical Novel*, trans. Hannah and Stanley Mitchell (Lincoln: University of Nebraska Press, 1983), p. 60.

[2] [Francis Jeffrey], 'Ivanhoe. A Romance. The Novels and Tales of the Author of Waverley', *Edinburgh Review*, 33 (January 1820), 1–54 (pp. 7–8).

[3] *Eclectic Review*, 13 (January 1820), in *Scott: The Critical Heritage*, ed. John O. Hayden (New York: Barnes & Noble, 1970), pp. 188–94 (p. 190).

or optical technology (mirrors, lenses). Like those phenomena, on the uncanny interface between the visible and the visionary, Scott's fiction 'inhabits the equivocal zone of "appearing": at once a manifestation and a simulacrum'.[4] Scaled for at-home consumption, historical romance became a portable analogue of the visual-media displays and devices that proliferated through the 1820s, like the 'Phantasmagoria Lantern' discussed by Phillip Roberts in Chapter 4 of this volume.[5] Other critics refer such effects to the increasing theatricalisation of political life in public spectacles and ceremonies, like the neo-Elizabethan pomp of George IV's coronation in 1820 ('a gigantic fancy-dress pageant on the theme of the *Faerie Queen*, in which George IV played the part of a male Gloriana') and the tartan-clad, retro-Jacobite pageantry Scott himself designed for the king's visit to Scotland in 1822.[6] Pageantry provides an aesthetic principle for Scott's second English historical novel, the Elizabethan romance *Kenilworth* – 'a clear-eyed meditation on the nature and uses of spectacle', according to Stephen Arata.[7] Andrew Lincoln views *Ivanhoe* and *Kenilworth* (both of which would hold the stage in multiple dramatic adaptations) as exercises in 'the politics of style and spectacle': converting the novelistic 'drama of inner development' into 'a drama of surfaces', Scott aims 'to reconcile traditional aristo-cratic styles of public display with newer, egalitarian styles of imagining national community' in response to the civil unrest of 1819–20.[8] For David Kurnick, disguise and performance in *Kenilworth* are tactical by-products of 'an unstable world in which theatricality goes all the way down'.[9] And Timothy Campbell argues that Scott's saturation of that

---

[4] Ina Ferris, '"Before Our Eyes": Romantic Historical Fiction and the Apparitions of Reading', *Representations*, 121 (Winter 2013), 60–84 (pp. 61, 80).

[5] Ferris (ibid. p. 62) cites Maurice Samuel's discussion of the context for French Romantic historical fiction (flourishing in Scott's wake) in 'new illusionist technologies of reproduction (for example, panoramas, dioramas, and wax displays), stage entertainments, exhibitions of historical paintings, [and] museum displays': *The Spectacular Past: Popular History and the Novel in Nineteenth-Century France* (Ithaca, NY: Cornell University Press, 2004), p. 164.

[6] See Mark Girouard, *The Return to Camelot: Chivalry and the English Gentleman* (New Haven, CT: Yale University Press, 1981), pp. 26–8; Boyd Hilton, *A Mad, Bad, and Dangerous People?: England, 1783–1846* (Oxford: Oxford University Press, 2008), pp. 31–6. For a comprehensive discussion of the period's media and performance culture, see Angela Esterhammer, *Print and Performance in the 1820s: Improvisation, Speculation, Identity* (Cambridge: Cambridge University Press, 2020).

[7] Stephen Arata, 'Scott's Pageants: The Example of *Kenilworth*', *Studies in Romanticism*, 40.1 (Spring 2001), 99–107 (p. 104).

[8] Andrew Lincoln, *Walter Scott and Modernity* (Edinburgh: Edinburgh University Press, 2007), pp. 69, 86.

[9] David Kurnick, 'Theatricality and the Novel', in *The Nineteenth-Century Novel 1820–1880*, ed. John Kucich and Jenny Bourne Taylor (Oxford: Oxford University

novel with descriptions of costume and décor installs a quintessentially modern mode of consumerist desire, bound to the cycles of fashion, which were not current in Britain before the mid-eighteenth century.[10]

Consequently, in Campbell's summary, Scott 'forges a historical "milieu" that is most fundamentally an anachronistic effect of commercialization'.[11] Nineteenth-century commentators noted a heightened visibility of anachronism in Scott's novels of the early 1820s, which they diagnosed as a by-product of the recourse to period surface. The author of *Ivanhoe* sets out to reproduce, 'with antiquarian fidelity, the manners and customs of the age': consequently, 'everything bordering upon palpable anachronism, must be avoided', or else 'the moment the antiquary is at fault, the pseudo-historian is detected in his forgeries'.[12] Sixty years later, Edward Augustus Freeman (Regius Professor of Modern History at Oxford) devotes an index entry in his *History of the Norman Conquest* to 'Ivanhoe, historical blunders in', which he blames for corrupting an actual work of history, Augustin Thierry's *Histoire de la conquête de l'Angleterre par les Normands* (1825).[13]

Scott himself was alert to the issue. 'It is extremely probable that I may have confused the manners of two or three centuries, and introduced, during the reign of Richard the First, circumstances appropriated to a period either considerably earlier, or a good deal later than that era', he concedes in the 'Dedicatory Epistle' to *Ivanhoe*, adding, 'It is my comfort, that errors of this kind will escape the general class of readers.'[14] He addresses the inescapable role of anachronism in historical fiction:

> It is true, that I neither can, nor do pretend, to the observation of complete accuracy, even in matters of outward costume, much less in the more important points of language and manners. But the same motive which prevents my writing the dialogue of the piece in Anglo-Saxon or in Norman-French,

Press, 2012), pp. 306–21 (p. 309). See also J. H. Alexander, 'Introduction', in Walter Scott, *Kenilworth*, ed. J. H. Alexander (London: Penguin, 1999), pp. xiii–xiv.

10 Timothy Campbell, *Historical Style: Fashion and the New Mode of History, 1740–1830* (Philadelphia: University of Pennsylvania Press, 2016), pp. 214–22. For this vein of commentary as cliché, compare Daniel Mendelsohn (reviewing Hilary Mantel's Tudor trilogy in the *New Yorker*, 16 March 2020): 'the Walter Scott approach . . . is to focus on exteriors, to dress things up with florid gold script and quaint period diction' (p. 82).

11 Campbell, *Historical Style*, p. 220.

12 *Eclectic Review*, in *Scott: The Critical Heritage*, p. 190.

13 Edward Augustus Freeman, *History of the Norman Conquest of England, its Causes and its Results* (Oxford: Clarendon Press), vol. VI (1879), p. 139; vol. V (1876), pp. 825, 839.

14 Walter Scott, *Ivanhoe*, ed. Ian Duncan (Oxford: Oxford University Press, 1998), p. 21. Future references to this edition will be cited in the text.

and which prohibits my sending forth to the public this essay printed with the types of Caxton or Wynken de Worde, prevents my attempting to confine myself within the limits of the period in which my story is laid. (p. 17)

An authentic mode of historical fiction, in Scott's view, is one that brings into play the relation between past and present, activating it on the textual surface, rather than – as in Thomas Chatterton's Rowley forgeries – covering it up: 'It is necessary, for exciting interest of any kind, that the subject assumed should be, as it were, translated into the manners, as well as the language, of the age we live in' (pp. 18–19). The principle informs Scott's stylistic innovation in *Ivanhoe*, the counterpoint of modern narration with a dramatic pastiche of antique speech, synthesised from English literary sources ranging from Chaucer (two hundred years after the novel's period setting) to Shakespeare (four hundred years afterwards). The medium of the 'modern antique romance' (Scott's own term, p. 505) is a 'mixed, artificially created language'.[15]

If *Ivanhoe* proceeds on the premise that England in the late twelfth century is remote enough, hence unfamiliar enough, that most readers will not notice anachronisms embedded within the story (as distinct from the interplay of narrative and dramatic styles on its textual surface), *Kenilworth* – published a year later, in January 1821 – flaunts its internal anachronisms, as if daring us to spot them.[16] Set in the summer of 1575, the novel has its characters refer to poetic and dramatic masterpieces of the Elizabethan age, by Edmund Spenser, Philip Sidney and William Shakespeare, which would not be printed or performed for another two decades. Shakespeare, born in 1564 and thus eleven years old according to the official chronology, is already at the height of his career in *Kenilworth*. His *Venus and Adonis* charms Philip Sidney; passages from *A Midsummer Night's Dream* and *Troilus and Cressida* are quoted by Walter Raleigh and Queen Elizabeth; other characters recite songs from *Hamlet*, *The Winter's Tale* and *The Tempest* (the latter not composed until 1612, according to Edmond Malone's still-authoritative chronology).[17]

[15] Graham Tulloch, *The Language of Walter Scott: A Study of his Scottish and Period Language* (London: André Deutsch, 1980), p. 14.

[16] For a list of anachronisms in *Kenilworth*, see John Sutherland, *The Life of Sir Walter Scott* (Oxford: Blackwell, 1995), p. 248.

[17] Edmund Malone, 'An Attempt to Ascertain the Order in which the Plays Attributed to Shakespeare Were Written', in *The Plays of William Shakespeare*, ed. Samuel Johnson and George Steevens, 5th edn, 21 vols (London: J. Johnson, 1803), vol. II, pp. 228–9. Malone's essay was published in the first edition of 1778. Scott owned the fifth: J. G. Cochrane, *Catalogue of the Library at Abbotsford* (Edinburgh: T. Constable, 1838), p. 210.

These anachronisms, planted within the historical *mise en scène*, are of a different order from the mode of anachronism noted by Campbell, in which the profusion of period detail triggers a modern affective relation between scene and reader, as well as from the analogous mode avowed by Scott himself in *Ivanhoe*, in which a modern narration encloses a simulation of antique speech: operations of anachronism that cross the diegetic frame, from the represented past to the present time of reading. Anachronism turns out to be a more complex and variable device, or suite of devices, than most commentary has recognised. Far from bearing a single effect, it assumes multiple forms and functions. Focusing on *Kenilworth*, this essay will explore the relation between anachronism and the new style of representation, oriented to period surface, that composes the turn in Scott's practice from the 'classical form of the historical novel' towards a different historicist aesthetic, one that has remained elusive to critical analysis, at the beginning of the 1820s.

*

Anachronism has been recognised as a primary technique of Scott's historicism since Lukács drew on the Hegelian concept of the 'necessary anachronism' for his analysis of the 'dialectic of contradictory development' in the Waverley novels.[18] The necessary anachronism 'can emerge organically from historical material,' Lukács notes, 'if the past portrayed is clearly recognized and experienced by contemporary writers as the *necessary prehistory* of the present.'[19] It forges a teleological link between the represented past and the present scene of writing – and, implicitly, the present scene of reading – by disclosing the present's immanence in the past. 'History is only ours,' Hegel affirmed in his *Lectures on Aesthetics*, 'when it belongs to the nation to which we belong, or when we can look at the present in general as a consequence of a chain of events in which the characters or deeds represented form an essential link'. Anachronism maintains that link by revealing 'the higher interests of our spirit and will, what is in itself human and powerful, the true depths of the heart', within 'what is strange and external in a past period'.[20] The past is made recognisable, imaginatively habitable, 'ours', by the revelation of a universal human spirit investing the contingent, transient forms of historical difference.

---

[18] Lukács, *The Historical Novel*, pp. 61, 182.
[19] Ibid. p. 61.
[20] G. W. F. Hegel, *Aesthetics: Lectures on Fine Art*, trans. T. M. Knox, 2 vols (Oxford: Oxford University Press, 1975), vol. I, p. 272.

Scott's first novel activates the necessary anachronism through a simultaneous discovery of the past in the present and the present in the past. *Waverley* reanimates a past social formation, Highland clan society, which appears as archaic within the novel's represented world as well as to the modern reader. During the 1745 Jacobite Rising, Lowland Scots and English witnesses view the clansmen (swarming down from their mountains) as savage remnants of a superseded historical stage. Meanwhile the novel's protagonist, equipped with modern liberal habits of sympathy and taste, acts as a proxy for the reader, dropped into the scenery of sixty years since. The intrusion of the modern visitor (an army officer in the guise of gentleman tourist) forecasts the clans' demise, while their primitive appearance confirms the ascendancy of his – and our – enlightened sensibility. Waverley himself, in short, is the vehicle of the necessary anachronism. Our recognition of the past as necessary prehistory of the present takes place through Scott's 'more or less mediocre, average' hero, who personifies the historical novel's mediation between then and now.[21] *Waverley* redeems its protagonist's untimely relation to the scenes through which he moves with a domestication in modern civil society which is realised by ourselves, in the act of reading, more than it is by him – and hence the novel's objective status, signalled in the necessary anachronism, as a work of fiction rather than 'real history'.

The teleological, domesticating function of anachronism, as realised in *Waverley*, thus differs from the alienating force ascribed to it in recent critical accounts of anachronism's effects of 'untimeliness and temporal heterogeneity', its disruptions of a linear, unified, progressive history of '"before" and "after"', cause and effect', and (hence) of 'the assumed futurity that useful history naturalizes'.[22] Scott brings this disruptive force to bear in some of the novels published between *Waverley* and *Ivanhoe*. The protagonists of *Old Mortality* (1816) and *The Bride of Lammermoor* (1819) inhabit what Ferris calls 'the time of the remnant', characterised by 'a suspension of connection and continuity that generates a curiously insubstantial existence in the present'. At odds with their historical moment, both characters struggle to reclaim the Waverley-hero's function as vessel of the necessary anachronism. Their passive disposition (in contrast to Waverley's) 'signals less the prudential reflex

---

[21] Lukács, *The Historical Novel*, p. 33.

[22] Justin Sider, '"Modern-Antiques," Ballad Imitation, and the Aesthetics of Anachronism', *Victorian Poetry*, 54 (2016), 455–75 (p. 458); Jeremy Tambling, *On Anachronism* (Manchester: Manchester University Press, 2013), p. 4; Mary Mullen, 'Anachronistic Aesthetics: Maria Edgeworth and the "Uses" of History', *Eighteenth-Century Fiction*, 26 (2013–14), 233–59 (p. 235).

of modernity's civil hero, than a disconnection from historical time altogether'.[23]

Scott restores the positive operation of the necessary anachronism in *Ivanhoe*, but at the cost of a drastic redistribution across the novel's character system. Its avatar is not the eponymous protagonist, Wilfred of Ivanhoe, but the Jewish heroine Rebecca. Debating Norman chivalry at the centre of the novel, Rebecca pleads for what modern readers are trained to recognise as humane, liberal principles, while Ivanhoe defends the institution's extravagance and violence – effects, to a modern point of view, of its moral obsolescence, its failure to transcend its era. 'In the dialectic between past and present values,' writes Alide Cagidemetrio, 'Rebecca consistently embodies contemporary England much more than does the novel's canonic mediator, Ivanhoe'.[24]

Yet historical necessity excludes Rebecca from the future national community convened at the close of the novel, banishing her to the prehistory of an unrealised present. The exclusion launches the most flagrant of all the anachronisms in *Ivanhoe*. Rebecca and her father prepare for an exile that will transport them not just through space but through time, three centuries into the future, to the court of 'Mohammed Boabdil, King of Grenada' (p. 499) – whose surrender to the Catholic monarchs Ferdinand and Isabella in 1492 will unleash the final expulsion of Jews and Muslims from the Iberian Peninsula. Reminding us that further cycles of persecution and exile await Rebecca's people, Scott's anachronism opens onto a sublime, turbulent, unfinished history of worldwide dispossession and vagrancy, in contrast to the English destiny of compromise and settlement that *Ivanhoe* is usually taken to be promoting. Rebecca personifies the Hegelian ideal of a universal human spirit which, now, cannot find its home within a national history fenced about by bigotry and xenophobia. Instead, the necessary anachronism poses a hard question to modern readers about the adequacy of their social and political order to the ethical values supposed to sustain it.[25]

*

---

[23] Ina Ferris, '"On the Borders of Oblivion": Scott's Historical Novel and the Modern Time of the Remnant', *Modern Language Quarterly*, 70 (2009), 473–94 (pp. 475, 482).

[24] Alide Cagidimetrio, 'A Plea for Fictional Histories and Old-Time "Jewesses"', in *The Invention of Ethnicity*, ed. Werner Sollors (Oxford: Oxford University Press, 1989), pp. 13–43 (p. 19).

[25] For a fuller treatment of anachronism in Scott's novels from *Waverley* to *Ivanhoe*, see my essay 'Scott's Anachronisms', in *Walter Scott at 250: Looking Forward*, ed. Caroline McCracken-Flesher and Matthew Wickman (Edinburgh: Edinburgh University Press, 2021), pp. 46–64.

Waverley rehearses a comic variant of the necessary anachronism, aligning the historical past with the gestation of the present. Subsequent novels (*Old Mortality*, *The Bride of Lammermoor*) experiment with an ironic technique that releases anachronism's alienating, dislocating force, casting characters adrift in history and unsettling our time of reading. In *Ivanhoe* Scott radicalises this exilic tropism for a critical and utopian mode of anachronism expressive of the separation of a spiritually evolved humanity from its historical homeland. More than a technical modulation of the 'classical form of the historical novel', *Ivanhoe* stages its ideological crisis, one in which the necessary anachronism splits the enlightened prospect of a humane civil society from the diminished – merely domestic – achievement of an ethno-national community. The crisis, depleting the past's teleological realisation in our present, accompanies the other kind of anachronism noted by critics of *Ivanhoe*: not the overlay of past and present, confirming their positive relation, which signals the necessary anachronism, but instead a more banal confusion of objects and styles from different periods, a misplacement of the past in the past, which we might call the local or contingent anachronism. If such anachronisms remain undetected by ordinary readers of *Ivanhoe*, as Scott protested, *Kenilworth* – to which I now turn – puts the device under scrutiny, activating anachronism's critical potential by making it obvious, unignorable.

Kenilworth does so by insisting on a date for its events, with a sharpened specificity new to the Waverley novels. We tend to think of the date as a defining topos of historical fiction – as in Victor Hugo's *Notre-Dame de Paris: 1482*, with its fanatically punctual opening, 'Il y a aujourd'hui trois cent quarante-huit ans six mois et dix-neuf jours que les Parisiens s'éveillèrent.'[26] But Scott's earlier historical novels are chary of specifying dates. While the informed reader of *Waverley* may track the convergence of the novel's plot with the public history of the Jacobite Rising, the narrator mentions 1745 only twice, in stances of retrospective distance from the narrated action (pp. 219, 363). The opening paragraphs of *Ivanhoe* immerse the novel's historical setting, 'a period towards the end of the reign of Richard I', in the more diffuse medium of 'ancient times', emanating from the primeval English greenwood – the chronotope of romance rather than history, haunted by legendary dragons as well as by Robin Hood (p. 25). *Kenilworth* also opens by evoking 'the old days of Merry England', *Ivanhoe*-style: but that legendary time dissipates as the action moves into the arena

---

[26] Victor Hugo, *Notre-Dame de Paris: 1482*, ed. S. de Sacy (Paris: Gallimard, 2002), p. 37.

of Elizabethan court politics.[27] 'It was the twilight of a summer night, (9th July, 1575,) the sun having for some time set, and all were in anxious expectation of the Queen's immediate approach', the narrator announces in volume three (pp. 284–5). The marking of date and time brings a frisson of urgency as the story marches to its crisis. It also calibrates the operation of the local anachronism to a micro-scale, a difference of a few years or decades within the period setting, rather than (as in *Ivanhoe*) across 'two or three centuries'. With the formula 'sixty years since', the span of a human lifetime, *Waverley* had marked the innermost boundary of a historical period, while acknowledging (in Scott's 'Postscript, which should have been a Preface') that the boundary is shrinking as the pace of historical change speeds up towards the present.[28] The anachronisms in *Kenilworth* notate a radically diminished temporal scale of historical event and period. They are expressions of 'the peculiar form of acceleration which characterizes modernity', in Reinhart Koselleck's analysis, within the longer-durational 'temporalization (*Vertzeitlichung*) of history' characteristic of 'the period in which modernity is formed'.[29]

Jonathan Sachs argues that the modern acceleration of historical time made itself felt through the industrial-scale increase of literary production and consumption in Romantic-period Great Britain: 'The regular appearance of an ever-proliferating quantity of printed materials – from books to broadsides, pamphlets to periodicals, annuals to almanacs, prints to playbills, newspapers to magazines – exacerbated the sense of hurry in commercial life.'[30] No one was more attuned to the phenomenon than Scott, financially bound to the firm that printed his own works. The calendrical spate of print – cresting in the 1820s – was manifest not only in the frenetic pace with which he was writing new novels (two per year, at this stage of his career) but also, now, in their repackaging in cheaper collected editions. Just one year after its initial printing *Kenilworth* was reissued in a new series, *Historical Romances of the Author of Waverley*, which would appear in two formats (eight volumes, octavo, 1822; six volumes, duodecimo, 1824), on the heels

---

[27] Scott, *Kenilworth*, ed. Alexander, p. 1; future references will be given in the text.

[28] On Scott's innovation of a period setting in the recent past, taken up by Victorian realism, see Helen Kingstone, *Victorian Narratives of the Recent Past* (Basingstoke: Palgrave Macmillan, 2017), pp. 142, 149–53.

[29] Reinhart Koselleck, *Futures Past: On the Semantics of Historical Time* (Cambridge, MA: MIT Press, 1985), p. 5. On the Romantic-period sense of history, see James Chandler, *England in 1819: The Politics of Literary Culture and the Case of Romantic Historicism* (Chicago: University of Chicago Press, 1998), pp. 100–17.

[30] Jonathan Sachs, *The Poetics of Decline in British Romanticism* (Cambridge: Cambridge University Press, 2018), pp. 70–1.

of a previous venture, *Novels and Tales of the Author of Waverley* (twelve volumes, octavo, 1819, 1822; sixteen volumes, duodecimo, 1821, 1825). Scott was already involved, in other words, in a commercial, chronological and taxonomical sorting of his ongoing oeuvre that recombined it into a new hybrid format of popular serial miscellany and classical author's edition (anticipating the later, better known 'Magnum Opus' edition, 1829–33), synchronised to the 'informational time' of an ascendant industrial capitalism.[31]

Meanwhile, the new collective name 'Historical Romances' reaffirms the generic category affixed to the first-edition title pages of *Ivanhoe: A Romance* and *Kenilworth: A Romance*, in avowal of their modal distinction from the 'Novels and Tales', based on modern Scottish history, that preceded them. 'Romance' signals the works' bondage to the accelerated time of modernity and an industrialising print market, in spite of a subject matter embedded in the deeper past of English history. Richard Cronin analyses the seeming paradox. Scott's historical novels satisfied contemporary readers' conflicted desire 'at once to be confirmed in, and relieved from, [their] own modernity' by offering them 'an experience of deep time, sometimes, as in *Ivanhoe* of 1820, very deep time', within a genre – the novel – that 'of all established literary genres had the shallowest history': its 'shallow time' exacerbated in the reprint format.[32]

This literary context provides for the other effect that distinguishes the local anachronisms in *Kenilworth* from those in *Ivanhoe*. Not only do they mark a micro-scale of historical misplacement (by years or decades rather than epochs): they obtrude upon our notice, demand (in short) to be read, insofar as they refer to literary history – a history that is 'ours' both spiritually, as a cultural heritage, and also materially, as a commodity in our possession, the novel we are reading, purchased or rented from a circulating library. Literary history presents itself as the medium both of the commodity form, with its accelerated temporality, and of Hegel's universal spirit, transcending time. Above all, it is a history that belongs to us (in Hegel's formulation) by virtue of its specific condensation in what Nassau Senior, reviewing *Kenilworth* in

---

[31] Sachs, *The Poetics of Decline*, p. 70; Peter Garside, '*Waverley* and the National Fiction Revolution', in *The Edinburgh History of the Book in Scotland, Volume 3: Ambition and Industry 1800–1880*, ed. Bill Bell (Edinburgh: Edinburgh University Press, 2007), pp. 222–31 (pp. 227–9).

[32] Richard Cronin, 'Magazines, *Don Juan*, and the Scotch Novels: Deep and Shallow Time in the Regency', in *Rethinking British Romantic History, 1770–1845*, ed. Porscha Fermanis and John Regan (Oxford: Oxford University Press, 2014), pp. 165–78 (pp. 173–4).

the *Quarterly Review*, called 'the pleasing anachronism of Shakspeare [*sic*]'.[33]

*

Shakespeare stands out from the other literary sources from which Scott concocts his stylistic pastiche. J. H. Alexander's notes to the Edinburgh Edition identify dozens if not scores of those sources, among which the Elizabethan dramatists are especially prevalent.[34] Many of these authors and works are known today only to specialist scholars, and they would have been more obscure in Scott's day – although *Kenilworth* rides on a Regency-era revival of interest in the Elizabethan and Jacobean drama, marked by Charles Lamb's anthology *Specimens of English Dramatic Poets* (1808) and Scott's own *The Ancient British Drama* (1810: a reissue of Robert Dodsley's *Select Collection of Old Plays*, 1744), as well as editions of Philip Massinger by William Gifford (1805), and of John Ford (1811) and Beaumont and Fletcher (1812) by Scott's protégé Henry Weber. These minor literary sources belong to the condition analysed by Campbell, for whom the modern fashion system, with its rapid commercial cycles of innovation and obsolescence, made the modern phenomenology of historical change legible to Scott and his contemporaries.[35] Like the minutiae of styles of dress and grooming, they too are lost from present view in the ephemeral cycles of production and obsolescence – absorbed, like mulch, into a generic period texture. The condition is extreme for the dramatists, whose works are extinct in stage history and hence only available as texts, secreted in the antiquarian archive unless harvested for anthologies or scholarly editions.

Shakespeare is the glorious exception. 'Not of an age, but for all time' (Scott quotes Ben Jonson in *Kenilworth*, although not this line), Shakespeare transcends the flux of fashion – hence his status as the anachronism we are supposed to recognise, the avatar of a history that 'belongs to us', as well as Scott's precursor in the proud practice of anachronism. (The notorious striking clock in *Julius Caesar* calls attention to the very question of historical punctuality.) By 1800 Shakespeare was established as the unassailable classic among British authors: a prize, consequently, in the intensifying culture wars of the Regency, fought over by rival party interests.[36] Furnishing 'the quoted banner, the originating sign', for Scott's own project of national historical romance on the title page

---

[33] *Scott: The Critical Heritage*, p. 253.
[34] See Alexander, Introduction to *Kenilworth*, p. xxii.
[35] Campbell, *Historical Style*, pp. 217–21.
[36] See Jonathan Bate, *Shakespearean Constitutions: Politics, Theatre, Criticism, 1730–1830* (Oxford: Clarendon Press, 1989), pp. 34–44, 102–4, 134–84.

of *Waverley*, in the form of an epigraph from *2 Henry IV*, Shakespeare would be a dominant allusive presence in the novels that followed.[37]

Scott evokes Shakespeare in different registers in *Kenilworth*. He figures as a historical character, on the edges of the action, hailed by the Earl of Leicester: 'Ha, Will Shakespeare – wild Will! – thou hast given my nephew, Philip Sidney, love-powder – he cannot sleep without thy Venus and Adonis under his pillow!' (p. 168). Other characters allude to him as already a living classic, cited by the queen herself:

'Think of what that arch-knave Shakespeare says – a plague on him, his toys come into my head when I should think of other matter – Stay, how goes it? –
    Cressid was your's, tied with the bonds of heaven;
    These bonds of heaven are slipt, dissolved, and loosed,
    And with another knot five fingers tied,
    The fragments of her faith are bound to Diomed.
You smile, my Lord of Southampton – perchance I make your player's verse halt through my bad memory.' (p. 163)

Shakespeare is also a sort of Renaissance Robert Burns, a snapper-up of popular tradition. 'But age has clawed me somewhat in his clutch, as the song says', someone quotes from the gravedigger's song in *Hamlet* (p. 247). Alexander's note (p. 442) tells us that the line is first recorded in a book of poems by Sir Thomas Vaux, printed in 1557, eighteen years before the action of *Kenilworth* and four decades before the first performance of *Hamlet* (according to Malone, who dates the play to 1596): ample time for it to have gone into popular circulation before being appropriated by Shakespeare. The voice of Shakespeare, sampling popular tradition, has the power to generate further allusions and anachronisms: the present speaker (the narrator cannot help himself) 'might have been the very emblem of the Wife of Bath' (p. 247).

Lastly, and most potently, Shakespeare functions as a model, a matrix of types and paradigms, available to shape the novel's characters and events: not just a passing period form but an abiding imaginative structure. What Diane E. Henderson calls Scott's 'Shakeshifting' creates 'a "modern" Shakespeare', in a symbiotic rather than parasitic reworking of the elder author.[38] Disaster ensues when Leicester falls into the role

---

[37] Judith Wilt, *Secret Leaves: The Novels of Walter Scott* (Chicago: University of Chicago Press, 1985), pp. 24–5. The *Edinburgh Edition of the Waverley Novels* maintains an online database of Shakespearean allusions and quotations: https://www.abdn.ac.uk/sll/documents/Shakespeare.docx (accessed 7 February 2022).

[38] Diane E. Henderson, 'Bards of the Borders: Scott's *Kenilworth*, the Nineteenth Century's Shakespeare, and the *Tragedy of Othello*', in *Collaborations with the Past: Reshaping Shakespeare across Time and Media* (Ithaca, NY: Cornell University Press, 2006), pp. 39–103 (p. 42).

of Othello, at the prompting of his Iago-like familiar Richard Varney, and succumbs to murderous jealousy of the innocent Amy Robsart. Presumably *Othello* has not been produced yet, in 1575 (Malone dates it to 1611; modern scholarship indicates a date between 1601 and 1604) – or if it has, Leicester has not seen it, otherwise he would surely have known better.

Shakespeare transcends the flux of fashion, as Scott's flourishes of anachronism remind us. At the same time, as virtuoso of a popular, commercial art, he belongs to it; it is his original medium. 'The public, ... in the widest sense of the word, was at once arbiter and patron of the [Elizabethan] Drama', Scott had written in his 'Essay on the Drama' (1819) for the *Encyclopaedia Britannica*. 'The effect of the genius of an individual upon the taste of a nation is mighty; but that genius, in its turn, is formed according to the opinions prevalent at the period when it comes into existence. Such was the case with Shakspeare', who '[composed] for the amusement of the public alone'.[39] In a witty set piece, Queen Elizabeth and her courtiers debate the merits of the new form of entertainment currently enthralling crowds on the South Bank (a hotbed of popular theatrical novelties in Scott's day, as in Shakespeare's). Placed where it is, at the very centre of *Kenilworth*, the scene glosses the social role and function of modern literature, including Scott's own art.

The debate opens with the presentation of a petition to the queen by the keeper of the royal bears, who complains that the playhouses are drawing audiences away from the adjacent bear-garden. (Scott mentions this episode, evidently historical, in his 'Essay on the Drama'.) Seconding the petition, the veteran Earl of Sussex dismisses the drama as 'all froth and folly – no substance or seriousness in it ... What are half a dozen knaves, with rusty foils and tattered targets, making but a mere mockery of a stout fight, to compare to the royal game of bear-baiting?' – a spectacle that yields 'the bravest image of war that can be shown in peace' (p. 174). In staging an actual bloody combat between beasts, the bear-baiting provides a more authentic mimesis of heroic violence than the drama, which features men who are only playing at it. Sussex supports his reactionary preference with the description of a fight between bear and mastiffs that reproduces the decorum of Homeric simile (embedding scenes of animal-on-animal violence, belonging to the domestic reality of the poem's audience, amid the epic narration of battlefield carnage) vividly enough to earn the queen's accolade.

---

[39] *The Miscellaneous Prose Works of Sir Walter Scott, Bart, Volume 6: Chivalry, Romance, the Drama* (Edinburgh: Robert Cadell, 1834), pp. 334, 337.

Nevertheless, the appeal to an older – primitive – epic regime fails to dislodge the ascendancy of the modern dramatic art, the power of which resides in its commercial, public and popular character. Leicester speaks up for the players:

> I must needs say that they are witty knaves, whose rants and jests keep the minds of the commons from busying themselves with state affairs, and listening to traitorous speeches, idle rumours, and disloyal insinuations. When men are agape to see how Marlow, Shakespeare, and other play artificers work out their fanciful plots, as they call them, the mind of the spectators is withdrawn from the conduct of their rulers. (p. 175)

Such entertainments are politically useful, in short, in that they distract their audience from thinking critically about government. (Elizabeth rejoins that she welcomes the people's scrutiny of her conduct, since 'the more closely it is examined, the true motives by which we are guided will appear the more manifest'.) A Puritan churchman objects that the plays, far from distracting public attention, promote 'such reflections on government, its origin and its object, as tend to render the subject discontented, and shake the solid foundations of civil society' (p. 175). The complaint is deflected rather than answered by Elizabeth's assertion that the new chronicle plays – Shakespeare's history cycle, the model for Scott's historical fiction – are wholesome combinations of amusement and instruction. Walter Raleigh then bolsters her approval by quoting the famous compliment to the queen (Oberon's vision of the 'fair vestal, throned by the west') inserted into Act 2 of *A Midsummer Night's Dream* (p. 176). The question of the political effect or function of the new art form is left unresolved, diverted, via the appeal to the Shakespearean exception, into courtly flattery. Scott's refusal to settle the question, in light of the struggle over Shakespeare as partisan trophy in his own time, no doubt reflects a desire to position his own art outside the fray. What the debate does establish is that these representations *are* political interventions, by virtue of their commercial medium – the public theatre – and their status as popular entertainment, addressed to the common people rather than a noble coterie. They may flatter a sovereign, promote harmless amusement and edification, distract the public from paying attention to politics, stir up discontent and sedition – all or any of these. They overflow the constraints that define literary production in the conditions of royal and aristocratic patronage – which are still potent enough, however, to motivate the 'fair vestal' passage in *A Midsummer Night's Dream*.

'By collaborating with Shakespeare, Scott creates a romanticized British tradition of authorship based on elective affinities', Henderson writes.[40] *Kenilworth* develops the theme, established in eighteenth-century poetry and criticism, of the Elizabethan age as foundation of a glorious, continuous national literary heritage.[41] Its great authors are at once classical and modern; Shakespeare, the greatest, inhabits both the shallow time of popular entertainment and the deep time of national culture – the amphibious temporality, according to Cronin, that Scott's historical fiction made imaginatively available to readers. Despite frequent comparisons of his art with Shakespeare's, Scott began to internalise complaints, on the rise through the 1820s, that the industrial-scale output of Waverley novels might relegate them to the class of ephemeral amusements, 'market commodities' rather than 'contributions to literature', after all.[42] This precarious double occupancy – of an age and for all time – rhymes with Lincoln's account of the pageantry in *Kenilworth*: 'an exclusive, privatized, hierarchical order that has to be defended by force, *and* the site of an inclusive national festival answering to the popular imagination' (p. 82). The popular festival opens the deep or transcendental time of national culture, providing legitimacy for a closed, corrupt, violent regime, in what amounts to Scott's invention of the modern 'heritage' concept.[43] And the revels at Kenilworth replicate (in fractal logic) *Kenilworth* itself: a novel that combines esoteric learning and literary game-playing with Gothic and melodramatic ingredients of suspense and terror, comedy and pathos, appealing at once to groundlings and to connoisseurs.

*

Except that the 'inclusive national festival' does not take hold. Having opened the arena of communal festivity, Scott steers his plot away from it. Bent on their missions, his characters bypass the 'throng and confusion' of 'players and mummers, jugglers and showmen of every description' converging on Kenilworth Castle (p. 252). The novel's avatars of popular culture, puckish Flibbertigibbet and onetime player Wayland Smith, fail to achieve the structural function of romance rescue they so vividly promise on their first appearance. Entering the plot as charismatic helpers from legend and folklore, they fade away again, distracted by the bustle of the revels (Flibbertigibbet) or depressed by an inability to translate theatrical performance into effective action (Wayland). Amy

[40] Henderson, 'Bards of the Borders', p. 92.
[41] See Jonathan Brody Kramnick, *Making the English Canon: Print-Capitalism and the Cultural Past, 1700–1770* (Oxford: Clarendon Press, 1999), especially chapters 4 (on Spenser) and 5 (Shakespeare).
[42] Cronin, 'Magazines, *Don Juan,* and the Scotch Novels', p. 173.
[43] Lincoln, *Walter Scott and Modernity*, pp. 82, 84–6.

Robsart herself restages the central romance scenario of an earlier Scott novel, *The Heart of Mid-Lothian*: the heroine's supplication, bypassing the traps of political justice, to the grace-bestowing sovereign. Once again, the performance fails, in part because of its literalisation as a theatrical performance. Mistaking Amy for a decorative nymph in one of the Kenilworth masques, Elizabeth interprets her passionate sincerity (the keynote of Jeanie Deans's eloquence) at first as an amateur actor's awkwardness and then, when the theatrical illusion is dispelled, as scheming or madness (pp. 318–26). As for the Kenilworth revels, these are not a public but a private entertainment, mounted by noble patronage for a royal audience of one. The popular crowd, in contrast to the Bankside audience that stands as 'arbiter and patron' of Shakespeare's art, is part of the show: supernumeraries in the pageant of national glory. The revels' brilliant magnification of Elizabethan court ceremony enhances the claustrophobic sense of the novel's action closing in, its redemptive options running out, as it drives toward catastrophe.

The pageantry culminates in a masque performed before the queen in which four bands of players represent 'the various nations by which England had at different times been occupied': 'aboriginal Britons', 'sons of Rome, who came to civilize as well as to conquer', 'Saxons, clad in the bear-skins which they had brought with them from the German forests' and 'knightly Normans, in their mail shirts and hoods of steel' (p. 349). The narrator explains: 'In this symbolical dance was represented the conflicts which had taken place among the various nations which had anciently inhabited Britain' (p. 350). Elizabeth herself supplies a gloss:

> '[It] seemed to her that no single one of these celebrated nations could claim pre-eminence over the others, as having contributed to form the Englishman of her own time, who unquestionably derived from each of them some worthy attribute of his character. Thus,' she said, 'the Englishman had from the ancient Briton his bold and tameless spirit of freedom,—from the Roman his disciplined courage in war, with his love of letters and civilization in time of peace,—from the Saxon his wise and equitable laws,—and from the chivalrous Norman his love of honour and courtesy, with his generous desire for glory.' (p. 351)

We read, in short, the ideological theme of British history that has informed Scott's preceding novels, most explicitly in *Ivanhoe*. However, this admirable compound of national virtue, synthesised from a prehistory of ethnic antagonisms and imperial conquests, is starkly at odds with actual English character as we read it in *Kenilworth* – splintered into poisonous shards of ambition, duplicity and cruelty by the factionalism of court politics. Neither ancient organic community nor modern civil society, the Elizabethan court musters a gangster-like formation of alliances and rivalries among nobles vying for the sovereign's favour. The ethical best option seems to be withdrawal into melancholy passiveness, exemplified by the novel's ostensible protagonist Tressilian; a Cornishman (the descendant of aboriginal Britons), he can do little more than act out the Waverley-hero's decline into worldly impotence.

All the world's the court, which destroys those it does not corrupt. Koselleck dates 'the period in which modernity is formed' as lasting from around 1500 to 1800: Elizabeth's reign, in other words, already belongs to modernity. Our period category 'early modern' was anticipated in Scottish Enlightenment stadial history, with its identification of modernity with the formations of a centralised state apparatus and commercial empire. The difference between the Elizabethan era and Scott's consists in the latter's having that historical transition available, at the culmination of the three-centuries-long *durée* of modernisation, as an object of retrospection and analysis – available, thus, for the formulation of a 'philosophy of historical process', the historiographic blueprint of the Scottish Waverley novels.[44] However, Scott's depiction of the age of Elizabeth in *Kenilworth* (in contrast to the Jacobean London of *The Fortunes of Nigel*, set fifty years later) does not open an active space of commercial, bourgeois culture – the engine of modern civil society – alongside the royal court. The court is absolute, the core of a world without political alternatives. The novel may register the emergent forces, as Lincoln contends, of a 'rapidly modernizing world' (a market economy, competitive individualism and social mobility, international trade and colonial expansion), but those forces remain enclosed within the absolutist system, not yet sustained and regulated by a civil society. The timeless domain of popular culture, outgrowth of an organic community residual with the folk, persists alongside or rather beneath the regime, harnessed by Shakespeare for his at once fashionable and universal art, but unavailable for the generation of a transformative politics.

This closed or absolute milieu affords a stark contrast with Scott's earlier novels, which model historical process through the 'dialectic of contradictory development' (Lukács) between residual and emergent social or anthropological stages, secured (in *Waverley*) by the necessary anachronism that aligns past with present, and in doing so produces the effect of historical depth. Here the old feudal moral economy (represented by Tressilian and Amy Robsart's ailing father) resides with faded remnants of the rustic gentry, while new commercial energies have yet to crystallise into the institutions of civil society. In abandoning (or

[44] Koselleck, *Futures Past*, pp. 16–17.

sidelining) the dialectical model, *Kenilworth* departs drastically from the 'classical form of the historical novel'. Historical alternatives are reduced from structural forces to forms, to (textually mediated) semblance and performance, as well as to thematic abstraction.

It is as though in *Kenilworth* Scott anticipates Lukács's vision of the lamentable collapse of historical realism, a generation later, in the wake of the failed European revolutions of 1848:

> [The] past appears, more so even than the present, as a gigantic iridescent chaos. Nothing is really objectively and organically connected with the objective character of the present ... And since history has been deprived of its real inner greatness – the dialectic of contradictory development, which has been abstracted intellectually – all that remains for the artists of this period is a pictorial and decorative grandeur.[45]

Kenilworth, however, stages this intellectual abstraction in front of us, quite literally, in the pageant of national history played before Queen Elizabeth. In rendering national history through official spectacle and ideological gloss, Scott's novel acknowledges its constructed, literary status and relocates his own historical theme to that medium: Tudor state propaganda, animated in the poetic and dramatic masterpieces of the Elizabethan age, revived as a poetic and critical topos in the eighteenth century.[46] The dialectic internal to historical process, the narrative motor of the Scottish historical novels, is extruded and flattened out in the present scene of entertainment. The operation analysed by Campbell, of a virtual emporium of period surfaces that solicits 'a romantic consumer's eye', enacts an implosion of the necessary anachronism which bears, however, a critical rather than merely symptomatic force.[47] (The 'romantic consumer's eye' may be an anachronistic projection of our own historical viewpoint more than it is of Scott's.) That critical force hollows out the ideological achievement of an 'end of history' which Scott commentators have ascribed to *Waverley* and its successors.[48] *Kenilworth* holds up a mirror to a cold, hard world without historical alternatives – lacking the utopian shimmer of a civil society to come, or still-glowing embers of primitive virtue.

---

[45] Lukács, *The Historical Novel*, p. 182.

[46] See, for instance, Howard D. Weinbrot on the 'national ode', in *Britannia's Issue: The Rise of British Literature from Dryden to Ossian* (Cambridge: Cambridge University Press, 1993), pp. 384–402.

[47] Campbell, *Historical Style*, p. 215.

[48] See, for instance, Ian Duncan, *Modern Romance and Transformations of the Novel: The Gothic, Scott, Dickens* (Cambridge: Cambridge University Press, 1992), pp. 53, 87–105; Jerome Christensen, *Romanticism at the End of History* (Baltimore, MD: Johns Hopkins University Press, 2000), pp. 157–75.

Acknowledgements

I thank Jon Mee, Matt Sangster and other members of 'The 1820s: Innovation and Diffusion' workshop for their comments on this chapter throughout the stages of composition; Paul Barnaby and Alison Lumsden for advice on Scott and Shakespeare; and Tara Ghoshal Wallace for her generous feedback.

Keyword: Power

Jon Mee

'Power' appears as a key term in a founding definition of Romantic studies: Thomas De Quincey's distinction between a literature of power and a literature of knowledge. De Quincey's version of this distinction first appeared in his 'Letters to a Young Man whose Education has been Neglected'. Published as a series of five letters over 1823 in the *London Magazine*, the letters frame an idea of true education against the mechanical acquisition of knowledge, associated in the second letter with the Dissenter Isaac Watts and 'the sectarian zeal of his party in religion'.[1] In the third letter, published in March 1823, De Quincey wrote: 'All that is literature seeks to communicate power; all that is not literature to communicate knowledge.' He went on to explain that by communicating power he meant to feel 'vividly and with a vital consciousness, emotions which ordinary life rarely or never supplies occasions for exciting.' A note gives credit for his use of the word 'power' to describe this interior resource to years of conversation with Wordsworth. Power for De Quincey comes to define 'literature' against what he calls 'anti-literature', defined in relation to the dizzying proliferation of print, 'our present enormous accumulation of books'.[2] Later elaborations of the distinction in a review of an edition of Alexander Pope for the *North British Review* in 1848 developed his complaint against mechanical systems into an opposition between 'a literature of power', identified with Wordsworth's poetry, and a 'literature of knowledge' explicitly associated with the steam engine: 'A good steam-engine is properly superseded by a better. But one lovely pastoral valley is not

---

[1] X. Y. Z., 'Letters to a Young Man whose Education has been Neglected. No. II', *London Magazine*, 7.38 (February 1823), 189–94 (p. 192).

[2] X. Y. Z., 'Letters to a Young Man whose Education has been Neglected. No. III', *London Magazine*, 7.39 (March 1823), 325–35 (pp. 333, 328).

superseded by another, nor a statue of Praxiteles by a statue of Michel Angelo.'[3]

The irony here is that when De Quincey first made his distinction in the 1820s the word 'power' was perhaps nowhere more prevalent in print than in discussions of the steam engine and the legacy of James Watt. Watt died in 1819, just two years before De Quincey first set out his distinction between 'power' and 'knowledge'. Although the opposition between Wordsworth and Watt was not explicit in De Quincey's first knowledge/power distinction, it haunts his antagonism to mechanical method, his concern about the proliferation of print, and may even lurk as a homophone in his swipe at Isaac Watts. Certainly, both the engineer and the Congregationalist divine tended to be venerated in the provincial manufacturing circles from which De Quincey had fled as a young man: circles that were increasingly understood as an emergent powerhouse for public opinion by the 1820s.[4] De Quincey's use of the word 'power' in relation to poetry might be understood as a deliberate attempt to reappropriate the word from this discourse. Francis Jeffrey was only one among many who eulogised Watt as a national hero at his death:

> It is our improved steam-engine that has fought the battles of Europe, and exalted and sustained, through the last tremendous contest, the political greatness of our land. It is the same great power which now enables us to pay the interest of our debt.[5]

The precise definition of this 'power' became an issue in the campaign to secure a monument to Watt in Westminster Abbey that ran for much of the 1820s.[6] Started in 1824, the campaign had originally sought a monument funded by the public, as the many and various celebrations of the Duke of Wellington had been. Jeffrey's celebration of Watt was a pointed rejection of Wellington as the hero of aristocratic martial virtues. The government refused to pay for a statue, but Lord Liverpool did condescend to chair a public meeting that would seek private subscriptions. Speeches were given by the Prime Minister himself; Robert Peel, whose cotton-spinning family had benefited from Watt's invention;

---

[3] 'The Works of Alexander Pope, Esquire', *North British Review*, 9.18 (August 1848), 299–333 (p. 304).

[4] See Donald Read, *The English Provinces c. 1760–1960: A Study in Influence* (London: Edward Arnold, 1964), p. 81.

[5] Francis Jeffrey, 'Character of Mr Watt', *The Scotsman*, 4 September 1819, quoted in Christine MacLeod, *Heroes of Invention: Technology, Liberalism and British Identity, 1750–1914* (Cambridge: Cambridge University Press, 2007), p. 95.

[6] See the detailed account of the campaign and its different constituencies in MacLeod, *Heroes of Invention*.

liberal Whigs like Henry Brougham and Sir James Mackintosh; and the President of the Royal Society, Humphry Davy. Davy granted Watt the genius of a savant. Mackintosh praised Watt as a genius of the diffusion of knowledge, but support for the campaign was, predictably enough, especially strong in manufacturing centres like Birmingham, Glasgow and Manchester (most of which got their own statues of Watt).

Outside of the question of how to commemorate Watt himself, 'the machinery question', to use Maxine Berg's phrase, came to the centre of public debate in the 1820s. Unlike the eighteenth century, when machinery was still largely relished as a novelty, by the 1820s the machine seemed 'responsible for the disharmony of rapidly expanding cotton towns, unprecedented population growth and the economic crisis of the post-Napoleonic years'.[7] Political economists, on the other hand, were starting to develop a more positive line, arguing that technology could vault the limits to growth and produce a new kind of society. Fascinated by a Stockport mill he visited in 1825, for instance, Nassau Senior opined that 'if the power of directing inanimate substances, at the same time to exert the most tremendous energy, and to perform the most delicate operations, be the test, that dominion and power are nowhere so strikingly shown as in a large cotton manufactory'.[8] In the same year, the Scottish economist J. R. McCulloch, satirised as Mac Quedy and associated with the Steam Intellect Society in Thomas Love Peacock's *Crotchet Castle* (1831), offered the paradigm of the machine to replace the traditional organic metaphor of the body politic: 'Like the different parts of a well-constructed engine, the inhabitants of a civilized country are all mutually dependent on, and connected with each other.'[9]

In 1819 the Manchester Literary and Philosophical Society had published an essay by John Kennedy, one of the town's leading cotton manufacturers, who praised the steam engine because 'instead of carrying people to the power', it allowed manufacturers 'to place the power amongst the people'.[10] Kennedy acknowledged the social dislocations involved in these changes, but presented a new kind of punctual being – disciplined, healthy and clean – as a compensation. Kennedy's essay was used as an authority in the account of the Manchester cotton industry

[7] Maxine Berg, *The Machinery Question and the Making of Political Economy 1815–1848* (Cambridge: Cambridge University Press, 1980), p. 1.

[8] Nassau Senior, *An Outline of the Science of Political Economy* (London: W. Clowes, 1836), p. 158.

[9] J. R. McCulloch, *The Principles of Political Economy with a Sketch of the Rise and Progress of the Science* (Edinburgh: William and Charles Tait, 1825), p. 90.

[10] John Kennedy, 'Observations on the Rise and Progress of the Cotton Trade', *Memoirs of the Manchester Literary and Philosophical Society*, 2nd series, 3 (1819), 115–37 (pp. 127–8).

McCulloch provided for readers of the *Edinburgh Review* in 1827. As he had also done in his influential textbook *Principles of Political Economy* (1825), McCulloch credited inventors up to and including Watt for 'the skill and genius by which these astonishing results have been achieved'. This genius of invention, located outside the traditional sources of authority, was lauded as 'one of the main sources of our power'.[11] In one sense, he was harnessing the power of the new manufacturing towns to his consolidation of political economy as a scientific discipline, a process Philip Connell sees as beginning in the 1820s.[12]

McCulloch's collocation of 'power' and 'genius' is a mirror image of De Quincey's, and one no less committed to a sublime transformation in human being. McCulloch believed that technical innovation would push progress – and not only economic growth – beyond the limits imagined by earlier political economists: 'There are no limits,' he argued, 'to the power and resources of genius.'[13] Power was rarely granted to the bodies and hands that did the work of supplying raw materials from plantations or working with the machinery in the factories. The faith in technological progress shown by McCulloch and his allies was a particular version of the faith in the march of the mind; it was also committed to the diffusion of knowledge in ways that De Quincey, with his quasi-religious emphasis on private revelation, was not. McCulloch's public lectures, popular publications like his *Principles of Political Economy*, his reviewing for the *Edinburgh*, the tracts he circulated for the Political Economy Club, not to mention his professorship at the new University of London, were all intended to spread a new gospel of redemption framed as a hard scientific discipline after the mathesis of David Ricardo, but his career benefited from the remarkable 'confluence', newly available in the 1820s, as Mary Poovey describes it, 'of print, extra institutional, and academic opportunities'.[14] In the context of the fundamental changes the power of the machine seemed to be making to society, De Quincey's response provided an attractive alternative to the perspective proposed by McCulloch and his allies. Understandably enough, perhaps, De Quincey's perspective has tended to hold sway in institutions of literary studies committed to the cultural project of Romanticism, but both he

---

[11] See [J. R. McCulloch], 'Rise, Progress, Present State, and Prospects of the British Cotton Manufacture', *Edinburgh Review*, 46 (June 1827), 1–39 (p. 2). McCulloch describes Kennedy as 'one of the most eminent and intelligent cotton manufacturers in the Empire' (p. 13) and refers to his 'valuable paper' (p. 3).

[12] Philip Connell, *Romanticism, Economics, and the Question of 'Culture'* (Oxford: Oxford University Press, 2001), p. 274.

[13] [McCulloch], 'Cotton Manufacture', p. 17.

[14] Mary Poovey, *Genres of the Credit Economy: Mediating Value in Eighteenth- and Nineteenth-Century Britain* (Chicago: University of Chicago Press, 2008), p. 226.

and McCulloch, in their very different ways, were involved in abstracting an idea of power from the hybrid innovations – in writing and in technology – emerging in the 1820s. Both occluded the energies of enslaved and exploited peoples that sustained their mirror images of liberal freedom. Both, also in their different ways, might be identified as prophets of a form of visionary Romanticism that played an important part in the culture of the 1820s.

Keyword: Diffusion

Matthew Sangster

In an 1812 review of George Crabbe's *Tales*, Francis Jeffrey, the editor of the *Edinburgh Review*, estimated that 'In this country, there probably are not less than two hundred thousand persons who read for amusement or instruction among the middling classes of society. In the higher classes, there are not as many as twenty thousand.'[1] In total, these groups represented less than two per cent of the British population at the time: the 1811 census counted 12,552,144 individuals.[2] Crabbe's potential audience seems a vanishingly small proportion by modern standards, but Jeffrey's estimate is not an inaccurate representation of the quantity of people with the leisure time, education and financial resources necessary to access new literature in the 1810s. For Byron's *The Corsair*, one of the most successful poems of the age, John Murray printed 29,500 copies of standalone editions.[3] However, for most verse volumes, one or two small runs of a thousand copies was the standard. Neither were novels more ubiquitous. William St Clair has claimed that '[d]uring the romantic period the "Author of *Waverley*" sold more novels than all the other novelists of the time put together', but he also estimates that only around half a million copies of Scott novels were printed prior to the commencement of cheap editions in the late 1820s.[4] Taking St Clair at his word, doubling this figure to a million and assuming that his Romantic period is thirty years long would indicate that around 35,000 new copies of contemporary novels appeared each year,

[1] [Francis Jeffrey], 'Crabbe's *Tales*', *Edinburgh Review*, 20 (November 1812), 277–305 (p. 280).

[2] Census data taken from original documents hosted on *Online Historical Population Reports*, http://histpop.org.uk (accessed 7 February 2022).

[3] Copies Ledger A of the publisher John Murray, 1803–1819, National Library of Scotland, Ms.42724, f.57.

[4] William St Clair, *The Reading Nation in the Romantic Period* (Cambridge: Cambridge University Press, 2004), p. 221.

or approximately one for every 360 people in Britain. Other sources do imply higher count. The *British Fiction 1800–1829* database lists 2,272 titles; assuming an average print run of a thousand would give a figure around twice that which St Clair indicates.[5] However, even taking this higher figure and factoring in the importance of circulating and subscription libraries in fiction consumption, it would still seem to be the case that new novels were rather restricted pleasures.

By 1832, the year of the Reform Bill, the situation had changed radically. The preface to the first volume of Charles Knight's *Penny Magazine* – sold for a tiny fraction of the cost of the *Edinburgh* and its ilk – testifies to a massive expansion of the reading public.[6] 'In the present year,' Knight writes, 'it has been shown by the sale of the "Penny Magazine," that there are two hundred thousand *purchasers* of one periodical work. It may be fairly calculated that the number of readers of that single work amounts to a million.'[7] The *Penny Magazine*'s vast circulation makes it apparent that an astonishing enfranchisement of new readers had occurred during the 1820s. While taxes on knowledge had made certain kinds of written political discourse less accessible, most forms of media circulated with considerably greater ease and reach. As David McKitterick has put it (perhaps with excessive caution), 'by about 1830 some of the major changes in manufacture, materials, market demands and economic possibilities had become sufficiently widespread for it to be possible to claim that a revolution of some kind had been effected'.[8]

A key facilitator of print proliferation was new technological efficiency. During the 1820s publishers began to make extensive use of steam-driven presses, which were both faster and less laborious than older hand presses. In 1824, the *Westminster Review* laid out the differences in stark terms, writing that from the invention of printing until the early nineteenth century,

> the printing-press produced at the ordinary rate of working 250 single impressions an hour ... By extraordinary effort and skill and frequent reliefs of men, this rate of despatch might be doubled. ... [However,] About ten years ago, Mr. [John] Walter the managing proprietor of the *Times* ... employed Mr. [Friedrich] Koenig to construct a machine, free from the inherent defects

---

[5] *British Fiction, 1800–1829: A Database of Production, Circulation, and Reception*, http://www.british-fiction.cf.ac.uk/ (accessed 7 February 2022).

[6] The first number of the *Edinburgh* was priced at five shillings in 1802, later rising to six shillings.

[7] 'Preface' to volume 1 of *The Penny Magazine of the Society for the Diffusion of Useful Knowledge*, ed. Charles Knight (London: Charles Knight, 1832), pp. iii–iv (p. iii).

[8] David McKitterick, 'Introduction' to *The Cambridge History of the Book in Britain, Volume 6: 1830–1914*, ed. David McKitterick (Cambridge: Cambridge University Press, 2009), pp. 1–74 (p. 3).

of the old presses, and to be moved by steam. After many failures and a discouraging amount of expenditure, the attempt succeeded to an extent which fully rewarded the perseverance of its projectors. This machine, in the first instance, produced about 12 or 1300 impressions an hour, but further improvements have enabled the mechanical presses to produce 2000, and when extraordinary speed is necessary upwards of 2500 impressions an hour.[9]

The writer helpfully goes on to do the sums: 'Ten times as many impressions can therefore be produced in a given time, as were made some time ago at the ordinary rate of printing, and five time as many as were made by the greatest exertions.'[10]

A conservatively estimated fivefold increase in the efficiency of presses was only one technological driver of cheap print. Fourdrinier paper-making machines substantially brought down the price of paper, often previously the highest single cost in book production processes.[11] Genuine mass production also became increasingly viable. While stereotyping dates from the early eighteenth century, it was finally adopted as a common practice in the early nineteenth, allowing publishers to respond more flexibly and economically to demand for publications popular enough for it to be worth making up the plates.[12] The developing network of canals and railways made it far easier to send printed materials around the country. While, as Joseph Rezek has argued, concentrations of capital infrastructure meant that provincial readers remained 'beholden to a London book trade that supplied the vast majority of texts', increasing ease of transportation also meant that British publishers faced competition from firms like John Anthony Galignani's business in Paris, which produced innovative cheap collected editions of British poets in a double-column format.[13]

Newly adopted technologies – supported by the increasing ease of illustration using lithography, wood block printing and steel engraving – swiftly catalysed the development of new forms and genres. In 1825, a *Gentleman's Magazine* article, 'On Cheap Periodical Literature', remembered that 'There was a time, when it was considered, even by the most opulent bookseller, a great hazard to undertake a periodical publication. Shareholders were convened, consultations held, and

---

[9] 'The Periodical Press of Great Britain and Ireland', *Westminster Review*, 2.3 (July 1824), pp. 194–212 (pp. 205–6).

[10] Ibid. p. 206.

[11] James Raven, *The Business of Books: Booksellers and the English Book Trade* (New Haven, CT: Yale University Press, 2007), p. 310.

[12] St Clair, *The Reading Nation*, pp. 100–1.

[13] Joseph Rezek, *London and the Making of Provincial Literature: Aesthetics and the Transatlantic Book Trade, 1800–1850* (Philadelphia: University of Pennsylvania Press, 2015), pp. 4–5.

deep calculations made before the speculation could be ventured on, which occupied as much attention as a modern project for forming a railway, or cutting a canal.'[14] However, cheaper print provided ample opportunities for periodicals and part-publications to burgeon. In 1834, *Tait's Edinburgh Magazine* recorded that '[t]he expensive quartos and octavos, which used to issue in such swarms from Albemarle Street, and The Row, and from the Edinburgh press in *Constable's* days, have given place to the *Waverley Novels, Lardner's Cyclopaedia, The Edinburgh Cabinet Library*, and some scores more of similar works, published in monthly parts, at cheap prices'.[15] This article in *Tait's* was designed to explain why the magazine had chosen dramatically to drop its price from half a crown to a shilling. Its success when it did so was indicative of the flourishing of a genuine mass print culture. The second-wave magazines (including *Blackwood's*, the *London* and the *New Monthly*) were early harbingers of this expansion, but it took in a far wider range of works. In order to 'render a . . . service to the future bibliographer', the 1825 *Gentleman's Magazine* article proposed to 'record the principal [cheap periodicals] now in existence'. Its helpful list gives a sense of these publications' subject matter and priorities: the *Mirror of Literature, Amusement, and Instruction* (one of the oldest, founded in 1822), the *Portfolio*, the *Nic Nac, Oxberry's Dramatic Biography*, the *Diorama*, the *Encyclopedia of Anecdote and Wit*, the *Universal Songster*, the *London Stage*, the *London Stage Edition of Shakespeare*, *Hone's Every-Day Book*, the *Drama*, the *Iris*, the *Mirror of the Church*, the *Mechanic's Magazine*, the *Mechanic's Register*, the *Register of the Arts and Sciences*, the *Pulpit, Knapp and Baldwin's Newgate Calendar*, the *Memoirs of Lord Byron*, the *Terrific Register, Legends of Terror, Endless Entertainment*, the *Literary Magnet*, the *Linguist*, the *Medical Advisor*, the *Chemist*, the *Lancet*, the *Theatrical Observer*, the *Dramatic Weekly Register* and the *London Mechanics' Register*.[16] In closing, the article also notes that 'several old standard publications have been issued in twopenny and threepenny numbers: among others the Arabian Nights Entertainments, British Novelists, Plutarch's Lives, Tales of the Genii, Cook's Voyages, Cowper's Poems, Hume's History of England, &c. There are also, in cheap weekly numbers, the Popular Encyclopedia, Biographical Dictionary, Stewart's Dictionary of Architecture, &c'. Alongside all these productions, gift annuals began to

---

[14] 'On Cheap Periodical Literature', *The Gentleman's Magazine*, new series, 95 (June 1825), pp. 483–6 (p. 483).
[15] '*Johnstone's Edinburgh Magazine*: The Cheap and Dear Periodicals', *Tait's Edinburgh Magazine*, 4 (January 1834), 490–500 (p. 492).
[16] 'On Cheap Periodical Literature', pp. 485–6.

proliferate; as Katherine D. Harris notes, the 1820s 'referred to by some scholars as dormant and unproductive, is in fact bursting with *Forget Me Nots, Friendship's Offerings, Keepsakes,* and *Literary Souvenirs*'.[17] In 1826, the Society for the Diffusion of Useful Knowledge was founded to harness the educational potential of cheap print, adding to the rush. Anthologies and miscellanies flourished, both in pleasurable forms, such as 'Beauties' volumes, and in more pedagogical guises.

These developments were registered at the time as having altered fundamentally society's terms of engagement with politics and culture. In his 1829 *Colloquies*, Robert Southey felt confident in remarking through the person of Sir Thomas More that '[a]ll classes are now brought within the reach of your current literature . . . on the quality of which, according as it may be salubrious or noxious, the health of the public mind depends'.[18] In his 1830 *On the Constitution of the Church and State*, Samuel Taylor Coleridge laid out a litany of 'new forces' that had impacted on the debate surrounding Catholic emancipation: 'Roads, canals, machinery, the press, the periodical and daily press, the might of public opinion, the consequent increasing desire of popularity among public men and functionaries of every description': all these, in Coleridge's view, were both causes and symptoms of a sea change in the relationship between print, knowledge and society.[19] As these accounts demonstrate, the 1820s was when print culture became ubiquitous. This transformed the horizons of hundreds of thousands of readers, causing substantial shifts in formats and contents and mandating the development of modern disciplinary frameworks as a means of accommodating and regulating a constant flow of new productions. When the Great Reform Bill finally expanded the franchise in 1832, it reflected the intellectual enfranchisement that cheap print had accomplished over the course of the previous decade. This had created and made visible a nation of readers whose potential for representation could no longer easily be doubted.

---

[17] Katherine D. Harris, 'The Legacy of Rudolph Ackermann and Nineteenth-Century British Literary Annuals', in *BRANCH: Britain, Representation and Nineteenth-Century History*, ed. Dino Franco Felluga, available at http://www.branchcollective .org/?ps_articles=katherine-d-harris-the-legacy-of-rudolph-ackermann-and-nineteenth -century-british-literary-annuals (accessed 7 February 2022).

[18] Robert Southey, *Sir Thomas More: or, Colloquies on the Progress and Prospects of Society*, 2 vols (London: John Murray, 1829), vol. II, pp. 362–3.

[19] Samuel Taylor Coleridge, *On the Constitution of the Church and State* (London: Hurst, Chance, and Co., 1830), p. 27.

Chapter 3

Feeding the 1820s:
Bread, Beer and Anxiety

Lindsay Middleton

Food has symbolic value within society and culture: it expresses social movements, power structures and patterns of living. Stephen Mennell argues that 'changing structures of social interdependence and changing balances of power within society have been reflected in one particular cultural domain, that of food'.[1] What Mennell's statement overlooks, however, is the way food not only symbolically reflects these structures, but has also been actively enlisted as a means of creating and disrupting them. In understanding the 1820s, a decade marked by unevenness and change, food can be a powerful tool for gaining insight into the different ways people attempted to both manifest and interpret that change. As such, this chapter turns to two texts that address food in the 1820s from markedly different perspectives. Friedrich Accum's *A Treatise on Adulterations of Food and Culinary Poisons: exhibiting the fraudulent sophistications of bread, beer, wine, spirituous liquors, tea, oil, pickles, and other articles employed in domestic economy, and methods of detecting them* was published in London in January 1820. It revealed and condemned the food adulteration undertaken in Britain, and particularly in London, by bakers, brewers and other food manufacturers. William Cobbett's *Cottage Economy* was published as a series of pamphlets in 1821 and 1822, and in book form in 1822. It was a rural management guide which aimed to radicalise food production by advocating the return to subsistence farming and self-sufficiency in response to increasing taxes and dependency on mass-produced goods. By paying attention to the adulteration and radicalisation of food within these texts, I demonstrate that both authors use morally charged language and dichotomies to elevate food's significance, playing with notions of nostalgia, sensation and fear to explore and construct contemporary

---

[1] Stephen Mennell, *All Manners of Food: Eating and Taste from the Middle Ages to the Present* (Oxford: Basil Blackwell, 1985), p. 17.

anxieties surrounding surveillance. Even something as vital to daily life as food could become a locus for the doubt that has been seen as the characteristic mood of the decade.

In the years leading up to the 1820s, food systems were unstable. Poor harvests in the 1790s meant wheat prices soared, leading to the extended bread riots of 1795 and 1796. During the Napoleonic Wars, the market economy and Napoleon's blockades on trading imported grains meant prices continued to climb. As Walter M. Stern notes, 'the average price of the quartern loaf stood at 1s. 0¼d. in 1795' but had risen to '1s. 5d. in 1812'.[2] An increase of nearly 5d was significant, and yet with peace the price of British grain fell dramatically. This resulted in the enactment of the 1815 Corn Laws, 'which allowed free entry [to the market] when the price of corn was above 80 shillings per quarter and prohibited entry when the price fell below 80 shillings'.[3] These import tariffs kept grain prices high and served the post-war British agricultural market. While they benefited landowners by creating a contingent monopoly, the Corn Laws faced massive public protest given the high price of bread for consumers. This culminated in the formation of the Anti-Corn Law League by Richard Cobden in 1839, while in 1845 the Irish potato failure and resulting famine eventually convinced prime minister Sir Robert Peel to revoke the Corn Laws, destroying the Tory Party. In the 1820s, however, people were still suffering from the high costs of food that percolated into the decade from earlier years.

Foodways were also changing as people moved to towns and cities in search of the opportunities afforded by mechanisation and because rural land use was slowly transforming to make life in the countryside difficult for the working classes. In 1801 only London, Bristol, Leeds, Liverpool, Birmingham and Manchester had over 50,000 inhabitants, but in 1851 around half of people lived in urban areas and seventeen more towns had expanded to house over 50,000.[4] This move meant landowners were under increasing pressure to feed urban populations. The distance between food producer and consumer also increased. Staple foodstuffs consumed by the British population before urbanisation were produced as part of a rural lifestyle. Since foods were kept within families or traded locally, it was unlikely they would be adulterated due to their

---

[2] Walter M. Stern, 'The Bread Crisis in Britain, 1795–96', *Economica*, 31.122 (1964), 168–87 (p. 168).

[3] Cheryl Schonhardt-Bailey, *From the Corn Laws to Free Trade: Interests, Ideas, and Institutions in Historical Perspective* (London: MIT Press, 2006), p. 9.

[4] Andrea Broomfield, *Food and Cooking in Victorian Britain: A History* (Westport, CT: Praeger, 2007), p. 89. See also John Burnett, *Plenty and Want: A Social History of Food in England from 1815 to the Present Day* (London: Routledge, 1989).

home-grown, untaxed nature. For the working classes, the rural diet in mainland Britain prior to urbanisation largely consisted of homemade '[b]read, butter, and cheese eaten along with cabbages or other greens', which 'kept labourers from going hungry' and meant that 'many lived to old age without debilitating diseases', according to Andrea Broomfield.[5] While this overlooks geographic specificities and the difficulties the rural poor faced sustaining themselves in times of famine or crop failure, it is true that home-grown diets were not sustainable within urban environments. Quickly expanding towns and cities created cramped conditions for the majority of the urban population, who lacked the indoor and outdoor space to produce food domestically. Moreover, technological innovations were not in place to address supply issues. As noted by John Burnett, the railway network quickly changed how food reached towns and cities, levelling geographic price variations and distributing resources across Britain to address scarcities.[6] However, until the opening of the Liverpool and Manchester line in 1830 and the mainstream adoption of rail, gaps between food and the people eating it were widening with no clear solution, and food had to travel great distances at slow speeds. As food became increasingly mass produced by those who needed to stretch ingredients and preserve it, food adulteration became a tangible reality.

Prior to the beginning of the nineteenth century, food adulteration discourses rarely gathered widespread attention. That is not to say that adulteration and its detection are absent from records before the nineteenth century, however, and mentions of adulteration can be traced as far back as ancient Athens and Rome, including records of Pliny the Elder being responsible for monitoring wine.[7] After this, spices, tea and luxury items were monitored to avoid tampering that increased their weight and decreased their quality. Even bread and beer were governed via policies like King John's 1202 Assize of Bread, the earliest British law that regulated food sales and attempted to control the price and quality of loaves sold by bakers. These regulations, however, were difficult to enforce and often unreliable. To take a comical example, in the fifteenth century some English towns had 'ale tasters' who were charged with gauging the quality of beer. To do so, the taster 'poured some of it on a wooden bench, and sat on the wet spot in his leather breeches. If his breeches adhered to the bench, it showed that sugar had been added'.[8] In the late eighteenth and early nineteenth centuries brewing was still

[5] Broomfield, *Food and Cooking*, p. 88.
[6] Burnett, *Plenty and Want*, p. 8.
[7] See Burnett, *Plenty and Want*, p. 86 and F. Leslie Hart, 'A History of the Adulteration of Food Before 1906', *Food, Drug, Cosmetic Law Journal*, 7.1 (1952), 5–22.
[8] Hart, 'A History', pp. 10–11.

a source of anxiety, though records show that practices had moved on from sticky breeches. James Sumner describes the brewery manuals and publican's guides that circulated during this time, which typically contained recipes and guidance about the laws relating to publicans, as well as 'warnings against the sharp practices of distillers and spirit-vendors, which included adulteration. These same practices, however, were employed by publicans themselves to extend their profits from drinkers, and so could not be straightforwardly attacked'.[9] Adulteration – warnings and guides to it – thus coexisted in texts just before the publication of Accum's *Treatise*. Even if adulteration did not gain publicity, it was discussed amongst those who were concerned with producing saleable products. While domestic brewing was prolific during this period, generating roughly half of British beer in 1801, 'from this time, the decline was both continuous and rapid', the pattern most homemade comestibles were following.[10] What brewing literature consolidates is that adulteration was most likely when foodstuffs were produced, sold and taxed on a large scale: '[i]ncrease in public revenue was of more importance than an increase in public health'.[11] The rapid expansion of towns and cities and widening gap between consumer and producer thus combined to facilitate decreasing self-sufficiency. As a result, the prevalence of food adulteration was accelerating in the 1820s, as was the anxiety that accompanied it.

While Accum was not the first to write about adulteration, he was the first to captivate the public imagination. Numerous critics labelled him a trendsetter.[12] Indeed, it was the combination of Accum's past achievements and the changing environment which positioned him perfectly to catch the crest of a rising wave of incipient anxiety. Accum was a German chemist who moved to London in 1793 and began working at an apothecary. He established himself as a lecturer, instrument-maker and author and was assistant chemical operator at the Royal Institution from 1801 to 1803, and then was in charge at the Surrey Institution. Sumner notes Accum's marriage of chemistry and commercialism, highlighting that his work was geared towards popular subjects and recording his connections with influential figures like the natural philosopher

---

[9] James Sumner, 'Retailing Scandal: The Disappearance of Friedrich Accum', in *(Re)Creating Science in Nineteenth-Century Britain*, ed. A. Mordavsky Caleb (Newcastle upon Tyne: Cambridge Scholars Publishing, 2007), pp. 32–48 (p. 40).

[10] Burnett, *Plenty and Want*, p. 7.

[11] Hart, 'A History', p. 12.

[12] Hart notes that Accum was 'The first pioneer on record to make [the exposition of adulteration] his life work' (p. 14); Burnett states that 'It was only in 1820, when Frederick Accum published his *Treatise on Adulterations of Food and Culinary Poisons*, that the subject was ventilated for the first time' (pp. 87–8).

William Nicholson.[13] As part of a vogue for domestic chemistry, particularly in terms of food and drink, Accum published treatises including *The Art of Brewing* (1820), *Culinary Chemistry* (1821), *The Art of Making Good and Wholesome Bread* (1821) and *The Art of Making Wine* (1821). These were published after the *Treatise*'s first edition, with Accum building upon the success it had gained. Since Accum's focus was on a widespread audience, it is not surprising he turned to food given the contemporary increase in texts addressing food and cooking. Later, in the mid-1830s, bestselling cookbook writer Eliza Acton would allegedly be told by Accum's publisher Thomas Longman: 'Don't bring me poems, madam, bring me a cookery book!'[14] Sheila Hardy notes the Acton story is hearsay, but accepts that 'Longman was responding, as publishers have always done, to what was considered to be the contemporary taste of the public'.[15] Longman's rival, John Murray, published Maria Rundell's *A New System of Domestic Cookery* in 1806 to huge success: the book's second edition had a run of 1,150 copies; by 1841 it was on its 65th British edition. Rundell's triumph sparked a wave of similar cookbooks, with examples like William Kitchiner's *Apicius Redivivus: The Cook's Oracle* (1817), Christian Isobel Johnstone's *The Cook and Housewife's Manual* (1826) and Mrs Dalgairn's *The Practice of Cookery* (1829) securing multiple reprints, making their authors household names.[16] Accum was thus wise to jump on this burgeoning trend and turn his chemical expertise to food, in keeping with his commercial drive.

Accum addresses his aspirations for a large audience in the *Treatise*'s preface: it was 'intended to exhibit easy methods of detecting the fraudulent adulterations of food' and it was for '[e]very person' to use.[17] He was successful in reaching a substantial fraction of the reading public: the book's first thousand-copy run sold out in a month. The second edition was published in April 1820, followed by another two between then and 1822. This was despite the *Treatise* presenting existing knowledge in a new format. Accum drew on a variety of other texts, which were

---

[13] Sumner, 'Retailing Scandal', p. 34.

[14] Sheila Hardy, *The Real Mrs Beeton: The Story of Eliza Acton* (Stroud: History Press, 2011), p. 89.

[15] Ibid. p. 89.

[16] *The Cook and Housewife's Manual* was published under the pseudonym 'Margaret (Meg) Dods', who was a character in Sir Walter Scott's novel *St. Ronan's Well* (1823). Meg Dods was an innkeeper in the novel; Scott wrote the cookbook's introduction.

[17] Friedrich Accum, *A Treatise on Adulterations of Food and Culinary Poisons: exhibiting the fraudulent sophistications of bread, beer, wine, spirituous liquors, tea, oil, pickles, and other articles employed in domestic economy, and methods of detecting them* (London: Longman, Hurst, Rees, Orme, and Brown, 1820a), pp. iii–iv.

often reproduced without attribution in the *Treatise*.[18] Accum does not hide his use of these sources, noting that to ensure his claims are accurate he has cited occasions of adulteration 'which are authenticated in Parliamentary documents and other public records'.[19] Nevertheless, Summer argues, Accum's use of these sources made him vulnerable to accusations of hackwork and influenced the scandal that followed the *Treatise*'s publication.[20] Accum was accused of cutting sections from the books of the Royal Institution's library and pocketing them. He was then expelled from the Institution and fled England while his work was discredited, the *Treatise* in particular. Some scholars connect the *Treatise*'s publication with Accum's dismissal, arguing that chemists were worried about being implicated in adulteration.[21] Sumner suggests that Accum's plagiarism and 'lurid devices' placed him outside the professional standards that chemists like Humphry Davy were establishing at the time.[22] Ironically, Accum's account of the fraudulent additions of food adulteration was composed of plagiarism and cut-and-paste repetition, as the form of his *Treatise* in this light mirrored its content. However, it was his mixing of genres and employment of 'lurid devices', I argue, that created a commercially successful text.

Accum's provocative textual intervention encouraged readers to deploy experimental processes within the home in order to demonstrate the dangers that lay in their pantries. The *Treatise* may be read as an 'anti-cookbook'; instead of listing recipes, Accum tells readers about the substances in foods and associated health risks, before instructing them how to decompose foodstuffs and analyse them for adulterates. He also disparages cookbooks for perpetuating dangerous practices: in the 'poisonous pickles' section, Accum criticises authors who write gherkin recipes that include copper or alum powder to colour pickles green.[23] By offering his text as an alternative, however, Accum situates himself in the cookbook marketplace – perhaps not unintentionally, given the genre's success. Indeed, like Rundell's cookbook, Accum's *Treatise* sparked an onslaught of exposition texts, including *Deadly Adulteration and Slow Poisoning Unmasked; or Disease and Death in the Pot and Bottle* (c. 1829), *Treatise on the Falsification of Food and the Chemical Means*

18 Sumner, 'Retailing Scandal', p. 36.
19 Accum, *A Treatise*, 1820a, p. v.
20 Sumner, 'Retailing Scandal', p. 36.
21 Burnett notes that 'there is a strong suspicion that there existed a deliberate conspiracy of vested interests determined to discredit and silence Accum, which succeeded in its object by driving him out of the country'; *Plenty and Want*, p. 90.
22 Sumner, 'Retailing Scandal', p. 33.
23 Accum, *A Treatise*, 1820a, p. 308.

Employed to Detect Them (1848) and *The Chemistry of Common Life* (1855).[24] The fearmongering titles echo Accum's *Treatise*, signalling an irrevocable change in the presentation of food adulteration that continued throughout the nineteenth century.

The *Treatise* is itself a mixed form, adulterating what could be colder natural-philosophical language with the vivid sensationalism of the Gothic. Accum's tendency towards the Gothic is instantly visible in the cover and frontispiece of the *Treatise*. The cover depicts a skull and crossbones with a verse from the Bible: 'There is death in the pot (2 Kings 4:38–41)'. Intertwined snakes surround a web, in the middle of which a spider eats a fly. Entrapment, poison, predation and death are conjured up for the reader. The *Treatise*'s second edition extends these onto the frontispiece which shows a skull above a pot inscribed with the biblical quotation from Kings (Figure 1).[25] Accum may well have deliberately ramped up the Gothic elements to further boost his sales. Ivy and a stone wall create the impression of a graveyard and the illustration pairs with the Gothic typeface used for 'Culinary Poisons' to create an image designed to spark the fear of death in the reader. Indeed, a review in the *British Review* claimed the cover was 'so frightful that more than one young lady of our acquaintance would think it necessary to scream at the sight of it'.[26] Moreover, the biblical reference positions food adulteration as an ungodly crime, ending in death. In the cited Bible passage, a poisonous vine is added to a pot of stew which results in the threat of death. The prophet Elisha adds meal to the pot, and as a result 'there was no harm in the pot'.[27] Through this reference, Accum likens himself to Elisha, framing himself as a prophet who provides the necessary means to prevent food adulteration. The repeated snakes evoke the Edenic serpent and the imagery works with the allusion to depict food adulteration as a sin. This paratextual material aims to elicit anxiety in the reader, as Accum reveals the danger invading their bodies via the foodstuffs they consume. Accum's *Treatise*, then, and even Accum himself, are positioned as saviours in the face of depravity,

---

[24] Judith L. Fisher, 'Tea and Food Adulteration, 1834–75', *BRANCH: Britain, Representation and Nineteenth-Century History*, ed. Dino Franco Felluga, available at https://www.branchcollective.org/?ps_articles=judith-l-fisher-tea-and-food-adulteration-1834-75 (accessed 7 February 2022).

[25] Friedrich Accum, *A Treatise on Adulterations of Food and Culinary Poisons: exhibiting the fraudulent sophistications of bread, beer, wine, spirituous liquors, tea, oil, pickles, and other articles employed in domestic economy, and methods of detecting them*, 2nd edn (London: Longman, Hurst, Rees, Orme, and Brown, 1820b), frontispiece.

[26] William Roberts, 'Accum on Adulterations of Food', *The British Review and London Critical Journal*, 15.29 (1820), 170–91 (p. 171).

[27] II Kings 4:39–41 (Authorised King James Version).

Figure 1   Frontispiece to Friedrich Accum, *A Treatise on Adulterations of Food and Culinary Poisons*, 2nd edn (London: Longman, Hurst, Rees, Orme, and Brown, 1820). Courtesy of The Lewis Walpole Library, Yale University.

and the language employed in the *Treatise* continues this tone of morality throughout. The sensationalism deployed by Accum seeks to elicit emotion from the reader: real fear at dangerous adulterated foods and exaggerated horror akin to reading a Gothic novel. As the quasi-satirical quotation in the *Review* shows, he succeeded.

Within the *Treatise* proper, accounts of adulteration and perform-at-home experiments make up the bulk of the text. It is debateable whether Accum's instructions were practical for people who may not have had food to spare. To expose poisoned pickles, Accum suggests they are minced and covered with liquid ammonia, which would run blue if copper was found in the food. Ammonia-drenched pickles would be inedible whether poisoned or not, meaning the reader following Accum's test risks rendering their food inedible even if it was not adulterated to begin with. Moreover, Accum's experiments often require specialist equipment and chemicals. To detect alum in bread, people should:

> Pour upon two ounces of the suspected bread, half a pint of boiling distilled water; boil the mixture for a few minutes, and filter it through unsized paper. Evaporate the fluid, to about one fourth of its original bulk, and let gradually fall into the clear fluid a solution of muriate of barytes. If a *copious* white precipitate ensues, which does not disappear by the addition of *pure* nitric acid, the presence of alum may be suspected.[28]

Readers here require a scale, means of distillation, a heat source, filter paper and two chemical solutions. It is unlikely the average reader would have the time, money, equipment or spare food to perform these experiments at home. Accum anticipated this, however, through his 'Amusement Chests', which were kits the public could buy to experiment at home. Brian Gee notes that Accum sold these from 1817 onwards and that, again combining science with consumerism and amusement, he 'enticed' listeners to purchase a chest 'for prices between ten and eighteen guineas and try the spectacle of chemistry for themselves'.[29] While exposing poisoned food was not the entertaining chemistry Accum originally imagined, encouraging non-scientific readers to perform experiments at home sees Accum once more blur the lines between science, commerce and domesticity. The expensive pricing of his chests, however, demonstrates that the practical use of the *Treatise* was predominantly reserved for a wealthy audience and the emerging middle class who had

---

28 Accum, *A Treatise*, 1820a, p. 147.
29 Brian Gee, 'Amusement Chests and Portable Laboratories: Practical Alternatives to the Regular Laboratory', in *The Development of the Laboratory: Essays on the Place of Experiment in Industrial Civilisation*, ed. F. A. J. L. James (London: Macmillan, 1989), pp. 37–60 (p. 38).

the income and leisure time to engage in these activities of experimentation and surveillance. The majority of the population would have been limited to reading about the horrible dangers lurking in their food, either in the *Treatise* or in its reviews and derivations in periodicals, without then having the means of performing the tests themselves.

Accum's rhetoric demonstrates that even if his *Treatise* was unlikely to be used, it elevates food to a level which encodes morality. The practices uncovered include 'blowing' meat, which involved butchers inflating meat with 'breath respired from the lungs, to make it appear white and glistening'.[30] Throughout these expositions, Accum repeatedly turns the dichotomies of sin and purity to the reader in question form, asking 'who can bear the notion of eating meat, the cellular substance of which has been filled with the air of the dirty fellow, who may at the same time perhaps be inflicted with the very worst of diseases'.[31] By framing judgement as a question Accum implicates the reader in the exchange, making it a moral quandary. He is not asking, 'who opts for fresh-looking meat?' but 'who would engage in a dirty act of consumption?'. Moreover, the use of 'cellular' to depict the biological structure of meat demonstrates the fusion of science and sensationalism in the text. Accum goes further than this, however. It is not just potentially diseased food the eater consumes, but the butcher's characteristics: the butcher is called 'dirty' before Accum mentions diseases. Given the long-standing etymological links between dirtiness and impurity, as in the definitions of dirty as '[m]orally unclean or impure' and 'stain[ing] the honour of the persons engaged; dishonourably sordid, base, mean, or corrupt', Accum's notion of dirtiness easily construes immorality.[32] There is also the implication that Accum is deriding the butcher as a lower-class tradesman, again suggesting he is writing for readers with middle-class sensibilities. If a person eats blown meat, they are as unhygienic and immoral as the butcher – consuming his disease and sinfulness. Polite society would certainly have avoided such social contamination. These questions are repeated throughout. By creating moral dichotomies Accum positions his reader so they become as disgraceful as food adulterators if they knowingly consume adulterated foods. Eating cleanly is the only course of action for honest readers. Despite these high moral stakes, however, 1820s life meant food adulteration was difficult to escape. People with limited funds, time and space would have to buy adulterated foods due

---

[30] Accum, *A Treatise*, 1820b, p. 36.

[31] Ibid. p. 37.

[32] 'dirty, adj. and adv.', *Oxford English Dictionary Online*, 3rd edn (Oxford: Oxford University Press, 2000–), www.oed.com/view/Entry/53367 (accessed 7 February 2022).

to lack of better options. The Adulteration of Food, Drink and Drugs Act would not pass until 1872, after several failed attempts, and after this there were still inconsistencies in practice. The Act made it illegal to change food unless labelled, but until that point food adulteration was unchecked, widespread and dangerous: not just to the eater's morality but to their health. Accum's language of life and death, then, conjured a fear that was not unfounded, but which was hard to escape.

Reviews of the *Treatise* highlight the idea that it foregrounded and profited from fear. The *London Literary Gazette* recounts chunks of it in a horrified tone, noting: 'It is so horribly pleasant to reflect how we are in this way be-swindled, be-trayed, be-drugged, and be-devilled, that we are almost angry at Mr Accum for the great service he has done the community by opening our eyes, at the risk of shutting our mouths forever.'[33] Despite the ironical tone, the *Gazette* highlights the problem Accum posed as his detailed expositions showed readers that most of their food was at risk of being adulterated. The *British Review* is sceptical of Accum's *Treatise,* but concedes that 'the money that is often laid out in the purchase of cookery books, which teach the art of exiting disease and pain by dubious combinations and culinary poisons, might, we think, be much better expended upon a book like the present: every page of which gives warning of some danger'.[34] Furthermore, the *Treatise*'s reception highlights that its fusion of chemistry, food and the Gothic was its most striking feature. W. J. Forbes's poem, 'Death (a Dealer) to his London Correspondent', was published in Richard Dagley's *Death's Doings* collection in 1826. The poem shows Death hypothesising about using adulteration to kill people, including the line 'As for coffee, Fred. Accum well knows the word means' and an illustration of Death surrounded by adulterants, with a document on the wall entitled 'Accum's List'.[35] The poem portrays Accum as party to adulteration, and similarities between the depiction of Death and the skull in Accum's frontispiece create visual links between the texts that establish Accum as a Gothic character himself – the evil chemist. Moreover, a *Blackwood's Edinburgh Magazine* review notes the *Treatise* is written in 'a spirit of dark and melancholy anticipation'.[36] The reviewer imagines Accum at home, where:

---

[33] William Jerdan, 'Poisoning of Food', *London Literary Gazette*, 4.156 (15 January 1820), 33–8 (p. 34).

[34] Roberts, 'Accum on Adulterations of Food', p. 187.

[35] W. J. Forbes, 'Death (a Dealer) to his London Correspondent', in *Death's Doings*, ed. R. Dagley, 2nd edn (London: J. Andrews, [1826] 1827), pp. 361–4 (p. 362).

[36] 'There is Death in the Pot', *Blackwood's Edinburgh Magazine*, 6.35 (1820), 542–54 (p. 543).

An imaginary sexton is continually jogging his elbow as he writes, a death's head and cross bones rise on his library table; and at the end of his sofa he beholds a visionary tomb-stone of the best granite – ON WHICH ARE INSCRIBED THE DREADFUL WORDS –[37]

Following this quotation is a plate showing Accum's tombstone: again, a skull harks back to the *Treatise*'s frontispiece. This characterisation of Accum as a haunted chemist once more positions him as a Gothic trope. Both literature and reviews thus responded to Accum's mixing of genres – critiquing it by using the same genre blurring. These reviews demonstrate that Accum scandalised the public imagination by accentuating the sensational, Gothic nature of his text. The dichotomies of sin and purity, frightening imagery and the adulterations Accum presented triggered worries about the consumption and production of modern food which had not entered mainstream British consciousness until that point.

The fear and worry Accum evoked through his use of Gothic motifs can be further situated in the 1820s when considered via the context of surveillance. The works of Jeremy Bentham, Edwin Chadwick and Elizabeth Fry emphasised surveillance, observation and transparency throughout the decade, looking to establish forms of mass observation in institutionalised settings and on an individual level.[38] The state, media and popular forms of entertainment were becoming increasingly geared towards the visual interpretation and quantification of the surrounding world. Food adulteration was a prime subject for this kind of self-surveillance as people increasingly sought to understand what they were buying and consuming. The very nature of Accum's text, with its expositions and experiments, thus played into the newfound fascination with inspection by highlighting the hidden dangers and fraudulent malpractice that obscured what the eater was really consuming. The *Treatise*'s Gothic tropes elicited an anxiety which encouraged readers to analyse their foodstuffs and equipped them with the tools they required to engage in their own forms of domestic and scientific surveillance. Indeed, when considering the use of science in the Gothic, as in Mary Shelley's *Frankenstein; or, The Modern Prometheus* (1818), Andrew Smith argues that '[s]cience in the Gothic functions repeatedly as a trope for rationality, moderation and creativity' and that '[s]cience therefore performs a type of politics in the Gothic, one which affirms that new models of reason are needed in order to fashion and sustain a new,

---

[37] Ibid. p. 543.
[38] The themes of surveillance and observation are explored further in the chapters by Porscha Fermanis and Sara Lodge in this volume.

utopian post-revolutionary world'.[39] If science is political within the Gothic, then within a scientific text the Gothic may do political work. When the *Treatise* is examined via its literary markings, Accum's use of Gothic tropes arguably creates a form of scientific discourse that represents the search for new systems of understanding that science, literature and the heightened focus on surveillance were reaching for in the 1820s. Through its blending of genres, metatextual references and alignment of chemistry with sales, the *Treatise* thus encapsulated tensions being played out that extended beyond food. The commercialisation of texts was problematising literary and scientific spheres and the *Treatise* represents this troubling of form versus content well. Its hybridity as a Gothic-scientific-exposition-cookbook unsettles the boundaries between genres that were dissolving at the time. Green pickles and white bread were just as deceptive as artificially segregated texts, and the form and content of Accum's *Treatise* demonstrated that both publications and ingredients could incorporate multiple genres or substances to ensure commercial gain: either in terms of book sales, or the successful deception of customers buying foodstuffs. Moreover, by its nature the *Treatise* showed readers that seeing (and tasting) could no longer be believing and further surveillance was needed to ensure one's safety even within the home. Food in Accum's *Treatise*, then, is used to expose doubt on textual, symbolic and physical levels.

While Accum's *Treatise* perpetuated the anxiety and heightened levels of surveillance that were occurring in the 1820s, William Cobbett's writing in *Cottage Economy* sought actively to resist the state's control and interference in the lives of individuals. While the *Treatise* brought Accum to fame, Cobbett was a household name long before *Cottage Economy*'s publication. Cobbett was the most famous and productive journalist of the late eighteenth and early nineteenth century, publishing an 'estimated twenty million words' throughout his career.[40] Growing up in rural England, working in London, serving in the military and living in France and North America, Cobbett's success came from writing about the American and French revolutions, before turning to political upheaval in Britain. His radical conservative ideas eventually became inextricable from a vision of pre-industrial Britain and the rural ways of life he petitioned to return to, as he presented his ideas and politics to a huge audience in *Cobbett's Weekly Political Register* (1802–36).

---

[39] Andrew Smith, 'Gothic Science', in *Romantic Gothic: An Edinburgh Companion*, ed. Angela Wright and Dale Townshend (Edinburgh: Edinburgh University Press, 2016), pp. 306–21 (p. 319).

[40] James Grande, *William Cobbett, the Press and Rural England: Radicalism and the Fourth Estate, 1793–1835* (Basingstoke: Palgrave Macmillan, 2014), p. 2.

Indeed, when individual articles were published as two-penny pamphlets, Cobbett sold 50,000 copies a week – indicating his vast readership. Cobbett's *Rural Rides* was serialised from 1821 to 1826 in the *Register*. The *Rides* recounted Cobbett's tours in southern England and demonstrate the way Cobbett fused genres, combining observation with a political call to arms. James Grande has described *Rides* as 'a mongrel genre, drawing on elements from a wide range of forms, including the pedestrian tour, picaresque novel, familiar essay, sentimental journey and agricultural report'.[41] Indeed, Cobbett's politics and influence were strengthened by his ability to weave voices together: as E. P. Thompson notes, Cobbett '*created* this Radical intellectual culture . . . he found the tone, the style, and the arguments which would bring the weaver, the schoolmaster, and the shipwright, into a common discourse'.[42] Critics have long debated the multifarious nature of Cobbett's politics and writing, but an examination of *Cottage Economy* demonstrates how powerful a subject food was when it was taken up by one of the most influential journalists of the 1820s.[43]

Cottage Economy turned Cobbett's observations of the English countryside into a guide, so readers could enact the lifestyles Cobbett encountered on his travels. Cobbett disliked the urbanisation and commodification of the working classes and his rural radicalism was an attempt to fight for a labouring class that was not debased by dependency on products. As outlined, the number of people who lived rurally had declined by the 1820s, so Cobbett's defence of rural living – while inspired by his touring – would have been imbued with nostalgia for readers forced to leave the countryside in pursuit of employment and for those who never had the chance to participate in such a lifestyle. *Cottage Economy* mobilises and radicalises nostalgia, however. In the introduction, Cobbett notes:

> The laws, the economy, or management, of a state may be such as to render it impossible for the labourer, however skilful and industrious, to maintain his family in health and decency; and such has, for many years past, been the management of the affairs of this once truly great and happy land.[44]

---

[41] Ibid. p. 148.

[42] E. P. Thompson, *The Making of the English Working Class* (London: Penguin, 1991), p. 820.

[43] Grande demonstrates how many labels have been ascribed to Cobbett's views and politics, noting that he has been 'variously described as reactionary radical, utopian reactionary, Tory radical, radical populist and proto-socialist', before labelling him a 'Burkean radical'; Grande, *William Cobbett*, p. 3.

[44] William Cobbett, *Cottage Economy* (Trowbridge: Verey & Von Kanitz, [1822] 2000), pp. 3–4.

By contrasting the mismanagement of England for 'many years past' with 'the once truly great and happy land' it was, Cobbett plays the past against itself, pitting the lengthy decline of labourers' lifestyles against a better life that is further in the past. Of course, Cobbett's readers may not have been alive to remember the happy times he describes, particularly because he creates an idealised version of times gone by. The state thus robs labourers of their current quality of life and of the reminiscences, nostalgia and national identity they would have had, had they experienced England before it was ruined. Nostalgia becomes something to reclaim, fight for and return to. As Ian Dyck notes: '*Cottage Economy* sought to rebuild the cottage as a viable economic organism at the same time as Cobbett campaigned against legislation prejudicial to labourers' independence and happiness.'[45]

Food is one of Cobbett's primary means of eliciting action within the text, as *Cottage Economy* petitioned readers to boycott manufactured foods and return to self-sufficiency. In the introduction, Cobbett continues using nostalgia, framing food with it:

> The people of England have been famed, in all ages, for their *good living*; for the *abundance of their food* and *goodness of their attire*. The old sayings about English roast beef and plum-pudding, and about English hospitality, had not their foundation in *nothing*. And, in spite of all refinements of sickly minds, it is *abundant living* amongst the people at large, which is the great test of good government, and the surest basis of national greatness and security.[46]

By highlighting the long-standing reputation of 'English roast beef and plum-pudding', which had been (in his depiction) the normal diet of English people, Cobbett again emphasises the food of the past as a way of engendering nostalgia. Cobbett is aware of the symbolic power food has and that most readers would not be able to eat beef and plum pudding because of their economic situation. Of course, this was also true in the past. Cobbett's version of the England of 'all ages' is a partial construction: he depicts a rose-tinted version of British life where everyone was well fed on an abundance of resources. Nevertheless, traditional English dishes take on symbolic resonance here which was particularly prominent in the cultural symbol of roast beef, coded with national pride, prosperity and homeliness, which is juxtaposed to the 'sickly minds' of the government who have diminished the potential for food's symbolic meaning to remain real.[47] Moreover, Cobbett accentu-

---

[45] Ian Dyck, *William Cobbett and Rural Popular Culture* (Cambridge: Cambridge University Press, 1992), p. 123.

[46] Cobbett, *Cottage Economy*, p. 4.

[47] On meat and British identity, see Nadja Durnbach, *Many Mouths: The Politics of*

ates his call to arms by interweaving descriptions of food with political statements, making them inextricable. If good food signals a good government, and Lord Liverpool's administration was failing to provide it, then lack of food signals the system's failings. Like nostalgia, then, food's meaning in *Cottage Economy* is myriad: it is a litmus test for effective governance, an indicator of national belonging and something that the labourer can reclaim via radicalism. *Cottage Economy* is a tool that readers can use to recover nostalgia, good food, heritage and the lifestyle they deserve. The emphasis on nostalgia and food in *Cottage Economy*, together and separately, creates a symbolic narrative of days gone by, but gives that symbolism potential by providing the instructions necessary to revitalise past realities once more. Food in *Cottage Economy* is radical – as Grande has noted, 'brewing your own beer, baking your own bread and avoiding taxed items such as tea become practical forms of opposition'.[48]

Within *Cottage Economy*, Cobbett's food-based resistance is framed through dichotomies of goodness and badness, just as Accum's food highlighted moral oppositions between sin and purity. In keeping with his political agenda, Cobbett's dichotomies are societal divisions: one microcosmic and one macrocosmic. On the smaller scale, food shows the difference between hard-working and slovenly people. On a political scale, Cobbett sets the needs of labourers against the state that has failed them. *Cottage Economy*'s structure repeatedly sets up these oppositions. The chapters follow a pattern whereby Cobbett outlines common practices – drinking tea over beer, for instance – and then proves how inefficient these are compared to home-grown alternatives. His means of proving this are sometimes questionable, given the scale of his calculations. Though not mathematically incorrect, Cobbett bases his economy on the time and cost that foodstuffs take to produce over a year. When discussing tea versus beer, his point of contention is the time they take to make. He notes: 'it is impossible to make a fire, boil water, make the tea, drink it, wash up the things, sweep up the fire-place, and put all to rights again in a less space of time, upon an

---

Food in Britain from the Workhouse to the Welfare State (Cambridge: Cambridge University Press, 2020), pp. 27–30; Nadja Durbach, 'Roast Beef, the New Poor Law, and the British Nation, 1834–63', *Journal of British Studies*, 52 (2013), 963–89 (p. 968); Nick Fiddes, *Meat: A Natural Symbol* (London: Routledge, 1991), p. 16; Ben Rogers. *Beef and Liberty: Roast Beef, John Bull and the English Nation* (London: Vintage, 2004), pp. 19–24; Julia Twigg, 'Vegetarianism and the Meanings of Meat', in *The Sociology of Food and Eating: Essays on the Sociological Significance of Food*, ed. Anne Murcott (Aldershot: Gower, 1983), pp. 18–30 (pp. 25–6).

[48] Grande, *William Cobbett*, p. 149.

average, than two hours'.[49] He shortens this to one hour, concluding that a woman will be making tea for 365 hours a year and her time would be better spent running the home instead. Cobbett then turns to brewing, assuring readers that 'brewing such as I have given the detail of above, may be completed in a day'.[50] Working through his process, however, and noting the timings Cobbett provides, shows him shortening and stretching time where it suits him. Cobbett's timings determine it would take roughly four days and seven hours from the start of brewing to enjoying your beer. After this there is a year's supply, but it is doubtful labourers could take four days off for brewing. Moreover, Cobbett decries the 'clattering tea-tackle' that tea requires, but in his account brewing demands a huge amount of equipment, including a thermometer, mashing tub, thirty-gallon tun-tub, cask and a forty-gallon copper.[51] These were costly and cumbersome; consequently, the majority of people would not have the time, space or money for home brewing. As with Accum, there is a disconnect between practicality and instruction. This problem is often repeated; Broomfield notes that Cobbett's meticulous instructions were 'tragically irrelevant' for most working people.[52] Quite unintentionally, then, Cobbett is similar to Accum in that he presented instructions that could only be followed by middle-class audiences with disposable income.

Despite potential flaws concerning temporality, equipment and his audience's economic capabilities, Cobbett's domestic model would have benefited labourers. He mentions food adulteration and that the rural diet he advocated bypasses these risks, while also reducing the tax burden the poor faced for shop-bought food and drink. Cobbett's instructions give the reader tools to avoid the need for the surveillance and suspicion of foodstuffs which are mass-produced: brewing beer yourself means you are not at risk 'of the poisonous drugs which that beer but too often contains'.[53] Cobbett continues to return to food-based dichotomies, however. Of tea, he says, 'I view the tea drinking as a destroyer of health, an enfeebler of the frame, an engenderer of effeminacy and laziness, a debaucher of youth and a maker of misery for old age.'[54] Of bread, he declares, 'how wasteful then, and indeed how shameful, for a labourer's wife to go to the baker's shop' and

---

[49] Cobbett, *Cottage Economy*, p. 14.
[50] Ibid. p. 44.
[51] Ibid. p. 14.
[52] Broomfield, *Food and Cooking*, p. 96.
[53] Cobbett, *Cottage Economy*, p. 16.
[54] Ibid. p. 19.

he calls the husband who allows this 'criminally careless'.[55] As with Accum, Cobbett's use of words that connote sickliness, weakness and criminality positions the reader so that their consumption of mass-produced goods amounts to a moral failing – one that jeopardises their place in a functioning society. Nostalgia for a better past is violently contrasted with the current reality, and Cobbett's rhetoric of good versus bad takes on an accusatory tone. His readers are given a scale on which to situate themselves, and if they are unable to produce their own foods then they are as much to blame for England's shortcomings as the government: wasteful, shameful, debauched and criminal. Baking bread and brewing beer are thus key to a wholesome life, but these activities are also signifiers of character for people in the 1820s.

Despite the discussions of food, instructions and inclusion of recipes, *Cottage Economy* is not a simple management guide or cookbook. Moreover, Cobbett's radical use of nostalgia does not situate his text in the past or outdate it. Rather, the fusion of radicalism, food, nostalgia and political commentary blurs genres in a way that speaks to the strug-gle to make sense of life in the 1820s. Cobbett's means of navigating the doubt and vast change of the period is to return to a model that worked in the past – but he gives it a new, radical meaning. The realities of increasing mechanisation, urbanisation and the struggle to live well rurally meant Cobbett's vision was unlikely – hence its tendency to be labelled 'nostalgic' in a passive manner. Yet food in this text is both personal and political, a matter of individual character and a matter of governmental care. Cobbett's methods of mobilising the symbolic potential of food demonstrates his persuasive, powerful style.

Reviews of *Cottage Economy* show it was divisive. The *Farmer's Magazine* notes its dichotomies, positing that 'its principal topics might be arranged under the two heads, of things forbidden and things required'.[56] This article's issue with *Cottage Economy* is the outdatedness of Cobbett's maxims: 'Cobbett's intention [is] to exclude the labouring classes, both male and female, from the knowledge of reading, writing and accounts, and to fix them down, like an Indian caste, to the condi-tion in which they were born.'[57] Cobbett indeed argues that labourers should teach children about self-sufficiency, rather than allowing them to pursue book knowledge. The article also notes the impracticalities of Cobbett's advice on brewing, concluding that Cobbett's instructions are unrealistic and overly political. The prestigious *Edinburgh Review*

---

[55] Ibid. p. 54.
[56] 'Cottage Economy', *The Farmer's Magazine*, 24.94 (1823), 222–34 (p. 222).
[57] Ibid. p. 222.

is less scathing, putting aside its usual suspicion of Cobbett's political populism because it saw his 'excellent little book' as encouraging labourers to self-improvement.[58] The expense of brewing it could justify as 'no considerable trouble, and . . . a most reasonable charge'.[59] Where it did diverge from Cobbett was on the matter of education, where it thought his ideas outdated. Taken together, these responses suggest that the reception of *Cottage Economy* was defined by the politics of food. Whatever the benefits of self-sufficiency, the nostalgic element to his writing seemed paradoxically to turn its back on the improvements it might bring; as the *Edinburgh Review* noted, Cobbett's advice 'can only be reaped, by those he addresses, through the very acquirement of reading, which he is disparaging'.[60]

By analysing the rhetorical strategies of these texts, it becomes clear that though food is their focal point, both Accum and Cobbett utilise its symbolism to evoke large-scale social and political discourses. Framed through the dichotomies of good and bad, food is transformed into an indicator of morality, which can elucidate an eater's (or buyer's) position in society. For Cobbett, this positioning is political; for Accum, moral. Moreover, food is explored via multiple genres within each text. Accum's Gothic motifs and sensationalism are mobilised through poisoned foods and his chemical experiments, giving him the literary appeal necessary to scandalise readers and create sales. Cobbett's radicalisation of food gives his readers the opportunity to reclaim the better lives they once had, or which they wish they could have now. By adopting his radical politics and sustaining themselves through food, readers could theoretically boycott the negligent state. Analysing food in this way therefore shows both *Cottage Economy* and the *Treatise* setting out to achieve numerous goals: political, commercial and personal. In terms of genre, they both elude definition as distinctive text-types, and this multiplicity highlights the authors' attempts to find new systems of living, understanding and eating in the 1820s. That both Accum and Cobbett turn to dichotomies of good and bad to convey their messages is also telling. These dichotomies implicate the reader in the new systems the authors are advocating, asking readers to position themselves and telling them how reprehensible they are if they do so wrongly. This tactic unavoidably creates doubt in the reader as to the way they should be living – particularly when the solutions Accum and Cobbett supplied were often not practical or even

---

[58] [Francis Jeffrey], 'Art V. Cottage Economy', *Edinburgh Review*, 38.75 (1823), 105–25 (p. 112).
[59] Ibid. p. 112.
[60] Ibid. p. 112.

possible. In an increasingly consumption-driven culture, people were cut off from both traditional ways of life and from certainty about the information they were being given. Even things as fundamental as food required individual analysis and selectivity to ward against fraud. Both texts thus participate in the decade's preoccupation with surveillance and truth by suggesting that emerging infrastructures and encroaching modernity did not have the individual's best interest at heart. While Accum perpetuates and profits from this uncertainty by foregrounding the deceit and danger which lurked in every meal, Cobbett fought against the state's intervention in people's lives by returning to or imagining a time where things were seemingly predictable in their simplicity. Life was changing on all levels, large and small, and a comparison of Accum and Cobbett demonstrates that even basics of life like bread, beer, tea and milk were immured in the doubtfulness of the decade.

Chapter 4

Light and Darkness: The Magic Lantern at the Dawn of Media

Phillip Roberts

In 1821 a Birmingham instrument maker called Philip Carpenter began selling a new kind of magic lantern. He named it the Improved Phantasmagoria Lantern – a little tin projector, complete with sets of hand-painted glass slides illustrating animals, religious scenes, views of the world, kings and queens, and astronomical diagrams.[1] For two pounds and eight shillings, purchasers could raise ephemeral images of life, the world and the universe. The lantern was wildly successful and helped to establish a public appetite for magic lanterns and domestic media consumption. A rapid succession of optical media instruments emerged between 1817 and 1833 – the Kaleidoscope, Phantasmagoria Lantern, Myriorama, Thaumatrope, Phenakistiscope, Stereoscope – each offering new powers to control images and play with perception, embedding long-rumoured visual deceptions in a new consumer framework.[2] Optical media technologies would soon be commonplace. Photography, lithography and rapid printing presses (later joined by phototelegraphy and moving pictures) all unrolled into a vast media network that changed how images and information could be transmitted and consumed.[3] This network began to coalesce in a series of commercial experiments in the 1820s, led by Philip Carpenter.

---

[1] See Phillip Roberts, 'Building Media History from Fragments: A Material History of Philip Carpenter's Manufacturing Practice', *Early Popular Visual Culture*, 14 (2016), 319–39; Phillip Roberts, 'Philip Carpenter and the Convergence of Science and Entertainment in the Early-Nineteenth Century Instrument Trade', *Science Museum Journal*, 7 (2017), doi: 10.15180/170707.

[2] See Helen Groth, *Moving Images: Nineteenth Century Reading and Screen Practices* (Edinburgh: Edinburgh University Press, 2013); Kate Flint, *The Victorians and the Visual Imagination* (Cambridge: Cambridge University Press, 2000).

[3] See Friedrich Kittler, *Discourse Networks 1800 / 1900*, trans. Micheal Metteert (Stanford, CA: Stanford University Press, 1990); Friedrich Kittler, *Gramophone, Film, Typewriter*, trans. Geoffrey Winthrop-Young and Michael Wutz (Stanford, CA: Stanford University Press, 1999).

The Improved Phantasmagoria Lantern was hugely influential, but its success was not some flash of commercial genius. Instrument makers had always made novelty items for curious consumers. The explosion of images and optical devices that followed Carpenter's lantern instead expressed something of the moment. New commercial possibilities were emerging as consumer appetites and manufacturing potentials shifted. Carpenter utilised a network of metalworkers and artisans that were rapidly increasing their production outputs as the economy began to recover from the post-war depression of the 1810s.[4] Mass production of scientific instruments was also becoming viable for the first time.[5] Novelty consumption was growing among the middle classes, providing new markets for instruments, printed paper toys and other trifles. Public interest in natural philosophy was on the rise, with famous scientific writers advocating for rational learning as a means to understand a fundamentally knowable world.[6] New printing technologies and innovations led to a flood of natural scientific, astronomical and religious-historical texts alongside general compendia and cyclopedia. Carpenter offered a machine that could project such knowledge into the air of a drawing room. It offered a public display of natural and scientific classification that could be applied to education as easily as to play.

But the magic lantern was old. Carpenter's machine was only the latest in a gallery of magic lanterns that stretched back to the seventeenth century. Lanterns were once cutting-edge optical instruments. They were staples in cabinets of curiosity; once commanding the attention of the great philosophers, they had come to be regarded with contempt by respectable opinion.[7] The lantern could not be used to investigate natural phenomena, nor generate new experimental knowledge, as more serious instruments could. What's more, it was associated with charlatans, magicians and (worse) poor people. The lantern had been highly diverse in its applications. In the seventeenth century it was a side-line sold by scientific instrument makers. In the eighteenth century it became a tool for poor travelling entertainers, and later a machine to

---

[4] François Crouzet, *The Victorian Economy*, trans. Anthony Forster (London: Methuen, 1982), pp. 24–69; Eric Hopkins, *Birmingham: The First Manufacturing Town in the World, 1760–1840* (London: Weidenfeld & Nicolson, 1989), pp. 25–39.

[5] Roberts, 'Philip Carpenter and the Convergence of Science and Entertainment'; A. D. Morrison-Low, *Making Scientific Instruments in the Industrial Revolution* (Farnham: Ashgate, 2007).

[6] Bernard Lightman, '"The Voices of Nature": Popularizing Victorian Science', in *Victorian Science in Context*, ed. Bernard Lightman (Chicago: University of Chicago Press, 1997), pp. 187–211; Bernard Lightman, *Victorian Popularizers of Science: Designing Nature for New Audiences* (Chicago: University of Chicago Press, 2007).

[7] Deac Rossell, *Laterna Magica* (Stuttgart: Füsslin Verlag, 2008), vol. I, pp. 71–3.

generate ghostly thrills. It lived alongside satirical prints and broadside ballads in the popular culture of common people, mocking the powerful and acting as a performative release for the energy and anger of the poor. But when Carpenter floated the little machine onto the emerging currents of consumer capital, he changed everything. The Improved Phantasmagoria Lantern became the latest must-have consumer novelty and found its way into middle-class homes across the country. The old travelling lanternists found it increasingly difficult to sell lantern shows to audiences that could now easily stage domestic performances of their own.

The lantern of the 1820s was both an emblem of a new world and a relic of the past. It conjured visions of ghosts, necromancers and scientists. It signified at once arcane and new knowledge, providing a space where the discourses and concepts of industrial and political transformation were contested. The poor saw very different lantern shows to the rich. The old travelling lanternists projected stories of satirical fury and grotesque wonder, while Carpenter's lantern, and the emerging optical entertainments of the 1820s, promoted curiosity about the principles and structures of the world. The magic lantern became the stage for a wider struggle between competing visions of life, as structural change and new economic opportunities opened amid deep unrest.

The Improved Phantasmagoria Lantern

Extinguish the lights. Stretch a sheet over the doorway and crouch behind it. Ball yourself up in the darkness. Hold your breath tightly and grasp this little tin box against your chest. This box is magical. Light a lamp inside and it can raise monsters. A great, razor-backed porcupine creeps out of the dark, eyes burning savage red. Watch it grow to five feet and more. Let it tower over the audience until, with a flick of the wrist, it drifts out of focus and shrinks away and dies.

The Improved Phantasmagoria Lantern arrived in 1821: a small lacquered-black tin lantern with a distinctive angled chimney and compound-lens arrangement of higher quality and complexity than the then typical single-lens bullseye lanterns. There were multiple sizes and types available.[8] One version came with a solar microscope attachment that could show living natural specimens. Another could be strapped to the

---

[8] Philip Carpenter, *A Companion to the Microcosm: Being a Concise Account of the Insects, Animalcules, Corals, Corralines, and Other Objects, Seen in the Microcosm of that Interesting Exhibition* (London: W. Glindon, 1827), p. 26.

lanternist with a belt to create elegant swooping effects across walls and ceilings. Initially, all of Carpenter's lanterns came with the same set of zoology slides, but by 1822 a whole catalogue of subjects was available – portraits of kings and queens, astronomical diagrams, botanical specimens, views of the world and religious scenes. Each set could be purchased with companion booklets that provided accompanying words and instructions.[9]

Carpenter had his lanterns cast, rolled, folded and riveted by the local Birmingham metalworkers. He fitted them with lenses ground by the garret glass grinders and boxed them up with an Argand lamp, slides and explanatory companion. The slides were printed using a new technique borrowed from the Black Country enamellers, then fired and painted. Every set carried the same sequence of animals illustrated after zoological prints by John Buego and Thomas Bewick.[10] Carpenter's sales strategy appealed to the notion of 'rational amusements', which sought to infuse novelty consumption with more worthy interests in optics and natural philosophy. Advertisements for the new lanterns appealed to their playfulness, beauty and technical ingenuity: 'This apparatus is not only productive of much amusement to the well-informed mind, but may provide a powerful auxiliary in the business of education, in teaching the elements of several branches of useful knowledge. The Lanterns and Sliders are complete in boxes, accompanied by a descriptive pamphlet.'[11] Carpenter's innovations made the magic lantern an everyday commercial instrument, encouraged further retailers and manufacturers to take it up, and helped establish the conditions for the emergence of a consumer trade in optical media technologies.[12]

The ability to play with vision, light and perception became commonplace, as techniques once shrouded in mystery, practised only by necromancers, polymaths and professional entertainers, were transformed into commercial opportunities. The Phantasmagoria Lantern brought immaterial visions of the distant world into the domestic sphere and was one of several contemporaneous instruments to offer the ability to control perception, optics and visuality. It contributed to a shift in the conceptual status of images in the 1820s and 1830s. The new optical machines and techniques, Jonathan Crary argues, led to a paradigm

---

[9] Philip Carpenter, *Elements of Zoology; Being a Concise Account of the Animal Kingdom, According to the System of Linnaeus* (London: Rowland Hunter, 1823).

[10] Phillip Roberts, 'The Emergence of the Magic Lantern Trade in Nineteenth-Century England' (unpublished doctoral thesis, University of York, 2018), p. 91.

[11] John Bywater, 'Carpenter's New Phantasmagoria Lantern, and Copperplate Sliders' [advertisement], *The Liverpool Mercury*, 12 April 1822, p. 327.

[12] Roberts, 'The Emergence of the Magic Lantern Trade', pp. 54–66, 191–222.

shift in perceptual knowledge, as the conditions of geometrically natural optics were undermined by new technical means of subverting vision.[13] Kaleidoscopes refracted whole objects into abstraction. Magic lanterns separated images from the materiality of form – life-size animals were now weightless and permeable as ghosts. The very conditions of natural vision were being captured and undermined by technology. The truthfulness of images was often undermined by the strange properties of visual technologies, which uncoupled appearance from physical matter.

Photographic experiments from 1825 through to 1839 would eventually come to invest images with a truth function derived from the indexicality of automatic reproduction, but the veracity of early photographic images was not guaranteed by chemical reproduction. The discursive formulation that enveloped photographic practice underpinned its claims to truth. Given that these early photographic practices often failed to meet expectations of legibility, early photographs were themselves often altered to better situate them within optical conventions. Pages of written explication were sometimes needed to justify how these muddy, dark and reflective chemical engravings constituted a true likeness.[14] The same was true of lantern images.[15] Carpenter underpinned his image's educational value with appeals to encyclopaedic knowledge.[16] His copperplate printing techniques further guaranteed the images accuracy and fundamental veracity by attaching them to an automatic reproduction method free from the errors of sloppy artists – 'the outlines can be given with a correctness which it is hardly possible to give with a pencil'.[17]

Carpenter used the copperplate printing process to standardise his slide output to a consistent series of recognisable images. The earliest surviving companion was called *Elements of Zoology* and provided zoological information and amusing stories to accompany the natural

[13] Jonathan Crary, *Techniques of the Observer: On Vision and Modernity in the Nineteenth Century* (Cambridge, MA: MIT Press, 1990).

[14] Susan S. Williams, 'The Inconstant Daguerreotype: The Narrative of Early Photography', *Narrative*, 4 (1996), 161–74.

[15] Or, indeed, of other visual materials – see Chapter 1 in this volume.

[16] Carpenter, *Elements of Zoology*, p. 16; Philip Carpenter, *A Compendium of Astronomy: Being a Concise Description of the Most Interesting Phenomena of the Heavens* (Bristol: Bagnal & Wright, n.d.), pp. 6–7; Carpenter & Westley, *A Compendium of Botany: Being a Concise Description of the Structure of Plants* (London: Carpenter & Westley, 1838), p. 6; Carpenter & Westley, *A Companion to the Improved Phantasmagoria Lantern* (London: Carpenter & Westley, 1850), p. 16.

[17] Philip Carpenter, 'A Short Account of the Copper-Plate Sliders, and a Description of an Improved Phantasmagoria Lantern' [1823], in *Light and Movement: Incunabula of the Motion Picture, 1420–1896*, ed. Donata Pesenti Campagnoni et al. (Gemona: Giornate del Cinema Muto, 1995), p. 126.

history slides (Figure 2). Both text and images reproduced contemporary concepts of collecting in a new commercial context, structuring the varied signatures of life into linear classifications for lantern performance. Carpenter's lantern pulled natural life into a sharp, consumable form in the space of its user's drawing room. Like the old cabinets of curiosity, it wrapped the signatures of an entire world in a grand parcel of knowledge. As Barbara Stafford argues, optical instruments were knowledge-generating machines in the tradition of cabinets and museums – compressing the world into a form that could be grasped in its entirety.[18] Carpenter exploited contemporary desires for classification to find a commercial application for the lantern's worldmaking power. He organised educational and imaginative content into standardised slide sets and interpretive companions. The lantern provided a different mode of information retrieval than a cabinet, or a textbook, but all drew on the same impulse towards classification and collecting. The lantern could be a system that contained the vastness of the natural world in a series of educational tableaux – equally adept at presenting classified sequences of animals, planets, plants or dead monarchs.

The format of *Elements of Zoology* is typical of popular zoology texts from this era. Intended for children and lay readerships, such books set species of animal into genera and orders and provided descriptions alongside woodblock, copperplate or lithographic illustrations.[19] Popular scientific writing provided (often disputed) conceptual systems to momentarily stabilise rapidly increasing circuits of information. Whenever new and more confusing animals emerged, naturalists and engravers rushed to locate them within the existing classification systems – setting the diverse signs of natural life into a neat structural framework.[20] The most popular zoological texts were *A General History of Quadrupeds* with illustrations by Thomas Bewick and George Shaw's *General Zoology*.[21] The Bewick book is oriented around numerous woodblock illustrations, with simple descriptive passages providing background information for the reader. The Shaw text is more detailed, setting out information on individual animals and building these into a classification system. Carpenter's companion similarly provides a framework to organise the

---

[18] Barbara Maria Stafford and Frances Terpak, *Devices of Wonder: From the World in a Box to Images on a Screen* (Los Angeles: Getty Research Institute, 2001), pp. 6–7.
[19] Harriet Ritvo, *The Platypus and the Mermaid, and Other Figments of the Classifying Imaginary* (Cambridge, MA: Harvard University Press, 1997).
[20] Ibid. pp. 1–50.
[21] Ralph Beilby and Thomas Bewick, *A General History of Quadrupeds* (Newcastle upon Tyne: S. Hodgson, 1790); George Shaw, *General Zoology, or Systematic Natural History*, 16 vols (London: G. Kearsley, 1800–26).

images into different kingdoms, orders and genera and then describes each individual animal within this wider structure. This makes sense, given the linearity of lantern performance. The lanternist had to move from one image to the next, providing explanation for each picture in a manner similar to the encyclopaedic zoology texts, but the lantern could supplement discursive content with playful tricks or optical distortions.

Various performative techniques were suggested by the companion booklets.[22] Carpenter's instructions for use encouraged lanternists to use a semi-transparent damp sheet for back projection, a technique that could make images seem to hang in the air (as in the old Phantasmagoria performances). Optical illusions could cause the animals to walk mysteriously out of the darkness, or move in great circular arcs about the room, or shiver. Carpenter framed the Phantasmagoria Lantern in a context of practical education to capitalise on broader developments in education, but he retained some of the lantern's long-standing associations with wonder and sensationalism. Natural history writing emphasised the pleasurable diversity of fauna or the transgressive appeal of a platypus. The opportunity to generate images to communicate zoological knowledge, using a machine with optical-scientific credibility of its own, had clear commercial potential.

Elements of Zoology exemplifies this tightrope walk between seriousness and playfulness. Its structure follows the standard Linnaean classifications but also adds often outlandish explanations of individual animals. This was common among the more dubious zoology textbooks. Louisa Lovechild's *Natural History* claimed that crocodiles were bulletproof and that eagles could carry away large animals and children.[23] The description of the ferret in the Bewick book notes its natural ferocity: 'such is it appetite for blood, that is has been known to attack and kill children in the cradle'.[24] By *Elements of Zoology* this has idea has escalated further: 'so great is its thirst for blood, that is has been known to grasp at the throats of infants in the cradle, and suck them till it has been completely gorged'.[25] Most of its descriptive content is more concerned with sensationalism than accuracy – crocodiles and condors are now both believed to be bullet proof.[26] The text took known characteristics of each animal (such as speed, strength or ferociousness) and amplified them to extreme degrees. The tortoise is claimed to be 'so tena-

---

[22] Carpenter, 'A Description of an Improved Phantasmagoria Lantern', pp. 129–31.

[23] Louisa Lovechild, *Natural History: Or, Zoological Sketches for the Amusement and Instruction of All Good Little Folk* (London: Orlando Hodgson, 1833), pp. 2, 8.

[24] Beilby and Bewick, *A General History of Quadrupeds*, p. 250.

[25] Carpenter, *Elements of Zoology*, p. 35.

[26] Ibid. pp. 76–7, 97.

cious of life, that one lived six months after its brain was taken out'.[27] Carpenter's commentary is a negotiation between existing zoological discourse and the lantern's more traditional function as a machine for sensational projections. Exciting ideas are lifted from other texts and further amplified for a new audience.

Rational Amusements

Carpenter's rhetorical focus on the lantern's educational value was a clever concession to the wider market for educational texts and to the domestic consumption of scientific instruments and optical toys. It also helped negotiate the magic lantern's relationship with older modes of performance now regarded as disreputable by the emergent values of the nineteenth-century middle classes. The lantern was once considered a machine for charlatans to fool the unwary and stupid. In an 1822 translation of Benvenuto Cellini's autobiography, Thomas Roscoe conjectured that a necromancer had used a concealed magic lantern to raise up armies of demons before the stunned sculptor.[28] Similar claims were made of the same episode by Samuel Hibbert and William Godwin in their studies of magical phenomena.[29] Godwin claimed 'the demons . . . were merely figures, produced by the magic lantern'.[30] Backward projection of modern optical techniques into history was common through the 1820s and 1830s. David Brewster suggested that all of the miracles and unexplained phenomena of the past may have been created by means of a cabinet of optical techniques and instruments existing as secretive, esoteric knowledge long before they were accepted by modern scientists. Citing the Cellini episode, he argued: 'Legions of devils were not produced by any influence upon the imaginations of the spectators, but were actual optical phantasms, or the images of pictures or objects produced by one or more concave mirrors or lenses.'[31] These critics set

---

[27] Ibid. p. 97.
[28] Benvenuto Cellini, *Memoirs of Benvenuto Cellini: A Florentine Artist*, trans. Thomas Roscoe, 2 vols (London: Henry Colburn & Co., 1822), vol. I, p. 233.
[29] Samuel Hibbert, *Sketches of the Philosophy of Apparitions: Or, An Attempt to Trace Such Illusions to Their Physical Causes* (Edinburgh: Oliver & Boyd, 1824), pp. 401, 456; William Godwin, *Lives of the Necromancers: Or, An Account of the Most Eminent Persons in Successive Ages, Who Have Claimed for Themselves, or to Whom Has Been Imputed by Others, the Exercise of Magical Powers* (London: Frederick J. Mason, 1834).
[30] Godwin, *Lives of the Necromancers*, pp. 371–2.
[31] David Brewster, *Letters on Natural Magic, Addressed to Sir Walter Scott* (London: John Murray, 1832), p. 73.

the provenance of the lantern in an obscure history of alchemy – one element in a larger field of arcane knowledge. Its users were, in Godwin's words, 'quacks, who in cool blood undertook to overreach mankind' by exhibiting their knowledge of optical principles as occult magic.[32] These texts reveal some of the associations that the magic lantern still held in the 1820s. Carpenter's marketing attempted to reverse them by framing his lantern as 'not only a most amusing and rational amusement, but a powerful auxiliary in the work of education'.[33] He offered a comparison with 'the common magic lantern' in his booklet on the Phantasmagoria Lantern:

> The magic lantern, which was formerly used merely to amuse children, by the exhibition of miserable caricatures and grotesque figures, has of late years assumed a different character by being adapted to the representation of subjects of natural history, astronomical diagrams, the costume of different countries, &c. &c.[34]

His argument rests on the clarity and accuracy of modern projected images, provided by a more advanced lens arrangement compared to previous lanterns. The copperplate printing process was also framed as more modern than older hand-painted slides. Reproducible projected images were a new phenomenon. Even though the line-printed illustrations still needed to be painted by colourists, the process lent the images the veracity of automatic reproduction.

The deeper implications of such rhetorical framing are the divestment of the older disreputable associations of the medium. Carpenter wanted to embed the lantern in contemporary discourses on rational knowledge. He offered accurate diagrams underpinned by modern optical and natural science, where the old lanternists offered only 'miserable caricatures'. Comparisons between modern and arcane magic lanterns became commonplace as the medium moved towards ubiquity. Later, J. S. Coyne dismissed earlier lantern culture as 'the degenerate predecessor ... to the modern magic lantern'.[35] There is a tension here between different discursive framings of the magic lantern that speaks to the period's relationship with knowledge and the struggle to embed Enlightenment rationalism into unfolding commercial structures. The magic lantern could be associated with both light – knowledge, learning, its institutions and metropoles – and darkness – charlatanism, uncer-

---

[32] Godwin, *Lives of the Necromancers*, p. 364.
[33] Carpenter, 'A Description of an Improved Phantasmagoria Lantern', p. 127.
[34] Ibid. p. 125.
[35] J. S. Coyne, 'Scenes in a Magic Lantern', *Illustrated London News*, 25 December 1858, p. 609.

tainty, low culture, the slums and the wide, dark country. This was not a simple opposition; contemporary discourses on rational science remained invested with ideas derived from older traditions of natural philosophy, while historical conceptions of magic and esotericism were hugely popular. Brewster's *Letters on Natural Magic* is perhaps the clearest expression of this tension, aligning the wonders and mysteries of the ancient world with modern optical knowledge. The work delights in the potential for satisfying optical deceits – simultaneously posting sublime ingenuity among the old magicians and stupidity among their unwitting victims. It is a textbook of optical principles, but also a work of rich fantasy, fascinated by the 'grand phantasmagoria' of unreal visions, spectres and illusions. Optical wonder remained a driving impulse among rational educational discourse.[36]

In 1807, thirteen gas-fired lamps were set along Pall Mall in London, running from St James's Square to Cockspur Street. They provided an early vision of a modern world, where mechanical science could banish a darkness that had seemed pervasive. Gaslight appeared with the splendour of a new age. Elsewhere, darkness remained thick. Whale oil lit the homes of the rich, but away from the metropolis, in the slums and backroads and new industrial towns, the night still rolled in with certainty. Street lighting had long been the responsibility of individual property owners and had only recently become a matter for urban gas companies. It is in this context that we should consider the magic lantern and its power. A dim, flickering figure on a sheet can be a miracle when the night outside is pitch dark. Optical wonders could be used to terrify, or coerce, or to raise extraordinary views of the life of the wide earth. The old magic lantern was associated with a darkness akin to ignorance that could now be dismantled and supplanted by a new rational lantern – later users sometimes preferred the title 'optical lantern'.

Carpenter was a practising Unitarian, one of Birmingham's successful dissenting businesspeople and brother of the famous minister Lant Carpenter, whose writings act as companion to the religious slide sets.[37] The rational Christianity of Unitarianism aimed to integrate modern scientific learning into religious belief. Scientific knowledge was the light of God and the dissemination of knowledge a kind of sacred mission.[38]

---

[36] Verity Hunt, 'Raising a Modern Ghost: The Magic Lantern and the Persistence of Wonder in the Victorian Education of the Senses', *Romanticism and Victorianism on the Net*, 52 (2008), doi: 10.7202/019806ar.

[37] Phillip Roberts, 'The Early Life of Philip Carpenter', *The Magic Lantern*, 6 (2016), 10–13.

[38] Stuart Andrews, *Unitarian Radicalism: Political Rhetoric, 1770–1814* (Basingstoke: Palgrave Macmillan, 2003).

In Birmingham, as in many of the new expanding industrial towns, Unitarians built artisans' libraries and mechanics' institutes, and used their trades and skills to increase the sum of wisdom around them. Carpenter's magic lantern was framed as a direct challenge to the older associations of the magic lantern as a disreputable instrument, all the while cleverly playing off the continued pleasures offered by a machine of such lowly status. The Phantasmagoria Lantern could be a weapon for illuminating the darkness.

The Travelling Magic Lantern

Today, we know far more of what happened to the lantern and optical media trades after Carpenter than we do of the media cultures preceding him. We know of itinerant lanternists in the eighteenth century and early use of the lantern among natural philosophers, but the evidence of this earlier period is dwarfed by the many surviving lanterns, slides, books and news reports from the later nineteenth-century trade.[39] Such evidential weighting skews our knowledge of the medium towards nineteenth-century entrepreneurs and knowledge institutions. Carpenter himself made a significant impression on the documentary record and this is one reason why his intervention is so visible.[40] Later, lantern shows at major institutions like the Royal Polytechnic and Egyptian Hall, and by famous showmen like Albert Smith and Charles Goodwin Norton, were recorded in detail. Lower-class lantern performers were less likely to leave a lasting impression. Our knowledge of the earlier itinerant lantern culture is dominated by reports made by more privileged observers, who were more likely to write down what they saw than the travellers themselves. The result is a literary record full of untrustworthy rogues and sentimental caricatures.[41]

The itinerant lanternists were variously known as Savoyards, Galantee Men and Raree Men. They were not all from Savoy, nor were they all men.[42] They came from the poor districts of Savoy, Piedmont, Auvergne and elsewhere; as Rossell says, anywhere 'where a hard life of precarious existence on the road offered hope beyond the certainty of endless

---

[39] Rossell, *Laterna Magica*, vol. I, pp. 63–140.
[40] See Roberts, 'Building Media History from Fragments'.
[41] Rossell, *Laterna Magica*, vol. I, pp. 102–22.
[42] Numerous illustrations and paintings after a study by Edmé Bouchardon show a woman with a barrel organ in her hands and a magic lantern on her back; Rossell, *Laterna Magica*, vol. I, p. 115; David Robinson, *The Lantern Image: Iconography of the Magic Lantern, 1420–1880* (London: Magic Lantern Society, 1993), p. 18.

impoverishment'.[43] They told stories, recounted major events, conjured monsters, spat satires and poked fun at the monied and the powerful. A report in the *Penny Magazine* recalled: 'The designs on their slips of glass were for the most part exceedingly grotesque; and their own personal appearance was scarcely less so.'[44]

A set of strange allegorical pamphlets survive in the National Library of Scotland, called *Thaumaturgus; Or, the Wonders of the Magic Lantern*, printed in Glasgow in 1816.[45] These outline the corruption and anxiety of the post-war years and call for reform and equal representation in parliament. Many such pamphlets were published in the early part of the century, but what is interesting about these is that a magic lanternist was chosen to articulate the author's reformist agenda. The main narrative voice is rather dull-witted and not very politically minded, but is converted to the reformist cause by a travelling entertainer, who uses their little projector to reveal the true state of the nation and the unease of its people.

The lanternist throws a landscape upon the screen, and then an English farmer, once 'wallowing in luxury' but now facing poverty from price rises.[46] He shows disbanded soldiers, and mechanics and their families – 'clusters of poor ragged men, women, and children, standing shivering in the cold'.[47] He shows a group of wealthy gentlemen, 'the men who encouraged the infatuated Pitt to enter into the late war, and who stood behind him clapping him on the back, and hallooing him upon the unfortunate French nation as butchers do a dog at a bull-baiting'.[48] These men chatter and debate over dinner. They petition against the income tax. 'There was not a word said about the war taxes, which grind the poor and middling classes. No, their whole energy was directed against the income tax, because by it they themselves were most affected.'[49] The lanternist diagnoses a corrupt society, where the upper classes care only for the welfare of their own pockets. The performance is still described as an 'amusement', but the lanternist summons a discontented nation and profound underlying social anxieties. This lantern compresses the signatures of the world in a different way than

---

[43] Rossell, *Laterna Magica*, vol. I, p. 102.

[44] 'Magic Lantern at Rome', *The Penny Magazine of the Society for the Diffusion of Useful Knowledge*, 14 (15 March 1845), 101–2 (p. 101).

[45] *Thaumaturgus; Or, the Wonders of the Magic Lantern; Exhibiting at One View the Distresses of the Country, and Some of the Consequences of the Late Just and Necessary War*, 3 vols (Glasgow: A. Napier, 1816).

[46] *Thaumaturgus*, vol. I, p. 6.

[47] Ibid. vol. I, p. 7.

[48] Ibid. vol. I, p. 11.

[49] Ibid. vol. I, p. 12.

the one imagined by Barbara Stafford. The author of *Thaumaturgus* brings together a variety of vignettes. The result is a kind of early political montage that communicates its ideas through the juxtaposition of different images.

Giving a travelling lanternist this role is significant for two reasons. First, it frames the lanternist as a reliable witness to the world around them. Magic lantern performances once introduced people to the visions and stories of the far earth, and so were a perfect vehicle to reveal the conditions of the working people. This is a different mode of knowledge to that generated by the Improved Phantasmagoria Lantern. The lantern of *Thaumaturgus* illuminated social hardships hidden beneath the metanarrative of rising liberal capitalism. A set of slides in the National Science and Media Museum show that such use of the magic lantern was not an invention of the pamphlet's writer. These show, with astonishing detail and subtlety, destitute figures, folk devils and soldiers marching on the Jacobites. Prints from the same era tend towards caricature but some of these slides present poverty in stark realism (Figure 3). Here are clusters of poor men shivering in the cold; one man warms his hands on a smoking pot; a women gazes forlornly at a single coin in her hand. Such images echo the lanternist of *Thaumaturgus*: 'Hunger will break through stone walls.'[50] Travelling lanternists were rural mountain-dwellers from southern Europe. They were poor, but were not themselves of the English labouring classes. This gave them a power to challenge authority from a place outside of national class structures. *Thaumaturgus* could use the magic lantern as a symbol for radical voices because it was a world-making machine. As professional travellers, itinerant lanternists could speak about a society without being fully part of it. Lanternists had the authority of observers and, being poor themselves, a natural kinship with the oppressed.

Second, the pamphlet suggests the role of performance in the circulation of radical discourse. Projected pictures, song, commentary and storytelling were powerful weapons for reimagining political and social realities. A magic lanternist could remake the world anew. An old itinerant's street cry once rang: *Chi vuol veder il Mondo Nuovo* – Who will see the New World?[51] Travelling lanternists could use fantasy and allegory to overturn power relationships and right wrongs that could not be challenged in everyday life. They made the powerful ridiculous and demanded that divine punishment intercede to restore natural

[50] Ibid. vol. I, pp. 7–8.
[51] 'Magic Lantern at Rome', p. 101.

Figure 2 Subjects in Natural History (Mammalia) – Porcupine, Brazilian Porcupine, Variegated and Spotted Cavies and Beaver; magic lantern slide by Frederick Cox, after Philip Carpenter, 1845–60. Phillip Roberts's collection.

Figure 3 Destitute figures; magic lantern slide by an unknown maker, 1790–1820. National Science and Media Museum collection.

justice. Many stories featured the devil as a restorer of everyday rights, who punished transgressors in ironic and delightful ways (Figure 4).[52] This made their stories heroic, cathartic and vulgar, depending on the spectator. Every image required interpretation and so could be varied with their audiences. Radical commentary could be buried in an old story or song. Obscenity would evaporate when the lantern's light was extinguished. Travelling lanternists could articulate the brewing radicalism of the later 1810s. People wanted political reform and the magic lantern was a machine that projected the world back onto itself in its fiercely contested variety.[53] Lanternists contributed to a wider network of political stories, songs, speeches, sermons and discussions rooted in personal and communal networks. Radical discourse continued through multitudinous everyday and unrecorded acts, with lantern performance as one space in which political experience and aspirations were drawn together and examined. Numerous reports, prints and satires confirm that the lantern was commonly used as a machine that generated political thought.[54]

The lantern was one of several key technologies of communication that helped structure the conditions of knowledge in the post-war era. Along with broadsides and popular song, it circulated in the lowest strata of society and offered libidinal pleasures, restorative justice and satirical ideas.[55] Lanternists could visualise new worlds that overturned hierarchies, guaranteed representation and enacted parliamentary reform; or that unleashed cathartic joy at the punishment of a greedy baker – 'bak'd like a hot-roll, burnt up like a pye crust' in hell's fire.[56] Later, following Carpenter's rearticulation of the lantern, the medium could support a new world of rational education, free-market liberalism and global empire. This battle would rage across all media for a century.

Theorists like Jonathan Crary have assumed that the effects of technology are homogeneous, theorising transformations in perception and subjectivity as soon as new apparatuses appear. In truth, the unrolling of

---

[52] Roberts, 'The Emergence of the Magic Lantern Trade', pp. 249–57.

[53] Rossell, *Laterna Magica*, p. 124; Roger Gonin, *Les Savoyards montreurs de lanterne magique* (Lyons: Cahiers de Vieux Conflans, 2016), pp. 64–5; Ian Haywood, '"The dark sketches of a revolution": Gillray, the *Anti-Jacobin Review*, and the Aesthetics of Conspiracy in the 1790s', *European Romantic Review*, 22 (2011), 431–51.

[54] Gonin, *Les Savoyards montreurs*, pp. 64–5; Anette Duller, 'The Magic Lantern as Political Instrument', in *Dutch Perspectives: 350 Years of Visual Entertainment*, ed. Willem Albert Wagenaar et al. (London: Magic Lantern Society, 2014), pp. 104–23.

[55] See Oskar Cox Jensen, *Napoleon and British Song, 1797–1822* (Basingstoke: Palgrave Macmillan, 2015).

[56] 'A New and Curious Dialogue Between the Devil and a Baker' [broadside ballad] (London: John Evans, 1796).

Figure 4 Pull Devil Pull Baker; magic lantern slide by Robert Bancks, 1795–1831. National Science and Media Museum collection.

new technological systems is much more uneven. Technologies appear, intersect with external paradigms and often disappear. They are not used by everyone; and even among their user base, they are not used in the same ways. The 1820s were significant as many older and newer discursive technologies intersected to negotiate the decade's key concepts, but there was not a dominant mode of media culture. Print circulation increased, magic lanterns shifted in form and a cycle of perceptual toys began to alter expectations of media technologies. All the while, older print and performance cultures persisted.

Friedrich Kittler argues that the magic lantern, in its very earliest days, was a weapon in an image war between reformation and counter-reformation.[57] It was a transmitting apparatus for circulating different articulations of truth. The lantern tunnelled into the unfolding political debates of each era. It was a technology for image communication and worldmaking. The next hundred years were not only about the networks becoming mechanised by new technologies, as Kittler argues. They were not only about the multiplication of new manufacturing and retail networks, and the technological systems generated by these networks. They were about each social, discursive, technical and political network grappling with all of the others. Media was already diverse, with optical technologies and visual novelties stretching back to the camera obscura and various anamorphic prints and illusions put out by commercial printers. The history of media does not follow a sequential progression from one age to the next. It was a continual negotiation between newly emerging potentials and long-existing cultures.

The Emergence and Decline of the Magic Lantern Trade

'Times are changed, and all for the worser.'[58] Sometime in the 1840s, Henry Mayhew interviewed a street showman and former magic lanternist. This old lanternist, 'a short thick-set man, with small, puckered-up eyes, and dressed in an old brown velveteen shooting-jacket', described his days as a travelling entertainer. He reflected on how the lantern business had changed, complaining that the old routines did not attract crowds as they once did:

---

[57] Friedrich Kittler, *Optical Media: Berlin Lectures 1999*, trans. Anthony Enns (Cambridge: Polity, 2010), pp. 70–89.

[58] Henry Mayhew, *London Labour and the London Poor: A Cyclopædia of the Condition and Earnings of Those that Will Work, Those That Cannot Work, and Those That Will Not Work*, 3 vols (London: Griffin, Bohn and Company, 1851), vol. III, p. 73.

A month before Christmas ... we went with a galantee show of a magic lantern. We showed it on a white sheet, or on the ceiling, big or little, in the houses of the gentlefolk, and the schools where they was breaking up. It was shown by way of a treat to the scholars. There was Harlequin, and Billy Button, and such-like. We had ten and sixpence and fifteen shillings for each performance, and did very well indeed. I have that galantee show now, but it brings very little.

Green's dead, and all in the line's dead, but me. The galantee show don't answer, because magic lanterns are so cheap in the shops. When we started, magic lanterns wasn't so common; but we can't keep hold of a good thing in these times.[59]

The public perception of the lantern changed over the decades. The instrument was welcomed into respectable society as a result of Carpenter's reinterpretation. The instrument's general visibility increased. More manufacturers followed suit and it became a device for domestic consumption. Professional lanternists became more prominent and would soon be regarded as educators and high-class showpeople.

Carpenter moved his business to Regent Street in Westminster around 1826, accruing the respectability of a London professional. After his death in 1833, his sister Mary Carpenter took control and formed Carpenter & Westley with her foreman William Westley. The business remained optical instrument makers, putting out huge quantities of spectacles and other commercial instruments, alongside various entertainment media devices. Their lantern business was spectacular. They supplemented their Phantasmagoria Lanterns with mechanical dissolving systems and improved lighting technology. They were among the most aggressive exploiters of the trend for Dissolving Views in the 1840s and 1850s, producing complex and dazzling transformation effects. The magic lantern was absorbed into the expanding theatrical and lecturing circuits.[60] By 1865 Carpenter & Westley were giving lantern shows at Windsor Palace. New lantern retailers sprung from the earth. By 1860 Newton & Co., Edward Wrench, John Benjamin Dancer, Lejeune & Perken, Benetfink & Co. and Barnard & Son, among many others, were doing a roaring trade in lanterns, slides and other optical media instruments.

The Galantee Men had tended to rely on the striking spectacle of lantern projection. In a world where everyone had lanterns at home, this was no longer so easy. The domestic Phantasmagoria Lantern presented a significant challenge to the survival of the poor lantern pedlars. This

[59] Mayhew, *London Labour and the London Poor*, vol. III, pp. 73–4.
[60] Richard D. Altick, *The Shows of London* (Cambridge, MA: Belknap Press, 1978), pp. 211–20.

is confirmed by the *Penny Magazine*, which invokes the multiplication of domestic lanterns as an explanation for the disappearance of the itinerants: 'Many of our young people have now better magic lanterns of their own within doors; and this fact may have driven away the old exhibitors by making their trade unprofitable.'[61] There were also more profound economic shifts making the business of peddling untenable. War, economic blockade and depression had had a severe impact on the peddling circuits over the first few decades of the century. New modes of sedentary retail were emerging and manufacturing centres were shifting away from the southern German states – key commercial centres that put legions of metalworkers at the heart of the trans-European itinerant circuits – and towards the new industrial towns of Birmingham, Sheffield and Manchester.[62]

There was no direct equivalence between the Galantee performances and their domestic counterparts, but the moment generated an ongoing tension between a reputable articulation of the lantern and its older life as the tool of itinerants and magicians. A new culture of slick professional lantern performance was emerging that was built on a shift towards respectability and popular middle-class consumption.[63] The consumer revolution triggered by the Phantasmagoria Lantern slowly drowned the struggling Savoyards and by late century they had become a cultural bygone. Frédéric Dillaye mourned: 'The toy sellers, by selling magic lanterns cheaply, have destroyed this industry of the streets.'[64] We find the itinerants scattered about the pages of later journals, chapbooks and prints. The visions that these lanternists raised were now the ghosts of an imagined past – of mythic street entertainers and shared pleasures. Recollections abound. *The Magazine of Science* remembers:

> The galanty show seems as it were engrafted in our earliest recollections of Christmas frolics. The grotesque figures—the terrific phantoms—and the magnificent processions displayed 'all on a white sheet', took too early and too vivid a hold on our fancies to be easily forgotten.[65]

---

[61] 'Magic Lantern at Rome', p. 101.

[62] David Alexander, *Retailing in England During the Industrial Revolution* (London: Athlone Press, 1970), pp. 61, 89–95; Laurence Fontaine, *History of Pedlars in Europe*, trans. Vicki Whittacre (Durham, NC: Duke University Press, 1996), pp. 140–63.

[63] Joe Kember, *Marketing Modernity: Victorian Popular Shows and Early Cinema* (Exeter: University of Exeter Press, 2009), pp. 44–83.

[64] Frédéric Dillaye, *Les Jeux de la Jeunesse: Leur origine, Leur Histoire et L'indication Des Règles Qui Les Régissent* (Paris: Hachette et Cie, 1885), p. 359; Laurent Mannoni, *The Great Art of Light and Shadow: Archaeology of the Cinema*, trans. Richard Crangle (Exeter: University of Exeter Press, 2000), p. 103.

[65] 'Magic Lanthorn and Phantasmagoria', *The Magazine of Science and School of Arts*, 1 (1839), 17–18 (p. 17).

These accounts made the old stories safe and nostalgic, no longer wondrous, terrifying or unsettling. The early lanternists sold wonder for a world beyond an audience's own experiences, or their own lives in sharper focus. The itinerant lanternists mythologised themselves, selling the pleasures of social transgression by entering into unfamiliar social strata. They traded on their own considerable personalities and the (sometimes fictional) grotesquery of their lowly status.

But things changed in the 1820s when Carpenter made a new form of reproducible images widely available in the shops. By the time of Mayhew's interview with the old man, the lantern had shifted from an unusual instrument to an established consumer device. The precariousness of their situation meant that the Savoyards and Galantee Men were hit hard by economic depression and changing ways of living. New entertainment patterns conspired to slowly drive the lanternists out of business. 'They have entirely disappeared from our streets,' laments the *Penny Magazine*, 'and their nocturnal cry, we believe, is no longer heard anywhere in England.'[66] The lives of working-class communities had also changed. As urban populations boomed, wage labour became the dominant mode of work and political activities shifted from clandestine agitation to organised social movements.

The history of the magic lantern is still being put together from a vast heap of material and discursive fragments. Over the few decades after 1821, this wreckage of material shows how magic lantern culture changed. Carpenter, and businesspeople like him, offered new conceptions of media entertainment as a rational, educational activity. Emerging technologies such as photography, rotary printing, stereography and telegraphy further transformed the relationship that people had with information and images. Pictorial reproductions of life would soon hold an indexical connection to the material world and become more common than at any time in history. A professional lantern trade emerged, driven by scientific instrument makers, slide publishers and entertainment halls. These same circuits drove the success of both photography and cinema.

But the old lantern was more complex than Carpenter and his successors dreamed. The Galantee show was intelligent, satirical and beautiful – so much so that one lanternist was forced to simplify his content to appeal to audiences raised on Carpenter's animal stories:

> To the sentimental folk I am obliged to perform werry steady and werry slow, and leave out all comic words and business. They won't have no ghost, no

---

[66] 'Magic Lantern at Rome', p. 101.

coffin, and no devil; and that's what I call spiling the performance entirely. It's the march of hintellect wot's a doing all this—it is, sir.[67]

An old and valuable mode of image culture was undercut and slowly destroyed. Carpenter and his contemporaries would have been pleased to see the end of these grotesque performances in favour of their own rational entertainments.

---

[67] Mayhew, *London Labour and the London Poor*, vol. III, p. 45.

Keyword: Performance

Jon Mee

The 1820s witnessed what contemporaries regarded as an unprecedented explosion of visual and theatrical spectacle. From the many panoramas of military and naval victories, especially of Trafalgar and Waterloo, to recently discovered marvels like the artefacts on display at Egyptian Hall in London from 1821, it was a decade where crowds flocked to novel forms of entertainment. These entertainments have sometimes been contrasted with an emptying-out of literary genres deemed more serious, but they were part of an emergent media ecology that placed great value on performance and included a wealth of writing about city life. Take Marguerite Blessington's *The Magic Lantern, or Sketches of Scenes in the Metropolis* (1822), which describes a series of fashionable cultural sites, including the model tomb at Egyptian Hall, but pays as much attention to the audience displaying itself as to the objects on display. Her title speaks to the idea of London as a show in itself, a series of novel scenes or sketches driven by new media technologies. As in Pierce Egan's more famous *Life in London* (1821), there was a growing sense of a newly expanded audience for culture as itself a performance that readers were invited to enjoy, a sense that started to inflect broader ideas of social being and personal identity.

The coronation of George IV in 1821 set the tone of a theatrical decade, soon followed by his royal tour of Scotland in August 1822, an event much reproduced as a theatre spectacle, just as the coronation itself was soon adapted into rival panoramic versions that competed over the number of figures they displayed. Not that all was acclaim: George IV continued to be the target of a torrent of visual and verbal satires that presented him performing a variety of roles from Macbeth in 1820 to the Great Joss in 1829.[1] Whatever the topical target of any

---

[1] See, for instance, *The Cauldron – or Shakespeare Travestie – 1820* (London: John Fairburn, 1820) and *The Great Joss and his Playthings* (London: G. Creed, 1829).

of these attacks, each played on the idea of the monarch as the presiding spirit of a society of empty display and pretentious self-importance. The idea of George IV as 'a sort of state-puppets [*sic*] or royal wax-work', in William Hazlitt's words, tapped into a broader fear about the precarity of personal identity.[2] Nevertheless, popular taste was drawn to forms that stressed their own ephemerality, most obviously in the rage for improvisation that peaked in 1824 with the London performances of Italian expatriates Gabriele Rossetti and Filip Pistrucci, who were exploiting the continental success of the great *improvvisatore* Tommaso Sgricci, famous for conjuring whole tragedies at the request of his audiences. Other languages followed the Italian lead. In English, the poet Theodore Hook already had a reputation as an improviser at the private parties of the beau monde, but he imported the improvisational style into his printed work of the 1820s.[3] Letitia Elizabeth Landon and her publicist William Jerdan used the fashion to boost her *Improvisatrice* volume (1824).

In these circumstances, Angela Esterhammer's suggestion that 'performance' ought to be understood as the decade's presiding media idea seems persuasive.[4] Performance as a practice transcended theatres and exhibitions – for instance, in the lecture circuits that became central to knowledge transfer in the 1820s, as Jon Klancher and Sarah Zimmerman have shown, not only in relation to the arts, but also to science, political economy and a vast range of other topics. As they became an important medium in the institutions of the metropolis, lectures were also drawing large audiences in the literary and philosophical societies and mechanics' institutes of the provinces for series that ranged from the Hieroglyphical Antiquities of Egypt to the Laws of Chemical Combination and Analysis.[5] Printed forms too were increasingly figured as time-bound events oriented towards an audience, often self-conscious about the precarity of the relationship, perhaps most obviously in the case of the

---

[2] William Hazlitt, 'On Personal Identity', in *The Complete Works of William Hazlitt*, ed. P. P. Howe, 21 vols (London: J. M. Dent, 1930–4), vol. XVII, p. 269.

[3] For more detail on Italian improvisation, Hook and Landon, see Angela Esterhammer, *Print and Performance in the 1820s: Improvisation, Speculation, and Identity* (Cambridge: Cambridge University Press, 2020).

[4] See Esterhammer, *Print and Performance*, p. 9.

[5] See Jon Klancher, *Transfiguring the Arts and Sciences: Knowledge and Cultural Institutions in the Romantic Age* (Cambridge: Cambridge University Press, 2013); Sarah Zimmerman, *The Romantic Literary Lecture* (Oxford: Oxford University Press, 2019). For a taste of the offerings at the Leeds Philosophical and Literary Society, founded in 1819, see E. Kitson Clark, *The History of the 100 Years of Life of the Leeds Philosophical and Literary Society* (Leeds: Jowett, 1924), p. 151. The lectures on the topics named were given in the 1827–8 season.

magazines and periodicals that came into being and died away across the decade.[6] These both provided a commentary on the rapid turnover of cultural forms and mimicked it by appearing to be written to the moment, often presenting themselves as the product of literary circles (sometimes actual, more often invented), as in the 'Table Talk' essays Hazlitt wrote for the *London Magazine*, founded in 1820 but struggling to survive within a few years, despite Charles Lamb's captivating performances in the persona of Elia.[7]

Hazlitt was a great theatre critic and an enthusiast for many of the shows of London. He could even celebrate pulpit oratory, if not without irony, as a variety of precarious performance: 'you now admire the skill of the artist,' he wrote of the Calvinist preacher Thomas Chalmers, 'and next tremble for the fate of the performer, fearing that the audacity of the attempt will turn his head or break his neck'.[8] Nevertheless, faced with the whirligig performativity of the metropolis, his essays often reflect on the fate of his own 'character' and the 'pith and marrow of his performances':

> What is it to me that I can write these TABLE-TALKS? It is true I can, by a reluctant effort, rake up a parcel of half-forgotten observations, but they do not float on the surface of my mind, nor stir it with any sense of pleasure, nor even of pride. Others have more property in them than I have: they may reap the benefit, I have only had the pain. Otherwise, they are to me as if they had never existed; nor should I know that I had ever thought at all, but that I am reminded of it by the strangeness of my appearance, and my unfitness for everything else.[9]

Many of Hazlitt and Lamb's essays operate with a nostalgia for lost certainties, often participating in the desire Mary Poovey identifies with their sometime friends Coleridge and Wordsworth in their attempt to define literary value against the market interest in '*popularity* or *demand*', but they also often register an idea of personal identity as more like social performance than essential being.[10] In Hazlitt's 'Actors and Acting', first published in 1817, the stage player has moved from the

---

[6] See David Stewart, *Romantic Magazines and Metropolitan Literary Culture* (Basingstoke: Palgrave Macmillan, 2011).

[7] On the fate of the *London*, see Tim Chilcott, *A Publisher and His Circle: The Life and Work of John Taylor, Keats's Publisher* (London: Routledge, 1972), especially, pp. 149–52.

[8] 'Mr Irving', published in *The Spirit of the Age* (1825), *Complete Works of William Hazlitt*, vol. XI, p. 46. The portrait of Irving originally appeared in the *New Monthly Magazine* in 1824 with others in the series.

[9] 'On Knowledge of Character', *Complete Works of William Hazlitt*, vol. VII, p. 305.

[10] Mary Poovey, *Genres of the Credit Economy: Mediating Value in Eighteenth- and Nineteenth-Century Britain* (Chicago: University of Chicago Press, 2008), p. 286.

inauthentic being of anti-theatrical prejudice to the paradigm of human identity, 'the motley representatives of human nature'.[11]

The core of human being was felt to be particularly vulnerable in the face of industrial transformation and the machinery question that was debated throughout the 1820s.[12] In this discourse, 'performance' was to do with efficiency, translation of invention into productive capacity, as J. R. McCulloch explained in his lectures on political economy in London, Liverpool and elsewhere. Although the word had been used in this way since at least 1598, it seems instructive that one of the *Oxford English Dictionary*'s illustrations is taken from John Nicholson's *Operative Mechanic* (1825): 'That there is a certain velocity . . . which will procure to an overshot-wheel the greatest performance.'[13] Numerous publications aimed at the working classes encouraged the diffusion of technical knowledge and the acceptance of the principles of political economy as irrefutable truths through the medium of mechanics' institutes and public lectures. Writing in the *Edinburgh Review* in 1827, McCulloch celebrated John Kay's invention of the flying shuttle because it allowed a weaver 'to perform on an average, twice the quantity of work he had previously been accustomed to perform'.[14] For McCulloch and economic liberals of his ilk, the question was cast in terms of human flourishing: the performance of the machine, they claimed, was liberating its operatives from filth and disease into a form of being contrasted with the empty show of the metropolis. For many others, of course, measuring human being against a standard set by the machine was simply a form of alienation. More generally, though, in its different iterations, the idea of performance suggests both the excitements associated with the dizzying possibilities of achievement in a period of rapid change and a deep uncertainty about the future. The audience of culture in the 1820s, like the astounded spectators of Hazlitt's Indian jugglers, were aware of the precarity of performance, including their own place on a tightrope where 'a single error of a hair's breadth, of the smallest conceivable portion of time, would be fatal'.[15]

---

[11] 'Actors and Acting', *Complete Works of William Hazlitt*, vol. IV, p. 153.
[12] See Maxine Berg, *The Machinery Question and the Making of Political Economy, 1815–1848* (Cambridge: Cambridge University Press, 1980). Berg makes the 1820s the key decade in the rise of political economy.
[13] John Nicholson, *The Operative Mechanic and British Machinist* (London: Knight and Lacey, 1825), p. 77.
[14] [J. R. McCulloch], 'Rise, Progress, Present State, and Prospects of the British Cotton Manufacture', *Edinburgh Review*, 46 (June 1827), 1–39 (p. 3). McCulloch became the *Edinburgh*'s principal writer on economics in the 1820s.
[15] 'The Indian Jugglers', *Complete Works of William Hazlitt*, vol. VIII, p. 78.

Keyword: Surveillance

Porscha Fermanis

The word 'surveillance' was first introduced into the English language around the turn of the nineteenth century, seemingly from the *comités de surveillance* that were formed in France from March 1793 to monitor the movements of foreigners and dissidents.[1] With the 'conspiracy hermeneutic' of the French Revolution towering over the period, 1790s Britain provided fertile ground for the emergence of systematic state surveillance and its legal codifications, beginning with the 1794 Treason Trials and 1795 Pitt-Grenville Acts, and culminating in the Six Acts of 1819.[2] The uncovering of the Cato Street Conspiracy to assassinate British cabinet ministers in February 1820 – largely in response to the Peterloo Massacre of 1819 and only two months after the Six Acts had been passed – further encouraged state surveillance of clandestine and radical societies into the 1820s. The presence of the Jamaican-born Afro-Caribbean William Davidson among the Cato Street conspirators extended the threat from home-grown radicals to emigrants from Britain's overseas settlements, where slavery and its resistance had already resulted in the implementation of pioneering surveillance technologies such as slave passes and biometric identificatory criteria.[3]

Continued efforts to counteract radical uprisings through the use of counter-intelligence, intercepted letters and other forms of espionage

[1] Colin Lucas, 'The Theory and Practice of Denunciation in the French Revolution', *The Journal of Modern History*, 68.4 (1996), 768–85.

[2] Orrin N. C. Wang, 'Introduction: Romanticism and Conspiracy', in *Romanticism and Conspiracy, Romantic Circles Praxis Series* (2007), available at https://romantic-circles.org/praxis/conspiracy/wang/owint2.html (accessed 7 February 2022), para. 3 of 7; John Bugg, *Five Long Winters: The Trials of British Romanticism* (Stanford, CA: Stanford University Press, 2013), p. 1.

[3] Ryan Hanley, 'Cato Street and the Caribbean', in *The Cato Street Conspiracy: Plotting, Counter-Intelligence and the Revolutionary Tradition in Britain and Ireland*, ed. Jason McElligott and Martin Conboy (Manchester: Manchester University Press, 2020), pp. 81–100.

raised ongoing questions about the limits of state intervention and the nature of governmentality.[4] Jeremy Bentham's 'Of Publicity', published posthumously in 1843 but written in 1791, advocated open government, arguing that 'secresy [*sic*] is an instrument of conspiracy; it ought not, therefore, to be the system of a regular government'.[5] At the same time, Bentham argued in 1822 that transparency in the form of a free press, accessible institutions and what he called a 'public opinion tribunal' needed to be offset by the right to reputation and privacy.[6] The seductively ambivalent practices of spying, peeping and prying were therefore increasingly understood as part of a potential dilemma that required careful balancing and evaluation: prying was both an 'embodiment of the [public] spirit of inquiry' and an unwarranted intrusion into private affairs. If, as David Vincent argues, the 1820s saw the emergence of a nascent self-regulating 'liberal polity', it was also a decade in which newly liberal subjects were still learning to 'interrogate the conditions of their freedom'.[7]

Alongside more direct modes of state surveillance, the density of urban growth in the 1820s did much to foster an alternative kind of surveillance associated by Max Weber and others with modern industrial capitalism and its 'relentless expansion of illumination'.[8] Linked to the spectacular 'phenomenology of urban modernity' and the rise of optical media technologies from the diorama to photography, the period's turn towards visibility increasingly went beyond the kind of individual flâneurial spectatorship celebrated by Pierce Egan, Thomas De Quincey and others towards forms of mass observation that were mediated through the infrastructures and institutions of the modern state.[9] The poor laws were 'an early test case' for how far the state could or should take class-based interventionist policies, eventually leading to more systematic attempts to monitor the 'dangerous classes'.[10] Edwin Chadwick's work to create a centralised police force in the 1820s and 1830s, for

---

[4] See, for instance, Jon Mee, *Romanticism, Enthusiasm, and Regulation: Poetics and the Policing of Culture in the Romantic Period* (Oxford: Oxford University Press, 2003).

[5] Jeremy Bentham, 'Essay on Political Tactics' (written 1791), in *The Works of Jeremy Bentham, Volume 2*, ed. John Bowring (Edinburgh: William Tait, 1843), p. 315.

[6] Jeremy Bentham, 'Securities Against Misrule' (written 1822), in *Securities Against Misrule and Other Constitutional Writings for Tripoli and Greece*, ed. Philip Schofield (Oxford: Clarendon Press, 1990), p. 121.

[7] David Vincent, *I Hope I Don't Intrude: Privacy and its Dilemmas in Nineteenth-Century Britain* (Oxford: Oxford University Press, 2015), pp. 121, 120.

[8] Chris Otter, *The Victorian Eye: A Political History of Light and Vision in Britain, 1800–1910* (Chicago: University of Chicago Press, 2008), p. 2.

[9] Otter, *The Victorian Eye*, p. 6.

[10] Vincent, *I Hope I Don't Intrude*, p. 119.

example, sought to draw policing, poor relief, urban sanitation and prison administration into an 'integrated inspection machine'.[11] Like the idea of rational self-surveillance embedded in his mentor Bentham's Panopticon inspection model, the system Chadwick envisaged in 'A Preventative Police' (1829) was one that combined observation and intelligence gathering with self-nomination, ultimately requiring 'the poor to administer themselves'.[12]

By 1825 London was probably the largest city in the world, with a population of nearly 1.5 million people. Partly from necessity, Chadwick's neo-Malthusian vision of urban population management was embedded in a new administrative and bureaucratic framework that sought to render territories 'transparent to knowledge' via quantifying and standardising technologies such as surveys, questionnaires and other methods of statistical record keeping.[13] Equipped with watches and report-books 'for the purposes of making the system of espionage more complete', the 'new police' used tools of time management, and reporting and interviewing techniques that recorded the names, ages, residences and habits of suspect individuals.[14] While the 'statistical moment' is usually associated with the 1830s and in particular with Chadwick's Special Board of Health (established 1832) and the Statistical Society (established 1834), it had a longer incubatory period in the growing cultural authority of demographic surveys such as the census, as well as in reforms of prisons, poorhouses and industrial factories, where work discipline required performance measurement and various forms of superintendence.[15] Statistical analysis and labour discipline took on a more racialised shape in Britain's 'Celtic peripheries' and overseas colonies. The Ordnance Survey of Ireland, which began in 1825 and replaced Irish place names with phoneticised English-language versions, pre-empted later attempts

---

[11] John L. McMullan, 'The Arresting Eye: Discourse, Surveillance and Disciplinary Administration in Early Police Thinking', *Social and Legal Studies*, 7.1 (1998), 97–128 (pp. 120–1); Roy Coleman and Michael McCahill, *Surveillance and Crime* (London: Sage, 2011), p. 50.

[12] Mary Poovey, *Making a Social Body: British Cultural Formation, 1830–1864* (Chicago: University of Chicago Press, 1995), p. 107; Edwin Chadwick, 'A Preventative Police', *London Review*, 1 (1829), 252–308.

[13] Patrick D. Joyce, *The Rule of Freedom: Liberalism and the Modern City* (London: Verso, 2003), p. 4.

[14] John Simpson at the Surrey Radical Association, 20 November 1836, quoted in Iorwerth Prothero, *Artisans and Politics in Early Nineteenth-Century London: John Gast and His Times* (Folkestone: Dawson, 1979), p. 273. My thanks to John Gardner for this reference.

[15] Martin Hewitt, *Making Knowledge in the Victorian City: The Visiting Mode in Manchester, 1832–1914* (Abingdon: Routledge, 2020), p. 11; Gregory Clark, 'Factory Discipline', *The Journal of Economic History*, 54.1 (1994), 128–63.

by Henry Mayhew and others to produce pseudo-ethnographic 'social maps' of population density, while the regimented schedules of planation colonies in the Americas and Caribbean were early examples of the 'rigid disciplinary structure of industrial time'.[16]

Bentham's prison Panopticon may have failed to gain parliamentary approval in 1810, but its physical, spatial and architectural mode of anonymous and unverifiable central inspection was gradually dispersed to institutions across the entire scale of social life from the domestic to the institutional, marking out what Michel Foucault has characterised as a shift from arbitrary forms of sovereign authority to the promotion of individual self-discipline.[17] Yet if Bentham and his protégés are now often seen as 'avatars of bureaucratic oppression', invigilist models of self-surveillance originally derived from a liberal and reformist desire to encourage more humane and effective means of punishment based on deterrence and prevention rather than on institutional coercion.[18] Like John Howard before him, Bentham's prison reform scheme promoted incentives for behaviour modification through positive rewards, reinforcement and education, as well as rejecting hard labour and solitary confinement. Architecturally, Bentham envisaged the Panopticon as a light and visually beautiful building, 'a lantern' or 'a glass beehive' that would resemble the rotundas of public pleasure gardens such as Ranelagh Gardens, thereby combining the disciplinary power of surveillance with the appeal of visual spectacle.[19] As Michael Meranze has pointed out, the period's reform of punishment was paradoxically both a 'forward-looking project' and one that required reformers to contain or eliminate anything that contradicted their enlightened, liberal vision.[20]

By the mid- to late 1820s, Bentham's liberal penology fell outside of mainstream views, with the influential Society for the Improvement of Prison Discipline (established 1816) increasingly promoting hard labour and solitary confinement. In his rejection of hard labour and transpor-

---

[16] Joyce, *The Rule of Freedom*, pp. 46–51; Rachel Hewitt, *Map of a Nation: A Biography of the Ordnance Survey* (London: Granta, 2010); James Beattie, Edward Melillo and Emily O'Gorman, 'Rethinking the British Empire through Eco-Cultural Networks: Materialist-Cultural Environmental History, Relational Connections and Agency', *Environment and History*, 20.4 (2014), 561–75 (p. 569).

[17] Michel Foucault, *Discipline and Punish: The Birth of the Prison*, trans. Alan Sheridan (London: Vintage, [1975] 1995), pp. 195–228.

[18] Priti Joshi, 'Edwin Chadwick's Self-Fashioning: Professionalism, Masculinity, and the Victorian Poor', *Victorian Literature and Culture*, 32.3 (2004), 353–70 (p. 353).

[19] Janet Semple, *Bentham's Prison: A Study of the Panopticon Penitentiary* (Oxford: Clarendon Press, 1993), pp. 116, 114.

[20] Michael Meranze, *Laboratories of Virtue: Punishment, Revolution, and Authority in Philadelphia, 1760–1835* (Chapel Hill: University of North Carolina Press, 1996), n.p.

tation, Bentham was joined by the Quaker prison reformer Elizabeth Fry and, on the issue of transportation, by her cousin Edward Gibbon Wakefield.[21] While professional bureaucrats such as Chadwick were hostile to the sort of individual agency and 'charismatic engagement' embodied by middle-class philanthropists and encouraged instead a 'displacement of political concerns from persons to places', Fry – as the 'angel of Newgate Prison' – was the compassionate middle-class face of social reform.[22] Her promotion of the direct observation and physical inspection of female prisoners is suggestive of the ways in which philanthropic endeavours increasingly coincided with monitorial and regulatory inspection regimes.[23] Yet as Chris Otter has rightly pointed out, inspection flourished as a viable way of producing knowledge in the nineteenth century precisely because it was a different form of oversight than either 'omniscient surveillance or furtive spying'. Invigilist models of social control confined their attention to overt acts and were thus able to monitor populations and encourage self-regulation without undermining the 'liberal tenets of subjective freedom' by prying into what Bentham referred to as 'the secret recesses of the heart'.[24]

---

[21] Robert Alan Cooper, 'Jeremy Bentham, Elizabeth Fry, and English Prison Reform', *Journal of the History of Ideas*, 42.4 (1981), 675–90 (pp. 688–9).
[22] Poovey, *Making a Social Body*, p. 106; Joyce, *The Rule of Freedom*, p. 67.
[23] See Chapter 5 by Sara Lodge in this book.
[24] Otter, *The Victorian Eye*, p. 20; Jeremy Bentham, *The Panopticon Writings*, ed. M. Božovi (London and New York: Verso, 1995), p. 94.

Paul Pry and Elizabeth Fry: Inspection and Spectatorship in the Social Theatre of the 1820s

Sara Lodge

The 1820s were an era of spectacle and conscious spectatorship, of gazing, ogling, perusing, peeping and prying. In 1780, there were six London theatres. By 1830, not only were there twenty-five new theatres, but the size of several individual theatres had doubled.[1] Many new opportunities for public gazing opened up after the Napoleonic Wars. The National Gallery opened in 1824; the Zoological Society of London first admitted public zoo-goers in 1828. From 1829, the Colosseum Panorama in Regent's Park offered visitors brave enough to ascend to its gallery a bird's eye view of London as if from the Dome of St Pauls. Vertiginously perched aloft, they might spot their own home depicted below on over an acre of canvas. Meanwhile, the mirror curtain of 1821, at the Royal Coburg Theatre, reflected the audience back to itself in sixty-three panes of glass and Regent Street – with John Nash's triumphal parade of colonnades inviting window shopping and discreet scrutiny of oneself and others – was completed in 1825. These burgeoning new forms of visual entertainment fostered a newly acute awareness, particularly in cities, of the street as itself a theatre crowded with types who might themselves be spies, impostors, gentlemen or 'flash coves' with links to the sporting fraternity and the criminal underworld. *Real Life in London* (1821), one of over sixty imitations of Pierce Egan's rowdy pub crawl of the capital's entertainments *Life in London*, advertised itself as 'exhibiting a living picture'.[2] Its dynamic, crowded illustrations invited readers to study audiences at a boxing match, a bear-baiting, a masquerade ball, and to enter the Fleet Prison, emphasising that to view and to be viewed was to join the fast-moving London scene.

---

[1] Frederick Burwick, *Playing to the Crowd: London Popular Theatre, 1780–1830* (Basingstoke: Palgrave Macmillan, 2011), p. 1.

[2] 'An Amateur', *Real Life in London*, 2 vols (London: Jones, 1821), with illustrations by Heath, Alken, Dighton and Rowlandson. Pierce Egan's original *Life in London* (1820–1) was memorably illustrated by George and Isaac Robert Cruikshank.

Periodicals flourished in the post-war marketplace, making it easier to pique one's curiosity about one's neighbours and increasing the range of visual material available to buy, whether a pin-up of a scantily dressed houri from a literary annual or a comic song illustrated by Cruikshank. Simultaneously, as Jonathan Crary has explored, this period saw a new preoccupation with scientific understanding of vision and experiments that would lead to new viewing technologies such as the diorama, first exhibited in London by Louis Daguerre in 1823.[3] In the Park Street diorama, top-lit pictures eighty feet long and forty feet high were suspended from the ceiling, while a darkened 'circular room, containing the spectators, was turned round, "much like an eye in its socket," to admit the view of each alternately'.[4] This experience, where the viewer became a 'component' in a viewing machine, reflects, Crary argues, an 'increasing abstraction of optical experience from a stable referent'.[5] Viewers were experiencing what it might be like to be a disembodied eye.

Into this world of energetic exhibition and shameless staring erupted the theatrical figure of Paul Pry. John Poole's comedy *Paul Pry*, first performed in September 1825, was the runaway theatrical hit of the 1820s. It starred the era's favourite 'low comedian', John Liston, in the role of Pry and Madame Vestris, a star singer and comedienne, as the maid, Phebe, who sang 'Cherry Ripe' and other popular numbers that helped to make the show the hottest ticket in London and, within weeks, throughout Britain. In this chapter I want to make a provocative pairing, thinking about *Paul Pry* and Elizabeth Fry's discursive text *Observations on the Siting, Superintendance and Government of Female Prisoners* (1827) as works that reflect the preoccupation of this decade with the act of looking – how viewing should be encouraged or regulated and how identity is conferred through the social gaze.

Poole's *Paul Pry* is, in many ways, a typical three-act comedy. There is a love plot featuring Eliza, daughter of Colonel Hardy, who is determined to marry her to a man she's never met. Eliza has meanwhile fallen in love with Harry Stanley, a man of her own choice. (By lucky accident, the man her father has in mind for her husband turns out to be the

---

[3] Phillip Roberts considers some of these new visual technologies in Chapter 4 in this volume.

[4] Edward Walford, 'The Regent's Park', in *Old and New London: Volume 5* (London: Cassell, Petter and Galpin, 1878), pp. 262–86. *British History Online*, available at http://www.british-history.ac.uk/old-new-london/vol5/pp262-286 (accessed 7 February 2022).

[5] Jonathan Crary, *Techniques of the Observer: On Vision and Modernity in the Nineteenth Century* (Cambridge, MA: MIT Press, 1992), p. 113.

same person.) Meanwhile, a wealthy gentleman, the elderly bachelor Witherton, a friend of Colonel Hardy, is being duped and tyrannised by his servants Mr Grasp and Mrs Subtle. This villainous steward and housekeeper have been for years stealing Witherton's correspondence, appropriating his money and turning him against his nephew, Edward Somers, whom Witherton has never met. The bad servants wish the nephew to be disinherited. Mrs Subtle intends, indeed, that Witherton should marry her. However, Edward Somers and his wife have secretly arranged to stay with Witherton under the assumed characters of Mr Willis and Marian, an assistant housekeeper, in order to understand why their letters haven't reached their uncle and to persuade him of their integrity and affection. Predictably, Mr Grasp and Mrs Subtle will be exposed, Witherton will see his nephew in his true light and the inheritance will pass to the young relatives who deserve it.

What makes this play fascinating and contemporary, however, is the character of Paul Pry. As Doubledot, landlord of the local pub complains, Pry is 'one of those idle, meddling fellows, who, having no employment themselves, are perpetually interfering in other people's affairs'. A servant complains: 'Aye, and he's inquisitive into all matters, great or small!' Doubledot responds: 'Inquisitive! Why he makes no scruple to question you respecting your most private concerns ... so he passes his days, "dropping in" as he calls it, from house to house, at the most unreasonable times, to the annoyance of every family in the village.'[6]

Pry's catchphrase is 'I hope I don't intrude'. But, of course, he does intrude – to the audience's delight. He passes the time by passing commentary on his neighbours:

> '. . . that's an uncommon fine leg of mutton the butcher has just sent up to your house. It weighs thirteen pounds five ounces.'
> Doubledot: 'And how do you know that?'
> Pry: 'I ask'd the butcher. I say, Simon, is it for roasting or boiling? ... Well, since you say you are busy I won't interrupt you: only, as I was passing, I thought I might as well drop in.'
> Doubledot: 'Then now you may drop out again. The London coach will be in presently, and —'
> Pry: 'No passengers by it to-day, for I have been to the top of the hill to look for it.'[7]

Pry is a busybody, a bore, an under-occupied man who is perpetually in the way, taking letters from the postman on the pretext that he will

---

[6] John Poole, *Paul Pry* (New York: Murden, 1827), p. 4.
[7] Ibid. p. 5.

assist by delivering them himself and then forgetting to pass them on for a week, asking servants whether they are on board wages, speculating about romantic and financial affairs, and poking his nose into the business of the community. He is perpetually punished and lambasted for his intrusions: chased over walls, his clothes besmirched, his motives insulted. Interestingly, however, Pry may create confusion and irritation but he also exposes the truth. His interfering shenanigans enable the marriage plot and the inheritance plot to succeed. Pry is impertinent in his questions, but pertinacious in his conclusions. He is a proto-detective, a Miss Marple *avant la lettre*.

John Liston, as Paul Pry, had a distinctive costume: he wore striped breeches and a top hat and carried quizzing glasses and a green silk umbrella with a goose handle. He is always depicted leaning forwards with his bottom sticking out: the literal butt of comedy. His umbrella is his quintessential prop. He uses it to shelter young ladies from rain and as an excuse to chat with them and to defend himself. But the umbrella is also an acted metaphor for 'intruding'. It is a potentially bawdy object; yet the green silk and goose head also defuse its phallic potential. Pry is a womanish old bachelor: gossipy and impotent. The quasi-sexual tension, then, between Pry's desire to intrude and the put-downs he suffers creates a vortex of audience delight, in which Pry represents the prick of curiosity that is perpetually aroused and rebuffed, entertained and punished.

As a figure representative of our desire to enquire – impertinent yet ubiquitous, selfish yet sociable – Paul Pry allows the audience to have a proxy for its own insatiable curiosity to see. This curiosity is expressed elsewhere in the play. It is notable that the characters who complain of Pry are equally (though less openly) engaged in trying to discover others' affairs. Simon and Doubledot, for example, speculate on who Eliza Hardy is in love with, since logically the object of her affection can't be a man she's never met. Simon observes: 'by putting this and that together, you know, we in the kitchen often know what's going forward in the parlour better than the parlour folks themselves'.[8]

Edward and Marian Somers are, meanwhile, pretending to be residents of the kitchen in order to understand what is going on in the parlour. Phebe, the maid, also listens at doors and wishes to attend masquerades. Pry devours the newspapers. When he meets a character who appears to be Colonel Hardy's nephew he observes: 'Not the shadow of a doubt what sort of a gentleman he is. Yet he looks like a gentleman — but what of that, every pickpocket now-a-days is described as a youth

[8] Ibid. p. 3.

of prepossessing appearance, and every disorderly woman taken before a magistrate is sure to be young and interesting.'[9]

Pry here notes how difficult it is to be certain about the class and credentials of those one meets, a thought he substantiates with the kind of remarks familiar in newspapers giving accounts of magistrates' courts. Mistaken and assumed identity is a familiar trope in stage comedy, but *Paul Pry* links it to forms of disguise and imposture that make it increasingly difficult to be certain about class identity in contemporary life. Is someone who looks like a gentleman really a gentleman? As H. E. Leblanc, the author of *The Art of Tying the Cravat* (1828), argued:

> in an age like the present, when the man of quality is so closely imitated by the pretender — when the amalgamation of all ranks seems to be the inevitable consequence of the '*March of Intellect*' now making such rapid strides amongst us, we think a more signal service cannot be rendered to the higher ranks of society, than by the production of such a work as this.[10]

Printing accounts of how to tie a cravat, however, surely threatened to assist the literate pretender.

Thomas Moore's *The Fudge Family in Paris* (1818) had placed Biddy Fudge in comic difficulties when she falls in love with a young man whom she believes to be the King of Prussia in disguise, but who is really a draper. Moore's epistolary satire inspired several imitations in the 1820s, where the inexperienced Fudges visit Edinburgh and Dublin, engaging in pretence about their social status and becoming, in turn, victims of scams. As Biddy remarks in *The Fudge Family in Edinburgh*:

> There are two sorts of creatures I hate and despise,
>   Those are *hypocrites* aping devotion
> To cover vile actions—the others are *spies,*
>   In families breeding commotion![11]

The Fudges' narrative, however, suggests that hypocrisy and spying go together. The ubiquity of social pretence and gaming requires a culture of covert observation to penetrate its realities.

Pry is a figure who, in embodying the need to peep and to speculate, enables audiences to view with pleasure their own ambivalent desires for privacy and scrutiny. In the play's closing remarks, Phebe the maid objects: 'Lord help me. You are too inquisitive for a husband.' Pry

---

[9] Ibid. p. 51.

[10] H. E. Leblanc, *The Art of Tying the Cravat* (London: Ingrey and Madeley, 1828), pp. iv–vii.

[11] Nehemiah Nettlebottom, *The Fudge Family in Edinburgh* (Edinburgh: Dick, 1820), p. 36.

retorts: 'Pooh, pooh! A spirit of inquiry is the great characteristic of the age we live in.'[12] One might add, with a nod to Hazlitt's *Spirit of the Age* (1825), that identification of the zeitgeist is essential to the zeitgeist of the 1820s: it is a time of enquiry about what it is legitimate to enquire about.

As Frederick Burwick points out, John Poole did not invent 'Paul Pry': a type-character of that name had appeared in children's books, and George MacFarren's one-act burletta, *Sir Peter Pry; or, Male Curiosity*, of June 1819 was followed that year by another entitled *Paul Pry*.[13] But Poole's new comedy of September 1825 gave Pry a distinctive appearance and verbal repertoire. The play caught on like wildfire. 'Paul Pry' became what we would now call a meme.

It immediately spawned publications in every conceivable genre, drawing attention to the possibility of total penetration of a multi-media market. By February 1826, the character had inspired a weekly journal, commenting on political and social affairs. The same year saw a variety of Pry plays, poems, a prose narrative and spin-off songbooks including *Paul Pry's collection of Choice Songs* and *The Vocalist, a new song book, being a choice collection of celebrated new songs, some of them sung by Mess. Liston and Mathews at various Theatres*. In 1827 *The Blunders of a Big-Wig or Paul Pry's Peeps into the Sixpenny Sciences* presented Paul Pry considering the subjects of hydrostatics, conic sections and various other mathematical topics in the Library of Useful Knowledge. Prefiguring the merchandising coup of Dickens's *Pickwick Papers*, Paul Pry also gave rise to porcelain figurines, public houses, racehorses and a fast stagecoach, the Paul Pry, which ran from Sheffield to London. David Vincent rightly identifies that Pry 'was first a play and then within weeks virtually every other category of cultural practice'.[14]

As Vincent explores, the 'sheer plasticity of Paul Pry' allowed him, 'however the boundary of the political nation was drawn', to be 'a presence on both the inside and the outside'.[15] His impertinent gaze could, for example, be invoked to remind citizens of how representatives of the state might 'drop in' in order to monitor and regulate their activities. In an article in the *Westmorland Gazette* of 1829, 'Paul Pry in the Highlands', a traveller is reported to have stopped for a whisky at a small roadside pub. When the stranger enquires if the excellent whisky he is drinking is legal, the owner discreetly replies: 'why, sir,

---

[12] Poole, *Paul Pry*, p. 68.

[13] Burwick, *Playing to the Crowd*, p. 202.

[14] David Vincent, *I Hope I Don't Intrude: Privacy and its Dilemmas in Nineteenth-Century Britain* (Oxford: Oxford University Press, 2015), p. 21.

[15] Ibid. p. 22.

that's a question!'.[16] The implication here is that such questions are best left unasked. Pry's unabashed nosiness could, however, also be used to describe the private citizen's right to examine the secretive workings of the state. In a rather different cartoon of 1826, 'Paul Pry's Peep into Chancery', the figure of Pry broaches a room piled with obfuscatory heaps of documents. Lord Eldon, identified with 'Power and Patronage', sits in the midst of Court Appointments, Cabinet Papers and private deeds, while Pry remarks, 'doubt if you'll ever get through it' and threatens to 'peep into the private accounts'.[17] On the wall are lists of Eldon's extravagant expenses set against income from Bankruptcies, Lunatics and Presents.

Britain in the 1820s was just beginning to use the word 'surveillance' in contexts that removed this foreign concept from the continental arena of French and Spanish politics to the sphere of domestic life. In 1825, for example, Theodore Hook would describe a tour as being 'under the surveillance of a tutor'.[18] It is very noticeable, however, that the British Newspaper Archive for 1800–9 lists 226 uses of the word in newspapers. Between 1810 and 1819 it records 1,260 uses; between 1820 and 1829 the number of occasions when the word is deployed has risen to 2,244.[19]

The jump in use of the word 'surveillance' in the 1820s may reflect national jumpiness. The Cato Street conspiracy drew attention to the actions of George Edwards, who had penetrated the Spencean movement and acted not only as a police informer but as an agent provocateur, inciting five radicals to actions for which they would be hanged.[20] Fear of unrest persisted in the wake of the Peterloo Massacre and the Six Acts (1819), as did fear of persecution by those who sought to suppress political meetings and radical publications. Amid talk of reforms

---

[16] 'Paul Pry in the Highlands', *Westmorland Gazette*, 24 January 1829, p. 3. The article says it is reprinted from the *Inverness Courier*, but I have been unable to verify this.

[17] Charles Williams, 'Paul Pry's Peep into Chancery' (London: Fores, 1826). British Museum, available at https://www.britishmuseum.org/collection/object/P_1868-0808 -8695 (accessed 11 May 2022).

[18] *Oxford English Dictionary* entry for 'surveillance' (accessed 10 September 2020): 'T. Hook *Sayings & Doings* 2nd Ser. I. 149'. This is the first usage cited in *OED* that is not explicitly political. Angela Esterhammer discusses Theodore Hook's *Sayings and Doings* in Chapter 1 of this volume.

[19] Compiled using https://www.britishnewspaperarchive.co.uk (accessed 10 September 2020). The context is one of significant growth in the overall number of newspaper pages, so even a blank search will show increased 'hits' between 1800 and 1830. Nonetheless, it is evident that the word 'surveillance' is gaining popular traction in this period.

[20] The *Sheffield Independent* referred to Edwards as 'the traiterous spy' and 'ruthless speculator in human blood' (27 May 1820, p. 3).

to the Police by Robert Peel, a writer to the *Morning Herald* in 1829 worried that Britain might adopt a plan whereby a register was kept of the inhabitants of all houses and the Police were empowered to make home visits: a system that if applied to the whole population of the metropolis 'would render it but one vast gaol'.[21] There were also more pettifogging busybodies to avoid. Lee Jackson draws attention to the professional informers operating in the 1820s who deliberately sought out obscure laws and prosecuted tradesmen for breaking quasi-obsolete statutes.[22] In 1828 Mr Botheroyd, a publican who ran a cock-and-hen club (a largely amateur forerunner of the Victorian music hall) above his premises, was prosecuted by the notorious informer Mr Green for operating without an entertainment licence. Green invoked the Disorderly Houses Act (1751), intended to control suburban pleasure gardens, but succeeded in having Botheroyd's respectable pub cabaret fined £100. It is easy to see why men like Green were detested by the ordinary citizen; they pocketed bribes while patrolling the border between public and private space.

A newspaper article of 1826, 'Paul Pry in the East', described a teenage actor, 'Edward Liston', who – meeting a pub landlord's son in the street and striking up an acquaintance – had performed sleight-of-hand conjuring tricks to an informal audience in the parlour of his friend's father's pub. Having succeeded with his magic show, Liston launched into a comic performance as Paul Pry. At this point, sadly, he was intruded upon by the local constable. The actor had, as witnesses asserted, done no necromancy, stolen nothing and charged no money for his impromptu act, receiving only the gift of breakfast. The magistrate could not charge him with any offence, but told him to go and get a proper job.[23] In another case of 1827, the proprietors of the Circus in Great Surrey Street were hauled up before the magistrate for having performed *Paul Pry and the Whimsicalities of Punchinello and Judith* to a crowded two-shilling house of around three hundred people. The character of Pry, mounted on a horse, transformed into that of Punch, delighting the audience but not neighbours in adjacent houses who 'considered the performances . . . illegal'.[24] The alignment between Pry and the traditional Punch and Judy show hints at how one popular character associated with comic misbehaviour could be incorporated

---

[21] 'Spirit of the London Journals', *Sun*, 1 January 1829, p. 4.
[22] Lee Jackson, *Palaces of Pleasure: From Music Halls to the Seaside to Football, How the Victorians Invented Mass Entertainment* (New Haven, CT: Yale University Press, 2019), p. 37.
[23] 'Paul Pry in the East', *Public Ledger*, 24 October 1826, p. 1.
[24] 'Police', *Morning Advertiser*, 22 November 1827, p. 3.

with another. However, these incidents, like the trial of Mr Botheroyd, demonstrate how unsympathetic many law enforcers of the period were towards theatre that operated in a liminal zone between licensed and unlicensed performance. *Paul Pry* raised various critical issues of the day: playfully staging debates about intrusive looking and private versus public space that also pertained to the boundaries of theatre and its regulation.

Moreover, Pry fits into a paradigmatic exploration in the 1820s of the self-reflexive quality of looking. Insistent depiction of the viewer as simultaneous visual subject and object signals a new self-consciousness about identity as constituted through the mutual gaze. In Thomas Hood's 1827 cartoon 'Unconscious Imitation', a giraffe and a human mirror each other's face and posture precisely as they bend forward to examine one another.[25] That mirror pose will be replicated in the youthful Edward Lear's sketch of parrots in the Zoological Gardens, circa 1830, staring back at the humans who come to gawp at them. Lear depicts the exotic macaws quizzically picturing the human zoo visitors as odd types and specimens.[26] Charles Lamb writing the obituary of Elia, his literary persona, or James Hogg's insertion of a newspaper article claiming the discovery of a mummified corpse that belongs to his novel's protagonist, the justified sinner Robert Wringham, also belong to an era that celebrates the self's acknowledgement of its own status as a rhetorical artefact, projected towards audiences whose viewing both confirms and interrogates it.

Paul Pry calls insistent attention to the self-referential qualities of the multi-media representations of his own figure. In one spin-off song, 'The Pryings of Paul Pry', Pry remarks: 'They've posted me in every picture shop in the metropolis / Caricatured me everywhere to please the vulgar populace.'[27] In another song, he affects to object: 'They've got me in the picture-shops, they have, upon my honour; / I'm next to *Venus*, which, they say, is quite a libel on her.'[28] The mention of Venus here hints at the pornographic nature of prints in shops like those of Holywell Street: prying can accompany various crimes, whether prig-

25 Thomas Hood, 'Unconscious Imitation', cut by Edward Willis, *Whims and Oddities*, 2nd series (London: Tilt, 1827), facing p. 148.
26 Edward Lear, 'View from the Parrot Cage', Houghton Library, Harvard, printed in Sara Lodge, *Inventing Edward Lear* (Cambridge, MA: Harvard University Press, 2018), p. 156.
27 W. H. Freeman, 'The Pryings of Paul Pry', in *The Vocalist, a new song book, being a choice collection of celebrated new songs, some of them sung by Mess. Liston and Mathews at various Theatres* (Newcastle: Marshall, 1825–31), p. 14.
28 'The Adventures of Paul Pry', in *The Universal Songster or Museum of Mirth*, 3 vols (London: Simpkin and Marshall, 1826), vol. III, p. 97.

ging pockets or plugging prostitutes. Joe Lisle's 1828 lithograph 'The Spectator' depicts a print shop. A gawper has his pocket picked while he stares at cartoons, including one by Joe Lisle himself, self-referentially placed in the window. Another of the images in the print shop is of Paul Pry. This lithograph reflects on the mutual vulnerability of viewing. As Brian Maidment notes: 'if there are traditional . . . elements in Lisle's "The Spectator" there is also a new sense of surveillance, exploitation and punishment'.[29] Although 'The Spectator' may contain an element of warning, it is also playful in its triangulation between the unconscious viewing performed by the print-shop gazer, the knowing view of the pickpocket within the lithograph and the ambivalent role of print itself, which both enables the crime and allows the cartoon's viewers to detect it. Like the ubiquitous character of Pry, printed material in this decade is outrageous in its incursions and yet often justified in its suspicions. It offends and enables justice simultaneously.

In the song 'Paul Pry', Pry tells us that the baker gives short weight, that the publican has got the barmaid with child and the parson has a mistress. He also turns to the theatre audience and announces:

A chap in the gallery's winking away
And thinks I don't notice his jerkings:
While he's answered in kind by a lady so gay —
Oh, I'm really asham'd Mrs Perkins.[30]

This calling out sexual flirtation in the audience reverses the spectatorship of the theatre, as the mirror curtain at the Coburg did, making the conscious viewer into the conscious object of view.

In *Paul Pry's Merry Minstrel or Budget of New Songs*, one of the offerings, 'Old and New Times' (1826), observes that:

Time was when you might have a chat, with a captain of light horse,
Without once thinking that your friend would print your words of course;
But now to Paternoster-row they go *sans* hesitation,
To publish forth to all the world your private conversation.[31]

Pry, as a meme, draws attention to the various ways in which speculation in print, whether penning gossip columns, cartooning, or producing lottery tickets, is part of a wider economy of spectatorship and speculation that has a cascading, domino effect. Pry's image was used to

[29] Brian Maidment, *Comedy, Caricature and the Social Order 1820–1850* (Manchester: Manchester University Press, 2013), p. 133.

[30] 'Paul Pry', *Vocalist*, p. 10.

[31] Orlando Hodgson, 'Old and New Times', *Paul Pry's Merry Minstrel* (London: Hodgson, 1825), pp. 15–16.

advertise a lottery on 6 December 1825, where four prizes of £30,000 were to be allotted in one day.[32] In the song 'The Misfortunes of Paul Pry', Pry stops by the bank to draw out his balance – about £15,000 – and the Banker says, 'this hour we've payment stopt'.[33] Pry is imaged losing all his money in the banking crash of 1825: he is a comic fall guy, who arrives just too late to preserve his savings. Yet, as someone whose runaway curiosity is the driver of all his actions, he isn't wholly a victim of the market: it is unchecked speculation, after all, that has produced the run on the bank.

John Poole's play is provincial in setting, but Pry quickly came to be associated with aspects of modern city life.[34] In 'Viaorama or The Way to St Pauls', a miniature printed diorama for home entertainment, produced by the lithographers Ingrey and Madeley in December 1825, the figure of Pry stands smiling at the gates of the capital, which are surmounted by the arms of the City of London accompanied by a cornucopia, suggesting the abundance of trade. The diorama is concertina-shaped and invites the viewer to 'peep' through the fan arch of the doorway, seeing a delightfully detailed, receding view of The Strand as it proceeds to St Pauls. The street is crowded; there are coaches passing, including the 'Tally Ho London to Paris'. Trade with France and travel have resumed after the Napoleonic Wars. Notices on the walls are part of the scene, as are vendors with trays. We view the architecture through the frame of whips of drivers of carriages and the bustle of shoppers, just as a real pedestrian might. The 'viaorama' is a miniature theatre, but one we participate in domestically. Charles Ingrey and George Edward Madeley had their own offices at 130 Strand and their name appears on an advertising sign within the viaorama, like Alfred Hitchcock in one of his own films.

So far as I am aware, this is the only known use of the word 'viaorama' and the pun is suggestive: it is a 'way of looking' that is at once a depiction of a real street and a viewing path. As practitioners of the new art of lithography, Ingrey and Madeley produced varied visual fare. Their lithographs included depictions of Madame Vestris and John Liston singing 'Buy a Broom' (1826), where Liston is depicted in female dress.[35] They also published an architectural 'Plan of the proposed

---

[32] See http://www.ephemera-society.org.uk/items/2012/jan12.html (accessed 7 February 2022).

[33] W. H. Freeman, 'The Misfortunes of Paul Pry', *Vocalist*, p. 15.

[34] In William Belch's illustrated comic book, *Paul Pry* (dated 1824, but must be 1825 or later), Pry is depicted in the urban street, being chased by geese and laughed at by urchins. National Library of Scotland Ms.992(22).

[35] Vestris was famous for her breeches roles. Her acting partnership with Liston in *Paul*

improvements at Charing Cross' and a lithograph of the execution of Chunee the elephant, who famously ran amok in 1826 during his Sunday walk along The Strand. Their 'viaorama' points to the world where Paul Pry rose to instant celebrity in the 1820s: drawing a pleasing connection between the streets of the metropolis and the theatre, showing how the two were linked by new modes of viewing the town as a performance space, a series of novel optical effects in which we are invited to join Pry as a compulsive looker-on.

In the song 'The Pryings of Paul Pry', Pry happens to be peeping into a shop when he sees thieves stealing from it. Unluckily, he is caught by the authorities holding the bag that the thieves were abstracting. Pry is found guilty of the crime and is sentenced to 'six months at the treading mill'. This is farcical. Yet it is also apt in representing the question of whether obsessive viewing is itself a form of break-in, which threatens the boundaries of civility, or whether it is continuous viewing – what we now dub 'neighbourhood watch' – that constructs and protects the civic space and its economy. To examine this question further and its signifi-cance in the 1820s, I'd like now to turn to the other text that I advertised at the beginning of this chapter: Elizabeth Fry's landmark publication *Observations on the Siting, Superintendance and Government of Female Prisoners* (1827).

This text constitutes, obviously, a different kind of investigation under the broad aegis of that 'spirit of enquiry' that Paul Pry defines as charac-teristic of the age. It is a discursive document designed to bring facts and recommendations regarding women prisoners to public notice and to effect positive change on the carceral system. However, the key words of the title – Observations, Siting, Superintendance – emphasise the highly visual nature of the project that Fry has undertaken. It concerns not only how female prisoners are housed and treated but how they are viewed.

Fry's *Observations* is, in many respects, a remarkably humane and progressive document. For example, she suggests that prisons must be properly heated to prevent inmates leaving with crippling diseases. She is opposed to capital punishment, both as an inhumane spectacle and one that by reducing the value of human life in people's eyes, adds to the numbers of murders and suicides; she rejects whipping as a form of punishment. She argues forcibly for prison education and against imprisonment for debt. And she stresses the importance of women acting as friends to assist and rehabilitate those who have just left prison and have no associates, as they will be exposed both to humiliations and

---

Pry doubtless intrigued audiences partly because Liston's male role was 'womanish' and Vestris's role as Phebe the maid was assertive.

temptations. In her *Report Addressed to the Marquess Wellesley, Lord Lieutenant of Ireland respecting their late visit to that country* (also of 1827, published with Joseph John Gurney), Fry would go further to petition for a sum of £50 annually, to assist Ladies' Committees in housing and providing initial support for destitute female prisoners after their release.[36]

However, Fry also insists that *'vigilant and unremitting inspection* is unquestionably one of the *most essential points* in a correct system of prison discipline'. This affords a *'certain and constant* check . . . on every vicious practice'. [37] There are certain points in Fry's argument about inspection to which a modern reader gladly assents: female prisoners, Fry insists, should not be under the superintendence of men who have the key to their apartments and can enter at any time, as this exposes them to inescapable sexual threat. Some local lock-ups threw prisoners of all kinds into one cell: a recipe for rape, assault and infection. Indeed, part of the regime of inspection Fry advocates is the regular inspection of warders and prison governors. Prisons are by their nature closed and to some extent hidden spaces but, in order for their management and systems to be more accountable, they need to be opened to the critical public eye. Only in this way can standards be improved and provision regularised throughout urban and provincial settings; Fry would write and publish separate accounts of prisons in Scotland, Ireland and England. In the wide sweep of her tours of inspection, her concern for greater standardisation and her desire to build new prisons with more spacious and sanitary conditions, we can see the reformist gaze as looking to expose and eradicate institutional corruption and neglect.

But the vigilant and unremitting inspection Fry advocates is not merely about ensuring reasonable standards of prison governance and prisoner safety. She advocates cutting female prisoners' hair and doing away with curls, fancy caps or any other departure from modest plainness in dress. Moreover, she insists that prisoners guilty of different types of offence should be classified, labelled and separated to prevent contamination. There will be four classes of prisoner, the highest of which have crimes of no deep moral dye and who may be permitted better clothing and less irksome labour. The fourth class is of the most hardened and desperate offenders. Fry recommends numbered tickets for each individual, with marks of approbation or disapprobation of conduct 'placed on parallel

---

[36] Elizabeth Fry and Joseph John Gurney, *Report Addressed to the Marquess Wellesley, Lord Lieutenant of Ireland, respecting their late visit to that country* (London: Arch, 1827), pp. 7–8.

[37] Elizabeth Fry, *Observations on the Siting, Superintendance and Government of Female Prisoners* (London: Arch, 1827), p. 33.

lines against their respective numbers'. Numbers, she notes, are given on convict ships in this way and promote 'that strictness of discipline which is essential to the order and regularity of the whole machine'.[38] This is a way of seeing prisoners that may be compassionate in its intention but risks depersonalising each woman in its determination to substitute for the marks of individual character, tickets that frame each prisoner systemically according to their relative badness.

The prisoner, in Fry's methodology, needs to be distinguished from others and put under constant surveillance – not just for her protection, but for her reformation.[39] Solitude at night is desirable, not for privacy but to afford prisoners 'sober, and often painful, reflection on the misery produced by their crimes'.[40] The possible comfort of touch and human warmth in repose, even where this has no sexual dimension, is discountenanced here as tending to distract from the pressing inner work of remorse and reform. Foucault contends that 'solitude is the primary condition of total submission'.[41] Reformers of this era wanted to believe that the offender was 'less deterred from crime by calculation of consequences, than by involuntary sympathy with others'.[42] The work of the prison visitor was, with gentleness, to model and cultivate sympathy. However, awakening sympathy for the middle-class 'good citizen' involved the prisoner internalising his or her own alienation. As Randall McGowen has argued, 'the 'criminal "other" must be made to feel a concern for those "other" than himself; he must learn to condemn his own otherness'.[43]

Fry is mistrustful of social activities in the prison outside of worship; she recommends labour and even hard labour, for both sexes, as preferable to 'corrupting idleness'.[44] Her notion of prison as an orderly and

[38] Ibid. pp. 35–8.
[39] Michael Meranze's *Laboratories of Virtue: Punishment, Revolution and Authority in Philadelphia, 1760–1835* (Chapel Hill: University of North Carolina Press, 1996) shows how debates about penal reform flourished on both sides of the Atlantic in the 1820s, with particular discussion of the value or folly of solitary confinement; the importance of hard labour; prison architecture and surveillance of prisoners; and separation of one type of prisoner from another. Meranze notes: 'Through the repetitive history of the expanded and intensified institutions of the 1820s, discipline, rather than simply being penal, extended further and further out into the wider social organization' (p. 254).
[40] Fry and Gurney, *Report*, p. 9.
[41] Michel Foucault, *Discipline and Punish: The Birth of the Prison*, trans. Alan Sheridan (Harmondsworth: Penguin, [1975] 1991), p. 237.
[42] 'Capital Punishment', *Edinburgh Review*, 35 (1821), 314–53 (p. 345).
[43] Randall McGowen, 'A Powerful Sympathy: Terror, the Prison, and Humanitarian Reform in Early Nineteenth-Century Britain', *Journal of British Studies*, 25 (1986), 312–34 (p. 330).
[44] Fry and Gurney, *Report*, p. 13.

regular machine is literalised in the Tread Wheel, which she advocates (not for women, but for male prisoners):

> a more general use of the Tread Wheel would, we think, be desirable. Every jail ought to be furnished with one; and the wheel ought, in all cases, to be large enough to receive the average number of male prisoners under sentence of confinement. It ought, moreover, to be divided into as many compartments as will ensure the continuance, during the hours of work, of the classification required by law.[45]

The Tread Mill, invented by William Cubitt in 1817, was not only a way of making fruitless labour into punishment, it was a way of ordering prisoners physically where they are definitely on view rather than viewing subjects. Fry, moreover, imagines each wheel being compartmentalised in such a way that every prisoner is present and every prisoner is separate. They become cogs, whose only relationality lies in the turn unwillingly produced by their collective action.

Fry's reports on the conditions she found in prisons opened up spaces previously dark and enclosed, subject to abuse, to positive public scrutiny. Yet the other side of the development she advocates is a prison society of constant surveillance, where privacy, personal appearance, right of association and marks of identity are punitively subjected to regularising frameworks that determine how one is seen.

A laudatory article of 1821 on Fry's life, 'her angelic mission' and prison visiting activities stressed that she was 'virtue made visible'.[46] As Helen Rogers had remarked, 'few women were made to embody the ideal of sisterhood in charity as much as the prisoner reformer, or would be more associated with lay constructions of saintliness'.[47] These hagiographic accounts emphasised the risks she undertook in entering, like Daniel into the lion's den, trustfully encountering groups of women who might rob, abuse or assault her and (implicitly) 'taming' these wild creatures through compassion and Christian charity. Mary Sanderson, the Quaker who accompanied Fry to the female wards, reported: 'she felt as if she were going into a den of wild beasts, and she well recollects quite shuddering when the door closed upon her, and she was locked in with such a herd of novel and desperate companions'.[48] Entering the

---

[45] Ibid. p. 13.

[46] 'Memoirs of Mrs Fry from Madame Adele du Thou's History of the Quakers', *Birmingham Chronicle*, 29 March 1821, p. 4.

[47] Helen Rogers, 'Elizabeth Fry and Sarah Martin', in *Making and Remaking Saints in Nineteenth-Century Britain*, ed. Gareth Atkins (Manchester: Manchester University Press, 2016), pp. 226–44 (p. 227).

[48] Thomas Fowell Buxton, *An Inquiry, Whether Crime and Misery are Produced or Prevented by Our Present System of Prison Discipline* (London: Arch, 1818), p. 118.

prison pregnant ('in a delicate condition'), Fry is being cast in the role of Elizabeth, mother of John the Baptist.

Doubtless, Fry was brave. Yet, to the modern reader, it seems as if Fry's offer of education for prisoners and their children, with financial aid for those who demonstrated submission and reform, came at a price. An article in the *Scotsman* of 1828 noted that each woman 'feels that her whole conduct is observed, but so obviously and unequivocally *for good*, that the conviction of this truth is the great agent of melioration'.[49] In this framework the prisoner is led and held to desire to be viewed always and viewed well. '*A monitor, chosen from among the most orderly, is intrusted with the particular oversight of each class*' – this monitor will observe, regulate and report her movements and behaviour, and any visitors she may receive, to the authority of the prison matron.[50] The prisoner's own power of looking and the objects she is permitted to view will also be restrained. Among the 'rules for regulating the conduct of female prisoners' within the new society Fry sought to get prisoners themselves to subscribe to was: 'Card-playing, and all other gaming – as also plays, *novels*, and other pernicious books, with all immoral songs – are strictly prohibited.'[51]

The commentator in the *Scotsman* noted with relief that this rule was not rigidly adhered to and there were two copies of *Robinson Crusoe* in the prison library he visited. He felt, however, that Mary Russell Mitford's domestic works ought to be there and worried that filling a library with didactic tracts expressly aimed at criminals might not be the best way to foster a love of literature. The notion of isolation breeding philosophical and moral reflection seems, however, to be embedded in *Robinson Crusoe* as the sole choice of permissible fiction. Fry's emphasis on abstracting the individual from the corrupting influence of those lower in the moral field, and prohibition on social pleasures such as card-playing or non-religious singing, suggests the extent to which her role as a prying middle-class visitor was also to be an arbiter of appropriate viewing. In this model, unremitting surveillance could be presented both as a signifier of care and value – like an omniscient deity, I see you and you are all of equal importance to me – and a deterrent, not only to committing offences on the statute book but more subtle forms of 'unacceptable' behaviour (such as singing lewd songs) that offered a constant reminder of the subject's guilt and their need to win back social approval by submitting to new levels of scrutiny and control.

---

[49] M., 'Mr Bentham_Mrs Fry_Prison Discipline', *The Scotsman or Edinburgh Political and Literary Journal*, 16 August 1828, p. 1.

[50] Ibid. p. 1.

[51] Ibid. p. 1.

Not all contemporary commentators on Elizabeth Fry were positive. Thomas Hood, whose comic poems of the 1820s often prefigure the political concerns of his later social protest works, argued in his 'A *Friendly* Address to Mrs Fry *in* Newgate' that it would be better to offer education to impoverished children at an earlier stage in life, before they became adults who resorted to crime:

> I like the pity in your full-brimmed eye;
> I like your carriage, and your silken grey,
> Your dove-like habits, and your silent preaching;
> But I don't like your Newgatory teaching.[52]

The pun on 'nugatory' is the sting in the tail. Hood's banner 'Fry for Ever' in his engraving *The Progress of Cant* (1825) is even sharper in its humour. It punningly suggests that Elizabeth Fry can go to hell. In this cartoon, a flag celebrating Fry becomes part of a parade of conscious advertisement on the urban street, whose proponents compete for visual space to push their views, producing unexpected conjunctions and unintended readings.

In Fry's own ideology of viewing, rather than a publicist, she is a restorer of modesty – the protective veil of female virtue. Under Fry's model regime, prisoners are urged to become agents in their own surveillance – monitors and informers. How they appear and deport themselves in prison will determine hierarchically how they are placed within the emergent categories of responsiveness to intervention and how society facilitates their return to the world outside its walls. Women had not only to 'stay clean' in terms of avoiding further crime; by Fry's rules they had to stay physically clean, too, and to keep their sober clothes and 'apartments' clean. Their language was also to be clean: no swearing was permitted. They were required to attend the 'work-room' regularly to hear portions of Holy Scripture, led thither by their monitor in forms of 'regular order' at the second ringing of a bell. The work of reform extended into leisure; it was, indeed, suspicious of leisure. Women were forbidden to look through the grating at which visitors appeared from the outside world unless visitors had specifically arrived for them. This level of order may have succeeded, in some cases, in making the woman's prison feel more like an intentional community, such as a nunnery: a quiet, safe, clean, tidy and predictable world governed by bells, spiritual reflection, the avoidance of disagreement and the aspiration to purity. Yet a prison is not a convent. Women who had

---

[52] Thomas Hood, 'A *Friendly* Address to Mrs Fry *in* Newgate', reprinted in *The Complete Poetical Works of Thomas Hood*, ed. Walter Jerrold (London: Frowde, 1911), p. 7.

'fallen' out of acceptable social view were admitted back only through the lens of a kaleidoscope in which they arranged themselves into a pleasing, orderly pattern of Christian self-restraint and humility that appealed to the patrons whose aid they required.

From the perspective of the Foucauldian critique of the will to discipline, it is telling that Thomas Fowell Buxton found that under Fry's 'rule of kindness' the female wards 'exhibited the appearance of an industrious manufactory, or a well regulated family'.[53] Arguably what is being manufactured in the reformed prison is an ideology of industry as morality and discipline as the machinery in which individual will must be subdued.

As Robert Alan Cooper has remarked, 'the ideas of Jeremy Bentham and Elizabeth Fry are remarkably similar, while the ideas of their supposed followers are also remarkably similar'.[54] Bentham's Panopticon and Fry's model prison are alike in basing their systems on continuous observation. Many of Bentham's and Fry's specific ideas were not put into practice by future legislators, but they remained influential in the swirl of reform that produced the Prisons Act of 1835 and the Poor Law Amendment Act of 1834, with their emphasis on greater uniformity and regular inspection, with the building of new collective workhouses, where basic relief was offered only on conditions of gender separation, labour, enforced cleanliness and uniform dress. In 'workhouses' – which remained ambiguously carceral and charitable settings throughout the century – submission to rules and privations was part of the deliberate humiliation designed to prevent the indigent from seeking aid unless they were in destitution so absolute that they had no alternative.

It is interesting that Fry is remembered as a heroine, whereas admiration for Bentham's legacy is more measured. Perhaps this is because Fry is little read; in the tradition of the good mother or selfless saint, her physical acts of compassion, nurture and education are considered to be her truest work. Her reports on prison governance show that compassionate looking and dispassionate looking – the statistical and the humane – cannot be teased apart in the context of reformist intervention. Both are bound up in this period with new technologies of vision, with a burgeoning print culture and with a post-war society that is looking about itself, fascinated by the pleasure and difficulty of reading others in the social encounter of the street, intrigued by the legitimate boundaries between public and private.

---

[53] Buxton, *Inquiry*, p. 127.
[54] Robert Alan Cooper, 'Jeremy Bentham, Elizabeth Fry, and English Prison Reform', *Journal of the History of Ideas*, 42.4 (1981), 675–90 (p. 675).

The 1820s, then, is a decade that stages its ambivalence about spectatorship. It is, as Thomas Hood pronounced in 1825, 'a masquing age' – an age of imposture and conscious performance.[55]

It is also an age of enquiry, of observation, speculation and detection, where self-reflexivity and performance emphasise how identity is constructed through mutual viewing. These two texts, read against one another, suggest the power of social viewing in the 1820s: a new 'spirit of inquiry' that uncomfortably combines the prurient activity of spying and the judicious activity of observation. Paul Pry and Mrs Fry may seem odd bedfellows, but they are equally characteristic figures in a scene where the process of looking is itself under scrutiny.

[55] Hood, 'Ode to the Great Unknown', *Poetical Works*, p. 16.

Chapter 6

Regional News in 'Peacetime': The *Dumfries and Galloway Courier* in the 1820s

Gerard Lee McKeever

In its 12 February 1828 issue, the *Dumfries and Galloway Courier* reports on a major art exhibition in the market town of Dumfries. Before moving into descriptions of individual paintings, the newspaper's editor John McDiarmid pays tribute to this 'important day in the town', using the event to mark the prosperity of a Scottish burgh that had long been at the forefront of a culture of civic improvement in the eighteenth and early nineteenth centuries.[1] Reviewing the exhibition in a characteristically studied prose, McDiarmid writes of 'the witchery which resides in the painter's art'. With quotations from Byron, he records 'a complete transformation' of the town's New Assembly Rooms:

> Walls that were formerly bare and unbroken, seemed instinct, for the first time, with life and feeling; and many an eye that had witched others, when 'music arose with its voluptuous swell,' and 'lamps shone o'er fair women and brave men,' now became witched in their turn.

These reflections say as much about the *Courier* itself as the exhibition. 'The genteel pretensions of Dumfries were well established' by the 1820s and supported by a whole range of improving activities from public lighting to police Acts, with the *Courier* itself a significant cultural institution.[2] While seeking to materialise the life of a community in southwest Scotland and to interpret global affairs on their behalf, the 1820s *Courier* consistently draws attention to its own efforts at 'witchery'. This newspaper does not reach the aesthetic overabundance of some of the decade's periodicals – notably *Blackwood's Edinburgh Magazine* – but it is highly conscious of the literary texture of its medium. 'Who

---

[1] See Bob Harris and Charles McKean, *The Scottish Town in the Age of Enlightenment 1740–1820* (Edinburgh: Edinburgh University Press, 2014).

[2] Ibid. p. 54. Harris and McKean note that Dumfries had lighting as early as 1733 (p. 94), while the Dumfries Police Act 1787 was 'almost certainly the first such measure for a Scottish provincial town' (p. 96).

would have known that Fingal fought, had not his countryman Ossian sung?' McDiarmid writes, making clear the artistic imperative in the successful manifestation of culture.[3] In pursuing its own work of literary geography, the *Courier* is a telling contribution to the periodical culture of the 1820s that mediates a complex sense of place from a specific regional perspective.

The first issue of the *Courier* had appeared in print on 6 December 1809, under the editorship of the Reverend Henry Duncan, minister of Ruthwell parish in Dumfriesshire.[4] Duncan is better known for the Ruthwell Parish Bank he instituted the following year (an influential early example of a savings bank) and under his stewardship the early *Courier* was also explicitly a vehicle of social improvement. Its political identity was established by the first issue, in a commitment to serve 'a free and enlightened country, where the very lowest of the people are capable of reasoning on moral and political subjects', while carefully 'preserving the subordination of ranks': in other words, socially liberal but politically circumspect. In this form it provided a counterpoint to the establishment Toryism of the *Dumfries Weekly Journal* (1777–1833), a rivalry that was underlined when on 31 January 1810 the *Courier* changed publication day from Wednesday to the *Journal*'s Tuesday. Moreover, in and beyond its social activism, the *Courier* took steps to promote local coverage as a mark of distinctiveness. Foreign intelligence was to take a lead role in the news, but domestic matters 'particularly respecting the Southern districts of Scotland' were also a priority. An early list of agents covers London, Liverpool, Edinburgh, Glasgow, Castle-Douglas, Kirkcudbright, Newton Stewart, Stranraer, New Galloway, Sanquhar, Moffat, Lockerbie, Langholm, Annan and Ecclefechan, reflecting a thorough coverage of southwest Scotland within the British newspaper world.[5] At the same time, the *Courier* was also 'to be distinguished, not merely as a vehicle of correct and useful information, but also as a source of elegant Amusement', encouraging 'Genius and Learning in whatever rank they may be found'.[6] This question of taste would prove integral to its imaginative geography.

---

[3] *The Dumfries and Galloway Courier*, 12 February 1828, p. 4. Henceforth 'Courier'.
[4] The *Courier* was produced in collaboration with printer and bookseller George Johnstone until January 1812, when Duncan entered into a new arrangement with Colin Munro. I have been unable to consult an entire copy of the 14 January 1812 issue, but Munro is identified as printer in that of 21 January 1812, p. 4. Munro's connection appears to continue until the issue of 18 April 1820.
[5] *Courier*, 13 December 1809, p. 4.
[6] *Courier*, 6 December 1809, p. 1.

Eight years into its run, on 28 January 1817, the *Courier* led with a piece signed by Duncan explaining that printer Colin Munro's recent ill health and his own 'numerous professional avocations' had prompted him to bring in the 'assistance' of John McDiarmid, to whom he was handing editorial control. McDiarmid, arriving from the newly established *Scotsman* in Edinburgh, represented an emergent class of professional journalists and would remain editor until his death in 1852. The paper took on a newly explicit liberal politics during McDiarmid's tenure and was vocal through the years of the reform debates, while shedding some of Duncan's paternalistic attention to welfare in the community. Under Duncan, the paper had always shown literary ambition in, for example, its 'Occurrences' column (retitled 'Miscellaneous' on 6 March 1810) and in its editorials. However, that component was developed by McDiarmid, who brought a distinctive brand of reflective prose to bear, pushing the title stylistically further towards the genre of the magazine, with its condition of 'semi-permanence' as compared to the ephemerality of news copy.[7] This would make the *Courier* a springboard for McDiarmid's entry into the world of monthly magazines with the short-lived *Dumfries Monthly Magazine* (1825–6), as well as other works including a collected volume of essays, *Sketches from Nature* (1830), and an extended study of locale, *Picture of Dumfries* (1832).[8] In his touchstone 1867 history of Dumfries, William McDowall describes McDiarmid as 'a thorough master of the literary amenities', with a 'quiet, playful, and florid' style suited to 'droll stories', 'illustrative anecdotes and pleasing scenic sketches'.[9] McDiarmid's *Courier* took on a newly lyrical voice, not least in a commitment to natural history, antiquarianism, tales, topography, biography, travel, curiosities, weather and other subjects, that activates a varied palette of place writing in the newspaper form.

This chapter focuses on tensions around both literary register and geography in the periodical press. The *Courier* of the 1820s engages resourcefully with the form of the weekly newspaper, reflecting, perhaps, what we will see was Henry Duncan's own prediction of a newly complex publishing milieu in this tempestuous decade. Politically, Marilyn Butler locates 'a curious period of relative stasis' in the 1820s, during which

---

[7] See Richard Cronin, *Paper Pellets: British Literary Culture After Waterloo* (Oxford: Oxford University Press, 2010), p. 139.

[8] John McDiarmid, *Picture of Dumfries & Its Environs* (Edinburgh: John Gellatly, 1832).

[9] William McDowall, *History of the Burgh of Dumfries* (Edinburgh: Adam and Charles Black, 1867), p. 853.

literature 'became ideologically apathetic or confused'.[10] That judgement feels out of step with current emphases on the experimental vigour of these years – and risks underplaying the degree of social unrest – but it speaks to Duncan's sense that an inevitable diffusion of public sentiment in an era of relative peacetime, not to mention an erratic economy, would force newspapers to find more creative ways to appeal to their readerships.[11] It is impossible to disentangle such influences on McDiarmid's *Courier* from other factors, including his own tastes as a versatile man of letters and erstwhile poet. Nevertheless, the *Courier* grapples creatively with a regional lifeworld emerging from within the local, national and global communications networks of this period. It develops an emphatic commitment to its titular area that is characteristic of a range of the era's periodicals but carries differently in those outside the major centres of population: the clarity of the place-making act in titles such as the *Courier* curiously underlines the dynamic, imaginative work of geography. Southwest Scotland is far from unique in bearing a significant regional print culture that has been largely overlooked by scholars to date.[12] Proper scholarly recovery of the many and varied periodicals of the 1820s will continue to underline place itself as one of the most hotly contested categories at work in the decade.[13]

*

Periodicals enable highly focused acts of place-making and this is especially true when their various commercial, aesthetic, political and moral motivations are closely bound to the iteration of a localised public

---

[10] Marilyn Butler, *Romantics, Rebels and Reactionaries; English Literature and its Background, 1760–1830* (Oxford: Oxford University Press, 1981), p. 173.

[11] We should not overlook conflicts fought against the Ashanti and Burmese empires in the 1820s, nor indeed the 'radical war' of 1820 that is a sign of social unrest in Scotland during these years. In the local context, McDowall describes, for example, an 1826 meal riot (pp. 772–4), while 'by far the greatest riot that ever occurred in Dumfries' took place when the famous murderer William Hare was transported through the town in 1829 (pp. 774–9).

[12] On the mid-nineteenth century, see Helen Sarah Williams, 'Scotland's Regional Print Economy in the Nineteenth Century' (unpublished PhD thesis, Edinburgh Napier University, 2018). Harris and McKean have articulated the culture of provincial enlightenment from which these publishing endeavours emerged in *The Scottish Town*. See also G. W. Shirley, 'Dumfries Printers in the Eighteenth Century, with Handlists of Their Books', *Transactions of the Dumfriesshire and Galloway Natural History & Antiquarian Society*, 3rd series, 18 (1934), 129–86.

[13] See for example Victoria E. M. Gardner's social history of newspaper production in *The Business of the News in England, 1760–1820* (Basingstoke: Palgrave Macmillan, 2016), and Hannah Barker on the politics of English journalism in *Newspapers, Politics, and Public Opinion in Late Eighteenth-Century England* (Oxford: Clarendon Press, 1998), both of which emphasise a provincial context in England.

sphere. The ubiquity of place names in regional or non-metropolitan titles is of more than passing significance. The *Dumfries and Galloway Courier* acquired both its identity and commercial viability in primarily geographical terms, where the London context meant that titles like the *Lady's Magazine*, or indeed the *Gazetteer and New Daily Advertiser*, could pitch to their demographic rather differently. Relatively limited circulations always affected editorial decisions: as Hannah Barker comments of 'provincial' newspapers in England, these journals became 'so closely associated with their place of production' in large part because 'locally made sales were of overriding importance'.[14] Even when actual local content was sparse, the regional marketplace emphasised local identity as a selling-point, in titles designed to cater sensitively and punctually to their immediate communities' reading appetites, while also accommodating constituencies of interested readers further afield.[15] Such commitments to the local were making a virtue of necessity, this being the point on which these newspapers and magazines could gain a competitive advantage.

This is not to ignore the profound acts of place-making in metropolitan periodicals: London is vividly materialised as a social text in the period's magazines and newspapers, a process in which regional titles collaborated through their cut-and-pasting of news from the London papers (although that flowed both ways). We need to be careful not to draw too firm a distinction between the London papers and their competitors, even if the former's market dominance rather suggests a binary metropole/province perspective; and even if London was sometimes described as inhabiting a unique condition of placelessness: 'indescribable and cacophonous', both 'everywhere and nowhere'.[16] In general, the fluidity of periodical print manifests less hierarchically ordered or networked spatial relations, such as have been championed by archipelagic criticism.[17] Indeed, one of the animating dreams of the newspaper as a form is the annihilation of distance as such. But there does remain a genuine difference in kind here between the milieu of

---

[14] Barker, *Newspapers, Politics*, p. 134.

[15] Allan Cunningham, living in London from 1810 until his death in 1842, evidently remained at least an occasional reader of the Dumfries newspapers. See, for example, David Hogg, *The Life of Allan Cunningham* (Dumfries: John Anderson, 1875), p. 174.

[16] Ian Newman and Gillian Russell, 'Metropolitan Songs and Songsters: Ephemerality in the World City', *Studies in Romanticism*, 58.4 (Winter, 2019), 429–49 (p. 430). For Thomas De Quincey, London's 'mighty labyrinths' meant overwhelming anonymity. See *Confessions of an English Opium-Eater and Other Writings*, ed. Robert Morrison (Oxford: Oxford University Press, 2013), p. 34.

[17] See John Kerrigan, *Archipelagic English: Literature, History, and Politics 1603–1707* (Oxford: Oxford University Press, 2008).

London or indeed Edinburgh – more liable to be coded as national or cosmopolitan – and that of southwest Scotland, less inscribed to begin with, being articulated ('imagined') primarily for the benefit of a local readership.[18] And, counterintuitively, the distinctive local attachment of a publication like the *Courier* can strangely accentuate the instability of cultural geography. Where we might expect to find the sense of place in its most tangible form, we are confronted not only with the dynamic melange of global spaces that constitute a single regional perspective, but also with the subjective and literary qualities of the act. Much the same insight might be adapted for news, as a genre where a (notionally) quotidian formal condition makes any sign of the literary imagination more conspicuous.

Many of the supposedly 'provincial' periodicals that were springing up across Britain and the anglophone world in this period were neither parochial nor conservative in their form. Regional space, in these texts, emerges from an interaction of local, national and global cultures. It is worth noting the degree to which newspapers were conceived in the 1820s as essentially a source of parliamentary and foreign news, a view implicit in John Mactaggart's 1824 description of a Galloway reader: 'Politics and newspapers he was always very fond of; still inquiring at those whom he thought skilled in these matters, how the war was coming on.'[19] The decade has also been identified in work on the English context as a moment in which newspapers helped to rebalance power away from London towards newly 'organized provincial interests, especially in Northern England and the Midlands', where cities like Manchester and Birmingham were to the fore.[20] At the same time, across their news coverage, advertisements, notices, editorials, original poetry, tales and other features, newspapers offered a key site for an evolving interest in particularised local experience.

Scholars of world-systems theory have long considered print the medium for a confrontation between the local and an emergent global information network in this period.[21] More specifically, the complex regionality developed by an array of periodicals like the *Courier* was closely bound up in their negotiation of the 'literary'. This involved a

---

[18] See below for the distinctive case of *Blackwood's* and Edinburgh.

[19] John Mactaggart, *The Scottish Gallovidian Encyclopedia* (London: Printed for the author, 1824), p. 55.

[20] See William Anthony Hay, *The Whig Revival, 1808–1830* (Basingstoke: Palgrave Macmillan, 2005), pp. 2–3; Donald Read, *The English Provinces c. 1760–1960: A Study in Influence* (London: Edward Arnold, 1964), p. 81.

[21] See, for example, Pascale Casanova, *The World Republic of Letters*, trans. Malcolm DeBevoise (Cambridge, MA: Harvard University Press, 2004).

long-standing continuum between the genres of the newspaper and the magazine, which were very often produced by the same people. From magazines' perspective, that hybridity was newly under pressure by a stamp duty of 4d on newspapers, part of a wider government attempt to regulate access to knowledge. On the newspaper side, the ascendant force of *The Times* was among titles setting new standards of reporting and analysis in the 1820s, but papers of all statures typically featured at least some diverting or lighter material, ranging from extensive original poetry and fiction to occasional stylistic flourishes, reprinted squibs and anecdotes. Still, emerging from an era marked by the increasing sophistication of the editorial article as a declaration of identity, the *Courier* is a strident example of an attempt to inject a coherent liter- ary personality into newspapers in a way that evokes a tradition of characterful magazine writing stretching back to Joseph Addison and Richard Steele that was being retooled for the 1820s in *Blackwood's*, the *London Magazine* and elsewhere. This porous generic condition was well adapted to a regional marketplace such as southwest Scotland, where a specialised literary periodical seems to have been less viable, as the failure of McDiarmid's own magazine venture suggests. In general, periodicals' interchange of registers (including fiction proper) heaps pressure on the boundary between the literary and the factual, with con- sequences for the places they presume to inhabit. Ian Duncan has made a claim for the novel, under the guidance of Walter Scott, as a site where 'romance' became a way of expressing modernity in the early nineteenth century, but the newspaper and the magazine both have at least as good a claim on a dramatic enabling of the literary imagination.[22]

*

When passing on the editorship of the *Courier* to McDiarmid in 1817, Duncan made clear that it would have to adapt to a changing environ- ment. Writing eighteen months after the Battle of Waterloo, he reflected on 'the increasing difficulty of conducting a Newspaper in times of peace and domestic embarrassment, so as to accomplish the important ends to which this great literary engine may be applied'. As he continued,

> During the late war, the public interest was so strongly excited towards one great object of paramount importance, and the whole energies of the state were so concentrated in one point, and so readily exerted in one direction, that the Editor of a Newspaper could not easily mistake the path of duty, or fail in gratifying the laudable curiosity, and in carrying along with him the

---

[22] See Ian Duncan, *Scott's Shadow: The Novel in Romantic Edinburgh* (Princeton, NJ: Princeton University Press, 2007), p. xii.

feelings, of his readers. But in such a period as the present, when sudden and total change in our political relations has been accompanied with a revulsion of public sentiment and a temporary depression of public prosperity, the part of those who conduct the vehicle of intelligence becomes more arduous and complicated.[23]

The year 1817 also saw the Burgh of Dumfries 'brought to the verge of bankruptcy': McDowall writes that the town had 'been living beyond its means' 'for a hundred years or more', and these financial difficulties would continue well into the next decade.[24] More generally, Duncan's statement now reads like a prescient forecast of the literary culture of the 1820s, which scholars increasingly characterise in terms of innovation and generative uncertainty, taking account of a tempestuous post-war economy that would eventually crash during 1825 and 1826. This is the environment in which David Stewart identifies the apex of an experimental, emergent magazine culture, as well as a poetics of 'doubt'.[25] It is the setting for what Ian Duncan calls a 'postmodern' phase in the Scottish novel, marked by texts like Walter Scott's *Redgauntlet* and James Hogg's *The Private Memoirs and Confessions of Justified Sinner* (both 1824).[26] It is a period characterised by Angela Esterhammer in terms of a pervasive culture of 'improvisation'.[27] This era of creativity was not confined to what we now think of as 'literary' textual forms. The new political stridency of the 1820s *Courier* may have substituted for the commercial reliability of war reportage, but the aesthetic turn of the paper also tallies with Henry Duncan's prediction that innovation would be a necessity as titles looked to meet a newly complex public taste. It was not alone in this respect: between 1817 and 1824, for example, the novelist Christian Isobel Johnstone was busy giving the *Inverness Courier* 'a literary distinction not usually found in provincial newspapers'.[28]

By January 1827, McDiarmid was announcing that, 'Notwithstanding the depression of the times', the *Courier*'s circulation was growing, then

---

[23] *Courier*, 28 January 1817, p. 1.

[24] McDowall, *History of Dumfries*, p. 755. Interestingly, Harris and McKean cite 'the new emphasis on loyal and patriotic celebration' in the 1790s as a factor in stretching the town's finances, suggesting the rather complicated domestic economics of war (*The Scottish Town*, p. 124).

[25] David Stewart, *Romantic Magazines and Metropolitan Literary Culture* (Basingstoke: Palgrave Macmillan, 2011), and *The Form of Poetry in the 1820s and 1830s: A Period of Doubt* (Basingstoke: Palgrave Macmillan, 2018).

[26] Duncan, *Scott's Shadow*, pp. 246–7.

[27] See Angela Esterhammer, *Print and Performance in the 1820s: Improvisation, Speculation, Identity* (Cambridge: Cambridge University Press, 2020).

[28] Fred Hunter, 'Johnstone [née Todd; other married name M'Leish], Christian Isobel (1781–1857), journalist and author', *Oxford Dictionary of National Biography*, 23 September 2004, doi: 10.1093/ref:odnb/14957.

at '1382 copies weekly'.[29] This suggests a degree of success in navigating the post-Waterloo landscape. Again, due deference must be paid to the longer-term cross-pollination of newspapers and magazines, and the transition between Duncan and McDiarmid was a modulation rather than a reinvention: the new, more polished *Courier* was building on and consolidating a range of existing elements. Poetry, for example, had always been a regular feature, while back on 20 December 1809, Duncan's editorial had printed a letter outlining what appeared to be a supernatural episode: a man riding through a storm is suddenly confronted by 'something bright dancing in the air', his 'whip-lash' catches fire and 'the sound of a foot' confirms that he must have encountered 'a *dead-light*, or an *elf-candle*', before the enlightened voice of the editor intervenes to explain the episode as a case of the '*Ignus fatuus*', 'called by the people in this country "*Will-a-wisp*"'.[30] This is news firmly inhabiting the generic territory of the tale or the antiquarian curiosity; or rather, it is an example of a porous relationship between such forms stretching back into the eighteenth century. Even so, the discrete, modern category of the 'literary' was reaching towards maturity in the 1820s and periodicals like the *Courier* were engaged in a conscious blending of genre.[31] Duncan, for his part, would go on to publish didactic fiction before turning his hand to the *Sacred Philosophy of the Seasons*, an ambitious piece of natural theology.[32] Building on Duncan's lineage at the *Courier*, then, a whimsical brand of reflective prose becomes McDiarmid's calling card in and beyond the editorial.

The 'Dumfries' editorial for 12 March 1822 begins, 'We have had another week of the most frightful weather', before continuing that, 'Among an agricultural and maritime population, a season of extraordinary inclemency, from whatever cause, never fails to form an era in the rustic's calendar.' This annalistic material is not without a 'harder' news quality: McDiarmid notes 'damages to the extent of nearly a million of money' caused by recent high winds, before moving into anecdotal reporting of the storms ('In Castle-Street, Dr Dalziel's house again suffered severely') and pointing to similar experiences in the other Scottish newspapers. Yet the digestion of all this in a polished piece that draws

---

[29] *Courier*, 2 January 1827, p. 4.

[30] *Courier*, 20 December 1809, p. 3.

[31] See David Duff, *Romanticism and the Uses of Genre* (Oxford: Oxford University Press, 2009).

[32] See, for example, Henry Duncan, *The Young South Country Weaver; or, A Journey to Glasgow: A Tale for the Radicals*, 2nd edn (Edinburgh: Waugh & Innes, 1821), and *Sacred Philosophy of the Seasons; Illustrating the Perfections of God in the Phenomena of the Year*, 4 vols (Edinburgh: William Oliphant, 1836–7).

out a clear moral ('feel grateful to Providence that things are not worse'), turns the editorial into a higher-status essay that happens to have as its subject the news; or put another way, it turns the raw data of the news into source material for incidental philosophy.[33] With his professional training, McDiarmid was equipped to provide a sophisticated, artful mediation of events in a way that might helpfully offset the overwhelming complexity of the 1820s media environment for the reader and he frequently does so by appealing to a poetics of the local.

The 3 June 1823 editorial begins with material on the war between Spain and France, before a piece that is critical of the Orange Order's persecution of Catholics in Ireland and a moral essay about 'boxiana': 'the prize ring is the true school of blackguardism'. Again, one of the effects of the regionality of a title like the *Courier*, with its particular grounding in a local circulation, is to illuminate the complex, transnational geography that a reader of the 1820s is being invited to share, casting the precise size and shape of locality as an ongoing, open question. Next, McDiarmid turns to the traditional celebration of 'Whitsun Wednesday' to reflect that, 'Time out of mind the Wednesday following the 26th of May has been celebrated as a sort of rural carnival by the respectable peasantry of Dumfries-shire and Galloway.' There is an evident change of tone here, as a breezier element that was beginning to shine through in the piece on boxing fully breaks out:

> It is meet and fitting, therefore, that those who have owed allegiance to the same roof-tree—who have toiled together through summer's heat and winter's cold—who have become, in a word, friends and acquaintance—should as Beattie says, enjoy 'one whole day of revelry and mirth,' before they separate,—never, perhaps to meet again, unless it be on some similar occasion.[34]

The uplift in style is not coincidental: as this editorial contracts from world news into local colour it expands proportionately in literary freedom. Local subjects potentially enable such aesthetic whimsy, which might be offensive in regard to more 'serious' matter. In this way, McDiarmid's authorial presence in the *Courier* suggestively articulates the intimacy of the local: often, perhaps, that which we are least able to remain detached about.

Still, the literary forces at work in the *Courier* countenance no strict boundaries. On 2 April 1822, the editorial recasts the news explicitly in the form of prose fiction, staging itself as a dialogue that begins, '"Well," said

---

[33] *Courier*, 12 March 1822, p. 4.
[34] *Courier*, 3 June 1823, p. 4.

Tom McTurk, (an old man-of-war's man, and mate of a foreign trading vessel) to his friend Jacob, the carpenter, "what do you think of this decision of Lord Stowel's?"[35] The strategy is reprised in the 15 October editorial (now 'Dumfries Courier'), which opens, 'In our last we left our whiggish friend Peter declaiming against the Holy Allies.'[36] Slippages between news and entertainment were not in themselves new for the 1820s, but this material is nonetheless indicative of a dissatisfaction with the narrower formal limitations of journalism, McDiarmid insisting that the profession exploit all the literary tools available to it. In November 1827, the *Courier* covers the death of a local women named Janet Williamson, described as a servant who had been wrongfully accused of theft. After a local man 'observed a female bonnet sticking amidst a mass of sand and sludge . . . her lifeless body was found in an upright posture, embeded [*sic*] in the spongy soil'. This might be Gothic enough, but McDiarmid, instructively, cannot resist a sequence of flourishes, speculating on Williamson 'wandering in the dark by the river side, meditating suicide, and yet afraid to commit the dreadful act', before noting that, 'If report may be credited, piercing cries were heard', though 'the sea-bird's scream or the fitful blast, alone answered to her dying wail'.[37]

Ongoing taxonomic decisions helped to shape McDiarmid's *Courier*. The presentation of a separate 'Weekly Summary' of the news, for example, could free up the editorial itself to take a more meditative approach.[38] In all, and despite the extensive coverage of both national and international affairs in the editorial as elsewhere as part of McDiarmid's curated regional geography, the literariness that distinguishes his stewardship is revealed nowhere better than in the *Courier*'s attention to the local. On 17 January 1826, the editorial moves from the 'only news of importance this week', regarding 'the individual who is to fill the Russian throne', into a longer piece headed 'Rural Affairs'. This article converts a notice of the recent 'Old New-year's-day' festivities into a piece of sentimental antiquarianism, in which the newspaper offers a polite mediation of events, with the day's activities framed by a picturesque contemplation of the surrounding countryside:

> The distant hills were covered with snow–the sky betokened a feeding storm– the cranreugh crept on every bush and blade–the plough rested midway in the furrow–and in a word, the wintry appearance of every thing without, added not a little to the snugness and bienness of every thing within.

---

35 *Courier*, 2 April 1822.
36 *Courier*, 15 October 1822, p. 4.
37 *Courier*, 17 November 1827, p. 4.
38 See *Courier*, 5 October 1819, pp. 3–4.

With Scots terms highlighting the switch in register, McDiarmid invites his readers into the familiar world of the local, activating as he does so readerly expectations about the connection between landscape and poetry. Subsequent notices about sales in the local cattle market are reframed by a history of these same markets in the editorial, just as a piece on curling matches is historiographical in tone, beginning: 'The two parishes of Carlaverock and Ruthwell have long been remarkable for the kindly disposition which the inhabitants entertain towards each other.'[39] Coming in the middle of a winter in which McDiarmid's editorials would eventually shift from self-congratulation that the financial crisis was avoiding Scotland to sharp concerns about its local impact ('a general death-blow' having 'paralyzed the whole activity of the country'), this issue contains a transitory vision of 'prosperous times'.[40] In general, it is symptomatic of the 1820s *Courier* in seeking to curate current events into the components of an irregular, ongoing essay on locale by the editor-author, with an implicit ambition to reward habitual readers much in the way that numbers of a magazine might sustain through-lines across and beyond collected volumes.

Back on 9 July 1822, the 'Dumfries' column had led with an essay on the agricultural condition of the southwest stimulated by the fact that, 'Within the last ten days we have traversed the greater part of Galloway.'[41] If the 'Romantic local was increasingly drawn into a discourse of domestic tourism and ethnographic objectification' in the 1820s, the *Courier* of this decade frequently acts like a purveyor of internal tourism, reflecting back (or rather, imagining) a view of Dumfriesshire and Galloway for the benefit of a section of its inhabitants, and in doing so apparently gratifying their 'complicated' tastes; while readers of the paper in Liverpool, London, Glasgow and Edinburgh are invited to share in this sense of proximate intimacy.[42] Mainland Europe may have been more accessible in these years than it had been under wartime conditions, but local attachments were evidently a hot commodity in the 1820s, when Scott's antiquarian fiction was selling in astonishing quantities and *Blackwood's* was reshaping the periodical culture with its distinctively performative tales of locale.[43] In 1830's *Sketches from Nature*, McDiarmid collected together writings on 'fragments of

---

[39] *Courier*, 17 January 1826, p. 4.

[40] *Courier*, 13 December 1825, p. 4; 28 March 1826, p. 4; 17 January 1826, p. 4.

[41] *Courier*, 9 July 1822, p. 4.

[42] Penny Fielding, *Scotland and the Fictions of Geography: North Britain 1760–1830* (Cambridge: Cambridge University Press, 2008), p. 161.

[43] For Scott's sales figures, see William St Clair, *The Reading Nation in the Romantic Period* (Cambridge: Cambridge University Press, 2004), pp. 632–44.

Scottish scenery and character', as well as 'anecdotes illustrative of the habits of animals', in a text that emerged out of the *Courier*'s editorial, with a governing emphasis on the southwest in articles ranging from 'The Mull of Galloway' to 'Gretna Green'.[44] Of course, literary matters of form, content and quality alone cannot explain a newspaper's success, but McDiarmid's editorial brand was committed to expressing regional identity in a way that would be both entertaining and useful for readers. And while the emphatic location of a journal like the *Courier* throws the global complexity of its sense of place into relief, it also helps to crystallise the fundamentally imaginative aspect of belonging: the idea of southwest Scotland it produces is often a self-consciously literary sign.

*

The *Courier* emerged from a rich print culture in southwest Scotland stretching back to the pioneering activities of the Rae family in the first part of the eighteenth century: Robert Rae's short-lived *Dumfries Mercury* (1721) is a remarkably early example of a town newspaper.[45] It is not possible to give an overview of the evolution of publishing in the area here, except to say that the *Courier*, the *Weekly Journal* and Dumfries-based magazines shared the 1820s from a local perspective with titles like the *Ayr and Wigtownshire Courier* (1818–c. 1825) and *Air [Ayr] Advertiser* (1803–), both of which were published in Ayr and thus compassed the western parts of Galloway within their own immediate catchments on a north–south axis. I do, however, want to pause to briefly introduce the *Castle-Douglas Weekly Visitor* (1823–32), a small journal under the stewardship of printer Anthony Davidson that flirted with the grey area between news and magazine writing, though the news elements were restricted to avoid incurring the stamp duty. Speaking from the perspective of the emerging small town of Castle Douglas, the *Weekly Visitor* openly advertised anxieties about parochialism while seeking to put Wigtownshire and Kirkcudbrightshire on the literary map, being 'the only periodical that has ever appeared in a quarter lying sae far distant frae the centre o' literary encouragement'.[46] Through its own rather more extreme vision of the local, the *Weekly Visitor* can help to illuminate the effects at work in the *Courier*.

The *Weekly Visitor* featured a version of 'Chit Chat', an established format in the period's magazines and a sign of the conversational

---

[44] John McDiarmid, *Sketches from Nature* (Edinburgh: Oliver & Boyd; London: Simpkin & Marshall, 1830), pp. 8–9.

[45] See Shirley, 'Dumfries Printers in the Eighteenth Century', pp. 131–40.

[46] *The Castle-Douglas Weekly Visitor, and Literary Miscellany*, 18 December 1829, p. 2. The journal was titled the *Castle-Douglas Miscellany* until 1829.

informality popularised by Leigh Hunt's *Examiner*. More specifically, the *Visitor*'s adaptation was one of the period's many homages to the 'Noctes Ambrosianae' in *Blackwood's Edinburgh Magazine*.[47] In place of the loose fictionalisations of John Wilson, James Hogg and others found in the 'Noctes', the *Visitor*'s reworking featured pseudonymous local characters engaged in a similar diet of gossip, literary criticism and miscellaneous horseplay. To understand the effect of this in the *Visitor*, we need to return to the April 1822 'Noctes', in which Christopher North half-jokingly describes London as 'the most provincial spot alive' before announcing: 'Our ambition is, that our wit shall be local all over the world.'[48] For all its hegemonic position in the nineteenth century, London, North declares, is in fact inward-looking and self-obsessed, while he envisages *Blackwood's* Edinburgh 'wit' forming a new, genuinely global consciousness, propelling the geographical designation in the journal's title into the condition of a household brand. The 'Noctes' aim at this universality in counterintuitive terms, however, deploying a barrage of thickly textured local detail that is designed to be incomprehensible to at least a significant proportion of readers. As Stewart comments, 'the joke is not the local references but the absurd nature of making local references in a broadly-circulated journal'.[49] We might recall here Joseph Rezek's argument that, by orienting their writings towards a mass market (specifically the publishing centre of London), 'provincial' authors in this period were helping to generate an 'autonomous' view of the aesthetic; that is, 'literature' in the idealised and commodified modern sense.[50] Certainly the example of the 'Noctes' suggests a mass experience in which *locality as such* begins to signify as much as actual local detail, presenting a register of authentic experience in a set of clues to something that may turn out to have been imaginary all along.

What happens, then, when this aestheticisation of the local (a version of what Roland Barthes calls 'reality effects') is taken up by other, more obviously local publications?[51] In the 8 January 1830 instalment of the

---

[47] See the March 1822 issue of *Blackwood's Edinburgh Magazine*, pp. 369–71, for the first appearance of the 'Noctes', which ran until February 1835. For the origins of this specific format, see 'Table-Talk', *The Examiner*, 9 May 1813, pp. 299–300.

[48] *Blackwood's Edinburgh Magazine*, April 1822, p. 488.

[49] Stewart, *Romantic Magazines*, p. 137.

[50] Joseph Rezek, *London and the Making of Provincial Literature: Aesthetics and the Transatlantic Book Trade, 1800–1850* (Philadelphia: University of Pennsylvania Press, 2015), pp. 14–15.

[51] Roland Barthes, 'The Reality Effect' [1969], in *The Rustle of Language*, trans. Richard Howard, ed. François Wahl (Berkeley: University of California Press, 1989), pp. 141–8.

Weekly Visitor's 'Chit Chat', the discussion turns on the landscape of the Glenkens valley in the northern part of Kirkcudbrightshire, which is presented as a 'pure specimen' of Galloway in a way that recalls attitudes to the Scottish Highlands as a reservation of national virtue. The piece foregrounds 'the laws o' association', with the valley emerging from an accumulation of associative detail including pastoralism, personal memories, lyrical commonplaces like 'the blue hills o' Galloway' and indeed the exotic counterpoint of the Alps. It thus insists upon the cultural quality of place, to the degree that the speaker Archie Fairnyear reflects anxiously that,

> Nae man wi' brains in his scull can open his ee on sic a landscape, but he maun feel his imagination growing teeming o' a' the shadowy, half-defined analogies that serve us to connect the warld o' matter wi' the warld o' mind . . . yet for a' that, I'm no very sure gif my extemporaneous description o' that grand panorama . . . might afford *you* a' the delight that my ain babblings gie to mysell.[52]

The distance between matter and mind, of course, is further complicated by the intercession of the literary, and Fairnyear represents solipsism as an extreme outcome of subjective forms of belonging, with his imaginative geography dangerously close to private 'babblings'. Writing, here, becomes a performance of communion with readers and with the environment in which 'Galloway' involves a precarious creative act. And in a publication that is emphatically both *by* and *for* a group of local people, in which the notion of a small community talking to itself is much less of an ironic ploy than in the 'Noctes', the text's intimate geography underlines rather than mitigates the work of the imagination. Inhabiting a periphery to a periphery, and in fact developing parochialism as a constitutive principle, the *Weekly Visitor* restores the Blackwoodian poetics of belonging to a defined local orbit where it becomes more rather than less strange. Parochialism does not cause 'Galloway' to resolve itself into phenomenological immediacy, but rather offers up the sense that local attachment is always a matter of projection. The same is true in a much less extreme way of the *Courier*: the force of location possessed by a journal with such a keen geographical orientation highlights both the complex horizons and the imaginative act involved in any manifestation of place.

*

Improvisational, doubt-ridden, proliferating: there is a growing scholarly consensus that the 1820s are a moment of ideological calibration,

---

[52] *Castle-Douglas Weekly Visitor*, 8 January 1830, pp. 2–4.

at least in the literary sphere. To whatever degree that historical narrative obtains, it was not confined to the remarkable high points in the development of the novel or the short story in this decade, but penetrated the full spectrum of periodical print, including newspapers. In the case of publishing endeavours in the southwest of Scotland, this saw the development of a long-standing commitment to registering and indeed mediating an experience of the region through the lens of text. Stylistically, the *Courier* of the 1820s nicely follows on from Henry Duncan's prognostication about this decade. While a continuum between news and magazine content, as well as creative literary strategies, had earlier been a feature of periodicals in southwest Scotland as elsewhere, McDiarmid's essayistic, unified and entertainingly literary approach to his newspaper was a key innovation locally that seems to have been conducive to its historical moment. From the perspective of the 1860s, at least, McDowall was convinced that, 'It was not the bare news itself, abundant as that was, which made the Courier so popular; but it was the style of the composition—so easy, quaint, and mellifluous—that rendered it a general favourite.'[53] Not long before McDiarmid's death in 1852, a poem titled 'Ode to our Marvellous Contemporary' appeared in *Punch*, proclaiming devotion to the paper's lively qualities:

> Thou art the Print for me,
> > *Dumfries Courier*;
> Such wondrous things in thee
> > Ever appear:
> Toads pent in solid trees,
> Enormous gooseberries,
> All sorts of prodigies,
> > Right through the year.[54]

The *Courier* played a part in the ongoing recalibration of the newspaper–magazine continuum in the nineteenth century and, per McDowall, obtained 'more than a district reputation' in doing so.[55]

Ruth Livesey has characterised nineteenth-century Britain in terms of a stage coach journey, which integrates diverse localities while remaining riven by 'halts' and 'stops'.[56] With its title alluding to a mail coach, the *Dumfries and Galloway Courier* inhabits one of those 'stops', conceiving the period's national and global interrelations from a thickly

[53] McDowall, *History of Dumfries*, p. 853.

[54] *Punch; or The London Charivari*, 19 June 1852, p. 256.

[55] McDowall, *History of Dumfries*, p. 853.

[56] Ruth Livesey, *Writing the Stage Coach Nation: Locality on the Move in Nineteenth-Century British Literature* (Oxford: Oxford University Press, 2016), p. 30.

textured, specific point of view. And in the end, what the regionality of the *Courier* suggests is neither the easy deference of the local to the national and the global, nor its parochial isolation, but a sense of place itself as a dynamic contingency. Following Benedict Anderson, the imagined community remains one of the most useful tools for understanding what newspapers do.[57] Yet one of the things that model tends to under-emphasise is the uneven nesting of such communities within and on top of each other, so that when newspapers sought to materialise publics in the 1820s, they did so in dialogue with what William E. Connolly calls 'eccentric' attachment, associated with modernity's compression of our experience of space and characterised by 'crosscutting allegiances, connections, and modes of collaboration'.[58] That complexity – a kind of spatial laissez-faire – is active in the *Courier*'s regional consciousness that is at once local, national and global. And with its promise of phenomenological immediacy, it is the emphatic grounding of this geography that powerfully underlines its 'eccentric' qualities, including the relationship of subjectivity and objectivity so strikingly materialised in newspapers. This is emblematised in the heading of the *Courier*'s editorial – whether 'Dumfries' or 'Dumfries Courier' – a location and literary-cultural text ('place') from which the world is mediated.

Reflecting on a 'Scarcity of News' in January 1826, McDiarmid noted the 'little shifts' that 'every news-vendor' must adopt from time to time.[59] There was hardly a scarcity of news in the 1820s, but the *Courier* was a regional newspaper that could cope regardless. It participated in a complex and wide-ranging culture of place writing in the 1820s in and beyond the periodicals that incorporated, for example, natural history, loco-descriptive poetry, fashionable 'Beauties' compendia and prose fictions inspired to varying degrees by Walter Scott, from John Galt's *Annals of the Parish* (1821) to Mary Russell Mitford's *Our Village* series (published in *The Lady's Magazine* from 1819 and collected in five volumes between 1824 and 1832). With its abundance of foreign news *and* decisive local bearing, the *Courier* registers the strain on local attachment in a period of increased mobility, but also its resilience as the supreme register of belonging. 'It would be easy to give a long list of names who, as soldiers, sailors, and civilians, acquired both fame and fortune abroad, and who after an absence, more or less protracted, returned to their native district, purchased land, planned, built, planted

---

[57] Benedict Anderson, *Imagined Communities: Reflections on the Origin and Spread of Nationalism*, 2nd edn (London: Verso, 1991).

[58] William E. Connolly, *Neuropolitics: Thinking, Culture, Speed* (Minneapolis: University of Minnesota Press, 2002), p. 186.

[59] *Courier*, 24 January 1826, p. 4.

and improved', McDiarmid explained in 1832.[60] His newspaper is a textual parallel to this experience, grounding an imperial consciousness in Dumfries. Apropos, having noted Captain John Franklin's latest expedition 'of discovery and adventure' accompanied by 'our friend and townsman Dr [John] Richardson', the *Courier*'s editorial for 22 February 1825 turns to the Dumfries horse fair: 'Since the conclusion of the war, a brisker or better Candlemas Fair has not been known . . . in the crowd of purchasers we recognised so few "ken't faces" that many of them must have come from a great distance.'[61] It is this context, in which the editor might realistically expect to recognise a wide cross-section of the local population, that renders the complex horizons of the *Courier*'s place-making so conspicuous. It also underlines the imaginative performance at work; as when, in celebrating another festive day, McDiarmid places 'dramatis personae' in amongst painterly scenery dominated in the background by 'gigantic Criffel, uncurtained, unnight-capped as befitted the occasion'.[62]

Alistair Livingston has described Dumfries and Galloway today as an 'unimagined community', constituted by local publics that are too 'tangible and concrete' to need the aid of a newspaper in their imagining. At the same time, he suggests that the region's idiosyncrasy is glossed over in both Scottish and British nationalisms, so that, in effect, it is a historical lifeworld lacking cultural superstructure.[63] There is an element of truth to Livingston's observations: the southwest as an entity is perhaps only hesitantly 'imagined', while region in general remains a less understood, less overtly meaningful signifier than nation. Nevertheless, there is a long history to the construction of southwest Scotland in the cultural imagination, including in a rich tradition of regional newspapers and magazines. The 1820s *Courier* participated in an emergent world-system, but it is a reminder that literary entrepreneurship in this period meant not only diffusion in content, influences and styles, but also a variety of new attempts to realise the category of the local. Fiona Stafford describes the Romantic era as a time 'when local detail ceased to be regarded as transient, irrelevant or restrictive, and began to seem essential to art with any aspiration to permanence'.[64] Yet this interest

[60] McDiarmid, *Picture of Dumfries*, pp. 7–8.

[61] *Courier*, 22 February 1825, p. 4.

[62] *Courier*, 30 August 1825, p. 4.

[63] Alistair Livingston, 'An Unimagined Community', *Bella Caledonia*, 21 March 2017, available at https://bellacaledonia.org.uk/2017/03/21/an-unimagined-community/ (accessed 7 February 2022).

[64] Fiona Stafford, *Local Attachments: The Province of Poetry* (Oxford: Oxford University Press, 2010), p. 30.

in the local was achieving many of its peaks in that most ostensibly impermanent of forms: periodical print.

Author's Note

This chapter is an output of McKeever's British Academy Postdoctoral Fellowship entitled 'Regional Romanticism: Dumfriesshire and Galloway, 1770–1830', based at the University of Glasgow between 2017 and 2020.

Keyword: Liberal

John Gardner

As Raymond Williams notes, the meanings of words belong to their time, although within that moment definitions are 'sectarian'.[1] Significations belong to differing factions. The Google Books Ngram viewer shows peaks in the use of 'liberal' in the 1780s and again in the 1820s. Uday Singh Mehta argues that, in this time frame, liberalism came out of a 'substantially European' tradition and became 'self-consciously universal as a political, ethical and epistemological creed'.[2] But, as D. M. Craig writes, even 'by the end of the eighteen-twenties . . . it remained unclear precisely what a "liberal" was . . . "liberals" were not a firmly defined group and "liberalism" did not securely mark out a single intellectual phenomenon'.[3] In the 1820s, liberalism could mean support for free trade, reform, Catholic emancipation and a pro-European stance. Liberalism signalled being neither a Tory, nor a member of the labouring classes.

Writing in 1819, William Hazlitt simply identified liberalism with tolerance: 'It always struck me as a singular proof of good taste, good sense, and liberal thinking, in an old friend who had Paine's *Rights of Man* and Burke's *Reflections on the French Revolution*, bound up in one volume, and who said, that, both together, they made a very good book.'[4] In 1827 Thomas Hodgskin took a similar view: 'I trust that our countrymen are now much too liberal and enlightened to be offended with the honest expression' of opinions.[5] However, for the weaver

---

[1] Raymond Williams, *Keywords: A Vocabulary of Culture and Society* (Oxford: Oxford University Press, 1985), p. 16.

[2] Uday Singh Mehta, *Liberalism and Empire: A Study in Nineteenth-Century British Liberal Thought* (Chicago: Chicago University press, 1999), p. 1.

[3] D. M. Craig, 'The Origins of "Liberalism" in Britain: The Case of *The Liberal*', *Historical Research*, 85.229 (August 2012), 469–87 (p. 482).

[4] William Hazlitt, 'Thoughts on Taste', *The Edinburgh Magazine and Literary Miscellany*, 5 (July 1819), 13–16 (p. 16).

[5] Thomas Hodgskin, *Popular Political Economy: Four Lectures Delivered at the London Mechanics' Institution* (London: Tait, 1827), p. xv.

poet Samuel Bamford, liberalism was something only the educated and enfranchised could enjoy, not the working classes. In his preface to *The Weaver Boy*, Bamford has 'Liberal' as a class-bound word, associated with a particular kind of education:

> The candid reader . . . will bear in mind, that he is not perusing the productions of one who has been blessed with a 'Liberal Education'. That tis not an 'Oxford Scholar' whom he is reading. That tis a *'Weaver Boy of Lancashire,'* one of old Burke's Pigs, who has the audacity to lift his snout on high in the congregation of the Public, and thus 'rebelliously' to grunt in the presence of his 'betters'.[6]

For Bamford, whose training was occupational, a '"Liberal Education"' marks a class barrier between him and his '"betters"'. This corresponds with Raymond Williams's description of 'liberal education' as 'predominantly a class term: the skills and pursuits appropriate . . . to men of independent means and assured social position, as distinct from other skills and pursuits . . . appropriate to a lower class'.[7] A need for differentiation in the kind of education given to the middle classes was asserted by the poet Thomas Campbell:

> [the] middling rich—that is, all above the working classes and beneath the enormously rich—form a momentously important mass of society . . . it is desirable that all positions of it should be well educated . . . to keep the most influential body of the people liberal in their opinions, solid in their information, and respectably intellectual in their tastes and opinions.[8]

Campbell argues for the needs of the middling classes as a group who are distinct from both the very rich and the working classes. In his 1821 *Elements of Political Economy*, James Mill also desires that the children of 'men of middling fortunes . . . receive the best education, and are prepared for all of the higher and more delicate functions of society, as legislators, judges, administrators, teachers, inventors in all the arts, and superintendents in all the more important works'.[9] The working classes are not included here. They might be the beneficiaries of paternalistic liberal reforms, but they are not among the enfranchised.

Distinctions between the 'middle ranks', who evidently felt that they constituted a distinct group, and those who got their hands dirty, were assiduously policed. The Reverend Lionel Berguer stated in 1819: 'a

---

[6] Samuel Bamford, *The Weaver Boy* (Manchester: Observer Office, 1819), n.p.

[7] Williams, *Keywords*, p. 179.

[8] Thomas Campbell, *Letter to Henry Brougham on the Subject of a London University* (London: Longman, 1825), p 1.

[9] James Mill, *Elements of Political Economy* (London: Baldwin, Cradock and Joy, 1821), pp. 48–9.

REVOLUTION will be either prevented, or induced, according as the MIDDLE RANKS bestir themselves during the REBELLION'.[10] The Salford Reverend Melville Horne addressed the same group in 1820, writing that 'the Higher and Middle Classes should be made to feel the *necessity* of Union, courage and exertion'.[11] Maintaining class distinctions and the division of labour is at the heart of much liberal thinking in this period. There was a desire, as Philip Connell points out, to differentiate 'the intellectual attainments and pursuits of the leisured yet virtuous middle class from the mental debilitation attendant upon the increasingly specialized and "mechanical" pursuits of the labouring classes'.[12] Liberalism, then, was essentially for the 'middling ranks'. Economic liberalism might suit those engaged in trade, but consequently there were times when the working classes and high Tories became allies in national protectionism. Thomas Hodgskin argued in 1826 that the Tory government had been 'illiberal' in departing from 'liberal principles of free trade', on issues such as the Corn Laws.[13] The notion of the 'highs' and 'lows' being capable of an alliance is something that Lord Byron picks up on in his drama *Marino Faliero, Doge of Venice* (1821), where the Doge disastrously allies himself with plebeian rebels against the state.

It would be careless to say that all liberals shared the same viewpoints in the 1820s. John Seed warns that within 'radical liberalism of the early nineteenth-century ... There were always countervailing ideological elements'.[14] Nonetheless, repressive post-war measures against the labouring classes, culminating with Peterloo and the Six Acts of December 1819, enabled a more inclusive liberalism to appear. Vic Gatrell points out that popular outrage against these events allowed middle-class politicians 'to initiate political debate without fear of ... [being] regarded as "noisy demagogues"', arguing that 'from 1820, serious radical debate even among the respectable became a legitimate if not a popular pastime'.[15] After Peterloo it was now possible for liberals to push for reform without being overly identified with radicals, such

---

[10] Rev. Lionel Thomas Berguer, *A Warning Letter to His Royal Highness the Prince Regent, Intended Principally as a Call Upon the Middle Ranks, At this Important Crisis*, 4th edn (London: Allman, 1819), p. 36.

[11] Rev. Melville Horne, *The Moral and Political Crisis of England; Most Respectfully Inscribed to the Higher and Middle Classes* (London: Hatchard, 1820), p. 36.

[12] Philip Connell, *Romanticism, Economics, and the Question of 'Culture'* (Oxford: Oxford University Press, 2001), pp. 119–20.

[13] Hodgskin, *Popular Political Economy*, pp. 216–17.

[14] John Seed, 'Unitarianism, Political Economy and the Antinomies of Liberal Culture in Manchester, 1830–50', *Social History*, 7.1 (1982), 1–25 (p. 24).

[15] V. A. C. Gatrell, 'The Commercial Middle Class in Manchester, c. 1820–1857' (unpublished PhD dissertation, University of Cambridge, 1971), p. 199.

was the popular backlash against the actions on St Peter's Field, which even establishment newspapers, such as *The Times,* deplored.

On the journal that Byron, Percy Shelley and the Hunt brothers published in 1822, *The Liberal: Verse and Prose from the South*, Raymond Williams writes that 'liberal . . . as a political term' was 'proudly and even defiantly announced in the periodical title'.[16] However, in his preface to *The Liberal* Leigh Hunt states that:

> The object of our work is not political, except inasmuch as all writing now-a-days must involve something to that effect . . . We wish to do our work quietly, if people will let us,—to contribute our liberalities in the shape of Poetry, Essays, Tales, Translations, and other amenities, of which kings themselves may read and profit[.][17]

Hunt then mentions King John, the Magna Carta, and professes to like 'certain modern Barons, as well as those who got the Great Charter for us'. Hunt's persona is opposed to monarchical power, although he identifies with the 'Barons' as like-minded allies pushing for reform. Hunt's elite position defines the kind of liberalism that Bamford and the working classes cannot access. The journal, which went through only four issues, was roundly vilified. Hazlitt thought it an 'obnoxious publication (obnoxious alike to friend and foe)'.[18] William Gifford decried the 'new-invented Liberal-ities' of the journal.[19] Hazlitt mocked the incongruity of an aristocrat like Byron founding a paper like *The Liberal* as an alliance between the 'Patrician and "the Newspaper Man["]'.[20] He castigates 'Lord Byron's preposterous *liberalism*' as he 'may affect the principles of equality, but he resumes his privilege of peerage upon occasion'.[21] Byron's liberalism is 'preposterous' because he is an aristocrat. Hunt later wrote that 'Lord Byron in truth was afraid of Mr. Hazlitt; he admitted him like a courtier, for fear he should be treated by him as an enemy' and would 'take pains to show his polite friends that he had nothing in common with so inconsiderate a plebeian'.[22] Byron and Hazlitt are at either end of the liberal spectrum, with one a Lord and

---

16 Williams, *Keywords*, p. 149.

17 Leigh Hunt, 'Preface', *The Liberal*, 1 (1822), v–xii (p. vii).

18 William Hazlitt, 'On the Jealousy and the Spleen of Party', in *The Plain Speaker: Opinions on Books, Men and Things*, 2 vols (London: Colburn, 1826), vol. II, pp. 409–47 (p. 440).

19 William Gifford, *The Illiberal! Verse and Prose from the North!! Dedicated to my Lord Byron in the South* (London: Holt, 1822), n.p.

20 Hazlitt, 'On the Jealousy and the Spleen of Party', p. 438.

21 William Hazlitt, 'Lord Byron', in *The Spirit of the Age; or, Contemporary Portraits* (London: Colburn, 1825), pp. 147–68 (p. 166).

22 Leigh Hunt, *Lord Byron and Some of his Contemporaries*, 2 vols (London: Colburn, 1828), vol. I, pp. 63–4.

the other an 'inconsiderate ... plebeian'. However, no matter how far apart Byron and Hazlitt might be, they are still members of an extensive middle-class liberal set that people like Bamford could never join.

The Liberal, writes Jane Stabler, had, from its outset, 'a daringly pan-European identity'.[23] That first number contains celebrations of European literature from British poets who felt they could no longer live in Britain, such as Shelley's 'May-day Night' translation from Goethe's *Faust*. As Élie Halévy has argued, the noun Liberal comes from the *Liberales* of Spain who in 1812 opposed the monarchist *Serviles*.[24] The association with 'the South' also makes the journal distinctly European: warmer and less British than opposing publications such as the Tory *Courier*. The first edition of *The Liberal* ends hotly with images of violence that echo the recent European revolutions, the final piece being one of Byron's epigrams on the death of Lord Castlereagh. The self-murder of Castlereagh has the symbolism of revolutionary Europe with neck cutting being mentioned three times in the eight-line poem. *The Liberal* ends with 'So *He* has cut his throat at last!—He! Who? / The man who cut his country's long ago'.[25] The final line emphasises that unreformed Tory Britain was dead and impossible to live in.

In the 1820s, liberalism was associated with political tolerance, Catholic emancipation, the abolition of slavery and the reform of Parliament, although not all liberals embraced all of these issues. In the coming decades, liberalism did not necessarily mean extending the franchise either. As Edward Luce writes, 'the most self-improving Victorian liberals recoiled in horror at the notion the labouring classes would get to choose who governed Britain'.[26] By 1839 the Spanish associations of *Liberales* were forgotten and Lord John Russell was writing to Queen Victoria calling the Whigs the 'Liberal party', although the change of name for the party did not occur until 1859.[27] In the 1820s, 'liberal' was a dirty word to many in the upper classes. It represented a growing middle class who saw themselves as neither Tory nor working class. During this decade the middle ranks recognised more fully that they now constituted a distinct class. Liberalism was an expression of the middle classes becoming a class for itself.

---

[23] Jane Stabler, 'Religious Liberty in the "Liberal", 1822–23', in *BRANCH: Britain, Representation and Nineteenth-Century History*, ed. Dino Franco Felluga, available at https://www.branchcollective.org/?ps_articles=jane-stabler-religious-liberty-in-the-liberal (accessed 7 February 2022).

[24] Élie Halévy, *The Liberal Awakening, 1815–1830* (New York: Harcourt, 1924), p. 81.

[25] Lord Byron, 'Epigrams on Lord Castlereagh', *The Liberal*, 1 (1822), p. 164.

[26] Edward Luce, *The Retreat of Western Liberalism*, (London: Abacus, 2018), p. 114.

[27] Ivor Jennings, *Party Politics*, 3 vols (Cambridge: Cambridge University Press, 1961), vol. II, p. 76.

Keyword: Emigration

Porscha Fermanis

According to Harriet Martineau, it was in the mid-1820s that emigration, 'in the modern import of the word, first began seriously to engage the attention of society'. Looking back at the social and financial adjustments required by Britain's turn from a war- to a peace-time economy in *The History of England During the Thirty Years' Peace: 1816–1846* (1849), Martineau characterises the years 1824–6 as critical ones for Britain's domestic situation, outlining a disturbing 'spectacle of intoxication and collapse' fuelled by a major financial crash, poor harvests and rising food prices.[1] Martineau estimates that in 1820 nearly 18,000 British people emigrated to the North American colonies, while 1,063 went to the Cape Colony and 19,000 to the Australian settlements, with the number of emigrants increasing nearly threefold between 1821 and 1826.[2] If, as a neo-Malthusian, she ties emigration more closely to domestic 'seasons of adversity' than emigration statistics now support, Martineau is right in suggesting that mass voluntary emigration began to gather force in the 1820s – one million emigrants had left Britain by 1840 and over six million by 1870 – and that the emergence of large-scale Anglo-Saxon settler diasporas in North America, Australasia and southern Africa coincided with a period of almost unprecedented demographic growth and popular unrest within Britain itself.[3]

Other than unsuccessful middle-class attempts to channel radical unrest into campaigns for assisted emigration, there was little direct correlation between emigration and events such as the Peterloo Massacre of 1819. However, state-sponsored emigration schemes in the early 1820s did respond to the domestic upheaval and sense of social crisis

---

[1] Harriet Martineau, *The History of England During the Thirty Years' Peace: 1816–1846*, 2 vols (London: C. Knight, 1849), vol. I, pp. 371, 352–3.

[2] Martineau, *A History*, vol. I, p. 411.

[3] Ibid. p. 371; James Belich, *Replenishing the Earth: The Settler Revolution and the Rise of the Angloworld* (Oxford: Oxford University Press, 2009), pp. 5, 12, 23, 51, 83.

Martineau outlines, particularly to rising pauperism, the politicisation of discourses surrounding the taxation of food and the radicalising effects of post-1800 industrialisation.[4] Spearheading the emigration scheme to the inauspicious eastern frontier of the Cape Colony in 1820, as well as organising two waves of voluntary state-sponsored emigration from Ireland to Canada in 1823 and 1825, Robert Wilmot-Horton, under-secretary at the Colonial Office, argued that the British and Irish pauper problem could best be relieved by continuous, planned emigration on a national scale, imagining the transformation of unemployed Britons into productive working-class communities of 'new world peasant proprie-tors' in terms very similar to Robert Owen's *Report to the County of New Lanark* (1820).[5]

Wilmot-Horton's ambitious Emigration Bill, which proposed the assisted emigration of 95,000 people, failed to find funding as the decade came to a close.[6] By the time that Edward Gibbon Wakefield came to promote his alternative view of 'systematic colonisation' in the late 1820s, the continued scarcity and high cost of white labour in the colonies had led many reformers and political economists, including Owen and Thomas Malthus, to become (or remain) sceptical of external settlement schemes, considering them 'misplaced solution[s]' to endemic domestic problems.[7] Approaching the settler colonies as a 'reformer or improver' within a Quaker family tradition and adopting Owen and Malthus's physiocratic view that emigration reform must go 'hand in hand with that of agricultural improvement at home', Wakefield's reasoning had less to do with poor relief and more to do with what, fol-lowing Adam Smith, he saw as the social regression of colonial depend-encies.[8] Adopting the rhetorical fiction of a duped 'insider' writing to a prospective emigrant, Wakefield's *A Letter from Sydney* (1829) argues that the brutalising effects of using convict labour, along with unmonitored emigration and land grants, had resulted in speculative

---

[4] On the politicisation of assisted emigration, see Robert Poole, *Peterloo: The English Uprising* (Oxford: Oxford University Press, 2019), pp. 217–18.

[5] Jack Harrington, 'Edward Gibbon Wakefield, the Liberal Political Subject, and the Settler State', *Journal of Political Ideologies*, 20.3 (2015), 333–51 (p. 339). On Ireland's problematic populousness, see Claire Connolly, *A Cultural History of the Irish Novel, 1790–1829* (Cambridge: Cambridge University Press, 2011), pp. 11–12.

[6] Karen O'Brien, 'Colonial Emigration, Public Policy and Tory Romanticism 1783–1830', *Proceedings of the British Academy*, 155 (2009), 161–79.

[7] Robert Grant, '"The Fit and the Unfit": Suitable Settlers for Britain's Mid-Nineteenth-Century Colonial Possessions', *Victorian Literature and Culture*, 33.1 (2005), 169–86 (p. 172); Harrington, 'Edward Gibbon Wakefield', p. 340.

[8] Harrington, 'Edward Gibbon Wakefield', p. 334; E. G. Wakefield, *A Letter from Sydney, the Principal Town of Australasia*, ed. Robert Gouger (London: Joseph Cross, 1829), p. x.

ventures, frontier violence against Indigenous peoples and a lack of cultural achievement in New South Wales, rendering 'men's minds as narrow as their territory is extensive'.[9]

Rejecting the period's 'progressive' tendency to valorise 'newness' and rejoice at 'every useful novelty, whether mechanical, moral or political', Wakefield's diagnosis of social and cultural barbarism in 1820s New South Wales is deeply entangled with his view of 'the public mind' in Britain as 'fermenting with colonial projects'.[10] While he makes no direct reference to frauds like the infamous Poyais scheme or to the bankruptcies and bank failures that led to the British financial crash of 1825–6, it was in the wake of this speculative financial panic (and his own imprisonment in Newgate Gaol for abducting an under-age heiress) that Wakefield formulated his theory of stabilising, systematic colonisation in *A Letter from Sydney*. In response to surplus population in Britain and labour scarcity in the colonies, Wakefield proposed dramatically to increase the number of voluntary white labourers while also restricting their access to land by curtailing land grants and keeping land prices artificially high.[11]

Wakefield's schema has rightly been described as an 'enormous speculation', but its distinctive features require further elaboration.[12] First, along with vast swathes of 'booster' or propaganda literature, Wakefieldian settlement schemes did much to challenge the view of emigration in the early 1820s as 'socially degrading', disentangling it from pauper relief and gradually emboldening a growing number of middle-class moneyed emigrants.[13] Middle-class emigration in turn drove the global proliferation of mobile media, carried to the colonies in a variety of printed forms and by practices of memorisation and recitation.[14] Emigration and its literatures thereby participated in a complex dialectic that linked the global movement of print to strategic attempts to mitigate the potentially destabilising effects of the mass movement of

---

[9] Wakefield, *A Letter from Sydney*, p. 63.

[10] Ibid. pp. 149–50, 203, 199.

[11] Ibid. pp. iv–xxiv (esp. p. xvii).

[12] Jonathan Lamb, *Preserving the Self in the South Seas, 1680–1840* (Chicago: University of Chicago Press, 2001), p. 291.

[13] Belich, *Replenishing the Earth*, p. 146; Ronald Robinson, 'Non-European Foundations of European Imperialism: Sketch for a Theory of Collaboration', in *Studies in the Theory of Imperialism*, ed. R. Owen and B. Sutcliffe (London: Longman, 1972), pp. 117–42 (p. 124). On emigration literature, see Fariha Shaikh, *Nineteenth-Century Settler Emigration in British Literature and Art* (Edinburgh: Edinburgh University Press, 2018).

[14] See Jason Rudy, *Imagined Homelands: British Poetry in the Colonies* (Baltimore, MD: Johns Hopkins University Press, 2017), and Chapter 7 by Lara Atkin in this volume.

people, including both metropolitan endeavours to promote regulatory models of national synchronicity and colonial attempts to invoke nostalgic notions of 'home' in the service of proto-national self-definition.[15]

Second, the professed humanitarianism of controlled settlement schemes managed to mollify, at least to some extent, the objections of anti-slavery campaigners and missionaries, some of whom had feared that mass emigration would lead to the persistence of chattel slavery and the extinction of Indigenous races.[16] While 'reverse' emigration schemes to return freed slaves proved controversial, few abolitionists in either Britain or America were opposed to emigration in any wholesale sense except in cases involving slavery, transportation or indentured labour migration.[17] More vociferous anti-emigration campaigns came from radicals such as William Cobbett, who argued that labourers were the lifeblood of Britain and should not be encouraged to leave, as well as from missionaries, who recognised that Indigenous peoples were likely to require protection from settlers.[18] Wakefield's schemes for settling South Australia and New Zealand in the 1830s and 1840s were explicitly anti-slavery and humanitarian in their outlook and tone, but they were also imbued with the kind of economic self-interest that was criticised by Samuel Marsden and Dandeson Coates of the Church Missionary Society.[19]

Third, schemes like Wakefield's appealed to moneyed capitalists and political elites within Britain. These groups recognised two potential advantages: first, controlled emigration was a national investment opportunity not only encouraging labour migration but also rendering working-class emigrants dependent on the owners of capital, thereby promoting a strategy of 'state-led, preemptive proletarianization' in the colonies; and second, Wakefield's endorsement of land commoditisation and cheap wage-labour offered a social and economic 'solution to the looming problem of abolition' in the 'ameliorative' decades of the 1820s and 1830s.[20] If Wakefield's price-fixing policies ran counter

---

[15] Jude Piesse, *British Settler Emigration in Print, 1832–1877* (Oxford: Oxford University Press, 2016), esp. pp. 2, 34, 37.

[16] On the anti-slavery movement, see the Introduction to this volume.

[17] See, for example, the scheme organised by the American Colonization Society in 1820 to return freed slaves from New York to Sierra Leone.

[18] Will Verhoeven, *Americomania and the French Revolution Debate in Britain, 1789–1802* (Cambridge: Cambridge University Press, 2013), pp. 291–2.

[19] Lamb, *Preserving the Self*, pp. 297–9.

[20] Onur Ulas Ince, *Colonial Capitalism and the Dilemmas of Liberalism* (Oxford: Oxford University Press, 2018), p. 9; Jane Lydon, '"Mr Wakefield's Speaking Trumpets": Abolishing Slavery and Colonising Systematically', *The Journal of Imperial and Commonwealth History*, 50.1 (2022), 81–112 (p. 81).

to mainstream political economy, his schemes more generally were compatible with new ideas encouraging the market-driven reciprocity of commercial interests between Britain and her colonies – an anti-mercantilist goal promoted in the 1825 Parliamentary debates on the 'Colonial Policy of the Country'.[21] Contrary, then, to accounts of the early to mid-nineteenth century as 'anti-imperial', the mutually self-sustaining nexus between emigration, abolitionism and liberal free-market ideology meant that the 1820s saw the beginning of significant, even 'relentless', growth in old and new forms of extra-European expansion, with emigration and its proliferating literatures encouraging mass settlement, the large-scale dispossession of Indigenous peoples, the creation of huge workforces of indentured labourers and the subsequent expansion of Britain's 'entrepôt empire into a world system in the making'.[22]

---

[21] Commons, 21 March 1825, *Hansard's Parliamentary Debates*, Second Series, 25 vols (1820–30), vol. XII, pp. 1097–1128. See also the various *Reports from the Select Committee on Emigration* (1826–8). My thanks to Maurice J. Bric for these references.

[22] John Darwin, 'Imperialism and the Victorians: The Dynamics of Territorial Expansion', *The English Historical Review*, 112.447 (1997), 614–62 (pp. 614, 627), and *The Empire Project: The Rise and Fall of the British World System* (Cambridge: Cambridge University Press, 2009), p. 45.

Chapter 7

(Re)settling Poetry:
The Culture of Reprinting and the
Poetics of Emigration in the 1820s
Southern Settler Colonies

Lara Atkin

Ever since Benedict Anderson's *Imagined Communities* (1991), it has become axiomatic to view print media as central to the formation of national consciousness. In the British Empire, newspapers functioned as what historian Chris Holdridge has termed a 'discursive mediator of identity' for those British emigrants who forsook the metropole for the settler colonies after the end of the Napoleonic Wars.[1] The function of newspaper poetry within this broader anglophone media ecology has been debated in recent years, as poetry's portability has re-established its importance to scholars interested in the role that print culture played in enabling the articulation of emerging national identities in the British settler colonies. Poetry's ability to traverse borders – both physically, as the portable property of emigrants or through the 'cut and scissors' reprint culture of nineteenth-century journalism, and imaginatively, through memorisation, reproduction and imitation – has led to a spate of recent studies that highlight the importance of poetry for the development of colonial literary cultures across the Anglo-world.[2]

---

[1] Christopher Holdridge, 'Circulating the African Journal: The Colonial Press and Trans-Imperial Britishness in the Mid Nineteenth-Century Cape', *South African Historical Journal*, 62.3 (2010), 487–513 (p. 489).

[2] See, for example, John O'Leary, *Savage Songs and Wild Romances: Settler Poetry and the Indigene, 1830–1880* (Amsterdam and New York: Rodopi, 2011); Mary Ellis Gibson, *Indian Angles: English Verse in Colonial India from Jones to Tagore* (Columbus: Ohio University Press, 2011); James Mulholland, *Sounding Imperial: Poetic Voice and the Politics of Empire, 1730–1820* (Baltimore, MD: Johns Hopkins University Press, 2013); Manu Samriti Chander, *Brown Romantics: Poetry and Nationalism in the Global Nineteenth Century* (Lewisburg, PA: Bucknell University Press, 2017); Jason R. Rudy, *Imagined Homelands: British Poetry in the Colonies* (Baltimore, MD: Johns Hopkins University Press, 2017); Nikki Hessell, *Romantic Literature and the Colonised World: Lessons from Indigenous Translations* (Basingstoke: Palgrave Macmillan, 2018).

As Jason Rudy has argued, the material form of poetry is central to its success as a globally circulating cultural commodity: poetry's portability 'meant it could circulate with ease through Britain's colonies, spaces that at first were not equipped to publish longer works'.[3] Throughout the nineteenth century, the most common way for poetry to be transferred from the private notebooks and memories of recently arrived emigrants to the public sphere was via colonial newspapers. In an era before the development of field-specific periodicals, colonial newspapers func-tioned as what Scotsman George Greig, the printer of the Cape Colony's first independent newspaper the *South African Commercial Advertiser*, termed 'a medium of general communication' connecting geographically dispersed settler communities to colonial hubs such as Cape Town and Sydney, as well as to metropolitan Britain.[4] Correspondence pages and 'poet's corners' featuring reprinted and original verse were the means through which settlers could participate dialogically in the public sphere debates that editors of colonial newspapers were shaping through their lead articles. As a result, poetry can be considered as an integral part of the nation-building project that colonial editors were actively engaged in through newspaper publication.

Both Rudy and Kirstie Blair have recently highlighted the role that emigrant verse played in enabling diasporic communities, fractured by the upheavals of emigration, to re-establish a sense of community in their new homelands.[5] One such example is a lyric by Thomas Pringle vari-ously titled 'The Emigrant's Farewell' or 'Our Native Land'. Written in 1819, the year that Pringle and his family left his native Roxburghshire as part of a group of 5,000 English and Scottish settlers bound for the Cape Colony in a government-backed emigration scheme, the poem first appeared in the appendix to volume three of John Struthers's anthology of ancient and modern Scottish songs, *The Harp of Caledonia* (1819). The inclusion of this brand-new emigration lyric, written in Scots and set to the traditional air 'My Guid Lord John', indicates that, by 1820, the 'emigrant farewell' was a generic sub-category of Scottish song that was recognised by songster compilers.

As it began its transmedial journey across the globe through the pages of colonial newspapers, Pringle's poem was also being widely reprinted in England, appearing in two further anthologies edited by Scottish poets but published in London: Allan Cunningham's *Songs of Scotland*,

[3] Rudy, *Imagined Homelands*, p. 16.

[4] George Greig, 'Prospectus of the *South African Commercial Advertiser*', 20 December 1823 (Cape Town: George Greig, 1823), p. 2.

[5] Rudy, *Imagined Homelands*, p. 22; Kirstie Blair, *Working Verse in Victorian Scotland: Poetry, Press, Community* (Oxford: Oxford University Press, 2019), pp. 128–9.

Ancient and Modern (1825) and Alaric Watts's *The Poetical Album; or, Register of Modern Fugitive Poetry* (1829). In his introduction to *The Poetical Album*, Watts is explicit about the role anthologisation plays in ensuring that poetry 'from sources of a temporary or fugitive character' acquires a broader circulation 'in a more popular and portable form' than the newspaper or periodical.[6] Like many of the metropolitan reprints that circulated promiscuously through the pages of colonial newspapers, Pringle's 'The Emigrant's Farewell' had already acquired considerable portability as a result of the publishing craze for anthologies of popular songs and fugitive verse facilitated by the cheap print boom of the 1820s. As such, it circulated through Britain and the settler colonies as part of a popular canon of 'emigrant farewells' that, as Jane Stafford has argued, were so numerous that they could be said to constitute a distinct poetic genre during the 1820s and 1830s.[7]

'The Emigrant's Farewell' is a nostalgic description of Pringle's native Teviotdale in which conventional pastoral evocations of the countryside operate synecdochally to represent the cultural history of the communities who inhabit the Scottish borderlands:

> Farewell, ye hills of glorious deeds,
> And streams renown'd in song!
> Farewell, ye blithesome braes and meads,
> Our hearts have loved so long![8]

Here, the generic landscape imagery evokes a nostalgic imagining of a homeland no longer physically accessible due to the distance and expense of long-distance travel, but imaginatively accessible through the forms and tropes of local poetic forms, in this case the Scots-language song. As Kirstie Blair has pointed out, 'the pose of missing Scotland from abroad' was a 'recognised literary stance' for Scottish emigrant poets in the nineteenth century.[9] It has become a truism in critical analysis of these poems to state that these poems are nostalgic, with sentimentalised representations of Britain providing an affective connection to the comforts of home and hearth so sorely missed by emigrants struggling to adjust to the privations of frontier life.[10] However, this pose of affectionate

---

[6] 'Preface', in *The Poetical Album; and Register of Modern Fugitive Poetry*, ed. Alaric Watts (London: Samuel Manning and Co., 1829), pp. vii–viii.

[7] Jane Stafford, '"No Cloud to Hide Their Dear Resplendencies": The Uses of Poetry in 1840s New Zealand', *Journal of New Zealand Literature*, 28.2 (2010), 12–34 (p. 20).

[8] Thomas Pringle, 'The Emigrant's Farewell', in *The Harp of Caledonia*, ed. John Struthers, 3 vols (Glasgow: E. Khull, 1819), vol. III, p. 445.

[9] Blair, *Working Verse*, p. 130.

[10] Ibid. p. 131.

nostalgia for home is the affective response to a condition of out-of-placeness experienced by many first-generation emigrants involved in the process of colonial nation building in the settler colonies during the 1820s and 1830s.

Prior to the mineral booms of the 1850s and 1860s, the success of the settler colonies was by no means assured. The 1820s proved a particularly turbulent time for both the Cape Colony and the Australian colonies. The banking system in New South Wales proved vulnerable to the economic shocks of the 1825–6 financial crisis, which took place at the very moment when the colony was beginning the process of rapid transformation from penal colony to a community of free settlers. Meanwhile, at the Cape, the 1820s marked a period of protracted crisis for the 5,000 British settlers who had migrated to the Eastern Cape in the 1820 government-backed settlement scheme. The sense of isolation and despondency engendered by the failure of the British agricultural settlement in the Eastern Cape is movingly articulated in the following letter signed 'A Tired-Out Emigrant' and printed in the *South African Commercial Advertiser* in 1829:

> Sir, – A British settler of 1820, is desirous to receive, through your columns, some information for himself and a numerous body of his friends, respecting the projected Settlement at Port Natal. Disgusted and disappointed with our reverses in the Colony throughout a series of nine successive years without any intermission, occasioned by Rust, Drought, Storms, and Locusts, to which there still appears no promise of conclusion, and terrified at the prospect of an *increasing Taxation upon decaying income*, it is not unnatural that we should cast our eyes upon some other asylum than that which has to us at least verified its old name of the *Cabo Tormentoso*.[11]

In response to both the geographical displacement of global emigration and the sheer precariousness of life on the agricultural frontiers of settlement, the trope of emigration-as-exile emerged in much original settler poetry, as Elizabeth Webby has shown in her analysis of early Australian settler verse.[12] This trope was also a recurrent theme in the British settler verse produced in the Cape Colony, suggesting an ambivalence on the part of recently arrived settlers to the project of colonial state building in which they were participating and a nostalgic longing for an idealised vision of home.

In her examination of the depiction of locality in nineteenth-century

---

[11] 'Letter from "A Tired-Out Emigrant"', *South African Commercial Advertiser*, 18 April 1829, p. 3.

[12] Elizabeth Webby, *Early Australian Poetry: An Annotated Bibliography of Original Poems Published in Australian Newspapers, Magazines and Almanacks before 1850* (Sydney: Hale and Iremonger, 2001).

fiction, Ruth Livesey argues that the use of the term 'nostalgia' was markedly different in the nineteenth century from today, denoting a feeling of 'acute homesickness', an affective 'yearning to smell, touch, hear, see the localities from whence they came' that was the result of 'a world on the move – out of local belonging and into global circulation'.[13] Livesey views the spatial displacements that resulted from increased global mobility as central to the experience of modernity in the nineteenth century, creating a tension between local attachments and a more expansive metropolitan modernity. In contrast, my interest is in the ways in which the global displacements caused by emigration created new forms of local attachment that involved settlers identifying not as part of a cosmopolitan British diaspora, but as citizens of specific colonial localities. Where early British settlers are concerned, global movement did not on the whole bring with it a particularly cosmopolitan consciousness. On the contrary, long-distance travel was expensive and impossibly inaccessible for the majority of settlers, who worked as either small-scale merchants or tenant farmers, often eking out a precarious existence on unproductive land. As a result, their worlds shrank. Their material concern with bare survival and the impossibility for most of ever returning home rooted them in their new localities whether they liked it or not. In this context, the rhetoric of exile emerged in emigrant verse as a poetic response to the nostalgia or homesickness brought about by the dislocation and out-of-placeness that was produced by the settler's position as an exile from the old world who was not yet ready to claim belonging in the new. Viewing nostalgia, as Livesey does, as 'rooted in the spatial rather than the historical' enables us to see why global mobility, the paradigmatic marker of modernity, paradoxically produced a turn towards interiority and containment that lyric verse was so well suited to articulating.[14]

Emigration lyrics, songs and ballads published in Britain and reprinted in colonial newspapers provided a counter-discourse to this solitary, inward-looking rhetoric of exile articulated in much settler-produced verse. If we turn to the full archive of verse printed in colonial newspapers during the 1820s, we find the majority of poems published were not original poetic productions but reprints from metropolitan newspapers and periodicals. This turn to metropolitan literary culture had much to do with the moral purpose colonial newspaper editors attached to their roles. Defining and shaping new forms of colonial identity was one of

---

[13] Ruth Livesey, *Writing the Stage-Coach Nation: Locality on the Move in Nineteenth-Century British Literature* (Oxford: Oxford University Press, 2016), pp. 5–6.

[14] Livesey, *Stage-Coach Nation*, p. 6.

the key purposes of colonial newspapers, with many editors viewing popular poetry as playing a central role in shaping what the printer of the *South African Commercial Advertiser*, George Greig, termed the 'taste and tone' of emerging colonial bourgeois public spheres.[15] This is made explicit if we turn to the 'Poet's Corner' section of *The Tasmanian and Port Dalrymple Advertiser* for 19 January 1825, where we find Pringle's 'The Emigrant's Farewell' reprinted. Uncoupled from its original title, the poem appears instead accompanied by the following headnote:

[The following beautiful lines, the production of Mr. Thomas Pringle, a Gentleman of great literary attainments, and formerly principal Editor of Blackwood's Magazine, on the prospect of leaving his 'native Teviotdale', for the Cape of Good Hope (where he is now a resident), cannot fail to gratify many of our Readers whose feelings, upon such an occasion, have no doubt been in unison with those of the Poet's.][16]

The paratext here provides a kind of authenticating narrative for the poem, containing an aesthetic justification for its inclusion in a specially designated 'Poet's Corner' based on Pringle's 'great literary attainments', including his brief role as the first editor of *Blackwood's Edinburgh Magazine* in 1817, a role he shared with James Cleghorn. Having established Pringle's literary credentials with reference to Edinburgh periodical culture, the biographical narrative contained in this editorial note stresses Pringle's status as an emigrant. In contrast to other Scottish poets such as Thomas Campbell, who also wrote a number of emigration lyrics in the 1820s, Pringle had actually experienced for himself the material and affective displacements that characterised emigrant experience. Ironically, given the inauthenticity of many metropolitan emigration poems reprinted in the colonies, it is the Pringle's own painful and well-documented experiences of the travails of settlement that enable the paper's editor, printer and publisher, George Terry Howe, to confidently assert that his readers' feelings 'have no doubt been in unison with those of the Poet's'. That Pringle's poem resonated with newly established British emigrant communities across the settler colonies is evidenced in the fact that between 1825 and 1842 it was reprinted in six colonial newspapers located in Sydney, Melbourne and Cape Town.[17]

---

[15] Greig, 'Prospectus', 20 December 1823, p. 2.

[16] George Terry Howe, 'Poet's Corner', *The Tasmanian and Port Dalrymple Advertiser*, 19 January 1825, p. 4.

[17] In addition to appearing untitled in *The Tasmanian and Port Dalrymple Advertiser* on 19 January 1825, the poem appeared under the title 'Our Native Land' in Watts's *The Poetical Album* (London), the *South African Commercial Advertiser* (Cape Town), 27 July 1829 and *The Australian* (Sydney), 21 October 1829. In 1842 it appeared in *The Colonial Observer* (Sydney), 10 September 1842, *The Teetotaller*

As well as providing the affective glue that enabled colonists to make sense of the estrangements of settlement, reprinted emigration lyrics could serve a more overtly polemical purpose. The arrival of foreign news by ship was an elongated form of information transfer as, during the 1820s, it took six weeks for a ship from London to reach Cape Town and four months to reach Sydney.[18] Cut off by the tyranny of distance from unmediated entry into metropolitan public sphere debates, colonial newspaper editors often used reprinted material from British newspapers and periodicals as a means of insinuating themselves into metropolitan news discourse, particularly when emigration and colonial affairs were discussed. To this end, colonial newspaper editors reprinted a vast quantity of what Fariha Shaikh has usefully termed 'emigration literature'. Shaikh's expansive definition includes both overt 'booster' literature that was primarily produced to publicly promote emigration and texts that were 'produced directly out of the practices of emigration', such as emigrant letters, poems and 'sketches' of colonial life published in colonial and metropolitan periodicals.[19]

Although most frequently published in London, narrative sketches of colonial life were frequently extracted in colonial newspapers. These extracts were often accompanied by acerbic editorials and letters critiquing what the Sydney-based *Australian*'s editor Robert Wardell termed the 'unscrupulous scribblers' who, in a quest to satiate the appetite for knowledge about emerging colonial societies, provided the metropolitan press with 'either overcharged pictures, or pure fictions' concerning the problems facing the settler colonies. In response to an anonymous letter purporting to be from a settler in New South Wales complaining of widespread crime and public disorder, which was published on the front page of the *Morning Chronicle* on 28 September 1825, Wardell argues in the *Australian* in June 1826 that the danger posed to the colony by these misrepresentations derives from the 'weight and authority' afforded to metropolitan newspapers such as the *Morning Chronicle*, causing readers contemplating emigration to 'necessarily come to the

and General Newspaper (Sydney), 14 September 1842 and finally in the *Port Philip and Melbourne Advertiser* (Melbourne), 22 September 1842. It also appears in two Scottish poetry anthologies during the 1840s, *The Book of Scottish Song*, ed. Alexander Whitelaw (Glasgow: Blackie and Son., 1843) and *Chambers' Miscellany of Useful and Entertaining Tracts*, ed. William and Robert Chambers (Edinburgh: Robert and William Chambers, 1847).

[18] Victor Isaacs and Rod Kirkpatrick, *Two Hundred Years of Sydney Newspapers: A Short History* (Sydney: Rural Press, 2003), p. 9.

[19] Fariha Shaikh, *Nineteenth-Century Settler Emigration in British Literature and Art* (Edinburgh: Edinburgh University Press, 2018), p. 5.

conclusion, that . . . New South Wales will not prove to them an eligible resting place'.[20]

In the broader discursive field of reprinted emigration poetry, optimistic, pro-emigration lyrics penned in the metropole extolling the virtues of colonial settlement created a counter-discourse to these metropolitan misrepresentations. One such example, titled 'Van Diemen's Land', was originally printed in England in *Woolmer's Exeter and Plymouth Gazette* and reprinted in the official government gazettes of New South Wales and Van Diemen's Land in October 1823 and January 1824 respectively. The poem takes the form of a secular prayer addressed to a departing emigrant in which the speaker begins by issuing a blessing for the journey: 'May fav'ring breezes fill thy sails, / And may no calm nor adverse gales, / Impede the on the main', before quickly shifting imaginatively to the site of colonisation, which is represented as a utopian scene of pastoral renewal. After the inevitable 'privations' of 'short duration', the emigrant will reap the domestic and economic benefits of the classic settler agrarian fantasy:

> May these, the comforts of this life,
> Soon smile on thee, thy babes and wife,
> And Heaven increase they wealth.
> There may your every plan succeed,
> Thy flocks and herds like rabbits breed
> . . .
> And may thy crops of wool and corn
> be to a ready market borne.[21]

These lines neatly encapsulate the ideology of free settlement in which the emigrant establishes himself at the centre of a domestic idyll while simultaneously participating productively in the market economy. In an era in which both Australian colonies were yet to break the shackles of their identities as penal settlements, the circulation of such aspirational images of prosperous settlement were central to concerted efforts to attract free emigrants to the colonies that were championed by editors and correspondents throughout the colonial press.

The status of such poems within the broader cultural economy of emigration booster literature is even more evident if we turn to the poem's publication in the *Sydney Gazette*. Immediately preceding the poem is a letter signed 'An Emigrant Settler' and dated 'Hunter's River, County of Durham, Aug 22 1823' in which the correspondent states 'no

---

[20] Robert Wardell, *The Australian*, 28 June 1826, p. 2.
[21] Anon.,'Van Diemen's Land', *Hobert Town Gazette and Van Diemen's Land Advertiser*, 9 January 1824, p. 3.

doubt [the following lines] will be thought characteristic by a portion of your Readers, as conveying the wishes of many a wooing friend'. The rest of the short letter goes on to praise the colony of New South Wales, 'where the industrious Emigrant Settler can look forward with a staple hope of being rewarded for his past cares, and present toil' with success in a colony where 'the Administration of Colonial Public Affairs' is 'so judiciously and well concerted'.[22] In an era of post-war retrenchment in which the British government was seeking to curtail expenditure on colonial administration, fledgling settler colonies such as New South Wales and the Cape Colony had to prove their economic worth to an ambivalent imperial administration in London. This created an atmosphere of intense inter-colonial rivalry in which colonial news-paper editors' selection criteria for original and reprinted material was governed to a large extent by the wish to present aspirational images of colonial life that would attract the interest of policy makers and investors in London, as well as increasing numbers of free emigrants. The presence of the letter and a reduced, eight-stanza version of 'Van Diemen's Land' on the front page of an 'Additional Supplement' to the *Sydney Gazette*, in which these emigration texts were the only content aside from classified advertising, clearly demonstrates the importance the *Gazette*'s editor Robert Howe placed in foregrounding these positive representations of the prospects of free emigrants in the colony of New South Wales (of which Tasmania was still a part in 1823).

In an editorial of 14 April 1824, John Fairbairn, editor of the *South African Commercial Advertiser*, explicitly addressed the difficulties posed to the Cape Colony by negative reports of the distress suffered by English settlers in the Eastern Cape, where three years of failed harvests had led Pringle to make an appeal to the British public to raise funds to alleviate distressed settlers. After reading Pringle's appeal in the pages of the *New Monthly Magazine*, a correspondent signing himself 'A Settler' wrote in to the *South African Commercial Advertiser* to complain that 'the colony is greatly in want of labourers, but the damaging and false reports circulated with regard to its internal state, deter emigrants from coming at all'.[23] In a discussion of a cluster of new emigration pam-phlets extolling the virtues of settlements in New South Wales and Van Diemen's Land, Fairbairn notes that just four years earlier such booster literature had been praising the Cape but that now 'the servants of

[22] 'Letter from "An Emigrant Settler"', *Sydney Gazette and New South Wales Advertiser*, 9 October 1823, p. 1.
[23] 'Letter from "A Settler"', *South African Commercial Advertiser*, 14 April 1824, p. 117.

Government . . . are not likely to continue to encourage their inquisitive and restless countrymen to settle in the Cape Colony by dilating much on its advantages'. Fairbairn acknowledges the cause of this neglect by stating that 'The English Settlers, who came into the Colony at a particularly unfortunate period, and were met by circumstances not likely to give them a favourable impression of it in any respect, have certainly the best reasons for dwelling on the dark side of the picture.'[24]

In an issue in which metropolitan misrepresentations of the realities of colonial settlement was a key note of both the lead editorial and correspondence page, Fairbairn elects to reprint a ballad titled 'The Poyais Emigrant' that had been hawked about the streets of London at the height of the Poyais emigration scandal in 1822–3 (discussed in Chapter 1 of this volume by Angela Esterhammer). The Poyais bubble, as Esterhammer notes, was textually constituted. In the court case brought to the King's Bench in January 1824, MacGregor attempted to sue the proprietors of the *Morning Herald* for printing claims made by Captain Joshua Antrim, one of the British captains responsible for repatriating emigrants evacuated from Poyais to the British colony at Belize, that the emigrants were deliberately misled and defrauded by MacGregor. Crucial to the case built by the defence was the fictitious emigration literature produced by MacGregor and his agents to build public confidence in the Poyais scheme. Acting on behalf of the defence, QC Mr Scarlett produced *Sketches of the Mosquito Coast* (1822) for the jury's perusal, stating that in this fabricated travelogue MacGregor 'had collected together all the most favourable accounts of this happy region, and had published them as if authenticated by an eye-witness, when the compilation, adorned with his own picture, was only from his own hand'.[25]

The association Scarlett builds between MacGregor's passing off a compilation of quotations as his own composition and the fraud practised on the emigrants through the Poyais land scheme clearly draws on a review of the work written by John Barrow in the *Quarterly Review* in October 1822, in which Barrow explicitly argues that the 'scissors-and-paste' practices of compilation disguised as authorship is the material embodiment of the fraud practised on guileless speculators and emigrants by MacGregor:

> Who 'Thomas Strangeways, K.G.C.' may be, we neither know nor desire to know; but if, as he tells us, 'a portion of his life has been spent in this fine

---

[24] John Fairbairn, *South African Commercial Advertiser*, 14 April 1824, p. 115.

[25] Anon., 'The Court of the King's Bench, Guildhall, Jan 9th 1824, McGregor v. Thwaites and another', in *The Annual Register of World Events: A Review of the Year*, 80 vols (London: J. Dodsley, [1762?]–1838), vol. LXVI (1824), pp. 17–23 (p. 21).

country,' we can only say that, within the covers of his *Sketch of the Mosquito Shore &c.* there will not be found a single particle respecting it, which bears the slightest testimony of his having ever set foot on it; in fact, he has gutted and garbled Bryan Edward's *Account of the West India Islands*, and Browne's *History of Jamaica*, and transplanted, word for word, the whole produce of these islands to Poyais, or rather into his pages.[26]

The 'gutted and garbled' travelogues passed off as original composition by MacGregor under the nom de plume Thomas Strangeways become the perfect metaphor for the tissue of deceptions underwriting his claims to legitimate authority over the land on the Mosquito coast, claims that Barrow systematically dismantles during the course of his review. But unwittingly Barrow also exposes the inherently fictive nature of all travel writing (including, perhaps, his own travelogues describing his residences in China and South Africa), which frequently consisted of large chunks of unattributed quotation as well as more transparent and fully attributed allusions to earlier works. The danger, Barrow and Scarlett imply, is that when such fictions are deployed as emigration 'booster' literature they can prove persuasive lures not only for 'romantic adventurers' but for 'all who are given to change'.[27]

It was not just the travelogue that acted as a primary vehicle for attracting the working-class Scottish emigrants to invest in MacGregor's Poyais scheme, but also a series of ballads written by Andrew Picken, himself one of the two hundred people persuaded by MacGregor to emigrate, and his sister, Joanna Belfrage Picken. In his testimony before the King's Bench, Picken gives the following description of the production of 'The Poyais Emigrant' and 'Lines to Poyais', two 'booster' poems produced by the Pickens:

> I first became acquainted with Sir Gregor in 1821; he engaged me as clerk, but promised me a cornetcy of lancers. Sir Gregor asked me to write something in favour of Poyais. I asked how it was to be done? He said, he understood I had a talent for poetry. I produced this (the 'lines to Poyais'), except a few lines at the end. The song, 'The Poyais Emigrant,' was written at his desire, by my sister. It was published and circulated by Sir Gregor, who said, the ballad was to be hawked through the streets to attract the vulgar.[28]

Here we have perhaps the most egregious historical example of emigration poetry produced explicitly as 'booster' literature to attract emigrants and investments. Quite how the poem made its way from a

---

[26] John Barrow, 'The Poyais Bubble', *Quarterly Review*, 28 (1822–3), 157–61 (p. 160).
[27] Anon., 'The Court of the King's Bench, Guildhall, Jan 9th 1824, McGregor v. Thwaites and another', p. 21.
[28] Ibid. p. 22.

broadside ballad hawked through the streets of Glasgow in 1822 to the newspaper office of John Fairbairn in Cape Town in 1824 is difficult to ascertain, but it seems likely that the poem was anthologised in one of the many compilations of 'fugitive verse' printed in London, given the amount of publicity the Poyais affair had gained in British newspapers and periodicals.

The poem itself is a utopian ballad deploying the classic trope of emigration as economic and cultural regeneration. It was written in the Scots dialect – a dialect that, Rudy has argued, had by the nineteenth century become a form of portable property that immediately signified an idea of Scotland rooted in a nostalgic yearning for a lost homeland.[29] This affective note of nostalgic attachment to an idealised agrarian past signified by the use of Scots and the generic choice of the ballad immediately situates MacGregor and the Poyais scandal within a broader cultural economy of internationally recognised Scottish song poetry that included the many poetaster imitators of Burns and the numerous anthologies of traditional Scottish songs and ballads that had flooded the British literary market place in the eighteenth and early nineteenth centuries.

Scots dialect songs were already popularly associated with a certain second-rateness and shabby inauthenticity, with songs produced and published in London dealing with 'rustic or humble life' frequently published generically as 'Northern' or 'Scotch' songs.[30] To 'genteel' London audiences, these fabricated songs presented to a metropolitan audience 'characterizations of the Scots as pastoral, virtuous, and simple, confined to a golden age long superseded by a developing Britain'.[31] These popular associations with Scots dialect song as a genre, combined with the infamy the Poyais scheme had gained through the pages of the British and imperial press, enabled Fairbairn to re-present 'The Poyais Emigrant' as the poetic embodiment of the fraud that had been perpetrated by MacGregor and his associates on unsuspecting emigrants. This point is reinforced by Fairbairn's insertion of the following editorial headnote: 'The following *morceau*, contrasted with the actual state of the Poyais settlement, and, indeed, of every other new settlement, gives a pretty accurate idea of the difference between poetry and matter of fact.'[32]

---

[29] Jason Rudy, 'Scottish Sounds in Colonial South Africa: Thomas Pringle, Dialect, and the Overhearing of Ballad', *Nineteenth-Century Literature*, 7:2 (September 2016), 197–214 (p. 199).

[30] Dave Harker, *Fakesong: The Manufacture of British "Folksong," 1700 to the Present Day* (Milton Keynes: Open University Press, 1985).

[31] Janet Sorenson, 'Alternative Antiquarianisms of Scotland and the North', *Modern Language Quarterly*, 70.4 (December 2009), 415–41 (p. 423).

[32] John Fairbairn, *South African Commercial Advertiser*, 14 April 1824, p. 118.

The portability of the internationally recognisable markers of Scottish song tradition combined with the political infamy that, by 1824, surrounded the Poyais emigration scheme, enabled 'The Poyais Emigrant' to stand metonymically for the propaganda and 'puff' literature produced during the 1820s emigration boom. This in turn enabled Fairbairn to enlist the poem in his own local propaganda war against metropolitan misrepresentations of the utopian possibilities of large-scale emigration to uncharted territories and virgin settlements. In so doing, he hoped to bolster the flagging fortunes of the Cape Colony to ensure that the plight of the emigrants at the Cape gained the attention of the British government.

Colonial ventures in the 1820s were inherently speculative, requiring both an investment of capital and the imaginative ability to project prosperous visions of future plenitude onto unseen lands. The literature of emigration blended fact and fiction in a way that was characteristic of what Esterhammer terms the 'hybrid genres' of 1820s periodical culture. In the final section of this chapter, I investigate the ways in which reprinted emigration poetry was invested discursively in this speculative, future-oriented vision of colonisation both imaginatively and materially. Emigration poetry's imaginative investment in projection is mirrored materially in its status as an internationally circulating commodity, imbricated in the same trans-imperial networks of commodity exchange that enabled other portable goods to circulate between Europe and the colonies. Poetry's status as a portable commodity that travelled through the same shipping routes as colonial commodities was explicitly recognised by colonial newspaper editors, affecting how it was positioned on the page and, by extension, how it was received and interpreted by colonial readers.

The transfer of literary texts between colonial hubs in the southern hemisphere and metropolitan centres was exclusively by shipping prior to the creation of a telegraph line between Australia and Europe in 1872.[33] As Anna Johnston has noted, the prominent position that 'shipping intelligence' occupied in all colonial newspapers 'reminds us of the crucial role mobility played in the formation of the colony, with the ocean world dictating the entrance and egress of people, goods and ideas'.[34] An advertisement from the *Hobart Town Gazette* in 1824 indicates that books were fully imbricated with these oceanic networks of commodity exchange, with settlers in Hobart or Cape Town able to

---

[33] Isaacs and Kirkpatrick, *Two Hundred Years of Sydney Newspapers*, p. 9.
[34] Anna Johnston, *The Paper War: Morality, Print Culture, and Power in Colonial New South Wales* (Crawley: University of Western Australia Press, 2011), p. 1.

acquire canonical works by Walter Scott and Tobias Smollett at the same merchants from whom they purchased their salt pork.[35] In early colonial newspapers compositors frequently positioned poetry on the front or back page, next to classified advertising and government notices. This meant these commercial and official notices were as much a part of the reception context for popular poetry as the journalistic writing that has hitherto attracted the attention of scholars interested in analysing the specific discourses surrounding newspaper poetry.[36]

One of the more substantial metropolitan emigration lyrics to be reprinted in the colonies was Thomas Campbell's 'Lines On The Departure Of Emigrants For New South Wales' (Figure 5). Published in the *New Monthly Magazine* in June 1829 and reprinted in the *Sydney Gazette* early the following year, signed and fully attributed, Campbell's poem represents colonisation in terms of metaphors of domestic virtue, and ultimately as a form of quasi-heroic liberal self-assertion. The 'pensive' emigrants are 'like children parting from a mother', but though the grief of familial parting and absence is likely to 'long' persist, it is a necessary departure, for they are leaving a 'home that could not yield them bread' for the prospect of creating their own domestic establishments which will in time far outstrip those of 'home'; indeed they will create a personal 'empire' for generations to come: 'There, marking o'er his farm's expanding ring / New fleeces whiten and new fruits upspring, / The grey hair'd swain, his grandchild sporting round, / Shall walk at eve his little empire's bound'.[37]

While the 'bond' of Britain as 'home' for the emigrant is repeatedly emphasised through the poem, it is a kind of proper filial fidelity that the 'homesick heart' must acknowledge but manfully overcome to secure the future for his children and subsequent generations. And the enterprise of the emigrant in transforming Australian 'wildness' into his own pastoral, patriarchal empire is rewarded by the fact that subsequent generations would be free of the pain of loss associated with emigration: 'not a pang that England's name imparts / Shall touch a fibre of his children's hearts'; for they will be 'bound to *that* native land by nature's bond'.[38] By 1830, newspapers like the *Sydney Gazette* were part of a

---

35 'Sales by Auction', *Hobart Town Gazette and Van Diemen's Land Advertiser*, 16 July 1824, p. 4.

36 See, for example, Natalie M. Houston, 'Newspaper Poems: Material Texts in the Public Sphere', *Victorian Studies*, 50 (2008), 233–42; Alison Chapman and Caley Ehnes, 'Introduction', *Victorian Poetry*, 52.1 (Spring 2014), 1–20.

37 Thomas Campbell, 'Lines on the Departure of Emigrants for New South Wales', *The Sydney Gazette and New South Wales Advertiser*, 25 February 1830, p. 4 (lines 44–7).

38 Campbell, 'Lines', lines 101–3.

Figure 5   Thomas Campbell, 'Lines on the Departure of Emigrants to New South Wales', *Sydney Gazette and New South Wales Advertiser*, 25 February 1830, p. 4. Courtesy of the National Library of Australia.

concerted push to encourage free emigration to the Australian colonies, and to advance the interests of the settler class there. It is notable that this poem praising the virtues of free emigrants was placed immediately before an extensive list of absconded convicts. The *Gazette*, still a semi-official publication, had an obligation to report lists of absconders and other aspects of penal administration. Campbell's poem – suggesting as it does that the sacrifice of free emigrants would lead to a splendid future for their children, who would in turn would become authentically Australian – directs readers to reflect on the promise of colonial success underpinned by free immigration, while also encoding the appropriate forms of sentiment for understanding the settler's place between the new world and the old. Yet reprinting Campbell's 'Lines' next to a list of convict absconders highlights the disjuncture between this idealised image of the colony's future produced in the metropole and the material conditions of New South Wales during the 1820s, where convicts and emancipists (freed convicts) vastly outnumbered free settlers.[39] This fact cannot have been lost on the *Sydney Gazette*'s editor Robert Howe, who was himself the son of an emancipist and campaigned vociferously in the pages of the *Gazette* for the granting of full civil rights to this class of colonists.

In the Cape Colony, where settler newspapers were published bilingually in English and Dutch, the immediate context in which reprinted poetry was read was even more complex. Another of Campbell's emigration lyrics, simply titled 'The Emigrant', was published in Cape Town's *South African Commercial Advertiser* in 1824 (Figure 6). In this conventional lyric, the speaker is an emigrant departing for Canada. Originally appearing in Campbell and Cyrus Redding's *New Monthly Magazine* in 1823, in both its British and South African publication contexts the poem was published anonymously, decoupling it from the biographical, historical and geographical contexts of its publication. The imagined addressee of the poem is deliberately vague, with the poem's lack of nominal or propositional referents enabling it to contain the possibility that it is addressed to a lover, a close friend or a family member. The dominant emotional registers of the poem's speaker are enduring love and a melancholic regret, with the generic references to the Canadian landscape serving less to map the geography of a colonial locale than to chart the contours of the speaker's sentiments. In this poem, the Canadian landscape is presented as an empty signifier ready to be filled by a set of stock sentiments that abounded in nineteenth-century emigration verse: the boundless grief of departure; the sense of estrangement from an alien and hostile natural world; and the nostalgic longing for home, as embodied in the figure of the imagined addressee.

---

[39] Anon., 'Abstract of the Population of the Colony of New South Wales . . . November 1828', *Sydney Gazette*, 26 September 1829, p. 1, available at https://trove.nla.gov.au /newspaper/article/2193488 (accessed 7 February 2022).

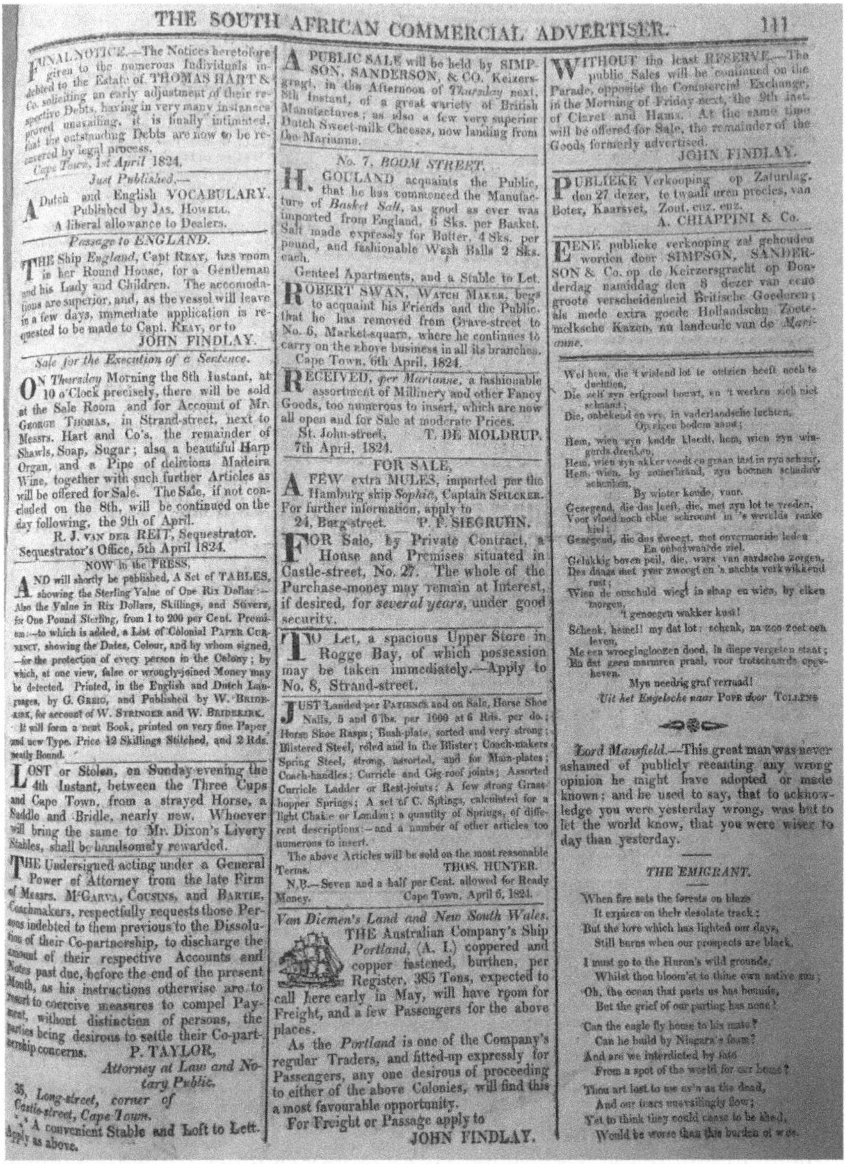

THE SOUTH AFRICAN COMMERCIAL ADVERTISER. 111

FINAL NOTICE.—The Notices heretofore given to the numerous Individuals indebted to the Estate of THOMAS HART & Co. soliciting an early adjustment of their respective Debts, having in very many instances proved unavailing, it is finally intimated, that the outstanding Debts are now to be recovered by legal process.
Cape Town, 1st April 1824.

Just Published.—
A Dutch and English VOCABULARY. Published by JAS. HOWELL.
A liberal allowance to Dealers.

Passage to ENGLAND.
THE Ship *England*, Capt REAY, has room in her Round House, for a Gentleman and his Lady and Children. The accomodations are superior, and, as the vessel will leave in a few days, immediate application is requested to be made to Capt. REAY, or to
JOHN FINDLAY.

Sale for the Execution of a Sentence.
ON *Thursday* Morning the 8th Instant, at 10 o'Clock precisely, there will be sold at the Sale Room and for Account of Mr. GEORGE THOMAS, in Strand-street, next to Messrs. Hart and Co's. the remainder of Shawls, Soap, Sugar; also a beautiful Harp Organ, and a Pipe of delicious Madeira Wine, together with such further Articles as will be offered for Sale. The Sale, if not concluded on the 8th, will be continued on the day following, the 9th of April.
R. J. VAN DER REIT, Sequestrator.
Sequestrator's Office, 5th April 1824.

NOW in the PRESS,
AND will shortly be published, A Set of TABLES, showing the Sterling Value of One Rix Dollar:—Also the Value in Rix Dollars, Skillings, and Stivers, for One Pound Sterling, from 1 to 200 per Cent. Premium:—to which is added, a List of Colonial PAPER CURRENCY, showing the Dates, Colour, and by whom signed, —for the protection of every person in the Colony; by which, at one view, false or wrongly-joined Money may be detected. Printed, in the English and Dutch Languages, by G. GREIG, and Published by W. BRIDEKIRK, for account of W. STRINGER and W. BRIDEKIRK.
It will form a neat Book, printed on very fine Paper and new Type. Price 12 Skillings Stitched, and 2 Rds. neatly Bound.

LOST or Stolen, on Sunday evening the 4th Instant, between the Three Cups and Cape Town, from a strayed Horse, a Saddle and Bridle, nearly new. Whoever will bring the same to Mr. Dixon's Livery Stables, shall be handsomely rewarded.

THE Undersigned acting under a General Power of Attorney from the late Firm of Messrs. M'GARVA, COUSINS, and BARTIE, Coachmakers, respectfully requests those Persons indebted to them previous to the Dissolution of their Co-partnership, to discharge the amount of their respective Accounts and Notes past due, before the end of the present Month, as his instructions otherwise are to resort to coercive measures to compel Payment, without distinction of persons, the parties being desirous to settle their Co-partnership concerns.
P. TAYLOR,
Attorney at Law and Notary Public.
35, *Long-street, corner of Castle-street, Cape Town.*
*** A convenient Stable and Loft to Lett. Apply as above.

A PUBLIC SALE will be held by SIMPSON, SANDERSON, & CO. Keizersgragt, in the Afternoon of *Thursday* next, 8th Instant, of a great variety of British Manufactures; as also a few very superior Dutch Sweet-milk Cheeses, now landing from the Marianne.

No. 7, *BOOM STREET.*
H. GOULAND acquaints the Public, that he has commenced the Manufacture of *Basket Salt*, as good as ever was imported from England, 6 Sks. per Basket. Salt made expressly for Butter, 4 Sks. per pound, and fashionable Wash Balls 2 Sks. each.

Genteel Apartments, and a Stable to Let.
ROBERT SWAN, WATCH MAKER, begs to acquaint his Friends and the Public, that he has removed from Grave-street to No. 6, Market-square, where he continues to carry on the above business in all its branches.
Cape Town, 6th April, 1824.

RECEIVED, *per Marianne*, a fashionable assortment of Millinery and other Fancy Goods, too numerous to insert, which are now all open and for Sale at moderate Prices.
St. John-street, T. DE MOLDRUP.
7th April, 1824.

FOR SALE,
A FEW extra MULES, imported per the Hamburg ship *Sophia*, Captain SPILCKER. For further information, apply to
24, Burg-street. P. F. SIEGRUHN.

FOR Sale, by Private Contract, a House and Premises situated in Castle-street, No. 27. The whole of the Purchase-money may remain at Interest, if desired, for *several years*, under good security.

TO Let, a spacious Upper Store in Rogge Bay, of which possession may be taken immediately.—Apply to No. 8, Strand-street.

JUST Landed per PATIENCE and on Sale, Horse Shoe Nails, 5 and 6 lbs. per 1000 at 6 Rds. per do.; Horse Shoe Rasps; Bush-plate, sorted and very strong; Blistered Steel, roled and in the Blister; Coach-makers Spring Steel, strong, assorted, and for Main-plates; Coach-handles; Curricle and Gig-roof joints; Assorted Curricle Ladder or Rest-joints; A few strong Grass-hopper Springs; A set of C. Springs, calculated for a light Chaise or Landau; a quantity of Springs, of different descriptions:—and a number of other articles too numerous to insert.
The above Articles will be sold on the most reasonable Terms. THOS. HUNTER.
N.B.—Seven and a half per Cent. allowed for Ready Money. Cape Town, April 6, 1824.

Van Diemen's Land and New South Wales.
THE Australian Company's Ship *Portland*, (A. I.) coppered and copper fastened, burthen, per Register, 385 Tons, expected to call here early in May, will have room for Freight, and a few Passengers for the above places.
As the *Portland* is one of the Company's regular Traders, and fitted-up expressly for Passengers, any one desirous of proceeding to either of the above Colonies, will find this a most favourable opportunity.
For Freight or Passage apply to
JOHN FINDLAY.

WITHOUT the least RESERVE.—The public Sales will be continued on the Parade, opposite the Commercial Exchange, in the Morning of Friday next, the 9th inst. of Claret and Hams. At the same time will be offered for Sale, the remainder of the Goods formerly advertised.
JOHN FINDLAY.

PUBLIEKE Verkooping op Zaturdag, den 27 dezer, te twaalf uren precies, van Boter, Kaarsvet, Zout, enz. enz.
A. CHIAPPINI & Co.

EENE publieke verkooping zal gehouden worden door SIMPSON, SANDERSON & Co. op de Keizersgracht op Donderdag namiddag den 8 dezer van eene groote verscheidenheid Britische Goederen; als mede extra goede Hollandsche Zoetemelksche Kazen, nu landende van de *Marianne.*

Wel hem, die 't wislend lot te ontzien heeft noch te duchten,
Die zelf zyn erfgrond bouwt, en 't werken zich niet schaamt;
Die, onbekend en vry, in vaderlandsche luchten,
Op eigen bodem aamt;

Hem, wien zyn kudde kleedt, hem, wien zyn wingerds drenken,
Hem, wien zyn akker voedt en graan last in zyn schuur,
Hem, wien, by zomerbrand, zyn boomen schaduw schenken,
By winter koude, vuur.

Gezegend, die dus leeft, die, met zyn lot te vreden,
Voor vloed noch ebbe schroomt in 's werelds ranke kiel;
Gezegend, die dus zwoegt, met onvermoeide leden
En onbezwaarde ziel.

Gelukkig boven peil, die, wars van aardsche zorgen,
Des daags met yver zwoegt en 's nachts verkwikkend rust;
Wien de onschuld wiegt in slaap en wien, by elken morgen,
't genoegen wakker kust!

Schenk, hemel! my dat lot; schenk, na zoo zoet een leven,
Me een wroeginglooze dood, in diepe vergeten staat;
En dat geen marmren praal, voor trotscharde opgeheven,
Myn needrig graf verraad!

Uit het Engelsche naar POPE *door* TOLLENS

Lord Mansfield.—This great man was never ashamed of publicly recanting any wrong opinion he might have adopted or made known; and he used to say, that to acknowledge you were yesterday wrong, was but to let the world know, that you were wiser to day than yesterday.

THE EMIGRANT.

When fire sets the forests on blaze
It expires on their desolate track;
But the love which has lighted our days,
Still burns when our prospects are black.

I must go to the Huron's wild grounds,
Whilst thou bloom'st in thine own native sun;
Oh, the ocean that parts us has bounds,
But the grief of our parting has none!

Can the eagle fly home to his mate?
Can he build by Niagara's foam?
And are we interdicted by fate
From a spot of the world for our home?

Thou art lost to me ev'n as the dead,
And our tears unavailingly flow;
Yet to think they could cease to be shed,
Would be worse than this burden of woe.

Figure 6 Thomas Campbell, 'The Emigrant', and Alexander Pope, 'Ode on Solitude' (Dutch translation by Hendrik Tollens), *South African Commercial Advertiser*, 7 April 1824, p. 111. Author's photograph of National Archives copy.

As with Campbell's 'Lines' in the *Sydney Gazette*, the poem is embedded in the classified section of the newspaper, a location that juxtaposes the poem's intra-imperial traffic in the stock sentiments of emigration poetry with the circulation of British and Dutch consumer goods in and out of the mercantile counting houses of Cape Town – so we have Simpson and Son advertising their 'Dutch sweet-milk cheeses' and John Findlay his 'Claret and Hams'. Canonical and modern verse's status as transnationally circulating commodity is even more obvious in the case of the Dutch-language poem printed alongside 'The Emigrant'. Printed without so much as a title, only the typographical layout of the verse on the page and the thickness of the dividing line separating it from the classified advertisement that proceeds it indicate to the reader that what they are reading is verse. The inscription 'Uit het Engelsche naar Pope door Tollens', indicates that the poem's assumed readership would be familiar with both Alexander Pope's original 'Ode on Solitude' and the reprinted poem – a Dutch translation of 'Ode on Solitude' by the Dutch poet Hendrik Tollens.[40]

The assumption of bilingual literacy and a working knowledge of popular poetry in both the Netherlands and Britain is indicative of the Whiggish *South African Commercial Advertiser*'s aspiration to reflect the literary tastes as well as the political and commercial interests of Cape Town's recently amalgamated Anglo-Dutch mercantile and bureaucratic elites. On an ideological level, it is a manifestation of the aspiration of the *Advertiser*'s Scottish editor, John Fairbairn, for what he later termed the 'cordial amalgamation' of the ethnically diverse European settlers of the Cape Colony into a single polity governed by British law, a call which echoed through the pages of his editorials in the *Advertiser* throughout the 1820s.[41] The reprinting in a Cape Town newspaper of a Dutch translation of an English poem that presents the embodiment of happiness as the man (and this is a quote from Pope's original) 'whose wish and care / A few paternal acres bound, / Content to breathe his native air, / In his own native ground' would seem, at first glance, to be asking to be read ironically.[42] Yet in a newspaper which celebrates the circulation and reconfiguration of the cultural and material productions of Britain and the Netherlands in the protean community of 1820s Cape Town, Pope's pastoral celebration of the putative joys of a settled life seems to ask to be read as a representation of the colonial ideology of settlement: a celebration of the independence and resilience of the rural yeoman that seems intended to imaginatively counter the despondency and disappointment articulated by British and Dutch emigrant farmers

---

[40] Hendrik Tollens, 'Uit het Engelsche naar Pope door Tollens', *South African Commercial Advertiser*, 7 April 1824, p. 111.

[41] John Fairbairn, *South African Commercial Advertiser*, 31 August 1825, p. 1.

[42] Alexander Pope, 'Ode on Solitude', *The Works of Alexander Pope: With Notes and Illustrations by Himself and Others,* ed. William Roscoe, 10 vols (London: C. and J. Rivington, 1824), vol. II, p. 54.

writing in the *Advertiser*'s correspondence pages and the speaker in Campbell's 'The Emigrant'.

A final alternative is offered in the juxtaposition between 'The Emigrant' and an advertisement offering passenger transport to the Australian colonies of Van Diemen's Land and New South Wales. In contrast to the timeless present of the lyric verse, this advert is future-oriented, offering 'a most favourable opportunity' to 'any one desirous of proceeding to either of the above colonies'.[43] In contrast to the romantic melancholy of Campbell's lyric, this text presents emigration as opportunity: with intra-imperial mobility framed as capitalist speculation, holding out the potential of economic reward to the speculating British emigrant. If the bursting of the Poyais bubble in 1823 alerted prospective emigrants to the potential for catastrophic loss through the risky enterprise of emigration to virgin settlements, the Australian colonies as textually constituted through both emigration literature and advertising offer a more secure prospect of success for the speculating British emigrant. The conventional sentiments of Campbell's 'The Emigrant' enabled it to stand for the despondency that affected early settlers in 1820s South Africa. Yet by reprinting it next to classified adverts and translated verse, the *South African Commercial Advertiser* was able to frame Campbell's melancholic lyric within a counter-discourse that focused on the material and cultural benefits to be derived from the transnational flows of people and goods facilitated by the 1820s emigration boom.

Poetry, as these examples of newspaper verse demonstrate, played an important role in the broader construction of new forms of settler-colonial identities that, although derived culturally from metropolitan Britain, were increasingly defined by the economic and political conditions of colonial life. As Rudy has persuasively argued, the very portability of popular poetry enabled the circulation of stock poetic genres and sentiments across the Anglo-world through the circulation of books in the book collections of emigrants, as well as republication in colonial periodicals.[44] By restoring these texts to their original colonial publication contexts, we can see more clearly that this traffic in stock tropes and sentiments was not merely a case of cultural replication and adaptation.

In the case of 'The Poyais Emigrant', John Fairbairn was able to repurpose a poem that had originally been penned as 'puff' literature

[43] 'Van Diemen's Land and New South Wales', *South African Commercial Advertiser*, 7 April 1824, p. 111.
[44] Rudy, *Imagined Homelands*, p. 16.

to promote the Poyais emigration scheme in order to further his own local propaganda war in support of the established settlers in the Cape Colony. He was able to do so by mobilising the trans-imperial literacy of his local readership, who he assumed would be familiar with the Poyais scheme and its tragic consequences, information they would have gained by reading the metropolitan newspapers and periodicals regularly shipped to the colony. In the Australian colonies also, editors such as the *Australian*'s Robert Wardell exploited the status of the nineteenth-century newspaper as a transnationally circulating commodity to attempt to write themselves into metropolitan emigration discourse. This was made possible in part through the networks of commodity exchange facilitated by the spread of Britain's informal and formal empire during in the 1820s, and in part through the culture of reprinting, which enabled British emigration literature to be extracted and extensively commented upon in the colonial press.

The culture of reprinting also had the potential to radically reconfigure the poetics of emigration. I have suggested that the poetics of emigration during the 1820s was characterised by a turn towards interiority and containment articulated in lyric verse that represents the emigrant as a perpetual exile who yearns for the landscapes of a homeland they can never return to. That global mobility, the paradigmatic marker of modernity, produced a poetics rooted in pre-modern forms such as the dialect song and the pastoral lyric, may seem paradoxical. Yet the ideology of settlement as articulated in emigration literature promoted an agrarian fantasy that enabled emigrants to imagine themselves as yeomen – lords or lairds of their own private empire. This ideology is, of course, deliberately blind to both existing Indigenous life-ways and sovereignties in what were presented as virgin territories and the transnational flows of capital that materially enabled colonial settlement to become a state-building enterprise. Attending to the material context for the reception of these works, as I have done in the case of the two Thomas Campbell lyrics, reveals how embedded they were with texts, such as classified advertising, that draw attention to the speculative economic practices that enabled British emigrants to be transformed, in a generation, into prosperous settlers.

As well as these perhaps accidental juxtapositions, the direct intervention of colonial editors, who used editorial notes, leaders and published correspondence to reframe popular metropolitan poetry to reflect the local concerns of protean settler societies, created new reception contexts for these works. Read in conjunction with the lead articles, government notices, correspondence and advertising with which they were juxtaposed, we can see how popular metropolitan poetry could be read against the grain as part of a deliberately constructed counter-discourse that drew the attention of colonial and metropolitan readers to the disjuncture between metropolitan representations of emigration and the material realities of colonial life.

Chapter 8

'Innovation and Irregularity': Religion, Poetry and Song in the 1820s

James Grande

Writing in the 1820s, William Hazlitt defined the 'spirit of the age' as 'the progress of intellectual refinement, warring with our natural infirmities'.[1] This two-part definition identifies the age with the kind of dialectical movements that have often since been taken to characterise the decade: progress and anxiety, reform and reaction, secularism and millenarianism – to name a few. The definition appears in Hazlitt's essay 'On the Pleasure of Hating', published in *The Plain Speaker* (1826) but written three years earlier, around the time that Hazlitt began the series of magazine portraits that appeared under the heading 'The Spirits of the Age'. This series launched with an essay on Jeremy Bentham in the *New Monthly Magazine* for January 1824 and would be gathered in a single volume as *The Spirit of the Age* (1825). In 'On the Pleasure of Hating', Hazlitt's evocation of the spirit of his age appears outside of the biographical form it would later come to be associated with; here, instead, the parenthetical definition is glossed by a discussion (as so often in Hazlitt) of deep-seated political and religious feeling:

> Even when the spirit of the age (that is, the progress of intellectual refine-ment, warring with our natural infirmities) no longer allows us to carry our vindictive and headstrong humours into effect, we try to revive them in description, and keep up the old bugbears, the phantoms of our terror and our hate, in imagination. We burn Guy Faux in effigy ... subscribe to new editions of *Fox's Book of Martyrs*; and the secret of the success of the *Scotch Novels* is much the same—they carry us back to the feuds, the heart-burnings, the havoc, the dismay, the wrongs and the revenge of a barbarous age and people—to the rooted prejudices and deadly animosities of sects and parties in politics and religion, and of contending chiefs and clans in war and intrigue.[2]

---

[1] William Hazlitt, 'On the Pleasure of Hating', in *The Plain Speaker*, 2 vols (London, 1826), vol. I, pp. 307–28 (p. 310).

[2] Hazlitt, 'On the Pleasure of Hating', pp. 310–11.

Hazlitt's vivid account of the pleasures of hating and the residual force of 'rooted prejudices', undermining the progress of refinement, emphasises the way that sectarian feeling continues to operate, in custom and culture.[3] In this essay, I want to use this conception of the spirit of the age as a means of thinking about the relative status of poetry and song in the 1820s and the way that both are shaped by a schismatic religious imaginary. Such sectarian prejudice might appear anachronistic in the decade that saw significant moves towards religious toleration through the Repeal of the Test and Corporation Acts (1828) and Roman Catholic Relief Act (1829), reforms which have often been seen to prefigure the expansion of the franchise in 1832. However, as Hazlitt's conjuring of a 'spirit of the age' suggests, to focus on progress and toleration over the 'animosities of sects and parties in politics and religion' is to tell only one side of the story.

David Stewart has given us a compelling account of poetry in the 1820s and 1830s as an 'age of doubt', of a poetic culture defined by its self-consciousness, 'uncertain about its own value in its contemporary market and in the future it hoped to reach'.[4] In what follows, I want to suggest that we should read this period as one of doubt but also, paradoxically, of fervent faith, as evident in the interrelated cultures of religious poetry and song.[5] For Protestant Dissenters from the Church of England, music had long been seen in deeply ambivalent terms, as at once central to Nonconformist identities and a continual source of anxiety, marked as it was by associations with luxury, commerce, ritual and unreason. Dissenting writers worried about the apparently irrational nature of music, its anti-mimetic qualities, or lack of semantic coding, as well as its vaunted power over the emotions and associations with both 'popish' superstition and the rituals of what William Blake derided as 'State Religion'. For many Nonconformists the sensuousness of music was indisputably at odds with the austere character of dissenting culture. As Hazlitt – among the most acute self-analysts of

---

[3] As Kevin Gilmartin writes, *The Spirit of the Age* 'teases the ingenuous reader and the disenchanted essayist alike with the possibility of a reformist spirit of the age, even as it defers fulfilment through a host of compromises and contradictions that leave revolution and reaction hopelessly intertwined in contemporary public life'. See *William Hazlitt: Political Essayist* (Oxford: Oxford University Press, 2015), p. 7.

[4] David Stewart, *The Form of Poetry in the 1820s and 1830s: A Period of Doubt* (Basingstoke: Palgrave Macmillan, 2018), p. 4.

[5] On the intensely evangelical character of the 1820s, see Boyd Hilton, *The Age of Atonement: The Influence of Evangelicalism on Social and Economic Thought, 1795–1865* (Oxford: Clarendon Press, 1988); D. W. Bebbington, *Evangelicalism in Modern Britain: A History from the 1730s to the 1980s* (London: Unwin Hyman, 1989), chapter 3, 'A Troubling of the Water'.

the dissenting sensibility – wrote in 1815, a 'distaste for pictures, music, poetry, and the fine arts in general' was part of the Puritan inheritance of Rational Dissent, a consequence (or so Hazlitt thought) of a dogmatic habit of mind and an 'affected disdain' for the fine arts 'as not sufficiently spiritual and remote from the gross impurity of sense'.[6]

At the same time, Dissenters and Methodists developed a musical culture of their own, centred above all on congregational hymn-singing.[7] To their detractors in the Church of England, however, this practice eroded the border between sacred and profane music through the appropriation of tunes from the stage, street and tavern. For many in the established Church, congregational singing was deeply suspect and routinely disparaged as an outpouring of enthusiasm. Even liberals such as Leigh Hunt routinely displayed their elite condescension towards Methodist culture:

> The Wesleyan Methodists are very much attached to social meetings, in which they pour out their souls to God and to each other. They have *watch nights* once a quarter, in which the thrilling calmness of midnight sheds a new enjoyment over the nuptials of the Church; on these occasions the most glowing hymns rise in delicious unison from male and female voices, the young men and women gaze on each other with looks of pity and devotion, and then of course walk home together through fields and lanes in the most comfortable manner possible.[8]

As Jon Mee writes, Hunt's 'liberalism perpetuates the dialect of enlightenment that casts popular forms of knowledge and experience as a threat to right reason and cultural value'.[9] Methodist singing is for Hunt a form of misplaced emotion, not directed towards any proper end.

In the history of hymn-singing in Britain, 1820 represents a break, signalling a sea change in Anglican attitudes towards congregational song. In contrast with the vibrant culture of hymnody among Dissenters and Methodists, the Church of England had long regarded congregational hymn-singing as unsanctioned, even prohibited. These concerns

[6] William Hazlitt, 'On the Tendency of Sects,' in *The Complete Works of William Hazlitt*, 21 vols, ed. P. P. Howe (London, 1930–4), vol. IV, pp. 47–51 (p. 49).

[7] See Misty Anderson, *Imagining Methodism in Eighteenth-Century Britain: Enthusiasm, Belief and the Borders of the Self* (Baltimore, MD: Johns Hopkins University Press, 2012). On the relationship between Methodism and Romantic literary culture, see Jasper Cragwall, *Lake Methodism: Polite Literature and Popular Religion in England, 1780–1830* (Columbus: Ohio State University Press, 2013); Helen Boyles, *Romanticism and Methodism: The Problem of Religious Enthusiasm* (London: Routledge, 2016).

[8] [Leigh Hunt], *An Attempt to Shew the Folly and Danger of Methodism* (London, 1809), p. 61.

[9] Jon Mee, *Romanticism, Enthusiasm, and Regulation: Poetics and the Policing of Culture in the Romantic Period* (Oxford: Oxford University Press, 2003), p. 266.

were brought to a head in 1820 when Thomas Cotterill, curate of St Paul's church in Sheffield, who 'had previously published "a Selection of Psalms and Hymns," which had become popular elsewhere', enlisted the aid of James Montgomery, Sheffield poet, newspaper editor, social reformer and one-time radical, 'in revising and improving the work for the service of his own congregation'. According to his Victorian biographers, Montgomery contributed 'not only the benefit of his judgment in the choice and amendment of available compositions from various quarters, but a number of his own best hymns: and in due course, the book was printed, and introduced to the seat-holders of St. Paul's Church'. The move quickly met with opposition from within Cotterill's church: 'so high did the spirit of resistance run ... that after many unedifying altercations among the parties, and several ineffectual attempts to settle the business by the mediation of friends', the case was brought before the Ecclesiastical Court at York in July 1820.[10]

Cotterill vs. *Holy and Ward* was not the most dramatic court case in a year that saw the trials of Henry Hunt after Peterloo, Queen Caroline on charges of adultery, and the Cato Street conspirators for their attempted assassination of the entire British Cabinet, but it carried its own significance.[11] In the introduction to *A Selection of Hymns for Public and Private Use* (Sheffield, 1819), Cotterill attempted to forestall claims that 'Psalms only are *authorized*, and that the introduction of Hymns is *Innovation and Irregularity*.'[12] The court heard, however, that Cotterill had introduced 'of his own pretended authority into the Public performance of divine service ... a certain selection of hymns and a metrical version of Psalms not set forth or allowed by law to be used in Churches or Chapels of the establishment of the Church of England or by any competent authority whatsoever'. On 28 July, the judge in the case ruled that hymns and metrical psalms were not permitted by the Thirty-Nine Articles or the Book of Common Prayer and had not since been legalised by the head of the Church. Even in the case of Sternhold and Hopkins's *Book of Psalmes* (1562), the so-called authorised version, the judge concluded, 'I can discover no regular authority, though perhaps it may be presumed from unquestioned usage'. He went on to add, however,

---

[10] John Holland and James Everett, *Memoirs of the Life and Writings of James Montgomery*, 7 vols (London: Longman, 1854–6), vol. III, pp. 158–60.

[11] For a detailed account of the political unrest of this year, see Malcolm Chase, *1820: Disorder and Stability in the United Kingdom* (Manchester: Manchester University Press, 2013).

[12] Thomas Cotterill, with the assistance of James Montgomery, *A Selection of Psalms and Hymns for Public and Private Use, adapted to the services of the Church of England* (Sheffield: The Editor, 1819), p. vii.

that 'so much advantage accrues from the prevalent usage of introducing into the church service Hymns and versions of Psalms more edifying and acceptable to the congregations than any compositions which have obtained the sanction of competent authority ... I should gladly have evaded the necessity of deciding the legality of this usage'.[13] He therefore suggested a compromise in which the archbishop of York, Edward Harcourt, 'acted as mediator between the parties; and, to put an end to contention, undertook to compile, for the use of that church, a new selection of Psalms and *hymns*, and to print them at his own expense'.[14] Cotterill and Montgomery's selection was withdrawn, but only to be replaced by an essentially identical edition, approved by and dedicated to the archbishop: 'in fact, the selection was ultimately revised by the very individuals who had originated it, and who conducted it through the press, Montgomery himself reading the proofs in Sheffield, as they came from the King's printer in London'.[15]

The case foregrounded the questions that hymn-singing provoked, as a cultural form uneasily situated between religious, literary and musical life. Was the hymn a private or a public genre, a confessional form of poetry intended for private meditation, or a form of collective song, to be used as part of public worship? The court case resolved that it was not the hymn texts, hymn tunes, or even the act of collective singing that was at issue but the question of authority. Once Cotterill and Montgomery's collection had received the stamp of episcopal approval, the decision was widely interpreted as sanctioning congregational hymn-singing within the Church of England, leading to a proliferation of new hymnals in the 1820s. Doubts on the subject still persisted among some high-church clergy, as the *Christian Observer* noted in July 1822, in reply to a pamphlet by the bishop of Peterborough:

> Should the plan of the bishop of Peterborough be adopted, all hymns which have not received the sanction of the king in council ... must be prohibited without exception: the Archbishop of York's must share the fate of the rest ... What a revolution would thus take place, in opposition to public taste and general feeling ... what is 'dignity' without utility? Let us beware how we realize the sarcastic prediction of certain Northern critics—'The Church of England will die of *dignity*.'[16]

---

[13] Jonathan Gray, *An Inquiry into Historical Facts, relative to Parochial Psalmody* (York: J. Wolstenholme, 1821), cited in Thomas K. McCart, *The Matter and Manner of Praise: The Controversial Evolution of Hymnody in the Church of England, 1760–1820* (Lanham, MD: Scarecrow Press, 1998), p. 100.

[14] *Christian Observer* (July 1822), p. 434.

[15] Holland and Everett, *Memoirs of Montgomery*, vol. III, p. 160.

[16] *Christian Observer* (July 1822), pp. 435–6.

The allusion here is to a prediction in an 1811 *Edinburgh Review* article by Sydney Smith, 'Hints on Toleration', which argued that the Church of England 'ought to be made more popular, or it will not endure for another half century'.[17] By 1820, congregational singing had come to be seen as an essential ingredient in any form of popular religion. The 'Archbishop's selection' went through at least twenty-nine editions and was followed by even more successful collections: as Nicholas Temperley writes, the Cotterill case 'opened the way for the flood of nineteenth-century hymn books'.[18] These were almost always collections of words, not tunes, which were published separately and not tied to specific hymns. Instead, hymns were set to any existing tune that fitted the metrical pattern, giving new meanings to old tunes.[19]

In 1820, another provincial clergyman, Reginald Heber, wrote to the bishop of London, William Howley, from his Shropshire parish, seeking approval for his own collection of hymns. Heber argued that,

> The fondness of the lower classes for these compositions is well known. Every clergyman finds that, if he does not furnish his singers with hymns, they are continually favouring him with some of their own selection; their use has been always the principal engine of popularity with the dissenters, and with those who are called the 'Evangelical' party.[20]

Howley prevaricated and Heber's collection remained unpublished, although his most well known hymn, 'From Greenland's Icy Mountains', was first published in 1820, after its impromptu composition the previous year. According to a story that would be endlessly retold, Heber was visiting his father-in-law, William Shipley, dean of St Asaph, in Wrexham. 'Half a dozen friends were gathered in the little rectory parlor one Saturday afternoon, when Dr. Shipley turned to Heber, knowing the ease with which he composed, and asked him if he could write some missionary lines for his church to sing the next morning', for a service in aid of the missionary Society for the Propagation of the Gospel. 'Retiring to a corner of the room', Heber composed four

---

[17] [Sydney Smith], 'Hints on Toleration', *Edinburgh Review*, 17 (February 1811), 393–402 (p. 398).

[18] Nicholas Temperley, *The Music of the English Parish Church*, 2 vols (Cambridge: Cambridge University Press, 1979), vol. I, p. 208.

[19] As Ian Bradley writes, the practice of printing words and tunes together, 'giving each hymn its own particular tune', only began with *Hymns Ancient and Modern* (1861). See Ian Bradley, *Abide With Me: The World of Victorian Hymns* (London: SCM Press, 1997), p. 72.

[20] Quoted in Amelia Heber, *The Life of Reginald Heber, D. D.*, 2 vols (London: John Murray, 1830), vol. II, p. 24.

verses on the spot, which were sung for the first time the following morning.[21]

'From Greenland's Icy Mountains' was destined to become one of the most popular missionary hymns of the nineteenth century, its expansive global ambitions and complacent evangelical sentiments reiterated through each performance:

> From Greenland's icy mountains,
>   From India's coral strand,
> Where Afric's sunny fountains
>   Roll down their golden sand;
> From many an ancient river,
>   From many a palmy plain,
> They call us to deliver
>   Their land from error's chain!
> . . .
> Salvation! oh, Salvation!
>   The joyful sound proclaim,
> Till each remotest nation
>   Has learn'd Messiah's name!

Like so many hymns, the lyric is self-reflexive, describing its own intended action in the world: the act of singing is itself the means of instruction, of spreading the 'joyful sound' to 'each remotest nation'. In 1819, Heber had not visited any of the places he confidently imagined the gospel spreading, but in 1823 he was appointed as the second bishop of Calcutta, with a diocese covering the whole of India, southern Africa and Australia. Over the next three years, he travelled widely across the Indian subcontinent, preaching for missionary societies, before his sudden death in February 1826 on a visitation to south India. *Hymns, Written and Adapted to the Weekly Church Service of the Year* (1827) was published a few months after his death, overseen by his widow. 'It was his intention,' Amelia Heber explained in her preface to the collection, 'to publish them soon after his arrival in India; but the arduous duties of his situation left little time, during the short life there allotted to him, for any employment not immediately connected with his diocese.'[22]

The history of Heber's *Hymns*, from Wrexham to Calcutta, underscores the extent to which the hymn had become a cultural object closely identified with the movement from provincial to colonial culture, often bypassing the metropolitan literary scene. As Chapters 6 and 7 in this

---

[21] Hezekiah Butterworth, *The Story of the Hymns* (New York: American Tract Society, 1875), pp. 40–1.

[22] Reginald Heber, *Hymns, Written and Adapted to the Weekly Church Service of the Year* (London: John Murray, 1827), p. vii.

volume show, the traffic between province and colony is a distinctive feature of 1820s print culture; by contrast, it is the metropolitan scene that often appears parochial. Over the next few decades, evangelical missionaries would become supremely adept at disseminating hymnals in vast quantities wherever they went.[23] They appeared to have harnessed the affective power of the eighteenth-century dissenting and Methodist hymn and directed it to missionary ends, in the process overwriting many of the earlier associations that hymn-singing had carried with enthusiasm and dissent. Heber maintained the propriety of his hymns: 'no fulsome or indecorous language has been knowingly adopted; no erotic addresses to him whom no unclean lips can approach; no allegory, ill understood and worse applied'.[24]

Heber's implied target here is the extraordinary and controversial eighteenth-century Anglo-German tradition of Moravian hymnody, characterised in musical terms by the collective improvisation of the congregation and in lyrical terms by visceral, often eroticised descriptions of the blood and wounds of Christ.[25] The following lines, for example, portray the marriage of Christ and the Church through a sensuous, even grotesque vision of the 'side-hole' of the lamb:

> We greet each other in the Side
>   Of our beloved Spouse,
> Which is ordain'd for his dear Bride
>   Her everlasting House
> . . .
> Blest Flock in th'Cross's Atmosphere,
>   You smell of Jesu's Grave,
> The Vapours of his Corpse so dear
>   Are the Perfume you have.
> Its Scent is penetrant and sweet!
> When you each other kiss and greet,
> This Scent discovers that you were
> To Jesu's Body near.

---

[23] This is not to say that hymns, in common with other forms of colonial culture, did not allow for anti-colonial resistance; on the subversion of the English book within the British Empire, see Homi K. Bhabha, 'Signs Taken for Wonders: Questions of Ambivalence and Authority under a Tree Outside Delhi, May 1817', *Critical Inquiry*, 12 (1985), 144–65. For Bhabha, 'the colonial presence is always ambivalent, split between its appearance as original and authoritative and its articulation as repetition and difference' (p. 150).

[24] A. Heber, *The Life of Reginald Heber*, vol. I, p. 371.

[25] As Sarah Eyerly has shown, eighteenth-century Moravians cultivated a form of collective improvisation as a spontaneous expression of religious feeling, based on a shared repertoire of hymns that had been memorised and internalised. See Sarah Eyerly, 'The Sensual Theology of the Eighteenth-Century Moravian Church', in *Christian Congregational Music: Performance, Identity and Experience*, ed. Monique Ingalls, Carolyn Landau and Tom Wagner (Farnham: Ashgate, 2013), pp. 155–68.

With thy Side's Blood quite cover me,
    And wet me thro' and thro';
For this I pant incessantly,
    And nothing else will do.
The Blood sweat in thy Agony
Come in full heat all over me,
Thy Body stretch its breadth and length
O'er me, and give me Strength.[26]

Small wonder such verses gave hymn-singing a bad name: in his influential *Life of Wesley* (1820), the Poet Laureate Robert Southey wrote that the 'most characteristic parts' of Moravian hymnody were 'too shocking to be inserted': 'even in the humours and the extravagances of the Spanish religious poets, there is nothing which approaches to the monstrous perversion of religious feeling in these astonishing productions'.[27] It was these associations that Anglican writers in the 1820s were keen to disavow, transforming the hymn into a respectable literary genre and an effective tool of missionary endeavour. Heber's *Hymns* are a manifesto for a chastened, Anglican hymnody, one that included hymns by Charles Wesley, William Cowper, Joseph Addison, Alexander Pope, John Dryden and Walter Scott alongside Heber's own compositions, many of which proclaim a martial Christianity.[28] Hymn-singing was now identified with the missionary project and with literary respectability. As J. R. Watson writes, 'such practical considerations were allied to the new affinities with Romantic poets, as hymn-writing became more closely connected with conceptions of inspiration (often prophetic, in the Ezekiel sense) and of imagination'.[29]

In the introduction to *The Christian Psalmist* (1825), a collection which includes his best-known hymn, the Christmas carol 'Angels from the Realms of Glory', James Montgomery argued that hymns are one of the fundamental forms of poetry, found across all known kinds of 'national mythology':

---

[26] *A Collection of Hymns of the Children of God in all Ages, From the Beginning till now. In Two Parts. Designed Chiefly the use of Congregations in Union with the Brethren's Church*, 2 vols (London, 1754), vol. II, pp. 349–50.

[27] Robert Southey, *The Life of Wesley; and the Rise and Progress of Methodism*, 2 vols (London: Longman, 1820), vol. I, p. 480.

[28] On this dimension of Heber's hymns, see Brian H. Murray, '"The Son of God Goes Forth to War": The Imperial Martyr's Hymnbook', in *Scripture and Song in Nineteenth-Century Britain*, ed. James Grande and Brian H. Murray (Bloomsbury, forthcoming).

[29] J. R. Watson, *The English Hymn: A Critical and Historical Study* (Oxford: Oxford University Press, 1997), p. 302.

Songs and Hymns, in honour of their Gods, are found among all people who have either religion or verse. There is scarcely any pagan poetry, ancient or modern, in which allusions to the national mythology are not so frequent as to constitute the most copious materials, as well as the most brilliant embellishments.[30]

Montgomery was educated at a Moravian school at Fulneck, Leeds and recalled the influence of the hymns he learnt as a child:

The hymns of the Moravians are full of ardent expressions, tender complaints, and animated prayers: these were my delight. As soon as I could write and spell I imitated them; and before I was thirteen, I had filled a little volume with sacred poems, though I was almost unacquainted with our great English poets.[31]

As one of the most widely disseminated forms of popular culture, hymn-singing would come to be deeply associated with ideas of national identity – writing a century later, D. H. Lawrence found a 'clue' to the 'ordinary Englishman' in an uncritical, childhood saturation in Nonconformist hymns. Here, however, it is the foreignness of Moravian hymns, their affective power and distance from 'our great English poets', that Montgomery emphasises.[32] Moravian hymnody is here an alternative tradition to 'our great English poets' and a formative one for Montgomery's later career as hymn-writer and poet, associated above all with intensity of affect.

While his reputation has long since been eclipsed, Montgomery was among the most popular poets of the early nineteenth century for his long poems on biblical and historical themes – his abolitionist *The West Indies* (1809) was into its sixth edition by 1823.[33] His five-canto (though unfinished) *Greenland* (1819) recounts the journey of Moravian missionaries to Greenland in 1733, opening with a scene of hymn-singing at sea:

---

[30] James Montgomery, *The Christian Psalmist; or, Hymns, Selected and Original* (Glasgow: Chalmers & Collins, 1825), p. v.

[31] Quoted in Watson, *The English Hymn*, p. 305.

[32] D. H. Lawrence, 'Hymns in a Man's Life' (1928), in *The Cambridge Edition of the Works of D. H. Lawrence: Late Essays and Articles*, ed. James T. Boulton (Cambridge: Cambridge University Press, 2004), 130–4 (p. 134). Reflecting on his own Congregationalist background and 'the rather banal nonconformist hymns that penetrated through and through my childhood', Lawrence writes that hymns learned as a child 'live and glisten in the depths of the man's consciousness in undimmed wonder, because they have not been subjected to any criticism or analysis' (pp. 130, 132). See also Lawrence's memories of domestic hymn-singing, and 'the insidious mastery of song', in 'Piano' (1918).

[33] William St Clair, *The Reading Nation in the Romantic Period* (Cambridge: Cambridge University Press, 2004), pp. 217–18.

Three humble voyagers, with looks inspired.
And hearts enkindled with a holier flame
Than ever lit to empire or to fame,
Devoutly stand:—their choral accents rise
On wings of harmony beyond the skies . . . [34]

While sometimes disparaged as 'the poet of the *sects*', as the *Monthly Review* described Montgomery on the publication of his evolutionary epic *The Pelican Island* (1827), his hymns were praised across denominational boundaries.[35] To Lucy Aikin, an old family friend who regretted Montgomery's intensifying evangelism through the 1820s, he was nonetheless 'at the head of living writers of this kind of poetry'. On receiving a new edition of his hymns in 1853, Aikin wrote to him warmly:

> Your Hymns have an earnestness, a fervour of piety, and an unmistakable sincerity, which goes straight to the heart. In the style, too, you are perfectly successful, and it is one in which few are masters. Clear, direct, simple, plain to the humblest member of a congregation, yet glowing with poetic fire, and steeped in Scripture.[36]

This description identifies Montgomery's hymns with the dissenting virtues of plain speech and sincerity, infused with poetic inspiration and scriptural authority.

For the poet Josiah Conder, writing in 1825 in the *Eclectic Review*, 'either Poetry is growing more religious, or Religion more poetical', a chiasmus that neatly levels the respective statuses of poetry and religion.[37] This trend reached an apotheosis two years later with the publication of John Keble's *The Christian Year*, which has some claim to being the bestselling book of English poetry across the nineteenth century. In the 'Advertisement' to the collection, Keble employs a recognisably Wordsworthian idiom to describe need for the kind of poetry he was supplying: 'in times of much leisure and unbounded curiosity, when excitement of every kind is sought after with a morbid eagerness', the effect of the Liturgy is lost 'on many even of its sincere admirers: the very tempers, which most require such discipline, setting themselves,

---

[34] James Montgomery, *Greenland, and Other Poems* (London: Longman 1819), p. 2.

[35] Review of *The Pelican Island and other Poems*, *Monthly Review*, 3rd series, 6 (September 1827), 83–9 (p. 84).

[36] Lucy Aikin to James Montgomery, Hampstead, 13 February 1853, in Holland and Everett, *Memoirs of Montgomery*, vol. VII, p. 228. My thanks to Jon Mee for this reference, and for much else in these paragraphs.

[37] [Josiah Conder], 'Sacred Poetry', *Eclectic Review* (October 1825), 354–63 (p. 354), quoted in Kirstie Blair, 'John Keble and *The Christian Year*', in *The Oxford Handbook of English Literature and Theology*, ed. Andrew Hass, David Jasper and Elisabeth Jay (Oxford: Oxford University Press, 2007), pp. 607–23 (p. 607).

in general, most decidedly against it'. Keble's own work is designed for a disciplinary form of private reading: 'The object of the present publication will be attained, if any person find assistance from it in bringing his own thoughts and feelings into more entire unison with those recommended and exemplified in the Prayer Book.'[38] Almost two decades later, John Henry Newman looked back on the first publication of Keble's collection:

> Much certainly came of the Christian Year: it was the most soothing, tran-quillizing, subduing work of the day; if poems can be found to enliven in dejection, and to comfort in anxiety; to cool the over-sanguine, to refresh the weary, and to awe the worldly; to instil resignation into the impatient, and calmness into the fearful and agitated – they are these.[39]

For Newman, writing soon after his conversion to Roman Catholicism, Protestantism was an essentially unpoetical religion; Keble supplied the missing poetry. Some of Keble's poems were also taken up as hymns, further blurring the boundary between religious song and verse.

Reading such accounts, we could conclude that readers in the 1820s were becoming increasingly pious. Alternatively, we might wonder whether Keble and Newman's prescriptive language betrays an anxiety about the need for regulation, for those who 'most require such disci-pline' to bring their 'own thoughts and feelings into more entire unison' with the Book of Common Prayer. This might be achieved by silent reading but perhaps even more effectively through song; indeed, while singing is often represented as an inspired expression of faith and com-munity, it can also serve as an effective means of disciplining minds and bodies.[40] As Roger Parker argues, the '*sending down* of vocal music', its 'controlled dissemination' through choral societies and other institu-tions, 'became a powerful propaganda tool' in the debate about the new industrial society.[41] Hymn-singing could function as a way of control-ling unruly subjects both in the British and colonial contexts, later aided by the development of the sight-singing movement and the Tonic sol-fa

---

[38] [John Keble], *The Christian Year: Thoughts in Verse for the Sundays and Holidays Throughout the Year* (London: W. Baxter, 1828), pp. v–vi.

[39] John Henry Newman, 'John Keble', in *Essays Critical and Historical*, 2 vols (London: Pickering, 1871), vol. II, p. 441, cited in Kirstie Blair, 'John Keble and the Rhythm of Faith', *Essays in Criticism*, 53.2 (2003), 129–50 (p. 129).

[40] See Erin Johnson-Williams, 'Musical Discipline and Liberal Reform', in *Music and Victorian Liberalism: Composing the Musical Subject*, ed. Sarah Collins (Cambridge: Cambridge University Press, 2019), pp. 15–36.

[41] Roger Parker, '"As a Stranger Give it Welcome": Musical Meanings in 1830s London', in *Representation in Western Music*, ed. Joshua S. Walden (Cambridge: Cambridge University Press, 2013), pp. 33–46 (p. 42).

method.[42] It could never be a totalising system, however, as the radical journalist William Cobbett suggested in his description of a Methodist meeting he encountered while travelling through the Kentish countryside in 1823:

> I was attracted, fairly drawn all down the street, by the *singing* . . . The *singing* makes a great part of what passes in these meeting-houses. A number of women and girls singing together make very *sweet sounds*. Few men there are who have not felt *the power* of sounds of this sort. *Eyes* do a good deal, but *tongues* do more . . . The parson seemed to be fully aware of the importance of this part of the '*service*'. The subject of his hymn was something about *love*: Christian love; love of Jesus; but, still it was about *love* . . . I am satisfied, that the singing forms great part of the *attraction*. Young girls like to sing; and young men like to hear them.[43]

For Cobbett, who maintained a reliably consistent antipathy to evangelicalism and dissent across the anti-Jacobin and radical phases of his career, communal singing could be a way to evade religious authority, as the slippage from sacred to profane love here suggests. This is a slightly different version of the scene Leigh Hunt described above: while equally hostile to Methodism, Cobbett is more sympathetic to the social pleasures the congregation find in song. Hymns carried many possible meanings – not all intended by their authors – and could be reclaimed by radicals, from the Paineite hymns 'To Reason' published in Richard Carlile's *Republican* (1817–26) to the Chartist hymnals of the 1840s.[44] In *Corn Law Rhymes* (1831), Ebenezer Elliott gives a powerful description of Primitive Methodists on the moors outside Sheffield, singing a hymn set to a tune from Robert Burns, in a scene that merges radical protest with millenarian zeal:

> To other words, while forest echoes ring,
> 'Ye banks end bra', o'bonny Doon,' they sing
> . . .
> The hymn they sing is to their preacher dear;
> It breathes of hopes and glories grand and vast . . . [45]

---

[42] See Charles Edward McGuire, *Music and Victorian Philanthropy: The Tonic Sol-Fa Movement* (Cambridge: Cambridge University Press, 2009). Congregational singing, along with other aspects of public worship, was also given new impetus by the postwar church-building programme that flowed from the Church Building Acts of 1818 and 1824.

[43] William Cobbett, *Rural Rides* (London: William Cobbett, 1830), pp. 176–9.

[44] On Chartist hymnody, see Mike Sanders, '"God is our guide! our cause is just!": The *National Chartist Hymn Book* and Victorian Hymnody', *Victorian Studies*, 54.4 (2012), 679–705.

[45] [Ebenezer Elliott], 'The Ranter', in *Corn Law Rhymes* (London: B. Steill, 1831), p. 9. My thanks to Tim Fulford for bringing this reference to my attention.

In spite of such radical reappropriations, the 1820s was the decade when hymn-singing escaped its controversial associations with sectarianism and enthusiasm to become a hegemonic cultural form, accompanied by the – not unrelated – emergence of a new form of devotional poetry.

How, then, do these changes relate to the broader literary culture of the 1820s? As Jerome McGann writes, the decade was once seen as a border zone or wasteland between the Romantic and Victorian:

> At best we track a series of wounded beasts – the failures or madnesses of Darley, Beddoes, Clare. For the rest, critics simply shut the book of a Romanticism that seemed to translate itself into a commercialized nightmare: the new craze for Gift Books and Annuals like *Friendship's Offering*, *The Keepsake*, *Forget-Me-Not*. Literary history averts its gaze from this spectacle – there is scarcely a better word for the scene – because culture cannot easily capitalize its values. It seems an elegant dumpheap of factitious and overpriced trash – poor imitations of the life of the great romantics.[46]

This view has since been substantially revised over recent years with Felicia Hemans, Letitia Elizabeth Landon and other 1820s poets no longer seen as 'poor imitations' of the great (male) Romantics. Similarly, the craze for keepsakes, anthologies and annuals inaugurated by Rudolph Ackermann's *Forget Me Not, a Christmas and New Year's Present* (1822) is now regarded as a more complex cultural phenomenon and not merely as a commercialised mode of literary production – a theme explored by Clara Dawson in Chapter 10 of this volume. The religious poets and hymn-writers, however, have eluded such critical recovery, with a few notable exceptions.[47] Their spiritual concerns might seem to elevate them above commercial imperatives, but we could instead view the annuals and hymnals of the 1820s as closely related through their pious sentimentality and mass appeal: twin cultural products of this decade, which have lacked critical-aesthetic prestige ever since.[48]

One of the points of connection between many of these collections and anthologies is their shared preoccupation with marking time, whether that takes the form of tracking the liturgical calendar (as with Heber and Keble) or presenting themselves as annual (Christmas or New Year's) gifts. Another common, and even more pervasive, theme is their obsession with poetry as song (and song as poetry) and the implications this holds for ideas of poetic voice. Much recent criticism has focused on

---

[46] Jerome McGann, 'Rethinking Romanticism', *ELH*, 59 (1992), 735–54 (p. 746).

[47] See, for example, Kirstie Blair's work on Keble, cited above.

[48] On the final, religious phase of Hemans's career, see Julie Melnyk, 'Hemans's Later Poetry: Religion and the Vatic Poet', in *Felicia Hemans: Reimagining Poetry in the Nineteenth Century*, ed. Nanora Sweet and Julie Melnyk (New York: Palgrave, 2001), pp. 74–92.

the ornate physical form and elaborate engravings of the annuals, with one account arguing that through 'their unequivocal embrace of visual culture, literary annuals represented a dramatic shift in how readers interacted with print'.[49] Such an emphasis risks overlooking the way that poets of the decade were equally concerned with an aesthetics of sound and voice. Poems such as Landon's *The Improvisatrice* (1824) belong to the genre of 'Romantic pseudo-song' identified by Terence Hoagwood, or alternatively to the form that Elizabeth Helsinger characterises later in the century as the 'song poem'. For Hoagwood, 'Landon's pseudo-songs exemplify common features of the genre in the Romantic period ... The imaginariness of the music is part of its charm, its sales appeal.'[50] Helsinger finds in her conflation of poem and song a more ambitious, less commercially driven set of cognitive demands: the song poem asks 'readers to think like song; to listen to the sound of a poem thinking'.[51]

In the leading article for the new *Westminster Review* in January 1824, the Unitarian minister William Fox surveyed English politics and culture. Turning to the poetry of the day, he wrote that Wordsworth 'seems rather to chaunt a demonstration to the initiated few than the many who should be sung to'. This phrase locates Wordsworth's voice somewhere between speech and song and within the contested religious politics of the 1820s.[52] Fox echoes Hazlitt's double-edged description of Wordsworth and Coleridge in 'My First Acquaintance with Poets', published a few months earlier in the *Liberal*, in which Hazlitt remembered meeting the poets of *Lyrical Ballads* in 1798 and hearing them read their work: 'There is a *chaunt* in the recitation both of Coleridge and Wordsworth, which acts as a spell upon the hearer, and disarms the judgment. Perhaps they have deceived themselves by making habitual use of this ambiguous accompaniment.'[53] As Lucy Newlyn has suggested,

---

[49] The Multigraph Collective, *Interacting with Print: Elements of Reading in an Era of Print Saturation* (Chicago: University of Chicago Press, 2018), p. 46.

[50] Terence Hoagwood, *From Song to Print: Romantic Pseudo-Songs* (New York: Palgrave Macmillan, 2010), p. 138.

[51] Elizabeth K. Helsinger, *Poetry and the Thought of Song in Nineteenth-Century Britain* (Charlottesville: University of Virginia Press, 2015), p. 2. See also Angela Leighton, *Hearing Things: The Work of Sound in Literature* (Cambridge, MA: Harvard University Press, 2018).

[52] [William Fox], 'Men and Things in 1823', *Westminster Review*, 1 (January 1824), 1–18 (p. 13). Wordsworth finally agreed to write for the annuals in 1829, unable to resist the offer of a hundred guineas for twelve pages of verse: see Peter J. Manning, 'Wordsworth in the *Keepsake*, 1829', in *Literature in the Marketplace: Nineteenth-Century British Publishing and Reading Practices*, ed. John O. Jordan and Robert L. Patten (Cambridge: Cambridge University Press, 1995), pp. 44–73.

[53] W[illiam]. H[azlitt]., 'My First Acquaintance with Poets', *The Liberal*, 3 (April 1823), 23–46 (p. 41).

'chaunt' here carries a range of meanings, from bardic primitivism to the 'oracular authority' of the Anglican Church, in opposition to the dissenting ideal of plain speech.[54] Hazlitt's identification of this sound as a source of suspicion, working alongside (or against) the lyrical content as a form of musical accompaniment, signals his own dissenting anxieties about musical meaning.

If Fox and Hazlitt were writing as dissenting critics, by the 1820s Wordsworth was himself attempting to capture and convey the new status of religious song: not so much '*creating* the taste by which he is to be enjoyed' but following in the wake of Montgomery, Heber, Keble and the final acceptance of hymn-singing in the Church of England.[55] In 'On the Power of Sound' (composed 1828–9, but not published until 1835), Wordsworth aligns his own poetry with the experience of religious song, 'the hymn / Of joy', which fills 'Innumerable voices . . . With everlasting harmony', bringing together semantic meaning with the affective force of 'inarticulate notes':

> Break forth into thanksgiving,
> Ye banded Instruments of wind and chords;
> Unite, to magnify the Ever-living,
> Your inarticulate notes with the voice of words![56]

The idiosyncratic 'argument' that precedes and glosses the ode imagines the ear 'as occupied by a spiritual functionary, in communion with sounds, individual, or combined in studied harmony' and speculates that 'sounds acting casually and severally . . . could be united into a scheme or system of moral interests and intellectual contemplation'. This desire is pursued first through the Pythagorean music of the spheres and then 'by the representation of all sounds under the form of thanksgiving to the Creator', followed by 'the destruction of earth and the planetary system' but 'the survival of audible harmony' (p. 310). Throughout the poem, sound is privileged over sight, in a way that revises and extends the argument of Wordsworth's earlier 'Immortality Ode', where the two senses exist in more equal relationship. In the final stanza, the 'visionary stir' we associate with Wordsworth's poetry is swept away:

> A Voice to Light gave Being;
> To Time, and Man his earth-bound Chronicler;

---

[54] Lucy Newlyn, *Reading, Writing, and Romanticism: The Anxiety of Reception* (Oxford: Oxford University Press, 2000), p. 339.

[55] William Wordsworth, 'Essay, Supplementary to the Preface', in *Poems*, 2 vols (London: Longman, 1815), vol. I, p. 368.

[56] William Wordsworth, *Yarrow Revisited, and Other Poems* (London: Longman, 1835), pp. 310–22 (pp. 321, 320).

A Voice shall finish doubt and dim foreseeing,
And sweep away life's visionary stir
. . .

O Silence! are Man's noisy years
No more than moments of thy life?

In the 'Immortality Ode', our 'noisy years' similarly tend to silence, but here this question is finally refuted by the vehicle of Logos and apocalypse: 'the Word, that shall not pass away' (pp. 321–2).

Wordsworth thought 'some passages in "The Power of Sound" equal to anything I have produced' and placed the poem at the end of *Yarrow Revisited* and as the last of the 'Poems of Imagination' in his collected works.[57] While most critics have not shared his own high valuation of the poem, some recent accounts have emphasised its significance: Tim Fulford reads 'On the Power of Sound' as 'an attempt to make a definitive statement on sound's place in the universe', one that 'straitjackets the more personal and experiential encounters with sound that had prompted Wordsworth to begin writing the poem', while for James Chandler it is as if Wordsworth 'were recomposing the straggling sounds of his earlier work into a sanctioned order'.[58] The context of the poem in the 1820s suggests that Wordsworth's strained attempt to retrospectively impose a structure on his earlier poetry is not only a sign of his own turn towards Anglican orthodoxy but a reflection of the elevated status of religious song in the 1820s and of a culture that valued such work as Heber's hymns and Keble's religious verse. Another poem in *Yarrow Revisited*, 'By the Sea-Side', one of Wordsworth's 'Evening Voluntaries', includes a less cosmic but still compelling evocation of pan-European hymn-singing:

> how gladly would the air be stirred
By some acknowledgment of thanks and praise,
Soft in its temper as those vesper lays
Sung to the Virgin while accordant oars
Urge the slow bark along Calabrian shores;
A sea-born service through the mountains felt
Till into one loved vision all things melt:

---

[57] Wordsworth to Alexander Dyce, 23 December 1837, in *The Letters of William and Dorothy Wordsworth, The Later Years, Part III, 1835–1839*, ed. Ernest de Selincourt, rev. Alan G. Hill (Oxford: Clarendon Press, 1982), p. 502.

[58] Tim Fulford, *The Late Poetry of the Lake Poets: Romanticism Revised* (Cambridge: Cambridge University Press, 2013), p. 235; James Chandler, 'The "Power of Sound" and the Great Scheme of Things: Wordsworth Listens to Wordsworth', in *"Soundings of Things Done": The Poetry and Poetics of Sound in the Romantic Ear and Era*, ed. Susan Wolfson, Romantic Circles Praxis Series (2008), available at https://romantic-circles.org/praxis/soundings/chandler/chandler.html (accessed 7 February 2022).

Or like those hymns that soothe with graver sound
The gulfy coast of Norway iron-bound;
And, from the wide and open Baltic, rise
With punctual care, Lutherian harmonies.[59]

The religious singing imagined here across Europe transcends differences of language and religion, to become one harmonious song.

John Stuart Mill famously described how reading Wordsworth helped him to recover from the nervous breakdown he suffered in the mid-1820s, brought on by his intensive utilitarian education. Wordsworth is also central to Mill's theorising of lyric in his 1833 essay 'What is Poetry?', which turns on a distinction between poetry and oratory, or 'eloquence':

> Poetry and eloquence are both alike the expression or utterance of feeling. But . . . eloquence is *heard*; poetry is *over*heard. Eloquence supposes an audience. The peculiarity of poetry appears to us to lie in the poet's utter unconsciousness of a listener. Poetry is feeling confessing itself to itself, in moments of solitude . . . Eloquence is feeling pouring itself forth to other minds, courting their sympathy, or endeavouring to influence their belief, or move them to passion or to action.
>
> All poetry is of the nature of soliloquy. It may be said that poetry, which is printed on hot-pressed paper, and sold at a bookseller's shop, is a soliloquy in full dress, and upon the stage. But there is nothing absurd in the idea of such a mode of soliloquizing.[60]

What Mill's distinction works to exclude, however, is the possibility of poetry as song, especially collective song, realised through performance. Indeed, by the late 1820s Wordsworth was himself working against Mill's conception of lyric through his attempts to capture and convey the experience of singing in unison. Song destabilises Mill's distinction between poetry and eloquence (or rhetoric), foregrounding the tension that Anne Janowitz identifies between the individual and communitarian impulses in Romantic poetics. For Janowitz, Mill's essay 'offers a structure of lyricism shorn of either social intention or musical accompaniment'.[61] The excluded communitarian lyric that Janowitz seeks to recover is the lyric of protest and solidarity; however, the history of hymn-singing in the 1820s points to the multiple possibilities that song can carry, from creating religious community to being used as an instrument of colonial control. Thinking about the hymn as a characteristic 1820s genre – one

---

[59] Wordsworth, *Yarrow Revisited*, p. 174.
[60] 'Antiquus' [John Stuart Mill], 'What is Poetry?', *Monthly Repository*, new series, 73 (January 1833), 60–70 (pp. 64–5).
[61] Anne Janowitz, *Lyric and Labour in the Romantic Tradition* (Cambridge: Cambridge University Press, 1998), p. 56.

that has rarely been the object of critical attention – can give us a richer understanding of the sectarian controversies of these years and of the transformation from early to mid-century poetry, between the epochs we label 'Romantic' and 'Victorian'.

Keyword: March of Intellect

Matthew Sangster

The increasing availability of education was one of the most contentious political issues of the 1820s. Responding to the King's Speech after the Duke of Wellington was installed as Prime Minister in 1828, the leading Whig politician Henry Brougham asserted that the current age had definitively moved on from the period of conflict in which the new premier had made his name:

> Let the soldier be ever so much abroad, in the present age he could do nothing. There was another person abroad,—a less important person,—in the eyes of some an insignificant person,—whose labours had tended to produce this state of things. The schoolmaster was abroad [cheers]! and he trusted more to the schoolmaster, armed with his primer, than he did to the soldier in full military array, for upholding and extending the liberties of his country.[1]

In this intervention, one much cited at the time, Brougham made an argument about historical progress that was fundamentally political. This was by no means an uncomplicated rejection of established systems of power or of British imperial ambitions – ideologically inflected instruction was, after all, a key element of Britain's national and global policies. Nevertheless, Brougham's assertion that large-scale education would promote liberal values made many commentators extremely uncomfortable. *The Age* – a conservative newspaper opposed to Catholic emancipation and Brougham's political agenda – made this obvious when it facetiously extended the encomium to the schoolmaster into a mock-heroic peroration on Brougham's ambitions for the March of Intellect:

> He has founded his university—he has established his Institutes—he is heard in the Senate, and at meetings for mutual instruction—he is the Crispin of Cobblers, and the "great toe to their assemblies"—the president of societies,

---

[1] HC Deb 29 January 1828, *Hansard*, Second Series, Volume 18, p. 58.

and the cavalier of the knights of the thimble—the Sampson destined to annihilate thousands, and the Hurcules to destroy the hydra of despotism.[2]

Brougham's praise and *The Age*'s mockery both speak to the currency and the imaginative power of the March of Intellect as a metaphor for cultural change. Technological innovation, economic development and demographic shifts were fundamentally redefining what knowledge was and what education meant. As Brian Maidment puts it, at its most expansive the March of Intellect can be taken as being the 'set of socio-economic, cultural, and scientific changes that underpinned the transformations in the class structure and economic base of British society in the first half of the nineteenth century'.[3] A satirical song in *The Age* provides support for Maidment's assertions about comprehensive change, seeing the March of Intellect as driving the whole country to moral degeneracy. The song asserts that 'Our Noble Lords now think it quite with their high rank compatible / To make love to each other's wives, if they're at all comeatable', but argues that the most worrying symptoms were expressed by the labouring classes, who 'Distracted now with *learned things*, home, wife, and work neglect'. For *The Age*, 'provinces grown haughty', the national debt and a wave of bankruptcies could all be blamed directly on the March of Intellect.[4] Nor was *The Age* alone. Decrying the effects of universal education in an 1829 pamphlet, the pseudonymous Scrutator frothed that Britain's travails 'shew[ed] the displeasure of Almighty God at the abuse of science and the march of intellect'.[5] The *Imperial Magazine* concurred, arguing that

> The besetting errors of the age in which we live, are scepticism and infidelity; these arise out of what is termed, "the march of intellect." Men are more generally informed in this age, than in any other recorded in history, and, alas, more proud, more confident, and more resolute.[6]

In the first issue of a short-lived fortnightly periodical entitled *The Censor*, the conductors contended that 'If intellect march much further, it is impossible to conjecture whither it will eventually carry us; it has already rendered those who were only qualified to serve behind counters

---

[2] 'The March of Intellect', *The Spirit of* The Age *Newspaper, for 1828* (London: A. Durham, 1829), pp. 92–3.

[3] Brian Maidment, 'Imagining the Cockney University: Humorous Poetry, the March of Intellect, and the Periodical Press, 1820–1860', *Victorian Poetry*, 52.1 (Spring 2014), 21–39 (p. 21).

[4] 'The March of Intellect', *The Spirit of* The Age *Newspaper, for 1828*, pp. 17–18.

[5] Scrutator, *The Mania of the Day; or The Effects of Universal Education* (Bristol: C. Goodchild for the Author, 1829), p. 58.

[6] 'On Reading.—No. IV', *Imperial Magazine*, 12 (1830), 344–8 (p. 347).

unfit even for that occupation; we really hope some *counter* attraction will shortly be discovered.'[7]

The notion of the 'March of Intellect' was employed in relatively neutral manners earlier in the century. As Alice Jenkins argues, it could stand both for improvements in disciplinary specialisation and for the scaling up of the intellectual franchise, 'progress across society as well as upwards towards perfection'. However, as Jenkins also acknowledges, 'the phrase played an important role in defining a sense of the difference between the early nineteenth century and all previous eras in British history, whether that difference [was] thought of as marking progress or the reverse'.[8] In the later 1820s, this discussion became sharply politicised as reform loomed, sharpening the popular sense that the new liberal age described by Brougham was rapidly coming into being. This was a cause of intense anxiety, even in those who were in principle sympathetic. In his comic poem *The March of Intellect*, William Thomas Moncrieff writes that

> We have had England's olden days,
>   When fought and bled her sons;
> We too have had her golden days,
>   These are her *learned* ones.[9]

Moncrieff echoes Brougham's assertion, but his succession of ages implies that while the past was marked out by military achievement and national glory, the achievements of the current age remain uncertain, open to questioning, mockery and doubt.

One manifestation of the March of Intellect was cheap literature in forms not always considered respectable by middle-class auditors. The *Gentleman's Magazine* opined that if the initial wave of supposedly improving publications was representative, the best course would be to 'halt, retrace our footsteps, and return, *if we can*, to the harmless simplicity—the darkest ignorance—of our dishonoured forefathers'. However, the magazine allowed that if education could manage to 'improve the understanding and correct the morals' of those to whom it was formerly unavailable, then the March of Intellect might 'be crowned with imperishable honour'.[10] The means of super-

---

[7] 'The March of Intellect', *The Censor*, 1.1 (6 September 1828), 13.

[8] Alice Jenkins, *Space and the 'March of the Mind': Literature and the Physical Sciences in Britain 1815–1850* (Oxford: Oxford University Press, 2007), p. 9.

[9] W. T. Moncrieff, *The March of Intellect: A Comic Poem* (London: William Kidd, 1830), p. 9.

[10] 'The March of Intellect', *Gentleman's Magazine*, new series, 98 (March 1828), 195–7 (p. 197).

intendence the more privileged classes sought to employ were often institutional, building on earlier organisations like the Sunday schools set up by Hannah More and others in the later eighteenth century and the mechanics' institutes founded both directly by workers and by middle-class interests. However, new institutional priorities were contentious. Just as Brougham and Wellington opposed one another in Parliament, they also opposed each other in pursuing educational projects. Brougham was instrumental in promoting mechanics' institutes, setting up the University of London and establishing the Society for the Diffusion of Useful Knowledge. Wellington played an important role in the foundation of King's College London. This was an institution designed to counter the University of London's levelling agenda, which sought to provide a space where 'an enlightened education may be obtained at a reasonable charge, and where persons of every religious persuasion may be freely admitted'.[11] The *London Magazine* saw Wellington's involvement in King's College as vindicating Brougham's project, arguing that 'Mr. Brougham, in having changed his opponents, first into pupils and then into co-operators in the same cause, has won a laurel more green and glorious, than if he had beaten them in argument a thousand times.'[12] However, more cynical operators continued to forecast a calamitous breakdown in the social order if current courses were adhered to. In a satirical article of obituaries purporting to be from sixty years in the future, *The Age* located Brougham's grave amid 'the ruins of the once noted London University', framing it in a very similar manner to the monument in Percy Bysshe Shelley's 'Ozymandias':

> the "wreck of matter" which is strewn around the spot where he sleeps, bears the most impressive testimony of the good his labours have accomplished. He has left behind him a sad memorial of the evil great men may do when their sole ambition is to rise, not by their own merit, but by the ruin of others. He promised to revolutionise the world, and had his life but stretched out another half century, the March of Intellect would have subverted every institution, civil and religious, which the wisdom of ages had pronounced pure and sacred.[13]

While the *London Magazine* dreamed of a time when 'every teacher and parish should have its school', evoking Scottish precedents to argue for

---

[11] *Statement by the Council of the University of London, Explanatory of the Nature and Objects of the Institution* (London: Longmans and John Murray, 1827), p. 8.

[12] 'The Two Colleges', *London Magazine*, 3rd series, 1 (July 1828), 480–6 (p. 486).

[13] 'An Obituary for the Year 1888', *The Spirit of* The Age *Newspaper, for 1828*, 66–9 (p. 69).

the huge social benefits of universal education, for others, the March augured chaos and societal collapse.[14]

The March of Intellect triggered both liberal utopianism and conservative doomsaying, but the truth was that few people in the 1820s knew confidently what to make of it. This ambivalent attitude might best be exemplified by the run of satirical cartoons produced in the late 1820s. In Robert Seymour's 'The March of Intellect' (Figure 7), London University strides confidently on, sweeping away elements of the Old Corruption; by contrast, in William Heath's 'March of Intellect' (Figure 8), a bewildering array of Heath Robinson-like contraptions speak to the confusing contradictions of an emergent metropolitan modernity. Commentators could agree that something big was happening and that this might be called the March of Intellect. However, while some were keen to assert what this would mean, many others rightly acknowledged that no one in the 1820s could fully understand what the ultimate consequences of these vast social innovations might be.

[14] 'The Two Colleges', p. 485.

Figure 7   Robert Seymour, 'The March of Intellect', [?1829]. Courtesy of The Lewis Walpole Library, Yale University.

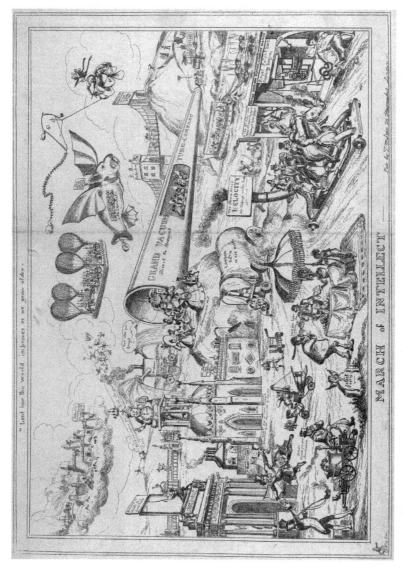

Figure 8 William Heath, 'The March of Intellect', 1829. Courtesy of The Lewis Walpole Library, Yale University.

Keyword: Doubt

David Stewart

Doubt, a matter of mixed feelings, self-consciousness and speculative enquiries, was a state that many in the decade found themselves in. I will begin this discussion of doubt in the 1820s with a quotation that is itself doubtful in content and form:

> when shall wonders have an end—when shall we become standard in knowl-edge when shall it be said—"The force of genius can no farther go"—the last forty days has left me behind a modern "Reading made easy"—where am I   the units & common place materials of things hardly know me in my astonishments—can it be so far in the year of the world as 5590—am I so far among the improvments of time & so ignorant[.][1]

The writer recounts and attempts to keep up with the 1820s catchphrase, the 'march of intelect' (p. 24): change, progress, improvement. Yet the march leaves the intellect spinning, unsure which way is forward. The prose gets lost, deranged. The Act for Ascertaining and Establishing Uniformity of Weights and Measures was written into law on 17 June 1824, and that should help: quantities fixed, comparisons possible, sub-jective experience of space and time regulated. Yet 'the units & common place materials of things hardly know me in my astonishments' (p. 27). That is not 'I do not know them', but those measurements have started to doubt *me*. 'Where am I', the writer asks, though he is also asking 'when am I' and 'who am I'. The reader may simply be asking 'what is this?'.

The quotation comes from an unsigned essay by John Clare, written (probably) in 1829, though it remained unpublished until 2001.[2] It is a product of the 1820s, and the difficulty we have in assigning it a date or even a form is an aspect of its relations with the decade's creative

---

[1] P. M. S. Dawson, 'Clare's "Letter to Allan Cunningham": An Unpublished Prose Work', *John Clare Society Journal*, 20 (2001), 21–37 (p. 27).

[2] For discussion of its likely dating, see Dawson, 'Clare's "Letter"', pp. 21–2.

innovations and uncertainties. It is a characteristic production of the 1820s in the doubts it raises rather than the answers it provides. The complaint one might make about writing like this is that, in its frantic chasing of an era of constant 'improvments', it loses shape. It is, one might say, deservedly ephemeral because it doubts its status so thoroughly. It has often seemed to be true of the decade as a whole: it does not shape itself in a way that is easily graspable, in part because it seemed so relentlessly focused on forward momentum and self-consciously concerned with its own future status. Its energy disperses and it leaves little trace. This keyword takes Clare's doubtful method of writing as its model. It seeks to show that the decade's own self-reflections provide a mode of thinking through the doubts about what we do when we name a decade, giving it shape, choosing and selecting, structuring and solidifying. Doubt offers readers of the 1820s an unusually flexible, if disorientating, way of thinking.

Clare's essay is headed 'On the Wonders of inventions curiositys strange sights & other remarkables "of the last forty days" in the Metropolis in a Letter to A Friend'. His friend Allan Cunningham (a colleague of Clare's on the *London Magazine* at the start of the 1820s, and himself a relentless experimenter in print culture) thought it might make Clare some money. The essay tries despairingly to keep track of speculations in printing, building, religion and even shaving, and the essay is itself a speculation aimed at the publishing trade.

It is hard to know how to frame or name this piece of writing. Calling it an essay, even, misses the way Clare combines genres and styles in unpredictable ways. But I would suggest that framing and naming undoes its 1820s quality, an era I have called elsewhere a 'period of doubt'.[3] Clare provides a method of writing that permits doubtful, speculative forms of thought. Steam innovations, he says, make Africa and even the moon seem to be within touching distance; yet this proves as much a matter of doubt (fear, uncertainty) as it does imperial confidence. We can date it to the end of the decade, but fixing the essay with a date seems perverse: the date he gives in the essay – 5590 – is accurate, providing you want the Hebraic year, though he's not quite sure about that. A collection such as this one is bound to think of literary culture in close relation to its historical moment of production, but an essay such as Clare's might help us think of the era's own uncertainties about the security of fixing time. Clare's writing talks of pushing forward to some chronological goal ('when will wonders have an *end*' [emphasis added])

---

[3] David Stewart, *The Form of Poetry in the 1820s and 1830s: A Period of Doubt* (Basingstoke: Palgrave Macmillan, 2018).

but his method of writing is powered by loops and circles, muddling time, place and identity. The essay threatens constantly to disperse, to lose its grip on its time and place and to become ephemeral. It was a common concern in a decade whose literary productions are characterised both by their technological solidity – steel-plate engravings, steam printing, wire-wove paper – and their frivolous ephemerality – silver-fork novels, light verse, magazine essays. Their methods of writing provide, I suggest, an epistemological guide for us.

Doubt becomes one of the animating spirits of the decade. The highly prominent place Clare gives religion is apt: 1827 saw the publication of John Keble's *The Christian Year*, one of many religious poems to enjoy huge sales. Looking back to the decade from the 1840s, Thackeray shows a young Pendennis and his mother reading Felicia Hemans, Bishop Heber and *The Christian Year*: 'son and mother whispered it to each other with awe'.[4] But even these seemingly doctrinaire poems seem unsure of themselves. Readings of Hemans, especially, seem both productively and perplexingly unsure: she is at once patriarchal and feminist, at once pro-colonial and anti-authoritarian.[5] Genres like annual poetry, magazines and the silver-fork novel build self-doubt about their status (how they are valued aesthetically and commercially, whether they will have any value for future ages) into their very structures. At the dawn of the decade Sydney Smith wrote playfully to Archibald Constable about the latest production of the Author of Waverley, *Ivanhoe*, that 'There is *no doubt* of its success.'[6] Scott was never so sure himself, and it might be that these novels, so exemplary of the power of the decade's print industry, helped readers navigate the decade's doubts. *Ivanhoe*'s Byronic sceptic, Brian de Bois-Guilbert, asks whether 'future ages [will] believe that such stupid bigotry [anti-Semitism] ever existed', and it is a question Scott turned towards his readers in 1820, while also being a question that looks forward to a succession of future eras in which that question will be posed again and again.[7]

Even architectural forms might be doubtful in this era of speculation

4 William Makepeace Thackeray, *The History of Pendennis* (London: Macmillan, 1901), p. 28.
5 On this feature of Hemans studies, see David Latané, 'Who Counts? Popularity, Modern Recovery, and the Early Nineteenth-Century Woman Poet', in *Teaching British Women Writers, 1750–1900*, ed. Jeanne Moskal and Shannon R. Wooden (New York: Peter Lang, 2005), pp. 205–23.
6 John O. Hayden, ed., *Walter Scott: The Critical Heritage* (London: Routledge, 1970), p. 172. See also Chapter 2, by Ian Duncan, in this volume.
7 Walter Scott, *Ivanhoe*, ed. Graham Tulloch (Edinburgh: Edinburgh University Press, 1997), p. 315. The novel was published at the end of 1819 – 18 December in Edinburgh, 31 December in London – with 1820 on the title page.

on building contracts: as Clare puts it, 'the wonders grows into nothing again or rather an enormous joke in stone' (p. 27). Gregory Dart describes the 'Cockney' aesthetics that lie behind John Nash's reconstruction of the West End, 'a construction that always seemed to be imagining its own ruin, even and perhaps especially in its pristine form', so that buildings seem to resemble the flash language and fashions of the era, 'a kind of optical illusion, functioning both as appearance and reality, aspiration and fulfilment'.[8] More generally in the decade, space is altered and regulated by the 'pristine' productions of new technology, but this has the strange and highly characteristic effect of making formal structures seem to be wavering by virtue of their insistent presentness.

Contemporary critics of a globalised world emphasise a view of space as a temporal flux of lines of movement rather than mappable entities.[9] The 1820s was an era of standardisation of measurement, but the decade's literature frequently finds space and time escaping its grasp. When Byron's Don Juan arrives in London, this 'mighty mass of brick, and smoke', he thinks of Bishop Berkeley and spins off into speculation about the proof that there was no matter, offering to 'stake' (to wager, to gamble) the world in a religious dispute (a doubt about the future state), and then comes to doubt: 'Oh Doubt! – if thou be'est Doubt, for which some take thee, / But which I doubt extremely'.[10] Clare, faced with yet another derangement of time and space, turns to doubt as a mode of mental exploration: 'If you was to tell me they were going to fetch the moon by steam for exebition to the egyptian hall should I doubt it – no – stirring & pokeing & pursuing my poor comprehensions into every cranny of my brain' (p. 28). Doubt can enable rather than inhibit thought. Doubting can be active, a matter of questioning. It can be baffled, almost a sense of wonder. It can be fearful. In Scots the word is used to mean suspect, expect, anticipate, believe to be true without quite having the proof: 'I doubt me, his wits have gone a bell-wavering by the road', says a character following an encounter with an apparition in Scott's *Monastery*, published in 1820.[11]

This is a decade that mobilises the idea of doubt by turning doubt

---

[8] Gregory Dart, *Metropolitan Art and Literature 1810–1840: Cockney Adventures* (Cambridge: Cambridge University Press, 2012), pp. 150, 124.

[9] For example, Tim Ingold, *Lines: A Brief History* (London: Routledge, 2007); Bruno Latour, *Science in Action: How to Follow Scientists and Engineers through Society* (Cambridge, MA: Harvard University Press, 1987).

[10] Byron, *Don Juan*, 10:82, 11:22. Cantos 9–11 were written in 1822 and published by John Hunt in August 1823. See vol. 5 of *Complete Poetical Works*, ed. Jerome J. McGann (Oxford: Clarendon Press, 1993).

[11] Walter Scott, *The Monastery* [1820], ed. Penny Fielding (Edinburgh: Edinburgh University Press, 2000), p. 74.

on itself. Thomas Carlyle called this the most 'self-conscious' society in human history: 'our whole relations to the Universe and to our fellow man have become an Inquiry, a Doubt'.[12] This fact was once used to write this decade off. Clare hopes to see a steam-driven razor blade invented, but he also wishes he had another improvement, a 'Reading made easy' to help him make sense of his age, to put it in order. We actually need, I'd argue, what Clare provides: a poetics of doubt that calls into being a culture obsessed with mapping, measurement and fact, but that seemed also to be spinning out of control.

---

[12] [Thomas Carlyle], 'Characteristics', *Edinburgh Review*, 54 (December 1831), 351–83 (p. 366).

Chapter 9

The Decade of the Dialogue

Tim Fulford

It is an 'age of personality', wrote Robert Southey in 1817, taking up a phrase of Samuel Taylor Coleridge's.[1] William Wordsworth agreed: for the Lake Poets, the post-Waterloo period represented the burgeoning of a print culture that preferred 'literary gossiping' to works of genius and unveiled poets' private lives rather than extolled their publications.[2] Dismayed by this trend, they understood its cause to be a boom of cheap periodical print aimed at an expanded reading public.[3] During the 1820s, the steam press made printing tenfold faster; the stereotype cut the cost of typesetting; the Fourdrinier machine slashed the price of paper. By 1832, it was possible to market a magazine for a penny and see it bought by 200,000 people, a tiny fraction of the price of the leading journals of 1820 – the *Edinburgh* and the *Quarterly* – which sold fewer than 10,000 copies each. The new mass readership was more plebeian and more likely to buy, 'in monthly parts, at cheap prices', encyclopaedias, annuals, novels and magazines than they were the expensive volumes of poetry of Wordsworth and his friends.[4] New periodicals such as *Blackwood's Magazine* profited from publishing intimate conversation between fictional versions of literary characters and from making personal attacks on the poets whose works they

[1] Robert Southey, *A Letter to William Smith, Esq., M.P.* (London: John Murray, 1817), p. 45.

[2] Samuel Taylor Coleridge, *The Friend*, ed. Barbara E. Rooke, 2 vols (London and Princeton, NJ: Routledge & Kegan Paul, 1969), vol. I, p. 210.

[3] On print's exposure, and consequent regulation, of the private, see John Brewer, 'This, That and the Other: Public, Social and Private in the Seventeenth and Eighteenth Centuries', in *Shifting the Boundaries: Transformation of the Languages of Public and Private in the Eighteenth Century*, ed. Dario Castiglione and Lesley Sharpe (Exeter: University of Exeter Press, 1995), pp. 1–21.

[4] '*Johnstone's Edinburgh Magazine*: The Cheap and Dear Periodicals', *Tait's Edinburgh Magazine*, 4 (January 1834), 490–500 (p. 492).

disliked.[5] In 1829, Southey noted the change: 'All classes are now brought within the reach of your current literature . . . on the quality of which, according as it may be salubrious or noxious, the health of the public mind depends.'[6]

Despite the proliferation of print, the democratisation of taste and the modest sales of their verse, the 1820s was the decade in which the Lake Poets' reputation was made. The cause of this seeming paradox is explained by Matthew Sangster on the basis of the decade's fetishisation of personality.[7] The old poets, Sangster suggests, were marketed to mass audiences in periodicals such as *Blackwood's* on the basis of intimate portraits. Purchasers could buy, through magazine articles, privileged access to the private man, and could thereby eavesdrop on a 'genius', vicariously sharing a relationship that was portrayed as being above the commercial fray that pertained everywhere else. Without having to read anything as demanding as *The Excursion, Thalaba the Destroyer* or *The Friend*, the magazine buyers consumed the essential poet, as revealed in his conversation. Thus to a degree, the 'real' poet was marketed so as to launder mass print: he gave an air of exclusivity to its ephemeral duration and cheap position in a commercial market. Ironically, having been dismissed in the old highbrow Reviews by such arbiters of traditional gentlemanly taste as Francis Jeffrey and George Canning, and having, in response, written obscure essays asserting their determination to 'create the taste' by which they would be relished, the Lake Poets were now popular – but as commodifications of genius in magazine pages rather than because their poetry sold heavily to the enlarged reading public.[8] As Sangster concludes,

> The propagation of Romantic genius thus operated through a kind of queasy symbiosis between the poets and their interpreters. Periodicals brought poets' work before a wider public, but did so by representing and misrepresenting those poets as objects of fascination in themselves. Readers and critics responded to poets' assertions of their exceptional natures with a curiosity that was as much social as it was aesthetic. Along with the conveniently-timed

[5] See Richard Cronin, *Paper Pellets: British Literary Culture after Waterloo* (Oxford: Oxford University Press, 2010).

[6] Robert Southey, *Sir Thomas More: or, Colloquies on the Progress and Prospects of Society*, ed. Tom Duggett, 2 vols (London and New York: Routledge, 2018), vol. I, p. 361. Henceforth cited as *Colloquies*.

[7] Matthew Sangster, *Living as an Author in the Romantic Period* (Cham: Palgrave Macmillan, 2021), pp. 325–32.

[8] From a letter of 21 May 1807, paraphrased in the 'Essay Supplementary to the Preface' (1815). *The Letters of William and Dorothy Wordsworth: The Middle Years 1806–20*, ed. Ernest de Sélincourt, revised by Mary Moorman and Alan G. Hill, 2 vols (Oxford: Oxford University Press, 1969–70), vol. I, p. 150.

deaths of the younger Romantic generation, this paved the way for a wave of articles that cemented poets as potentially glamorous subjects of interest, but which also subjected their lives and habits to intense scrutiny.[9]

The poets found this unexpected development bittersweet: on the one hand, they seized the opportunity that publicity gave to cash in by supplying verse to the intellectually lightweight, high-paying annuals that became popular in the 1820s; on the other, they deplored the exposure of their private lives in gossipy articles (however complimentary the journalist). All too often, moreover, the journalist was not complimentary but either critical, or embarrassing, or both. De Quincey, confessing his own opium addiction in the *London Magazine*, hinted at Coleridge's – the first reference to it in print.[10] He implied that if Coleridge, was, as claimed, an original genius, he was a damaged one who dishonestly concealed his problem. Hazlitt, provoked by their self-elevation to a position above criticism, detailed Wordsworth's and Coleridge's conversations with him, and with each other, in Alfoxden in 1798 – only to lament the passing of Coleridge's brilliance.[11] He also revealed the poets' onetime political radicalism and attacked them for attempting to cover it up while pretending their politics had remained consistent. His former idols and mentors, he suggested, had enchanted him by their presence but had subsequently revealed feet of clay: their claims to brilliance were smokescreens to hide their retreat and decline. Neither Hazlitt nor De Quincey was forgiven by the poets for thus publicising the private information known to him as a friend.

It was Southey who found himself most completely exposed by the proliferation of cheap print. In 1817 a pirate edition of the revolutionary play he had written in 1794, *Wat Tyler*, was published without his knowledge – for the sum of two shillings (about a fifth of the typical price for books of verse of its size). Its appearance was followed by speeches in Parliament and articles in the press identifying him as a turncoat and a hypocrite. His efforts to suppress the publication in the courts failed, and further pirate editions were then produced. Richard Carlile's edition, priced at threepence, sold over 20,000 copies; together, in William St Clair's estimate, the editions sold between twice and three

---

[9] Sangster, *Living as an Author*, p. 327.

[10] *Confessions* appeared in the *London* in September and October 1821 and in book form in 1822. On De Quincey's exposure of Coleridge, see Nigel Leask, *British Romantic Writers and the East: Anxieties of Empire* (Cambridge: Cambridge University Press, 1992), pp. 170–228.

[11] William Hazlitt, 'My First Acquaintance with Poets', *The Liberal*, 1 (1822), 23–46.

times as many copies as all Southey's other works put together.[12] The text, and his reputation with it, had spiralled out of his control.

Finding their past lives and present selves public property when old writings and private conversations appeared in print, the Lake Poets were provoked into attempting to take back control of their images. Rather than simply rail at the new print culture or write memoirs telling things their way, they published conversational dialogues designed to debate and exemplify a healthier model of discussion and dissemination than did the magazine portrait. It is this 1820s genre – an effort to beat the marketers of intimacy and personality at their own game – that is the subject of this chapter. Prose rather than verse, it has Wordsworth's *Excursion* (1814) as its trigger (as did several of the magazine portraits that objected to that poem's critical portrait of political radicals who resembled the Wordsworth of the 1790s). Like that poem, it typically features several characters in conversation, sometimes seen in situ in hill country, debating what they happen to see and feel – and reflecting on how they come to see and feel it. It is not, that is to say, Socratic dialogue or its eighteenth-century descendants, which work dialectically through a particular philosophical question with each 'speaker' merely a mouthpiece for a particular position and with setting and context largely absent.[13] Rather, it represents in writing the conversational interaction of the now-distant old relationships – interaction that had fostered poems (and had, to some extent, been thematised in those poems). In reviving old conversations in new, virtual form, it recollects past collaborations self-reflexively – both acknowledging their passing and considering its own form as a testament to them. In the process, as a print discourse, it offers readers a taste of the friendly talk that had sponsored the old poems that they were now coming to appreciate (placing the public, as if guests, within the coterie from whose conversations those poems had arisen). Unlike Hazlitt's magazine articles, however, it does so at one or two removes and omits personal information. It also features two further characteristics, to greater and lesser degrees. First, it often models for readers how they may receive the writing of the author and his contemporaries. Thus, instead of lecturing readers on how to read the new poetry, as Wordsworth had done in the 1815 'Essay Supplementary to the Preface', or inveighing against the publishing of private lives, as Coleridge had done in *Biographia*

---

[12] William St Clair, *The Reading Nation in the Romantic Period* (Cambridge: Cambridge University Press, 2004), pp. 317–18.

[13] This tradition, and its ending, is outlined in Michael Prince, *Philosophical Dialogue in the British Enlightenment: Theology, Aesthetics, and the Novel* (Cambridge: Cambridge University Press, 1996).

Literaria (1817), the dialogue features characters discussing how to read the poems and why they are worth reading. What is said unlocks the characteristics of the poetry, and the way it is said suggests that the poetry is best understood through intimate conversation between intellectuals. Second, the dialogue models the acquisition of knowledge as a process of mutual questioning between particular writers of the present and from the past, rather than as the assemblage of isolated facts or formulation of abstract principles. Knowledge is embodied and subjective and is shared in writing and talk; it is not coldly systematic or detached from personal discourse. Against utilitarian liberalism, the dialogues seek to exemplify conservative historiography and to intervene in social, political and religious argument on that basis.

It was Southey who first planned to write dialogues; his idea was taken up by his friends and the first publication in the genre was Walter Savage Landor's *Imaginary Conversations* in 1824 (further series saw print in 1828 and 1829, with later expansions). Humphry Davy's *Salmonia* appeared in 1828 (with a second edition in 1829); his more ambitious sequel *Consolations in Travel* came out after his death in 1830. Southey responded to Landor's work in *Sir Thomas More: or, Colloquies on the Progress and Prospects of Society* (1829). Coleridge's *Aids to Reflection* (1825), a work comprising marginal commentary on the prose of Archbishop Leighton, is a related form. These works not only comprise dialogues between various authors but also maintain a dialogue with each other. Coleridge's posthumously published *Table Talk* (1835) was a further related publication – not dialogue, but one side of many conversations recorded by his nephew Henry Nelson Coleridge. This work was a family attempt to bring 'the peculiar splendour and individuality of Mr. Coleridge's conversation' before the public, as Hazlitt had done for himself in the *Table Talk* volumes he published in 1821 and 1822.[14] The aim of this attempt to print talk 'too subtle to be fettered down on paper' was to reveal 'something of the wisdom, the learning, and the eloquence, of a great man's social converse', in order to give it 'a permanent shape for general use'. The immediate context for this vindication of the lasting value of Coleridge's words was an effort to counter the reputational damage caused by De Quincey's *Tait's Edinburgh Magazine* exposé of 1834,[15] which showed his philosophical works to contain plagiarisms.

---

[14] Preface to *Specimens of the Table Talk of the Late Samuel Taylor Coleridge*, 2 vols (London: John Murray, 1835), vol. I, pp. v–vi.

[15] On this episode, see Alan Vardy, *Constructing Coleridge: The Posthumous Life of the Author* (Basingstoke: Palgrave Macmillan, 2010), pp. 26–44.

Landor's *Imaginary Conversations*

From the late 1790s, Southey thought of Landor as his ideal interlocutor. He was highly excited by *Gebir* (1798), regarding it as exactly the innovation in the traditions of epic and romance that he was himself hoping to achieve in a series of long poems based on the myths and legends of the East. He sought Landor out and the two men debated poetry in a series of intense conversations while walking round Landor's country estate, Llanthony. They corresponded regularly and it was Landor's encouragement (and offer to bankroll the publication) that motivated Southey to finish his Hindu epic *The Curse of Kehama* (1810). Southey, in return, counselled Landor over his involvement in the Peninsular War.

It was from the relationship with Southey that the *Imaginary Conversations* came about. In 1817, Landor, who had moved to Italy, hosted his friend, who was still grieving for the son who had died the year before. Landor later remembered Southey's sadness and the fellow feeling that it generated:

> Southey, a sorrowing guest, who lately lost
> His only boy. We walk'd aside the lake,
> And mounted to the level downs above,
> Which if we thought of Skiddaw, named it not.
> I led him to Bellaggio, of earth's gems
> The brightest.
>   We in England have as bright,
> Said he, and turn'd his face toward the west.
> I fancied in his eyes there was a tear,
> I knew there was in mine: we both stood still.
> Gone is he now to join the son in bliss,
> Innocent each alike, one longest spared
> To show that all men have not lived in vain.[16]

Evidently, Southey told Landor about his attempt to write himself out of sorrow by producing 'a poem as desultory as the Task, & containing my mind as that contains Cowpers. Consolation might be a proper title'.[17] This 'monument in verse for him & for myself' had Boethius's *Consolations of Philosophy* as well as *The Task* as its model.[18] It

---

[16] 'To Sir Roderic Murchison' (1863). Quoted in R. H. Super, *Walter Savage Landor: A Biography* (New York: New York University Press, 1954), p. 139.

[17] *Collected Letters of Robert Southey*, ed. Lynda Pratt, Tim Fulford and Ian Packer (Romantic Circles Electronic Edition, 2009–), letter 2776, 1 May 2016. Henceforth cited as *CLRS*.

[18] *CLRS* 2761, 18–[19] April 1816.

envisaged, that is to say, a dialogic form – a conversation between the mourner and a consoling spirit.[19]

As well as arousing sympathy, the visit renewed enthusiasm. Southey brought his completed Spanish poem *Roderick, the Last of the Goths* (1814); he also rhapsodised about Wordsworth's poetry and, after his return to Britain, sent Landor *The Excursion*, the *Collected Poems* (1815) and *The White Doe of Rylstone* (1815). Reading these, Landor became convinced of Wordsworth's genius, writing that 'In thoughts, feelings, and images not one amongst the ancients equals him, and his language (a rare thing) is English.'[20] In subsequent letters, Southey widened the conversation, telling Landor that Wordsworth had 'as just a sense of your ~~Genius~~ powers as a poet, as you have of his'.[21] He then sent the *Peter Bell* volume and, in a letter wherein he worried about the dangers of mob rule, updated Landor on the Consolations project: 'One of my occupations at this time is a series of Dialogues, upon a plan which was suggested by Boethius. The motto will explain their object, – it is three words which I found somewhere quoted from St Bernard, – Respice, aspice, prospice.'[22]

'Look back, look around, look forward': St Bernard's motto would become Southey's watchword for dialogic prose that took the measure of the present and of the future from conversation between friends, real and imaginary, now and then. He had enabled Landor to 'look around' to Wordsworth, and Wordsworth to Landor; he had himself been enlivened by both. Now, in the face of death in his intimate circle, the trashing of his personal reputation in the *Wat Tyler* affair and his fear of anarchy on a national level, he would extend this consoling dialogue from conversation and correspondence into print, and from personal friends to historical figures.

Southey, however, was anticipated in his plan by Landor, who began working on what became the imaginary conversations soon after receiving the letter. He acknowledged Cicero and *The Excursion* as models,

---

[19] Sections were published after his death as 'Fragmentary Thoughts Occasioned by his Son's Death' in *Oliver Newman: A New-England Tale (Unfinished): With Other Poetical Remains* (London: Longman, Brown, Green, & Longmans, 1845), pp. 93–5, and 'Additional Fragment, Occasioned by the Death of his Son', *Poetical Works of Robert Southey. Complete in One Volume* (London: Longman, Brown, Green, & Longmans, 1850), p. 815.

[20] Quoted in Super, *Walter Savage Landor*, p. 145.

[21] CLRS 3443, 20 February 1820.

[22] CLRS 3524, 14 August 1820. 'Look to the past, the present, the future'. This motto appeared on the title page of volume I of *Colloquies*. On Southey and Landor's joint development of dialogues, see Duggett's introduction to *Colloquies*, vol. I, pp. liv–v.

but the hallmark of his work was the Southeyan idea of conversations between present and past figures, some personally known to the author and some from remote times and places. For Southey, this form enacted the continuity between past and present that he thought threatened by laissez-faire liberalism and democratic radicalism in the country at large. The dialogue was a literary relative of the historical institutions and history writing that, by containing debate and difference within a single organised tradition, preserved national stability and kept reform gradual. As such, it sat alongside the fictionalised history that he and Wordsworth, as if in dialogue via print, were separately publishing. Wordsworth's *Ecclesiastical Sketches* (1822) and Southey's *Book of the Church* (1824) would reinforce each other's insistence on renewing the spirit of the national past by making plain the inherence of that spirit in the organic institution of the national church (and by embodying that spirit in their verse and prose).

When *Imaginary Conversations* appeared, Wordsworth's talk had recently been made public property in Hazlitt's 'My First Acquaintance with Poets'. Whereas that magazine article recollected the actual discussions and real scenes of 1798, in Landor's work a fictionalised Southey was deployed as a speaker vindicating Wordsworth's poetry in a dialogue with the sceptical figure of Richard Porson, the classical scholar. Porson had in fact died in 1808, before the imaginary conversation supposedly took place: the figures, then, were clearly fictional equivalents of the actual people and the dialogue's purpose was not to gossip about 'real' events. Instead, the conversation advances a Wordsworthian poetics, dramatising, only to dispel, the typical criticism that Wordsworth claimed too much of small-scale incidents and vulgar themes:

PORSON. In my opinion your friend is verbose; not indeed without something for his words to rest upon, but from a resolution to gratify and indulge his capacity. He pursues his thoughts too far; and considers more how he may shew them entirely, than how he may shew them advantageously.... . Wordsworth goes out of his way to be attacked. He picks up a piece of dirt, throws it on the carpet in the midst of the company, and cries '*This is a better man than any of you.*' He does indeed mould the base material into what form he chooses; but why not rather invite us to contemplate it, than challenge us to condemn it? This surely is false taste.
SOUTHEY. The principal and the most general accusation against Wordsworth is, that the vehicle of his thoughts is unequal to them.... . You admire simplicity in Euripides; you censure it in Wordsworth: believe me, sir, it arises in neither from penury of thought, which seldom has produced it, but from the strength of temperance, and at the suggestion of principle. Take up a poem of Wordsworth's and read it; I would rather say, read them all; and, knowing that a mind like yours must grasp closely what comes within it,

I will then appeal to you whether any poet of our country, since Shakspeare, has exerted a greater variety of powers with less strain and less ostentation.[23]

Porson is made to voice the scepticism about Wordsworth that readers, guided by reviewers such as Jeffrey, had inherited. Porson also voices the tendency of classically educated gentlemen to assume that modern poetry must imitate the ancients and should be judged in the ancients' terms, only for Southey to reply:

> Whom did they imitate? If his genius is equal to theirs he has no need of a guide. He also will be an ancient; and the very counterparts of those, who now decry him, will extoll him a thousand years hence in malignity to the moderns. Whatever is good in poetry is common to all good poets, however wide may be the diversity of manner, . . . Our feelings and modes of thinking forbid and exclude a very frequent imitation of the old classics, not to mention our manners, which have a nearer connection than is generally known to exist with the higher poetry.[24]

Here 'Southey's' heartfelt plea appeals, beyond Porson's pedantic periodisation, to the reader's sense of modernity. In this way the dialogue dramatises, for public consumption, the kind of debate on Wordsworth's significance that Southey and Landor (like Porson a classicist) had enjoyed in person and by letter. It promotes Wordsworth's poetry, old and new, and positions Southey as its sympathetic interpreter. It lets the reader into an apparently private discussion by two public figures, placing her inside the hermeneutic community within which the poetry was written and received. It gives Southey the best lines and thus vindicates the stylistic, thematic and formal innovations of the 1790s for the 1820s. But it does not give access to the poet's personal life. In this way it models a mode of reception of poet and poetry for a readership that is educated enough to want (and wealthy enough to be able) to buy books as well as magazines. Dialogue but no embarrassing detail; Landor lets the reader into a high-minded conversation that portrays the speakers and their subject as thinkers rather than personalities.

The *Imaginary Conversations* were successful enough in their positioning to help 'create the taste' by which the Lake Poets would be relished as modern geniuses. They were priced to be accessible to young intellectuals, and sold well enough to go through several instalments and many editions.

---

[23] Walter Savage Landor, *Imaginary Conversations* (London: Taylor and Hessey, 1824), pp. 47–8.
[24] Landor, *Imaginary Conversations*, p. 50.

Southey's *Sir Thomas More; or, Colloquies on the Progress and Prospects of Society*

Southey's dialogic work of 1829 emerged from continuing discussion of society, history and literature with Landor in letters, and from the consolation project that had precipitated *Imaginary Conversations*, the manuscript of which Southey read for the publisher. It also developed, in a still more personal, conversational direction, the history writing that Southey had published in the popular form of biographies of Nelson and Wesley. In the *Colloquies* the inter-personal transmission of history is modelled by a book that aspires to be talk. The speakers in *Colloquies* are just two – 'Montesinos' (man of the mountains) and the ghost of Sir Thomas More; they speak to each other and thus, implicitly, to the reader, who is positioned as if overhearing a conversation he could join rather than distantly reading a text. They have more character about them than Landor's figures and invite readers into a recognisable Lake District, where Southey was known to live. The book includes narratives of family excursions in the Lakeland hills; these appeal to readers by exemplifying, in ordinary activities, the virtues of a retired, domestic life. They also establish the credentials of Montesinos/Southey as a spokesman for the place – its geography and history. By these means, *Colloquies* responded to the magazine attacks on Southey's character more directly than Landor's dialogues did, whilst refraining from revealing reveal intimate details as Hazlitt and others were wont to do. Montesinos is and is not Southey; he is a persona and so is his interlocutor – Sir Thomas More – another version of the author.[25] The aim is to lift the gossipy magazine portrait onto a higher plane – the characters discuss poetry, society, history – and to model the proper reception of the Lake Poets. The dialogues suggest that conversation on public issues that begins in and returns to the personal is the poets' mode of proceeding and is also the best way to receive their works.

Southey's method is epitomised by a discussion that emerges from a walk in the northern Lake District. The speakers are prompted by what they see en route to consider the place's historical associations, and this leads to a meditation on how history is transmitted. At the centre of the discussion is a quotation from Wordsworth's 'Song at the Feast of Brougham Castle', the 1809 poem in which a local bard is imagined singing, to the assembled Clifford clan, of the deeds of their ancestor,

---

[25] See Tom Duggett, '"Et in Utopia ego": *Sir Thomas More* and "Montesinos," a Southey Mystery "Solved"', *Romanticism on the Net*, 68–9 (2017), doi: 10.7202/1070621ar.

who renounced baronial feuding and espoused peace. The quoted lines associate the song, the 'good Lord Clifford' and the place – Threlkeld – where Montesinos and Sir Thomas More stand:

> Love had he found in huts where poor men lie;
> His daily teachers had been woods and rills,
> The silence that is in the starry sky,
> The sleep that is among the lonely hills.
>
> In him the savage virtue of the Race,
> Revenge and all ferocious thoughts were dead:
> Nor did he change; but kept in lofty place
> The wisdom which adversity had bred.
>
> Glad were the vales, and every cottage-hearth;
> The Shepherd-lord was honoured more and more;
> And, ages after he was laid in earth,
> 'The good Lord Clifford' was the name he bore.[26]

Quoted in Southey's dialogue, the poem positions Wordsworth, like the bard, as a storyteller for a community – the Lakelanders and Britons more widely. Song, it appears, animates history, passing it down as legend in the hearts and minds of local people as their inheritance. Wordsworth's language of feeling connects people imaginatively to their forebears and derives lessons from those forebears; the places it invests become enworded – repositories of meaning where people are enabled to consider their own conduct, as Lakelanders, as Englishmen, in the light of their ancestors. Here Wordsworth represents the notion of history that the *Colloquies* as a whole sets out to recommend and exemplify: his poems achieve what Southey's dialogues attempt: they pass history down as a way of thinking and being centred both on places and in persons – a transmission of voice. Story and legend are central: they enable present identity to be derived from past generations; they intensify loyalty to locality. This Burkean conservative organicism is directly opposed to the new languages of power in the commercialising and industrialising nation – the languages of laissez-faire economics, free market liberalism and Benthamite utilitarian rationalism.

If Wordsworth is honoured as a bard, rather than revealed as a private man, historical transmission is also shown to stem from scholars who bring to voice the old books that they study. Southey has Montesinos praise Landor's ability to derive, from his reading of Isaac Casaubon's *Epistles*, 'one of the most pleasing of his Conversations; [Casaubon's] letters had carried him in spirit to the age of their writer, and shown

---

[26] *Colloquies*, vol. I, p. 250.

James I. to him in the light wherein James was regarded by contemporary scholars'.[27] Imaginatively transported by his reading, Landor had found convincing voices for Casaubon and James, reanimating debates about religious government that were highly relevant to the 1820s' debates about Catholic emancipation. Paying tribute to Landor, Southey shows that his imaginary dialogue has in turn seeded his own: he not only has his speakers discuss Casaubon and the Catholic question but also has More ask, 'Is there no message to [Casaubon] from Walter Landor's friend?'. Montesinos replies that More should take a message from Southey back to the spirit world: 'Say to him, since you encourage me to such boldness, that his letters could scarcely have been perused with deeper interest by the persons to whom they were addressed than they have been by one, at the foot of Skiddaw, who is never more contentedly employed than when learning from the living minds of other ages.'[28] Here, referring to himself through his speaker, Southey imagines the present as being able to speak to the past. Textuality's time-out-of-time creates a virtuous circle: Landor's dialogue, animating past characters, sponsors his own. In this fantasy of transmission, books are a starting point for conversation and the past learns from the present just as the present does from the past. Historical transmission is here a question of the animation – the personification – of print into a fantasy of conversation. The reader becomes so familiar with the words of a writer that he is possessed by and ventriloquises him. Southey's speakers are the imaginary embodiments – the ghosts – of past writers insofar as those writers are discernible in the prose of their books. As Tom Duggett puts it, Sir Thomas More is a 'spectral manifestation of the archive'.[29]

Colloquies thus represents historical learning not as the absorption of lessons from a past master but as writing so deeply informed by reading that the writer vocalises himself as both now and then. His is a selfhood of present and past speaking to each other – two voices in one. The animating power of the fictional – dramatic prose and lyric poetry – brings about this dialogic self by embodying the past in imaginary characters. Its effect, Southey argues in the concluding section, is socially vital, for it prevents the debasement that besets a society that is uninformed by the past because the past has become unfelt, a mere dead letter:

> Poetry in this respect may be called the salt of the earth; we express in it, and receive in it, sentiments for which, were it not for this permitted medium, the usages of the world would neither allow utterance nor acceptance. And who

---

[27] *Colloquies*, vol. I, p. 346.
[28] Ibid.
[29] Duggett, Introduction to *Colloquies*, vol. I, p. xxviii.

can tell in our heart-chilling and heart-hardening society, how much more selfish, how much more debased, how much worse we should have been, in all moral and intellectual respects, had it not been for the unnoticed and unsuspected influence of this preservative? Even much of that poetry, which is in its composition worthless, or absolutely bad, contributes to this good.[30]

Davy's *Salmonia* and *Consolations in Travel*

Humphry Davy had known Southey, Coleridge and Wordsworth since 1799, when he had arrived in Bristol to work as a chemical experimentalist. He had written poetry in dialogue with them, then and afterwards, and had climbed the Lakeland fells with them on several occasions. His rise to fame, however, was far more spectacular than theirs. After his isolation of the alkali metals and of chlorine and iodine (1807–13), he was hailed across Europe as the greatest ever chemist; by 1820, as the newly elected President of the Royal Society, he had become the most powerful scientist in Britain. By the later years of the decade, however, he was in trouble. A quarrelsome marriage made him quick-tempered in public and this created enemies; when, in 1826, his efforts to protect naval shipping from corrosion by electrochemical devices were judged a failure, articles complaining of his arrogance appeared in the press. Stressed by these, at the end of the year he suffered a stroke and was forced thereafter to retire and live the life of an invalid, travelling in Italy and the Alps in search of the mild temperatures that alleviated his ill health. It was in this period, expecting to die, that he composed two dialogic works, *Salmonia* and *Consolations in Travel*, in which he reflected on the natural world into which he had formerly enquired experimentally. He seems to have picked up the concept when walking and talking in the Lake District in 1816, when Southey, in the wake of his son's death, was initiating his consolations project, and in 1825, when he again visited and Southey's plans were further advanced.

Salmonia and *Consolations* were dialogic in form as well as content, presenting enquiry as a wandering conversation between friends who were geologising in the landscape, angling along river valleys, or standing on hilltops. In *Salmonia* Davy doubled down on his dialogic form, having one of his characters allude, as an instance of prophetic insight into the natural world, to the poetic dialogue between Wordsworth and Coleridge that had been printed in *The Friend* (1809).[31] In that journal, Coleridge had published his prose description of skaters on a frozen lake

---

[30] *Colloquies*, vol. I, p. 381.
[31] *Friend*, ed. Rooke, vol. II, pp. 257–9.

at Ratzeburg, originally sent by letter to Wordsworth in 1798. He followed this with Wordsworth's verse description of skating on Esthwaite
water, originally sent to him by letter in return (and not yet published in
The Prelude). To cap the verse dialogue, Coleridge had included some
lines from the poem he had written in 1807 after hearing Wordsworth
recite the unpublished 'poem on the growth of my own mind' in which
the skating passage was included. These lines, calling *The Prelude* 'an
Orphic tale indeed / A tale divine of high and passionate thoughts /
To their own music chaunted', paid tribute to Wordsworth's prophetic
power not only by what they said, but by their very existence – they
were a token of the seminal power of the 'poem to Coleridge' (another
of Wordsworth's working titles for *The Prelude*) to inspire answering
verse from its addressee. The poetic conversation, they implied, was
self-renewing. Quoting them in *Salmonia*, Davy summoned an old conversation between friends that he had subsequently joined in person and
in his own verse.[32] Now, in 1829, quotation acted as a conversation
between books, renewing the old dialogues in which a cross-fertilisation
of talk, verse and scientific enquiry had taken place. The further implication was that the textual dialogue, like the spoken dialogues recorded in
these texts, made possible new thought processes and new writings as
one person replied to another, modifying his discourse. In Davy's own
case, these new thought processes and writings included new scientific
hypotheses. His experimental enquiry, Davy suggested, was stimulated
and shaped by hill and waterside conversations and by the fanciful and
fictional writings to which those conversations gave rise. For instance, in
Consolations in Travel, the friends looking from mountainside towards
distant river each describe their slightly different perspectives, creating a composite view via a spoken conversation that becomes written
dialogue:

> PHIL—You are most unreasonable in imagining additions to a scene which
> it is impossible to embrace in one view and which presents so many Objects
> to the senses, the memory and to the imagination; yet there is a river in the
> valley between Naples and Castel del Mare; you may see its silver thread and
> the white foam of its torrents in the distance; and if you were geologists you
> would find a number of sources of interest, which have not been mentioned,
> in the scenery surrounding us. Somma which is before us, for instance, affords
> a wonderful example of a mountain formed of marine deposits, and which
> has been raised by subterraneous fire, and those large and singular veins
> which you see at the base and rising through the substance of the strata

---

[32] Humphry Davy, *Salmonia: or Days of Fly Fishing. In a Series of Conversations.
With Some Account of the Habits of Fishes Belonging to the Genus Salmo*, 2nd edn
(London: John Murray, 1829), pp. 5–6.

are composed of volcanic porphyry, and offer a most striking and beautiful example of the generation and structure of rocks and mineral formations.[33]

Because it is a composite of scenes that cannot all be seen at once, the view as reconstituted by Davy's prose is an act of imagination or vision, as one of the characters goes on to acknowledge: 'I consider it in fact as a sort of poetical epitome of his philosophical opinions, and I regard this Vision or dream as a mere web of his imagination in which he intended to catch us his summer-flies and travelling companions.'[34] In another twist, however, this web of imagination is presented not merely as a way of intriguing travelling companions but also as a consciously shaped version of the dreams and visions that are experienced unwittingly when asleep, or gravely ill. As such, it appears as a form of structured mental activity that prepares the imaginer to intuit real relations between things and is thus, to an extent, prophetic. The implications for the practice of science are that the enquirer is prepared for insights and discoveries by the call upon his imagination actively to develop and supplement the real. This call is made when he is exposed to new spatial and temporal stimuli: the mountain prospect gives new vantage on landforms (and therefore on the ancient movements of an earth that at first seems static). It also offers a new perspective on human activity (not only present and seen but historical and imagined), the traces of which are marked on the landscape just as the geological past is. Dialogue turns out to be vital to this activity, for it allows a multi-perspectival engagement with nature to become a shared reflection on it and on the viewing process. Knowledge here is characterised neither as elements found by directed pursuit nor by modelling nature in laboratory experiment but as a dialogue which responds to and in turn develops a mental process in which shared reflection is both summative (the friends add to or shift each other's perspective until a communal vision is generated) and initiatory (new relationships are forged by the shared way of thinking that dialogue produces).

[33] Humphry Davy, *Consolations in Travel, Or, The Last Days Of A Philosopher* (London: John Murray, 1830), pp. 63–5. The generic mixing of the text is discussed in Kurtis Hessel, 'Humphry Davy's Intergalactic Travel: Catching Sight of Another Genre', *Studies in Romanticism*, 54 (2015), 57–78.

[34] Davy, *Consolations in Travel*, p. 67.

Coleridge's *Aids to Reflection*

Textual dialogue is the mode of this 1825 work, which takes the form of commentaries by Coleridge on texts by Robert Leighton. The intention is that the text practises what it preaches: it reflects upon faith, and holy living, as a text reflecting another text. In this way, Coleridge seeks to aid the practice of reflection in its target readership of young intellectuals (such as the men who came to hear him talk on Thursday evenings in Highgate). *Aids* is more bookish than *Colloquies* and *Salmonia*; there are no speakers and no *mise en scène*. There is less tension and disagreement than in *Imaginary Conversations*; Coleridge's tendency is to acknowledge difference only to transcend it in unity (as he himself put it, the book is a 'oneversazioni' rather than a conversazioni).[35] Opposition is subsumed rather than refuted or left standing – yet the text is not dialectical: it operates more by textual melding than through argumentative synthesis. Frequently, Leighton's and Coleridge's texts are merged, with Coleridge inhabiting Leighton's words and modifying them – or just replaying them – as part of his own declarations. It becomes hard to tell which is which; identification ceases to be the point. The merged Leighton/Coleridge discourse is a verbal enactment of close intellectual companionship and of a theory of reading in which the reader voices the writer so that what he reads becomes his own internal discourse.

One of the elements subsumed is Wordsworth's poetry. Regretting the Unitarianism of his past, Coleridge recruits 'Lines Composed a Few Miles above Tintern Abbey' in the service of faith in a personal, biblical god rather than a nature-spirit. Despite a disclaimer in parenthesis, the quotation suggests a more explicitly Christian reading of that verse than either Wordsworth or he held when it was written:

> But many do I know, and yearly meet with, in whom a false and sickly *taste* co-operates with the prevailing fashion: many, who find the God of Abraham, Isaac, and Jacob, far too *real*, too substantial; who feel it more in harmony with their indefinite sensations

---

[35] Samuel Taylor Coleridge, *Collected Letters of S. T. Coleridge*, ed. Earl Leslie Griggs, 6 vols (Oxford: Oxford University Press, 1956–71), vol. VI, p. 790. Cf. Jon Mee on Coleridge's and Wordsworth's 1790s 'conversation' poems: 'the evacuation of social space and incorporation of verbal exchange into a dialogue with the self appear in their conversation poetry of the 1790s, as they did in many other forms of writing. A democratic sphere beyond the mediations of social difference may be glimpsed in these imaginings, but often at the cost of elevating literary culture beyond the diversity of talk'; *Conversable Worlds: Literature, Contention, and Community 1762–1830* (Oxford: Oxford University Press, 2011), p. 200.

To worship Nature in the hill and valley, Not knowing what they love:—
and (to use the language, but not the sense or purpose of the great poet of our
age) would fain substitute for the Jehovah of their Bible
                    A sense sublime
Of something far more deeply interfused,
Whose dwelling is the light of setting suns,
And the round ocean and the living air;
A motion and a spirit, that impels
All thinking things, all objects of all thought,
And rolls through all things!

Here Coleridge's textual dialogue is opposed in its effects to Hazlitt's.
Whereas 'My First Acquaintance with Poets' harks back to the conversations of 1798 in order to suggest that Wordsworth and Coleridge have
reneged on their radicalism, Coleridge quotes a poem of that period so
as to promote a Trinitarian Christianity that he did not then espouse but
that he now regenerates in dialogue with a seventeenth-century divine.
He recommends a new faith for himself and for his readers by reflecting
– recontextualising – Leighton's and Wordsworth's old words in the light
of each other and of his own responses to each.

Conclusion

As related works, the 1820s prose dialogues successfully defended the
1790s authors against the age of personality produced by the proliferation of cheap print. In modelling the desired reception of their own
poetry, they showed how imaginative writing, fantasising the author/
reader relationship as conversation, effected historical transmission
through the production of a dialogic self in whom the past speaks
(the other becoming a familiar spirit and vice versa). This presented
the process of learning as a living relation, a two-way encounter
rather than the inculcation of facts. It suggested a multi-perspectival
self: the dialogues made from spoken (or, in Coleridge's case, textual)
conversation serving as a literary means for making new discoveries
by allowing one self to entertain multiple perspectives – to vocalise
many voices.

If this was a recollective process, the older writers reworking the
fertile exchanges of their earlier years in the medium of print, it
was nevertheless successful in finding a niche market: neither the
consumers of magazines wanting 'personality', nor the purchasers
of literary annuals looking for light verse, but young, university-
educated, intellectual men like J. S. Mill and John Keble, who found
the prevailing utilitarian and empiricist philosophies heartless and

simplistic.[36] Coleridge became a draw for such men; there was, as De Quincey testified, a 'tumult of anxiety ... to "hear Mr Coleridge", or even to talk with a man who *had* heard him'.[37] Among those who visited Highgate to converse with the author of *Aids* were Thomas Carlyle and Ralph Waldo Emerson. A stream of admirers also came to Keswick and Rydal to hail the writers of *The Excursion* and the *Colloquies* and to walk and converse in the hills and valleys that the Lake Poets had portrayed. Evidently, the taste by which Wordsworth's poetry would be relished had now been created, in no small part owing to the modelling of its reception offered in the prose dialogues. By 1830, he and his circle were established as high-end writers who offered spiritual guidance rather than cranks peddling puerilities (the view of Jeffrey as late as 1814) or commercial commodities whose private lives were revealed while their public writing was ignored. Their works were no longer vilified in reviews and now sold much better than before. Though relatively expensive, it was accepted that they were worth paying more for because they were of higher moral, aesthetic and intellectual value than the sea of popular print that surrounded them. To new generations less interested than Hazlitt and De Quincey in their transition from radical youth to conservative middle age, to buy their books demonstrated discernment and seriousness. The Lake Poets had attained the status of original geniuses and national bards to which they had long aspired, but had done so, ironically enough, by virtue of their prose.

---

[36] On the publication strategy of seeking a smaller, higher-spending niche market for Wordsworth's poems, see Lee Erickson, *The Economy of Literary Form: English Literature and the Industrialization of Publishing, 1800–1850* (Baltimore, MD: Johns Hopkins University Press, 1996), pp. 49–70.

[37] Samuel Taylor Coleridge, *Table Talk*, ed. Carl Woodring, 2 vols (London and Princeton, NJ: Routledge & Kegan Paul, 1990), vol. I, p. lix.

Chapter 10

Butterfly Books and Gilded Flies: Poetry and the Annual

Clara Dawson

Gift annuals were an important medium for the most significant poets of the 1820s, Felicia Hemans and Letitia Landon. That the annual overtakes the single-authored book as the dominant medium for poetry in the 1820s has been established, but the proliferation of poetry brought about by this new publishing format was often described in derogatory terms.[1] The gift annual's decorative and luxurious appearance conflated it with the body of the middle-class woman on display in drawing rooms, and its association with women readers caused it to be regarded as lacking in seriousness. Much recent scholarship on gift annuals has demonstrated their importance and the sophistication of annual writers' contribution to aesthetic and political questions of the 1820s and 1830s. However, the significance of the poetic experiments that take place in and through the annuals for Victorian poetry has not yet been fully acknowledged. The post-Romantic presence in Victorian poetry has tended to separate into twin strands of a male and female literary tradition and the significance of late Romantic woman poets is often confined to their influence on Victorian woman poets.

This gendered separation of post-Romantic influence may be in part responsible for the idea that the 1820s, a decade dominated by the success of women poets, is an 'aesthetic lacuna', a perspective that this book wholeheartedly challenges.[2] It is a critical view that leaves annual poetry

---

[1] Lee Erickson pinpoints 1825 as the year when 'the literary Annuals were coming to dominate the gift-book market that poetry had previously dominated': *The Economy of Literary Form: English Literature and the Industrialization of Publishing, 1800–1850* (Baltimore, MD: Johns Hopkins University Press, 1996), p. 40. More recently, David Stewart develops a 'more nuanced view of the market' for poetry in the 1820s and 1830s. See particularly chapter 1, 'The Genius of the Times': Sales, Forms, and Periods', in *The Form of Poetry in the 1820s and 1830s* (Basingstoke: Palgrave Macmillan, 2018), pp. 19–63.

[2] Mary A. Waters, 'Letitia Landon's Literary Criticism and her Romantic Project:

lingering on the margins of literary history, merely a localised phenomenon of the decade that has no bearing on later nineteenth-century poetry. In this chapter, I examine two aspects of annual poetry that I argue do, in fact, shape the course of Victorian poetics: first, the transmission of thought, feeling and sensation from poet to reader through a medium subject to commercial imperatives and mass audience demand; and second, the new temporalities the fast-paced publishing world imposed on poetry, disrupting ideas about fame, posterity and the present and future status of poetry, as well as the time frames of reading and memory.

Annual poets engaged with the relation between poet and reader through the dramas of reception in their poems, the multiple ironies created by the juxtaposition of engraved illustrations, poems and short stories, and by exploring the materiality of transmission through print media. There is a tension between striking an intimate note which embraced the individual reader and creating a relation with a mass audience of consumer-readers. Poetry written in the annuals responded by exploring the new contract between poet and reader and expanding the possibilities of this innovative medium.

Annuals were published in a yearly cycle, released in November for the Christmas market in order to maximise sales. They marketed themselves in part on lasting bonds of friendship and sisterhood and on their long duration as objects in the home. One of the temporal contradictions of the annuals was this need to present an aura of enduring value whilst disguising the commercial imperative that promoted buying annuals anew every year. In the ninth annual volume of *Friendship's Offering* in 1832, the editor concedes the repetitive nature of the annual, writing that 'to claim in indulgence for the ninth time would be preposterous, and to return thanks wearisome'.[3] To justify publication, he writes that 'it is our ambition to produce, not a certain number of unconnected annual books, but a uniform work in a series of consecutive volumes'.[4] The annual poet therefore must write for the present, for an audience whose reception is immediate and potentially ephemeral, in that it must be renewed on a yearly basis. The same is true of weekly and monthly magazines, which are also reiterative and cyclical, but the annual strove for a stronger sense of lasting value than the more disposable weekly and monthly magazines, appearing at more stately intervals and encouraging readers to preserve older volumes for the coming years.

L.E.L's Poetics of Feeling and the Periodical Reviews', *Women's Writing*, 18.3 (August 2011), 305–30 (p. 305).

[3] Thomas Pringle, 'Preface', in *Friendship's Offering* (London: Smith, Elder & Co., 1832), p. v.

[4] Pringle, 'Preface', p. vi.

These aesthetic conditions are at odds with the qualities prized by earlier Romantic poets; consequently, two competing models for poetry emerge in the 1820s. On the one hand, there is the solitary genius inspired by nature, oblivious to the market and uncontaminated by it, writing for a small number of refined and sophisticated readers unswayed by consumer trends, aiming for the lofty heights of posterity rather than the unruly mass audience of the present. On the other, there is the poet who writes weak, inferior poetry for a large audience of women, which, at best, is pretty and decorous, but is ultimately subordinate to the demands of publishers for a quick profit. Of course, these perceptions were more critical construction and poetic performance than fixed positions. Nonetheless, these two poetic modes circulated through literature and literary reception, and were often divided by gender, where the feminisation of poetry by women poets garnering a large share of the market threatened a supposedly stable male tradition.[5] The earlier generation of male Romantic poets still in circulation in the 1820s, as Tim Fulford shows in Chapter 9, ironically profited from 'the air of exclusivity' their biographical portraits gave to the 'ephemeral duration and cheap position' of literary magazines.

The two modes also divide around the material nature of their publication, the feminine associated with publication in annuals, periodicals and magazines, the latter with the single-authored book.[6] The gift annuals were collaborative, multi-generic (containing short stories, poems and illustrations), expensive, decorative, hugely successful in sales and marketed to female readers.[7] Poems were especially subordinated to the exigencies of publishers: they were often commissioned to respond to the engraved illustrations, which were more expensive to produce, and therefore poems were perceived to be written on demand rather than from original inspiration. Networks of women editors and authors were able to operate through annuals and they were key to developing women's careers by enabling them to find an audience. Even while male authors

---

[5] Mary A. Waters describes how reviewers in the 1820s 'frequently sought to police out of literature the corruption of what they viewed as inauthentic, conventional, feminized sentimentality': 'Letitia Landon's Literary Criticism', p. 305.

[6] In his chapter on Landon, Browning and Darley, David Stewart argues that the latter is concerned with the 'metrical form of the poem, and the other with the material form of the book'; 'The Genius of the Times', p. 91.

[7] Paula R. Feldman draws the interesting conclusion from archival research that 'it would seem to have been permissible for a male to have given a female a literary annual and for a female to have given another female a literary annual, but ... it was *not* permissible for a female to have given an adult male one of these volumes'. 'Women, Literary Annuals, and the Evidence of Inscriptions', *Keats-Shelley Journal*, 55 (2006), 54–62 (p. 57).

contributed to annuals, critics point to what Alison Chapman describes as 'the format's association with femininity – both with women's participation in the literary market as producers and consumers, and also with the aesthetics of beauty and luxury, taste and ornament'.[8]

By contrast, the single-authored volume sought to retain the aura of the isolated male genius of Romanticism, inhabiting the eternal present of the lyric poet and oblivious to the demands of the audience in the contemporary moment. This performance of lofty indifference to the contemporary is of course a pose, as Andrew Bennett discusses in his work on the significance of posterity.[9] But Linda K. Hughes notes how publishing formats such as the periodical or annual heightened a sense of crisis for lyric: 'the lyric . . . could in this context offer only a contingent rather than transcendent perspective, forced as it was to compete with other voices and views for authority'.[10] In the annuals, the poet of pure lyric can only be a performance staged within the framing discourses of epigraphs and editorial prefaces, the juxtaposition with other authors and artists, and the temporal imperatives of immediate profit. The idealised lyric poet exists in the past, and the annual poet is necessarily belated, writing in a present in which a pure lyric mode has been disrupted by the medium itself.

Christina Lupton has written about literature and time in the eighteenth and nineteenth centuries and her diagnosis of a 'lag' in the temporality of books as opposed to newer forms of periodical and pamphlet publication is a useful framework here.[11] The idea that 'writing emerges as a historical medium and expires as the medium of current communication' is more usually applied to the end of the nineteenth century. Using terms from Friedrich Kittler, who argues that 'writing . . . can never participate in real time: its temporality is always symbolic (linear, alphabetic)', Lupton suggests that 'the reading of books was already opposed throughout the century to the "quicker" and more appealing consumption of pamphlets, periodicals, newspapers, and letters, suggesting the lag that makes them in media historical terms impossible

---

[8] Alison Chapman, 'Robert Browning and the Keepsake', *Victorians: A Journal of Literature and Culture*, 124 (Fall 2013), 82–97 (p. 85). Feldman points out that 'while male authors . . . appeared in the annual, they were one of the main venues for women authors' (p. 54).

[9] Andrew Bennett, *Romantic Poets and the Culture of Posterity* (Cambridge: Cambridge University Press, 1999).

[10] Linda K. Hughes, *The Cambridge Introduction to Victorian Poetry* (Cambridge: Cambridge University Press, 2010), p. 8.

[11] Christina Lupton, *Reading and the Making of Time in the Eighteenth Century* (Baltimore, MD: Johns Hopkins University Press, 2018), p. 26. All the following quotations are from p. 26.

to livestream'. The exploration of temporalities in both the book and annual poems that I discuss below is indeed connected with the impact of time on transmission between poet and reader. The 'suspension of time' and the solitude of the poet associated with lyric and book pub- lication meant the channel of communication between poet and reader might be temporally blocked.[12] Yet the deadlines and cycles imposed by commercial imperative on annuals created only a short window of time to connect with readers within a culture of disposability where one publication was quickly superseded by the next.

In this chapter, I compare poems by Landon and Tennyson in annuals and in their single-authored books in order to examine how they experi- ment with these different media. They exemplify the contrasting modes of poetry that dominated the late Romantic and early Victorian period: Landon irrevocably associated with her navigation of the commercial marketplace of the annuals, Tennyson with the loftier tradition of the Victorian prophetic mode. Yet both published across the differ- ent formats of single-authored books, periodicals and annuals. Reading across their poetry in these formats, the lines between these two modes become blurred and the aesthetic innovations of annual poetry ulti- mately fertilise the ostensibly separate tradition of masculine, single- authored poetry volumes.

Some critics have sought to gloss over the influence of the annuals. Richard Cronin argues that Keats, Shelley, Byron and Wordsworth were 'the poets who were to exert the most powerful influence on their nineteenth-century successors'.[13] For this critical tradition, Hemans and Landon are secondary to these male poets, confined to writing within frameworks established by Scott and Byron and lacking any originality of their own. Cronin contends that 'formally, neither poet was particu- larly innovative', their 'femininity . . . the one possible vessel for the life of the affections, and . . . the only sources of those values that poems enunciate', although he also contends that they 'nevertheless . . . effected a startling transformation of English poetry'.[14] More recent scholarship has challenged the correlation between women poets who are commer- cially successful and a lack of formal innovation. Jerome McGann has pushed against the 'critical assumption . . . that sentimental writers are simply deficient writers' and asks instead, 'what if we assume that the style has been deliberately chosen?'[15]

---

[12] Scott Brewster, *Lyric* (London: Routledge, 2009), p. 81.
[13] Richard Cronin, *Romantic Victorians* (Basingstoke: Palgrave, 2001), p. 10.
[14] Cronin, *Romantic Victorians*, p. 10.
[15] Jerome McGann, *The Poetics of Sensibility: A Revolution in Literary Style* (Oxford: Oxford University Press, 1996), p. 138.

In 1828 Landon released a new single-authored book, *The Venetian Bracelet*, whilst continuing to publish in gift annuals. Comparing 'A History of the Lyre', a longer poem in *The Venetian Bracelet*, with 'The Bridal Morning', included in the 1828 volume of the annual *Forget Me Not*, reveals Landon's sophisticated understanding of the distinctions within print culture. Both poems examine different kinds of poetic transmission and relations with an audience, probing the temporalities and material nature of poetry in different media. 'A History of the Lyre' narrates the tale of Eulalie, a young Italian poetess who wastes her gift by rejecting fame and who is fated to an early death. She has a number of speeches in the poem, but her story is narrated in retrospect by an Englishman travelling through Italy with his new bride. Eulalie sings only for her friends at social gatherings or on her lonely wanderings through the ruins of Rome by night and chooses not to write down or publish her poetry. Her poetic qualities coincide with those of the idealised Romantic poet, her 'ready song' the spontaneous 'o'erflow' of inspired feelings produced by the natural world.[16] 'All was association with some link / Whose fine electric throb was in the mind' (214–15): she is deeply attuned to the poetic and spiritual truths immanent in the world around her. Eulalie echoes Shelley's Prometheus – 'the deep truth is imageless' – in the lines 'I may not image the deep solitude / In which my spirit dwells' (248–9).[17] However, this 'may not' becomes symptomatic of her inability to turn her perceptions into socially transmissible truths. Her audience remains that of a small, intimate coterie of listeners to her spontaneous, oral performances and when the English narrator overhears her in the ruins, she is 'scarcely audible' (76).

The poem offers two perspectives on Eulalie's choice to remain an oral singer rather than a written poet: that of Eulalie herself and the thoughts of the English narrator. He finds it 'sad and strange, / To see that fine mind waste itself away' (126–7) and accuses Eulalie of 'vanity' (151). Although she acknowledges the 'wasted bloom' (199) of her womanhood, which has been fruitful neither poetically nor romantically, she defends her decision on the grounds of female weakness. Her reasons for rejecting the fame she might find in poetic success fall in line with gendered expectations of female modesty. She tells the narrator 'it is such pain to dwell upon myself' (155) and argues that women are like lilies of the valley, needing 'support and shelter from man's heart' (188).

---

[16] Letitia Elizabeth Landon, 'A History of the Lyre', in *Letitia Elizabeth Landon: Selected Writings*, ed. Jerome McGann and Daniel Reiss (Ontario: Broadview Press, 1997), lines 12, 24. All other quotations from this poem will be given line numbers from this edition.

[17] *Percy Bysshe Shelley: The Major Works*, ed. Michael O'Neill and Zachary Leader (Oxford: Oxford University Press, 2003), Act 2, iv, l. 116.

By exposing herself to the noonday glare, she has begun 'to wither' and by dwelling 'too much in the open day', she will 'droop or die' (198, 200, 201). Exposure to an even wider audience is renounced because humanity is mixed 'with base alloy' (276) and to offer her poetry to such would make Eulalie herself impure. She deems the audience for poetry unworthy: they are 'vain', 'curious', 'idle' (289–91) people, who offer only 'neglect' and 'scorn' (292), filling poets full of 'envy', 'discontent' and 'weariness' (293, 298, 303). After reaffirming her choice not to publish her work, Eulalie soon dies, in a reversal of the Pygmalion myth. She shows the narrator a statue of herself designed to mark her grave, seeming to morph into it while still alive. 'She wore / The beauty of a statue' (411–12) and when she leans next to the statue, ''twas hard to say / Which was the actual marble' (435–6).

The dispute about waste and value between Eulalie and the narrator engages with different time frames of reception. She idealises the poets whose words survive death, triumphing over mortality to survive gloriously 'on others' lips' (140). Her argument that 'such speaking dust / Has more of life than half its breathing moulds' (143–4) is countered by the narrator's assertion when it comes to her own song:

> Your songs sink on the ear, and there they die,
> A flower's sweetness, but a flower's life.
> An evening's homage is your only fame; (148–150)

By privileging a speculative future, Eulalie fails to gain temporal traction on the present, her songs disappearing in the moment of their singing. The narrator's questioning of Eulalie's decision figures in terms of Landon's own career as the rejection of the isolated poet whose name is writ in water. The poet who withholds from the present because of an unworthy audience is not celebrated as the great poet of posterity but mourned for wasting her gift. Eulalie figures herself in terms of being out of sync with the present – 'too soon my heart . . . had pointed to a later hour / Than time had reached' (202–4) – but by turning away from the contemporary moment, she becomes a passive statue, an object of the spectator's gaze rather than a voice of thrilling power. She has handed over her representation to a male agent, who frames her by offering the reader a 'rudely-framed sketch' (5) and has the last word. His final lines ask for 'peace to the weary and the beating heart / That fed upon itself' (448–9), implicitly criticising Eulalie for feeding upon herself rather than feeding others. But the greatest indictment comes in the pronouncement that 'her thrilling voice / Had lost its power, but still its sweetness kept' (413–4), suggesting Eulalie has succumbed to her own beliefs that she can be only one of those 'delicate flowers' (182) rather than thread the 'stormy path' (176) of Fame. The poem dramatises a woman poet who cannot navigate audiences or speak with a voice of power without compromising her purity and domestic role, ultimately expiring under the weight of these pressures.

However, Eulalie is clearly distinct from Landon herself. The poem adds a third voice in the epigraph to the Englishman's narrative, which presents an ironic commentary on his sketch of Eulalie. By opening with the exclamation, 'Sketches indeed' (i), it scrambles the reading order by seeming to respond sarcastically to the narrator's lines which follow beneath. His crude 'sketch' (5) which recalls 'a host of pleasant thoughts / And some more serious' (6–7) contrasts in its mildness and diffidence with the 'passionate page' of a 'woman's heart' (i, ii) perceived by the poet of the epigraph. Her desire to portray Eulalie's woman's heart is more ambitious:

> I fain would trace
> Its brightness and its blackness; and these lines
> Are consecrate to annals such as those,
> That count the pulses of the beating heart. (vi–x)

Unlike the dead material of 'speaking dust' (143) which Eulalie idealises, the epigraph poet seeks to write poetry that counts 'the pulses of the beating heart', not the dead one. Working to animate the present, the poem exposes the mediation of the lyric mode, revealing that the pure voice of spontaneous song is impossible, particularly for a woman poet, to voice. Eulalie is unable to inhabit the full potential of her thrilling, powerful voice, but Landon's lines are 'consecrate', suggesting that she herself may well be able to do so (and the slippage between 'annals' and annuals point to what the latter might enable). Typical of the sophisticated, nested discourses of her poems, she thus produces an ironic commentary about the kinds of relations women poets could have with their audience, and the temporal consequences for their poetry.

If 'A History of the Lyre' reveals that a woman poet will not gain power when working within the ideals of a masculine poetic tradition, 'The Bridal Morning' grapples directly with the terms on which she can succeed and the costs involved. Patricia Pulham suggests that comments about women annual poets 'are informed by the language of the market, of prostitution and enslavement, which both contaminates and reflects the woman poet's engagement with the literary economy'.[18]

---

[18] Patricia Pulham, '"Jewels – Delights – Perfect Loves": Victorian Women Poets and the Annuals', in *Victorian Women Poets*, ed. Alison Chapman (Cambridge: Brewer, 2003), pp. 9–31 (p. 20).

Many poems and stories in the annuals depict situations where women must choose between loveless marriages with rich men or worthy but poor suitors (although the poor suitors often turn out to be rich, revealing their disguise only when the woman has proved her moral worth by accepting them on the basis of poverty). Often the 'language of the market' works to incorporate both women poets and women circulating on the marriage market. Landon's 'The Bridal Morning' is one such poem, using the financial transactions of marriage to explore the conditions of writing poetry in a highly commercialised system.

The poem portrays a woman dressing on the morning of her wedding, contemplating the poor lover she has betrayed and rejected in favour of a wealthier suitor. The narrator's address to the 'you' of the young woman creates a voice which moralises and pronounces judgement on her, in keeping with the moral probity of the annuals, which sought to encourage virtuous behaviour. She appears to condemn the bride for her mercenary decision and ends with a lament that money is now 'prevailing over love' and women's faithfulness is weakening.[19] However, the elaboration on the emotional costs of this financial transaction bears not only upon the young bride, but upon poetry itself. The imagery used to depict money coincides with diction associated with the annual's decorative nature – 'gems', 'golden letters' and 'baubles' (103, 105, 104). If we read the poem as condemning the bride's avarice, then it also condemns the poet who sells her emotions and sensations for a contract 'writ in golden letters' (105).

The poem portrays a temporal split between an idealised past characterised by selfless love and the present state of corruption by money. This split between past and present emphasises the commercial conditions from which women, whether seeking a husband or an audience, cannot escape. The opening stanza, with the repetition of 'last' in 'the last braid of thy tresses wreathing' and the 'last white pearl' (103), conveys the sense of an ending rather than a beginning (as one might expect on a wedding day) and suggests that, once made, the contractual exchange of the bride for financial security cannot be undone and will have irrevocable effects. Stanzas 4 to 6 explore what is lost:

> But thou art yet less fair than pale—
> Pale!—it is but a bride's sweet sorrow;
> Fling over her the silver veil—
> That cheek will be more bright to-morrow (103)

---

[19] L.E.L., 'The Bridal Morning', in *Forget Me Not, A Christmas and New Year's Present for 1828*, ed. Frederic Shoberl (London: R. Ackermann, 1828), p. 105. References will be given as page numbers, as there are no line numbers in the original.

Initially, the poet suggests the bride's paleness is temporary and can be covered over with a veil, but the silver veil implies coin as well as colour and permanently erases the natural brightness of her cheek:

No more, no more!—the rose hath said
Farewell to that pale cheek for ever;
  Those gems may cast a meteor red
Upon that face, but the heart never.

Those eyes have tears they may not weep,
Those lips words never to be spoken:
  As weak as frail, thou canst not keep,
Nor yet forget, vows thou hast broken. (103)

'No more, no more' reinforces the irrevocable loss from which there can be no recovery. The capacity of the heart to produce a blush has gone, and what now creates the blush is secondary, an external reflection from the gems rather than an internal expression of vitality and purity. The replacement of the heart with gems as the animating principle of the bride's beauty is mirrored by the woman poet who sells her poetry to gift annual editors and has her work mediated by the gem-like annual. The stopping up of tears suggests that the transmission of true sensibility from woman poet to reader is disrupted. Words which will not be spoken from lips foreground the expanded distance between poet and readers in a culture of mass print, where the immediacy of oral song is attenuated.

Annual prefaces sought to create the impression of bonds of friendship between editors and readers: is this vow of friendship between poet and reader broken if the poetess is negotiating sales contracts for her poems? The poet who has accepted silver coins to publish in the annual appears diminished by the financial system in which she works, only able to transmit a reflected version of herself to readers. Landon also figures the temporal status of annual publication in stanza 9:

The curl he took, the ring he gave—
The vow that bound your hearts together!
  O froth, such is on ocean's wave!
O change, such is in April weather! (104)

The bride's fickleness in breaking her vow is expressed through the idea of seasonal change, a temporality linked to the annual's cyclical publication and the ephemerality of the frothy waves, which disperse immediately upon making contact with the shore, stands in for annuals' disposability. The contract that is 'writ in golden letters' (105) and its rhyme with 'fetters' (105) is a contract that applies to poet as well as bride and under these conditions, the 'heart must still its beating' (105), becoming less vital.

Although the poem appears to mourn the corruption of money, the questions, dashes and exclamation marks throughout open up an inter-pretation that is sympathetic to the bride's plight, or at the very least, draws attention to the difficulties and contradictions of the social system she inhabits. 'The Bridal Morning' speaks also to the unavoidable con-ditions that a profit-making publishing system imposes on the poet. Although appearing to present the case that the poet–reader relation is fatally compromised and weakened by the contractual nature of the annual, the poet signals that there may be compensation for these losses. The final stanza laments that 'even woman's faith is failing' (105) but it uses, for the first time, the pronoun 'we', eschewing the judgemental 'I'–'you' pronominal relation between narrator and female subject for the more inclusive collective pronoun. As the question acknowledges the impossibility of escape – 'Great curse! where shall we fly from thee?' (105) – it brings together poet and reader as part of a community of shared experience and values. While Eulalie's voice fades out, losing its power, the poet of 'The Bridal Morning' finds her relation to women readers precisely by navigating the commodity culture of the annual. By doing so, she is able to reflect upon and question a social system in which marriage was the dominant mode of economic survival for middle-class women.

Alison Chapman argues that 'while conforming to heterosexual, middle-class virtues and values, many of the [annual] texts teach female resilience . . . The doubleness—decorative yet empowering—was intrin-sic to the annuals, which commodified, celebrated and circulated the feminine ideal as well as female authors'.[20] Landon employed this dou-bleness to explore the different temporal frameworks available to the woman poet and the different ways she might connect with an audience. The privileging of a temporality pure from commercial motive and too lofty to connect with the present is a mode in which the woman poet will suffer, but when she builds a community of readers through the annual, she must accept the financial conditions it imposes. If the annuals offered such a community to women poets, what did they offer the many male poets who also published in them? Critical work on Coleridge and Wordsworth demonstrates that the annuals had a rejuvenating effect on their stalled careers in the 1820s. Although male authors protested vehemently in letters about the degradation of contributing to annuals, this new medium developed their poetry in ways that go beyond a mere

[20] Chapman, 'Robert Browning and the Keepsake', pp. 85–6.

financial transaction.[21] Tennyson, too, clearly took note of the importance of shaping a presence in the media channels of the period. Kathryn
Ledbetter's work on Tennyson and his relation to periodical publication
throughout his career demonstrates his focused attention on controlling
his reception and his awareness of the importance of different kinds
of publication. Ledbetter demonstrates that while Tennyson showed
'ambivalence' and even 'hatred' for the annuals, he recognised the need
'to seek out popular forms of publication to reach a larger audience to
support himself as a poet'.[22] The following selection of poems published
in the first few years of the 1830s demonstrate this ambivalence and
awareness of the conditions which structure the production and reception of his poetry.

In the 1831 volume of *The Gem*, Tennyson published a pair of poems,
the first of which was 'No More':

> Oh sad *No More!* Oh sweet *No More!*
>> Oh strange *No More!*
>> By a mossed brookbank on a stone
> I smelt a wildweed-flower alone;
> There was a ringing in my ears,
> And both my eyes gushed out with tears.
> Surely all pleasant things had gone before,
> Lowburied fathomdeep beneath with thee, No More![23]

The poem partakes in the atmosphere of melancholy and romantic loss
characteristic of much annual poetry.[24] Yet the miniature drama also
compresses the experience of the belated Romantic poet, trapped in the
eternal present of the lyric, unable to formulate or transform his experience except through a negation. The poet is actively engaged with the
natural world through his sense of smell, which produces the sensations
of 'ringing' in his ears and gushing of tears. Repetition of 'No More'
both echoes Landon's 'The Bridal Morning' and prefigures the negative

---

[21] See Peter Manning, 'Wordsworth in *The Keepsake*, 1829', in *Literature and the
Marketplace: Nineteenth-Century British Publishing and Reading Practices*, ed. John
O. Jordan and Robert L. Patten (Cambridge: Cambridge University Press, 1995),
pp. 44–74; Tim Fulford on Coleridge and annual poetry in *The Late Poetry of the
Lake Poets: Romanticism Revised* (Cambridge: Cambridge University Press, 2013),
pp. 153–96. See also the essays by Fulford and Tom Toremans in this volume.
[22] Kathyrn Ledbetter, *Tennyson and Victorian Periodicals: Commodities in Context*
(Aldershot: Ashgate, 2007), p. 9.
[23] Alfred Tennyson, 'No More', in *The Gem: a Literary Annual* (London: W. Marshall,
1831), p. 87.
[24] Ledbetter argues that his contribution to annuals 'places him in a bourgeois book
product that markets such emotions and the aesthetic of loss as proper and common
with young women': *Tennyson and Victorian Periodicals*, p. 27.

chorus in 'Mariana' ('he will not come').[25] These dramatic situations of silence and unresponsiveness are scattered through Tennyson's early work. The capitalisation and address to 'thee' in proximity to 'No More' has the effect almost of personifying it, so that the syntax suggests the poet himself is buried with 'No More'. 'Fathomdeep' correlates with the internal nature of the sound of ringing and with the presence of noises and music circulating more generally in Tennyson's early poems. This deeply internal music is present in 'The Lotos-Eaters', where there is more gush in the 'gushing of the wave' and voices are buried: 'if his fellow spake, / His voice was thin, as voices from the grave'.[26] Keeping in mind Isobel Armstrong's critical encouragement 'to get away from the gush of the feminine regarded simply as a consent to nonrational and emotional experience', the gush in 'No More' is arguably a way of thinking through the poet's contemporary situation.[27] 'No More' brings to the fore Tennyson's experience of the distance between poet and reader which characterises the dramatic situations of many of his poems in his 1832 and 1842 single-authored volumes and enables him to formulate a poetic response in which the lyric poet is isolated and melancholy.

'Anacreontics' follows 'No More' as the second poem in a pair and presents the opposite emotional mood:

> With roses musky breathed,
> And drooping daffodilly,
> And silverleaved lily,
> And ivy darkly-wreathed,
> I wove a crown before her
> For her I love so dearly,
> A garland for Lenora.
> With a silken cord I bound it.
> Lenora, laughing clearly
> A light and thrilling laughter,
> About her forehead wound it,
> And loved me ever after. [28]

---

[25] Alfred Tennyson, 'Mariana', in *Tennyson's Poetry: Norton Critical Edition*, ed. Robert W. Hill (London: W. W. Norton, 1999), line 81.

[26] Alfred Tennyson, 'The Lotos-Eaters', *Tennyson's Poetry: Norton Critical Edition*, lines 31, 33–4.

[27] Isobel Armstrong, 'The Gush of the Feminine: How Can We Read Women's Poetry of the Romantic Period?', in *Romantic Women Writers: Voices and Countervoices*, ed. Paula R. Feldman and Theresa M. Kelley (Hanover, NH: University Press of New England, 1995), pp. 13–32 (p. 15).

[28] Alfred Tennyson, 'Anacreontics', in *The Gem: a Literary Annual* (London: W. Marshall, 1831), p. 131.

The analogy of weaving with poetic creation present in this short poem anticipates the central conceit of 'The Lady of Shalott'.[29] In contrast to his solitude in 'No More', the poet weaves his creation in the presence of the beloved. The plants surrounding him also differ: where the moss, the brook and the wildweed are pristinely natural and wild, silver and silk gesture to the luxurious bindings and gilt of the annual, roses and lilies to a domestic scene of house or garden. Reading the analogy of weaving with writing poetry, the poem suggests that if Tennyson can create art with the materials of the annual, he will win the love of his female readers. Accepting the crown with 'thrilling laughter', Leonora becomes an active participant, winding the garland around her head, symbolising both the female reader who rewards the poet with eternal love and favour, but also hinting at the power of the female poet. Her 'thrilling laughter' echoes Eulalie's 'thrilling voice' and 'thrill' is a word that often marks the passage of sensation from one person to another. As the poem probes the possibilities that female voice and the feminised medium of the annual might offer, Tennyson simultaneously situates his short poem in a tradition of light verse forms. An Anacreontic is an easy, short, lyrical poem which deals with love or wine, and is thus eminently suitable for the annual. Jane Moore comments that the Anacreontic ode is 'based on imitation, rather than innovation', on 'friendship and coop-eration' rather than an 'aggressive rivalry ... of literary inheritance'.[30] In a poem that appears to concede to the conditions of writing for women readers of the annual, Tennyson attempts to undermine his poetic prowess by associating himself with this easy or slight form, lacking in innovation.

This pair of poems offers a stark choice: continue with the lyric voice of the poet singing alone in nature and be buried alive in that negated state or demean yourself by writing with the materials of the annual to seduce the female reader and thus ensure your survival. Yet at the same time, the confrontation with the conditions imposed by the annual produces the metaphors and sensations which are central to Tennyson's early poetry, as the connections with 'The Lady of Shalott' and 'The Lotos-Eaters' demonstrate. The ambivalent relation to female poetic experience in the annual is also explored in the sonnet published in

---

[29] Katie Garner has demonstrated how Tennyson's 1832 poem 'The Lady of Shalott' 'participates in a shared discourse' with annual poems by Letitia Landon and Louisa Stuart Costello: *Romantic Women Writers and Arthurian Legend* (Basingstoke: Palgrave Macmillan, 2017), p. 247.

[30] Jane Moore, 'Thomas Moore, Anacreon, and the Romantic Tradition', *Romantic Textualities: Literature and Print Culture, 1780–1840*', 21 (Winter 2013), 30–52 (p. 34).

Friendship's Offering in 1832. It presents another melancholy situation where the poet mourns his distance from the woman he loves. Their experiences of sorrow are defined through temporal difference:

> Me my own fate to lasting sorrow doometh:
>   Thy woes are birds of passage, transitory,
>   Thy spirit, circled with a living glory,
> In summer still a summer joy resumeth.[31]

The woman's feelings are described as both cyclical and transitory, time frames connected to annual publication. As in 'No More', the poet inhabits an everlasting time frame but one which brings him sorrow rather than joy. He is like 'a lone cypress . . . From an old garden where no flower bloometh'. If the flowers are symbolically linked to annual poems, which they commonly were, the poet is trapped in a literary past which no longer produces fruit for the present.

The final six lines continue to depict male and female experience in opposition:

> But yet my lonely spirit follows thine,
>   As round the rolling earth night follows day:
> But yet thy lights on my horizon shine
>   Into my night, when thou art far away.
> I am so dark, alas! and thou so bright,
> When we two meet there's never perfect light.

He is in thrall to the woman who sets the direction in which he must follow and who is again linked to the cyclical time frame of the annual. She has immense creative force, demonstrated by the power to shine her light from a great distance, whereas he lacks such power and has no light of his own. When 'we two meet' might suggest a meeting of male poet and female poet or reader, but his darkness and her light fail to create a marriage of minds. A woman exerting her power over cyclical time and ruling the lives of men in thrall to her is also present in 'Tithonus' (written in 1833, not published until 1860), where Tithonus wastes in the shadow of the powerful goddess of the dawn, Aurora.

Rather than merely being dashed off to take advantage of a generous financial offer or as a concession to an audience which held buying power, these poems are significant works for Tennyson's poetic development. His exploration of the relation between the poet and his audience along with the materials and temporalities of contemporary print culture are formed in the crucible of these annual poems. In the light of

---

[31] Alfred Tennyson, 'Sonnet', in *Friendship's Offering and Winter's Wreath* (London: Smith and Elder, 1832), p. 367.

these readings, I turn now to 'The Palace of Art', a poem in his 1832 volume considered central to Tennyson's early aestheticism. It has been read in terms of Harold Bloom's anxiety of influence and a number of critics point to the poem's male literary precursors.[32] I argue that 'The Palace of Art' is also engaged with the aesthetic conditions brought into being by the annuals. It presents a poetic 'I' who tells the reader about the palace he builds for his soul, a palace which contains many rooms and scenes and artworks; within its walls, the soul indulges her senses but later becomes sick of the palace and leaves, finishing the poem with the plea that she might one day return to the palace with others when she has 'purged' her guilt.[33]

'The Palace of Art' begins with an act of spiritual and artistic construction: 'I built my soul a lordly pleasurehouse / Wherein at ease for aye to dwell'.[34] The poet aims to create an everlasting dwelling for the soul and the poem later refers to 'gilded galleries / That gave large view to distant lands' (XXXII). The poem is concerned with the relation of poetry's materiality to the mind of the poet (and by implication, the reader), literally, how and where the poem will be housed (and the word 'gilded' creates an association with the gilded annuals) and its ability be transported through time and space to distant places. 'The Palace of Art' elaborates on the different scenes which each room contains, ranging across wildly varied geographical locations and touching on Arthurian, German and Greek myths. Isobel Armstrong argues that the series of rooms creates an 'environment . . . at once overdetermined and fragmented . . . since each representation is simply the equivalent of another they exist in a self-enclosed system. Hallam's "pure" art thus becomes drained of meaning and history, a "pure" luxury commodity'.[35] I would go further to suggest that Tennyson's portrayal of a multiplicity of scenes unconnected by any logical system bar the poem itself reflects not just any luxury commodity, but specifically the gift annual. The soul finds herself in a palace that resembles the aesthetic world of the gift annuals, crowded with myriad different locations, myths and writers. An earlier

[32] Christopher Ricks cites the King James Bible, Herbert, Shelley and Milton as allusions, in *The Poems of Tennyson*, ed. Christopher Ricks (London: Longman, 1969), pp. 400–1; Herbert Tucker describes Shelley as 'the clearest of analogues' in *Tennyson and the Doom of Romanticism* (Cambridge, MA: Harvard University Press, 1988), p. 122.

[33] I refer to the original version of 'The Palace of Art', published in the Moxon 1833 edition, rather than the revised version published in 1842.

[34] Alfred Tennyson, *Poems* (London: Moxon, 1833 [1832]), stanza I. As there are no line numbers in the original edition, stanza numbers will be cited.

[35] Isobel Armstrong, *Victorian Poetry: Poetry, Poetics, and Politics* (London: Routledge, 1993), pp. 78, 79.

pun on the engraved 'plates' of the annual occurs when the speaker describes 'long sounding corridors' that are 'roofed with thick *plates* of green and orange glass' (VII).

The scenes described by Tennyson resemble those typically found in the annuals: a hunter with a bugle horn, a pastoral scene with an English cottage, shipwrecks in stormy seas, a man walking in desert sands, a maiden with 'babe in arm' (XIV) are all familiar scenes in the engraved illustrations of the annuals. The way in which these geographically distant landscapes are suddenly brought into proximity corresponds to the extensions of time and space in the gift annual poem. The speaker also describes hanging paintings of writers in the palace rooms, which brings together Milton, Shakespeare, Dante and Homer in one quatrain. Turning these writers into visual images and crowding them together corresponds to the manner in which famous writers such as Shakespeare were incorporated in the gift annual, where they were often quoted as epigraphs to stories or poems. Tennyson is seeking a way to incorporate the male poetic tradition into the expanded space of poetic print culture opened up by the annuals.

Tennyson's image depicting how delight within the speaker's 'deep heart / Moved in my blood and dwelt, as power and might / Abode in Samson's hair' (LX) recalls Landon's concern with the heart and pulse as sources of poetic power, which can be weakened, as they are in 'The Bridal Morning'. In Tennyson's poem, the poetic soul has become a fountain that has dried up and stagnated. His soul is 'a still salt pool, locked in with bars of sand . . . that hears all night / The plunging seas' (LXV) and she shrieks 'No voice breaks through the stillness of this world' (LXVII), lamenting also that 'There comes no murmur of reply' (LXXIV). An obstructive force evoked by the bars of sand plays into the idea of print as an impediment between poet and reader. However, the soul is unable to find a way to break through the barriers of the printed medium to join the 'starry dance' (LXVI) or to speak and be heard by another. It is in this failure of communication that 'The Palace of Art' differs from the annual poems by Landon.

If, in the gift annual poems, the impediments to connection between poet and reader are explored, there is also the compensation of different and new kinds of communication. 'The Palace of Art' ends with an attempt at redemption involving a community of others, but it feels less convincing. While the soul says 'Perchance I may return with others there' (LXXVI), the two conditional words weaken the possibility that this will happen and no vision is offered for how or when this might take place. 'The Palace of Art' contends with the legacy of the annual, of how the transformation of the material nature of poetry and the struggle that this creates for Tennyson in formulating his own poetic voice, particularly as a male poet striving for the audience of female readers that the annuals had captured.

Lindsey Middleton's chapter in this volume explores concerns around the adulteration and contamination of food in the 1820s. Fears of the contamination of both poetry and food come together forcefully in Tennyson's 1855 poem, *Maud*, where 'chalk and alum and plaster are sold to the poor for bread'.[36] The correlation between food and poetry suggests that the relation between producers and consumers across disparate sectors of society is key to defining the culture of the 1820s. There are a number of consequences for Victorian poetics: the different media of 1820s poetry led to the lyric poet becoming the object of verse, with the development of poetic personae intensely conscious of these new media. The process resulted in the dramatic monologue, where the impossibility of pure lyricism made way for an 'objective' voice. The disruption of lyric temporality precipitated by weekly, monthly and annual publication necessitated an exploration of the time of writing. The vexed relation between public demand for poetry that responded to problems of the age (poetry oriented towards the present) and a timeless lyric sensibility follows Tennyson throughout his career and informs the arguments about Spasmodic poetry between Matthew Arnold, Elizabeth Barrett Browning and Arthur Clough in the 1850s. Tom Toremans's argument in the next chapter that the Victorian prophetic mode developed as a way of evading the problems of transmission inherent in this diffuse media culture is another example. The increasing tension between the material book and the literature within it can thus be traced through a whole series of nineteenth-century debates about commercial and aesthetic value.

---

[36] Alfred Tennyson, *Maud*, in *Tennyson's Poetry: Norton Critical Edition*, I, i, 39.

Chapter 11

'Still but an Essayist': Carlyle's Early Essays and Late-Romantic Periodical Culture

Tom Toremans

In the final pages of *Scott's Shadow*, Ian Duncan stages Thomas Carlyle's *Sartor Resartus* as a signpost marking the end of an Edinburgh post-Enlightenment literary culture dominated by Walter Scott's historical novels. To fully appreciate the transitional position of Carlyle's work, Duncan argues, it is imperative to reconstruct the 'Scottish genealogy' that has been obscured by the almost exclusive critical emphasis on 'the Anglo-Irish and German traditions Carlyle himself alludes to'.[1] Duncan is by no means the first to posit *Sartor Resartus* at the end of the Romantic period, nor to foreground its Scottish context.[2] However, his observation that the critical neglect of the latter repeats 'the work's own, programmatic suppression of its local literary circumstances' suggests the need for a re-interrogation of the peculiar self-reflexivity of *Sartor Resartus*, which has traditionally been approached in terms of (Romantic or deconstructionist) irony.[3] The partial restoration of *Sartor*'s Scottish context has led to philosophical reassessments of the work as an antithesis to Scott's historical romances or in relation to the

---

[1] Ian Duncan, *Scott's Shadow: The Novel in Romantic Edinburgh* (Princeton, NJ and Oxford: Princeton University Press, 2007), pp. 308, 309.

[2] See, for example, Janice Haney's '"Shadow-Hunting": Romantic Irony, *Sartor Resartus*, and Victorian Romanticism', *Studies in Romanticism*, 17 (1978), 307–33. On the Scottish context, see Ralph Jessop's *Carlyle and Scottish Thought* (London and New York: Macmillan, 1997).

[3] Duncan, *Scott's Shadow*, p. 308. For discussions of *Sartor Resartus* in terms of irony, see Anne K. Mellor on *Sartor Resartus* as a 'self-consuming artefact': *English Romantic Irony* (Cambridge, MA: Harvard University Press, 1980), p. 131; and J. Hillis Miller's designation of the work as 'a speaking which, in one way or the another, discounts itself in its act of being proffered': '"Hieroglyphical Truth" in *Sartor Resartus*: Carlyle and the Language of Parable', in *Victorian Perspectives*, ed. John Clubbe and Jerome Meckier (London: Macmillan, 1989), pp. 1–20 (p. 7)). For a re-evaluation of *Sartor*'s self-reflexivity in terms of translation, see my '*Sartor Resartus* and the Rhetoric of Translation', *Translation and Literature*, 20.1 (2011), 61–78.

Scottish Common Sense philosophy.[4] Equally important has been the recovery of its relation to late-Romantic periodical culture. Duncan, for example, traces back *Sartor*'s 'formal and stylistic, mixed-metaphorical heterogeneity' to its original serial publication in *Fraser's Magazine* (between November 1833 and August 1834) and, by extension, to the magazine culture of the 1820s:

> *Sartor Resartus* can be viewed as the ultimate *Blackwood's* article – the most hyperbolic of those experimental fusions of cultural criticism with fictional form and the most drastic alternative to the Scottish historical novel to emerge from the Blackwoodian crucible.[5]

Mark Parker's more elaborate re-evaluation of *Sartor Resartus* sees it as a 'culmination of . . . the innovative and flexible essay fostered in the literary magazines of the 1820s' that 'completes the first phase of British periodical literature in the nineteenth century' and chimes with Duncan's recontextualisation of the work in late-Romantic Scottish periodical culture. Both invite a critical return to Carlyle's active engagement with this culture in the 1820s.[6]

While Carlyle's early essays have mainly been studied in terms of his emergence as 'the Voice of Germany', recent scholarship on the genre of the Romantic essay allows for a critical reappraisal of their dynamic and essentially ambivalent interaction with their immediate context of publication.[7] Tim Milnes's discussion of Charles Lamb's and William Hazlitt's respective engagements with the genre of the essay, for example, not only highlights 'their ambivalent relationship with the print culture on which their journalistic careers depend', but further extends this ambivalence to the ways in which both authors navigate 'a space between . . . the pragmatic empiricism of Hume and Jeremy Bentham, and . . . the transcendental aesthetics of some of their poetic contemporaries'.[8] Milnes derives

---

[4] See, for example, Duncan's *Scott's Shadow* and Jessop's *Carlyle and Scottish Thought*.

[5] Duncan, *Scott's Shadow*, pp. 309, 307–8. For a detailed account of the history of publication of *Sartor Resartus*, see Rodger L. Tarr's introduction to the Norman and Charlotte Strouse edition: Thomas Carlyle, *Sartor Resartus. The Life and Opinions of Herr Teufelsdröckh in Three Books*, ed. Rodger L. Tarr and Mark Engel (Berkeley, Los Angeles and London: University of California Press, 2000), pp. xlii–lxxv.

[6] Mark Parker, *Literary Magazines and British Romanticism* (Cambridge: Cambridge University Press, 2006), p. 158.

[7] G. B. Tennyson, *Sartor Called Resartus. The Genesis, Structure, and Style of Thomas Carlyle's First Major Work* (Princeton, NJ: Princeton University Press, 1965), p. 7. A recent exception that discusses Carlyle's essays in their periodical context is Joanna Malecka, 'Thomas Carlyle's Calvinist Dialogue with the Nineteenth-Century Periodical Press', *History of European Ideas*, 45.1 (2019), 15–32.

[8] Tim Milnes, *The Testimony of Sense: Empiricism and the Essay from Hume to Hazlitt* (Oxford: Oxford University Press, 2019), pp. 200, 194.

this duality from Duncan's distinction between the 'Humean-empirical' literary mode 'with no projected foundation beyond that of cultivating consensus through communication', on the one hand, and 'the Kantian-transcendental' mode, in which 'aesthetic experience acquires a recuperative function, compensating for the loss of epistemic foundations and their replacement with transcendental conditions', on the other.[9]

Mapping Duncan's analysis of post-Enlightenment literary culture onto the development of the Romantic essay, Milnes provides a compelling framework for a reconsideration of Carlyle's late-Romantic essays as marked by an essential ambivalence, not only towards the periodical culture in which they participated, but also, and more fundamentally, towards the genre of the Romantic essay itself. Central to this ambivalence is the critical programme behind Carlyle's essayistic interventions, which was primarily aimed at articulating an anti-Humean, transcendentalist critique of contemporaneous criticism, primarily as exemplified by the critical practice of the *Edinburgh Review*. This critique forces Carlyle's essayistic practice, which predominantly took place in the *Edinburgh Review*, into an increasingly self-critical and ambivalent position, to the point of becoming incompatible with the genre of the periodical essay, anticipating its performative implosion in *Sartor Resartus*.

Interestingly, the critical neglect of the periodical context of Carlyle's early works rehearses a repressive gesture made by Carlyle himself in the late 1830s. After the success of *The French Revolution* (1837), Carlyle collected a selection of his essays in the four-volume *Critical and Miscellaneous Essays* (1838–9).[10] As the early essays migrated from their original periodical context to that of the essay collection, they also migrated from late-Romantic Edinburgh to early-Victorian London, a move mirroring Carlyle's permanent resettlement in London in 1834. As was the case with *Sartor Resartus*, the later critical neglect of the periodical context of the essays' original publication was thus partly prompted by the altered material format of their republication in the late 1830s, a period which marked a definitive shift in Carlyle's career from

---

[9] Milnes, *Testimony of Sense*, p. 193.
[10] The idea had presented itself to Carlyle as early as 1830 but only came to fruition in the wake of the success of *The French Revolution* (1837). The collection was first published by James Munroe in Boston (who had published the first book edition of *Sartor Resartus* two years earlier) and subsequently by James Fraser in London. On the publication of the *Critical and Miscellaneous Essays*, see *The Carlyle Encyclopedia*, ed. Mark Cumming (Madison, NJ: Fairleigh Dickinson University Press, 2004), pp. 106–9. It is interesting to note that in the Norman Strouse edition of Carlyle's collected works, the essays are also dispersed over different volumes and thus isolated from their periodical context.

the essay format to that of the book, with his last extensive reviews (on Scott and Karl August Varnhagen Von Ense) appearing in the *London and Westminster Review* in 1838.

Unlike Thomas De Quincey, Hazlitt and Lamb, who engaged with the genre of the essay prolifically and for a variety of purposes, Carlyle exclusively produced review essays, from his earliest contributions to the *New Edinburgh Review* to his reviews for the *Edinburgh Review* and the *Foreign Review* in the second half of the 1820s. From his settlement in Edinburgh in 1818 onwards, Carlyle actively built a network of booksellers and editors that would allow him to enter the reviewing industry. Carlyle's entry into the Edinburgh publishing scene was initiated by two letters of introduction provided to him by Henry Duncan, minister of Ruthwell Parish in Dumfriesshire and founder of the *Dumfries and Galloway Courier*.[11] A first letter introduced him to David Brewster, who in February 1819 commissioned a translation (of an article by Swedish chemist Jacob Berzelius) for his *Edinburgh Philosophical Journal*. Between 1819 and 1823 Carlyle contributed more 'wretched little translations [and] compilations' to Brewster's *Edinburgh Philosophical Journal* and *Edinburgh Encyclopaedia*.[12] Brewster additionally commissioned a book-length translation of Legendre's *Elements of Geometry and Trigonometry*, which Carlyle finished in December 1821 and published in 1824. As he complains in a letter to his brother (14 March 1821), this early practice as translator brought little or no gratification: it mainly 'brings grist to the mill' and 'besides the money that springs from it, no other benefit, no increase of reputation or even notoriety, is attached to it in any sense'.[13] In the same letter, however, Carlyle announced a first opportunity for more 'original' work, which presented itself on the basis of Duncan's second letter of introduction, to Edinburgh bookseller Baillie Waugh. Carlyle had met Waugh in 1819, deeming him 'a very flimsy vapouring sort of character' and expecting to 'hear no more of him', yet when Waugh relaunched his *New Edinburgh Review* as a quarterly, he commissioned Carlyle to write a review of Joanna Baillie's *Metrical Legends of Exalted Characters*,

---

[11] Thomas Carlyle, 'Letter to Margaret A. Carlyle, 17 December 1818', in *The Carlyle Letters Online*, available at DOI 10.1215/lt-18181217-TC-MAC-01 (accessed 17 May 2022). Gerard McKeever discusses Duncan and his paper in Chapter 6 of this volume.

[12] Thomas Carlyle, *Reminiscences*, ed. K. J Fielding and Ian Campbell (Oxford and New York: Oxford University Press, 1997), p. 263. For a full list of Carlyle's contributions to the *Edinburgh Encyclopaedia*, see Tennyson, *Sartor Called Resartus*, pp. 340–2.

[13] Thomas Carlyle, 'Letter to Alexander Carlyle, 14 March 1821', in *The Carlyle Letters Online*, available at DOI 10.1215/lt-18210314-TC-AC-01 (accessed 17 May 2022).

which had appeared earlier in 1821.[14] While working on the articles for Brewster's *Encyclopaedia* and on translations of Schiller, Carlyle finished a first draft of his review by April and saw it appear in print in October. When the parcel with the proofs of the review reached him in September, it was accompanied by 'a copy of somebody's translation of Faustus by Goethe — "for criticism"'.[15] Carlyle's review of *Faust* appeared in the April issue of the *New Edinburgh Review*, with no further reviews appearing until 1827. Apart from a series of articles on 'Schiller's Life and Writings' for the *London Magazine* between October 1823 and September 1824 (republished one year later as *The Life of Friedrich Schiller*), Carlyle mainly produced translations, most notably of Goethe's *Wilhelm Meister's Apprenticeship* (1824) and of German short stories and novellas for the collection *German Romance* (1827). While the latter was favourably reviewed in the *Examiner*, it was the former that established Carlyle's reputation as promulgator of German literature and attracted the attention of Francis Jeffrey.

Through a letter of introduction by Bryan Waller Procter (Barry Cornwall), Carlyle first met Jeffrey in 1827, a meeting that proved the start of an unlikely friendship between 'the intense, late Romantic' aspiring author and 'the self-conscious pupil of a *laissez-faire* eighteenth-century sociability'.[16] In June and October of the same year, Carlyle published his first two review essays in the *Edinburgh Review*. The first review, of a biography of Jean Paul Richter, led to Carlyle's introduction in *The Kaleidoscope* as 'universally acknowledged to be the first German scholar of which the country can boast', while eliciting a more mixed review by De Quincey, who in the *Edinburgh Saturday Post* admitted that '[t]he critique is . . . frequently able and original in its style of thinking' while charging 'the Reviewer with . . . an imperfect

---

[14] Thomas Carlyle, 'Letter to Robert Mitchell, 18 November 1819', in *The Carlyle Letters Online*, available at DOI 10.1215/lt-18191118-TC-RM-01 (accessed 17 May 2022).

[15] Thomas Carlyle, 'Letter to Thomas Murray, 2 October 1821', in *The Carlyle Letters Online*, available at DOI 10.1215/lt-18211002-TC-TM-01 (accessed 17 May 2022). In 2007 the translation in question was attributed to Coleridge and republished as *Faustus: From the German of Goethe: Translated by Samuel Taylor Coleridge*, ed. Frederick Burwick and James C. McKusick (Oxford and New York: Oxford University Press, 2007). This attribution, however, has been contested, for example by Roger Paulin, William St Clair and Elinor Shaffer in their review essay '"A Gentleman of Literary Eminence": *Faustus, From the German of Goethe, Translated by Samuel Taylor Coleridge*, edited by Frederick Burwick and James C. McKusick' (Institute of English Studies, School of Advanced Study, University of London, 2008), available at https://sas-space.sas.ac.uk/4530/1/stc-faustus-review.pdf (accessed 7 February 2022).

[16] William Christie, *The Edinburgh Review in the Literary Culture of Romantic Britain: Mammoth and Megalonyx* (London: Pickering & Chatto, 2009), p. 178.

acquaintance with John Paul's writings'.[17] Before the end of the decade, Carlyle contributed two additional essays to the *Edinburgh Review*: a review of John Gibson Lockhart's biography of Robert Burns in 1828 and his social commentary 'Signs of the Times' in 1829. After being introduced to William Fraser, again by Procter, Carlyle published eight additional essays in the *Foreign Review*: seven on German literature – on Zacharias Werner, Christian Gottlob Heyne and two on Johann Wolfgang von Goethe in 1828; on Novalis and 'German Playwrights' in 1829; and a second one on Jean Paul Richter in 1830 – and one on Voltaire in 1829.

Carlyle's almost exclusive focus on review essays in the later 1820s begs the question as to why he refrained from using the format of the magazine article. Especially noteworthy in this respect is that Carlyle never contributed to *Blackwood's*, not only because the magazine obviously inspired the formal extravagance of *Sartor Resartus*, but also because its 'German literary offensive' extended from the earliest issues in 1817 well into the late 1820s.[18] In the same month in which Carlyle's first Schiller article appeared in the *London Magazine*, *Blackwood's* reprinted Coleridge's translation of *Wallenstein*, and in 1824 Lockhart favourably reviewed Carlyle's translation of Goethe's *Wilhelm Meister*. Carlyle had been familiar with *Blackwood's* at least since September 1817 and became acquainted with its main editors John Wilson and Lockhart, yet this never led to collaboration of any kind.[19] Part of his reluctance to collaborate with *Blackwood's* was based on moral indignation, as can be glimpsed in a letter of 1823:

> The 'Literary news' of Edinr were of very small account. Blackwood's Magazine is said to be going down; the sale is lessening I hear; and certainly the contents are growing more and more insipid. I hope yet to see it dead: it is

[17] 'Foreign Review', *The Kaleidoscope: Or, Literary and Scientific Mirror*, 8.397 (5 February 1828), 258–9 (p. 258). Thomas De Quincey, *New Essays by De Quincey: His Contributions to the Edinburgh Saturday Post and the Edinburgh Evening Post*, ed. Stuart M. Tave (Princeton, NJ: Princeton University Press, 1966), p. 38.

[18] Diego Saglia, *European Literatures in Britain, 1815–1832: Romantic Translations* (Cambridge: Cambridge University Press, 2019), p. 48. For the congruity between *Sartor Resartus* and *Blackwood's*, see Duncan's suggestion that the former can be read as 'the ultimate *Blackwood's* article' and my analysis of the ways in which *Sartor Resartus* re-enacts scenes of pseudotranslation in *Blackwood's*: 'Pseudotranslation from *Blackwood's* to Carlyle: Dousterswivel, von Lauerwinkel, Teufelsdröckh', in *Authorizing Translation*, ed. Michelle Woods (London and New York: Routledge, 2017), pp. 80–95.

[19] For Carlyle's acquaintance with Wilson, see the *Reminiscences*, pp. 410–26. On the friendship between Carlyle and Lockhart in the 1820s and its cooling after 1830, see Cumming, *The Carlyle Encyclopedia*, pp. 492–4.

a disgrace to the age and country. Talent joined with moral baseness is at all times painful to contemplate.[20]

In a later remark on *Blackwood's*, recorded in a notebook in September 1830, Carlyle expands this moral judgement into a broader criticism of the medium of the literary magazine and its tendency towards playful performance, 'Impudence' and the pursuit of commercial success:

> Last night came a whole bundle of 'Fraser's Magazines' &c.: two little papers by my brother in them, some fables by me; and on the whole such a hurly-burly of rhodomontade, punch, loyalty, and Saturnalian Toryism as eye hath not seen. This out-Blackwoods Blackwood. Nevertheless, the thing has its meaning—a kind of wild popular lower comedy, of which John Wilson is the inventor. It may perhaps (for it seems well adapted to the age) carry down his name to other times, as his most remarkable achievement. All the magazines (except the 'New Monthly') seem to aim at it; a certain quickness, fluency of banter, not excluding sharp insight, and Merry Andrew drollery, and even humour, are available here; however, the grand requisite seems to be impudence, and a fearless committing of yourself to talk in your drink. *Literature* has *nothing* to do with this; but printing has; and printing is now no more the peculiar symbol and livery of literature than writing was in Gutenberg's day.[21]

Carlyle's sharp demarcation of 'literature' from 'printing' and his figuration of the literary magazine as the intoxicated performance of a 'lower comedy' condemns the format as symptomatic of an industrialised periodical culture driven by fast production and the commodification of print.[22]

At the same time, however, his judgement has become more ambivalent than the straightforward moral condemnation earlier in the decade. Carlyle's admission that 'the thing has its meaning' subtly anticipates his eventual decision, made three years later, to publish *Sartor Resartus*

---

[20] Thomas Carlyle, 'Letter to James Johnston, 20 December 1823', in *The Carlyle Letters Online*, available at DOI 10.1215/lt-18231220-TC-JJ-01 (accessed 17 May 2022).

[21] Quoted in James Anthony Froude, *Thomas Carlyle: A History of the First Forty Years of His Life, 1795–1835* (Cambridge: Cambridge University Press, 2011), p. 89. The clown figure of the Merry Andrew, the 'hurlyburly' and the intoxicated crowd return in *Sartor Resartus*, when Teufelsdröck remembers 'the annual Cattle-fair' in Entephul, the town where he grew up: 'Here, assembling from all the four winds, came the elements of an unspeakable hurry-burly. . . Ballad singers brayed, Auctioneers grew hoarse; cheap New Wine (heuriger) flowed like water, still worse confounding the confusion; and high over all, vaulted, in ground-and-lofty tumbling, a particolored Merry Andrew, like the genius of the place and of Life itself' (*Sartor Resartus*, pp. 74–5).

[22] On the performative dynamics of literary magazines in the context of 1820s periodical culture, see Angela Esterhammer, *Print and Performance in the 1820s: Improvisation, Speculation, Identity* (Cambridge: Cambridge University Press, 2020), pp. 28–60.

in *Fraser's Magazine*, the magazine that 'out-Blackwoods Blackwood'. In a letter to John Stuart Mill (1834), Carlyle justified this choice precisely by defending the performative mode of the magazine, something that has 'struck [him] much of late years in considering *Blackwood* and *Fraser*':

> both these are furnished as it were with a kind of theatrical costume, with orchestra and stage-lights, and thereby alone have a wonderful advantage; perhaps almost their only advantage. For nothing was ever truer than this: *Ubi homines sunt modi sunt*; a maxim which grows with me in significance the longer I meditate it; modifying innumerable things in my Philosophy.[23]

When Carlyle subsequently criticises the 'most prosaic' and 'barren' style of the Radicals (referring to the recently founded *Tait's Edinburgh Magazine*) as 'almost more afflicting, only that it is *not* poisonous, than the putrid fermenting mud of *Fraser*', his defence of the Blackwoodian literary magazine bathes in ambivalence, balancing between 'repulsion and admiration', moral indignation and the pragmatic pursuit of effect.[24] This structural ambivalence towards its own form is essential to *Sartor*'s self-consummation and is a constituent part of its repression of the immediate material means of production that are provided by the culture it aims to reform. What has remained unobserved, however, is that this structural ambivalence is a culmination of similar, more subtle, self-critical gestures in Carlyle's review essays. Perhaps the most direct instance occurs in 'Characteristics', published in the *Edinburgh Review* in December 1831:

> Nay, is not the diseased self-conscious state of Literature disclosed in this one fact, which lies so near us here, the prevalence of Reviewing! ... now your Reviewer is a mere *taster*; who tastes, and says, by the evidence of such palate, such tongue, as he has got, It is good, It is bad. ...Far be it from us to disparage our own craft, whereby we have our living! Only we must note these things: that Reviewing spreads with strange vigour; that such a man as Byron reckons the Reviewer and the Poet equal; that at the last Leipzig Fair, there was advertised a Review of Reviews. By and by it will be found that all Literature has become one boundless self-devouring Review; and, as in London routs, we have to do nothing, but only to *see* others do nothing. — Thus does Literature also, like a sick thing, superabundantly 'listen to itself'.[25]

[23] Thomas Carlyle, 'Letter to John Stuart Mill, 20 January 1834', in *The Carlyle Letters Online*, available at DOI 10.1215/lt-18340120-TC-JSM-01 (accessed 17 May 2022); quoted in Parker, *Literary Magazines*, p. 163.

[24] Parker, *Literary Magazines*, p. 163.

[25] Thomas Carlyle, 'Characteristics', in *The Works of Thomas Carlyle*, ed. Henry Duff Traill, 30 vols (Cambridge: Cambridge University Press, 2010), vol. XXVIII, pp. 1–43 (pp. 24–5), doi: 10.1017/CBO9780511697234.001.

Whereas Carlyle's critique of literary magazines staged them as perform-ative spectacles, the periodical reviews are designated as driven by a par-alysing self-consciousness and unbridled proliferation, and as such are symptomatic of an all-pervasive moral and social malaise. Interestingly, this critique of the periodical review forces the essay into a self-reflexive twist, as it explicitly indicates its inevitable complicity in the periodical culture it criticises. This self-reflexive ambivalence that marks Carlyle's writings in the early 1830s is the culmination of an increasingly critical attitude in his essays, not only towards the commodification of literature in periodical culture, but also towards its prevailing critical practice and the generic restrictions imposed by the genre of the review.

Carlyle's earliest reviews, of Baillie and Goethe for the *New Edinburgh Review*, display a strict adherence to generic prescriptions. As the editors of the recent edition of Carlyle's *Essays on Literature* argue, the review of Baillie's *Metrical Legends* remains 'largely descriptive, with extensive summary and quoted extracts' and 'does not stray into a general discus-sion of drama'.[26] This absence of an extensive argument or original voice beyond the description and assessment of the works under review probably explains their exclusion from the *Critical and Miscellaneous Essays*. At the same time, however, both reviews already display some degree of critical reflection on the matter of genre. As Porscha Fermanis has suggested, Carlyle's review of Baillie should be read against the backdrop of 'a new sense of generic competition between history and fiction', a competition that became increasingly prominent in Carlyle's biographical and historiographical writings leading up to the *French Revolution*.[27] Similarly, while Carlyle's review of *Faust* largely consists of descriptive summary and evaluative comments, it also foregrounds the issue of genre. Although '[w]e scarcely know under what class to arrange it' and despite its 'want of unity', Carlyle argues that *Faust* exhibits 'a union of poetic and philosophical powers' that allows it to generate 'a vague emblem of the great vortex of human life'.[28] Both this emphasis on the aesthetic unity of the Goethean literary work and the related critique of the generic boundaries between poetry, philosophy,

---

[26] Thomas Carlyle, *Essays on Literature*, ed. Fleming McClelland, Brent E. Kinser and Chris Ramon Vanden Bossche (Berkeley, Los Angeles and London: University of California Press, 2020), p. xiv.

[27] Porscha Fermanis. 'Countering the Counterfactual: Joanna Baillie's *Metrical Legends of Exalted Characters* (1821) and the Paratexts of History', *Women's Writing*, 19.3 (2012), 333–50 (p. 334).

[28] Thomas Carlyle, 'Faustus: from the German of Goethe. London. Boosey and Sons, 1821, 8vo pp.86', *New Edinburgh Review*, 2.4 (April 1822), 316–34 (pp. 331, 319, 332, 319). Available at http://www.friendsofcoleridge.com/CarlyleFaustusNER.pdf (accessed 7 February 2022).

history and biography will resurface as key elements in Carlyle's critique of contemporaneous criticism.

When Carlyle, after producing his translations of *Wilhelm Meister* and the stories collected in *German Romance*, returns to the practice of reviewing and makes his entry into the *Edinburgh Review*, his relative adherence to the generic requirements of the review makes way for a more intricate critical performance that targets both the critical practice of the periodical in which it appeared and the genre of the review essay as such. This critical shift is most legible in the essays 'The State of German Literature' (1827) and 'Signs of the Times' (1829). Published in October 1827, four months after Carlyle's first contribution to the *Edinburgh Review* on Richter, 'The State of German Literature' reviews two books on the history of German literature by Franz Horn. Commenting on Horn's 'affected style' and 'antithetic jests', the essay quickly abandons the works under review and expresses its intent to introduce 'that strange Literature itself; concerning which our readers probably feel more curious to learn what it is, than with what skill it has been judged of'.[29] Modern critical readers of the essay have indeed considered the essay as primarily an exposition on German literature, rather than as a critique of its contemporaneous reception.[30] Yet, as much as the essay deals with the recent history of German literature and its promise of moral reform, it also critically repositions itself *against* the critical practice of the very medium in which it appears. This is most apparent in the much-overlooked polemical motivation behind the essay. As a close reading of the essay's argument demonstrates, it develops a systematic response to Jeffrey's review of Carlyle's translation of Goethe's *Wilhelm Meister's Apprenticeship*, published in the August 1825 issue of the *Edinburgh Review*. Structurally, Carlyle's essay broadly rehearses Jeffrey's argument as it develops from a cosmopolitan consideration of German literature in the broader context of European culture to a fiery critique of 'the peculiarities of German taste' and Goethe's work as 'conversant only with incomprehensible mystics'.[31] Goethe's *Meister*, Jeffrey argued, is 'eminently absurd, puerile, incongruous, vulgar, and affected' and 'one flagrant offence against every principle of taste, and every just rule of composition'. This 'radical, and apparently irreconcileable [*sic*] disagreement' between English and German principles of taste Jeffrey attributed to

---

[29] Thomas Carlyle, 'The State of German Literature', *The Edinburgh Review*, 46.92 (October 1827), 304–51 (p. 305).

[30] See, for example, Tennyson, *Sartor Called Resartus*, pp. 100–4.

[31] Francis Jeffrey, '*Wilhelm Meister's Apprenticeship*, a Novel', *The Edinburgh Review*, 42.84 (August 1825), 409–49 (p. 415).

the comparative newness of original composition among that ingenious people, and to the state of European literature when they first ventured on the experiment – and in part to the state of society in that great country itself, and the comparatively humble condition of the greater part of those who write, or to whom writing is there addressed.[32]

If Jeffrey thus invokes 'the state of European literature' and 'the state of [German] society' in order to present German literature as both culturally and socially backward, the title of Carlyle's essay already presents itself as a response to this criticism.

While Carlyle never explicitly refers to Jeffrey's review, his implicit references to the latter are legible in the opening remarks of his essay. The observation that 'the commerce in material things has paved roads for things spiritual', for example, rehearses Jeffrey's cosmopolitan view of European literatures. The condemnation of France as 'a nation that ... isolates itself from foreign influence, regards its own modes as so many laws of nature, and rejects all that is different as unworthy even of examination' also echoes Jeffrey's remark that the French 'are far more disposed than any other people ... to circumscribe the rules of Taste to such as they themselves have been able to practise, and to limit the legitimate empire of Genius to the provinces they have explored'.[33] In his subsequent argument, however, Carlyle carefully articulates his disagreement with Jeffrey. Although it cannot be alleged, Carlyle continues, that 'our countrymen have erred much in this point', the English openness towards other European cultures, and to German culture in particular, suffers from a lack of knowledge which is to some extent 'natural', given that 'many readers should draw conclusions from imperfect premises, and by the imports judge too hastily of the stock imported from'. Carlyle's subsequent elaboration on German literary history corrects Jeffrey's claim that the Germans had 'neglected their native literature for two hundred years'.[34] Against Jeffrey's claim that the Germans mainly 'wrote huge Latin treatises on Law and Theology – and put forth bulky editions, and great tomes of annotations on the classics', Carlyle retorts that one should not assume that 'the Germans were idle; or altogether engaged, as we too loosely suppose, in the work of commentary and lexicography', providing Martin Luther and Jakob Böhme as counterexamples and explaining the seventeenth-century downturn as a consequence of the 'horrors of the Thirty Years' War' and the 'French

---

[32] Jeffrey, '*Wilhelm Meister's Apprenticeship*', pp. 414, 415.
[33] Carlyle, 'The State of German Literature', p. 307; Jeffrey, '*Wilhelm Meister's Apprenticeship*', p. 413.
[34] Carlyle, 'The State of German Literature', p. 307; Jeffrey, '*Wilhelm Meister's Apprenticeship*', p. 415.

influence [that] lay like a baleful incubus over the far nobler mind of Germany'.[35] Having established that 'for all profitable purposes of national intercourse, correct knowledge is the first and indispensable preliminary', Carlyle proceeds by countering the two main objections against recent German literature, '*Bad Taste*' and '*Mysticism*' – not coincidentally the key terms structuring Jeffrey's review.[36]

Again, Carlyle implicitly refers to Jeffrey when he states that 'even among men of sense and liberality we have found so much hallucination, so many groundless or half-grounded objections to German literature, that the tone in which a multitude of other men speak of it cannot appear extraordinary'.[37] Jeffrey's first assumption, that Germans 'are still in a rather coarse and uncultivated state of mind', simply results from a lack of knowledge and the reduction of the literary production of Germany to the genre of the Gothic. Imagine, Carlyle asks his reader, 'a German critic that selected his specimens of British literature from the *Castle Spectre*, Mr. Lewis's *Monk*, or the *Mysteries of Udolpho*, and *Frankenstein or the Modern Prometheus*':

> till some author of acknowledged merit shall so write among the Germans, and be approved of by critics of acknowledged merit among them, or at least secure for himself some permanency of favour among the million, we can prove nothing by such instances. That there is so perverse an author, or so blind a critic, in the whole compass of German literature, we have no hesitation in denying.[38]

Carlyle's subsequent affirmation that '[t]wo nations that agree in estimating Shakspeare as the highest of all poets can differ in no essential principle, if they understood one another, that relates to poetry' responds to Jeffrey's rhetorical question 'Can we be wrong, after this, that there are diversities of national taste that can never be reconciled, and scarcely ever accounted for?'.[39] Carlyle then extensively dwells on the 'quiet little theory' that explains the 'bad taste' of German literature by referring to the fact that its authors 'are generally very poor' and 'cannot acquire the polish of drawing-rooms, but must live in mean houses, and therefore write and think in a mean style'.[40] When Carlyle extensively counters this claim by insisting that 'with the culture of a genuine poet, thinker or other artist, the influence of rank has no exclusive or even

---

[35] Jeffrey, '*Wilhelm Meister's Apprenticeship*', p. 415; Carlyle, 'The State of German Literature', pp. 309, 308.

[36] Carlyle, 'The State of German Literature', p. 312.

[37] Ibid. p. 312.

[38] Ibid. p. 313–14.

[39] Ibid. p. 314; Jeffrey, '*Wilhelm Meister's Apprenticeship*', p. 425.

[40] Carlyle, 'The State of German Literature', pp. 314–15.

special concern', he is again directly responding to Jeffrey's claim that 'the writers . . . in that country belong almost entirely to the plebeian and vulgar class'.[41]

If 'The State of German Literature' thus presents itself as an extensive response to Jeffrey's negative assessment of German literature in general and of Goethe's *Wilhelm Meister* in particular, it also engages in a more fundamental critique of the critical principles underlying Jeffrey's reviewing practice. Observing that *Wilhelm Meister* and *Faust* are considered by 'men of deeper views' as 'full of bad taste', Carlyle attributes this misreading to a misdirected and flawed critical praxis:

> We have heard few English criticisms of such works, in which the first condition of an approach to accuracy was complied with;—a transposition of the critic into the author's point of vision, a survey of the author's means and objects as they lay before himself, and a just trial of these by rules of universal application.[42]

Proceeding on the basis of differences in national taste, Jeffrey had professed to 'judge of the work only according to our own principles of judgment and habits of feeling' and to express 'what we, and I really believe most of our countrymen, actually think of this *chef d'oeuvre* of Teutonic genius'.[43] In Jeffrey's view, this radical incompatibility between German and British 'principles of judgment' resulted from the former modelling itself after 'the exaggerated sentiment of Tristram Shandy – the mawkish morality, dawdling details, and interminable agonies of Richardson – the vulgar adventures, and . . . fantastical speculations of John Buncle'. German writers have tended to exaggerate the 'peculiarities' of these British examples and

> to mix up with them a certain allowance of their old visionary philosophy, misty metaphysics, and superstitious visions – and to introduce a few crazy sententious theorists, to sprinkle over the whole a seasoning of rash speculation on morality and the fine arts.[44]

Against Jeffrey's nationalistic juxtaposition, Carlyle posits the necessity of 'literary and intellectual intercourse' and defends the 'new Criticism' that has emerged in Germany by highlighting its 'universal tolerance' and its tendency 'to give due honour' to '[e]very literature in the world'.[45]

---

[41] Carlyle, 'The State of German Literature', p. 316; Jeffrey, '*Wilhelm Meister's Apprenticeship*', p. 418.

[42] Carlyle, 'The State of German Literature', p. 314.

[43] Jeffrey, '*Wilhelm Meister's Apprenticeship*', p. 414.

[44] Ibid. p. 417.

[45] Carlyle, 'The State of German Literature', pp. 310, 325, 326.

Moreover, German criticism distinguishes itself both from the British eighteenth-century emphasis on 'qualities of diction, the coherence of metaphors, the fitness of sentiments, the general logical truth, in a work of art', and from the current British focus ('usual with the best of our own critics at present') on questions 'of a psychological sort, to be answered by discovering and delineating the peculiar nature of the poet from his poetry'. German criticism, Carlyle argues, supersedes both approaches (as 'the *garment*' and the '*body*' of poetry, respectively) by incorporating them into 'a question on the essence and peculiar life of the poetry itself', which involves the '*soul* and spiritual existence, by which alone can the body, in its movements and phases, be *informed* with significance and rational life'.[46] As such, 'the practice or science of Criticism' that has emerged in Germany is 'distinctly, and even considerably in advance' in Europe.[47] Contra Jeffrey, Carlyle adds German criticism as a serious contender to the 'grand controversy . . . so hotly urged between the *Classicists* and the *Romanticists*' and stages it as providing a remedy for the current stagnation of English criticism.

In a key gesture that will condition Carlyle's own intervention as one that occurs in the British critical context, his critique subsequently takes on a decisively formal dimension. The 'vague effort on the part of our best critics everywhere to express some still unexpressed idea concerning the nature of true poetry', Carlyle argues, indicates 'a pure glory, nay, a divineness' of poetry 'for which they had as yet no name and no intellectual form'.[48] The current poor state of British criticism thus comes to bear on the very form of that criticism to the extent that it lacks the language to address properly the 'invisible and immaterial' essence of poetry. In the absence of this form, 'The State of German Literature' formulates as 'the task of Criticism' to 'devise new means of explanation' and 'guide his reader up to the perception' of the 'invisible idea'.[49] It is in this context that Carlyle's extensive excursions into Schiller, Johann Gottlieb Fichte and Immanuel Kant can more fully be understood as part of a critical response to Jeffrey's appeal to the Humean tradition as superior to the 'old visionary philosophy' and 'misty metaphysics' of the Germans. When for the articulation of a new intellectual form Carlyle refers to the Kantian concept of Reason as 'the highest faculty in man' that does not proceed 'by logic and argument' but 'requires a far finer culture for its development', he is doing so not primarily to

[46] Ibid. pp. 323–4.
[47] Ibid. p. 323.
[48] Ibid. p. 325.
[49] Ibid. pp. 324, 340.

deliver a philosophical counterargument, but to articulate an philosophical basis for a new criticism.[50] Carlyle's idiosyncratic version of Kantian 'Reason' not only provides a philosophical basis for Carlyle's emphatic presentation of a German 'science of Criticism' that proceeds 'by rigorous scientific inquiry', but it also recasts Jeffrey's argument on the divergence of taste among European literatures in terms of the varied adherence to Reason and Understanding.[51] The observation that Kantian philosophy, 'in direct contradiction to Locke and all his followers, . . . commences from within, and proceeds outwards' generates an alternative picture of the state of European literature and criticism.[52]

What is especially interesting in Carlyle's articulation of a new critical form is that it ultimately gestures away from the genre of the review to the literary text itself. Carlyle's prime example of the advanced state of German criticism is Goethe's discussion of *Hamlet* in *Wilhelm Meister*, which 'may be called the poetry of criticism'. Criticism, Carlyle argues, 'is in some sort also a creative art; aiming, at least, to reproduce under a different shape the existing product of the poet; painting to the intellect what already lay painted to the heart and the imagination'.[53] Significantly, the choice of this particular fragment is also part of Carlyle's response to Jeffrey, who in his own commentary had praised Goethe's digression on *Hamlet* as 'at once so poetical, so feeling, and so just' and had claimed that '[n]othing as so good as this' can be found 'in any of our own commentators'.[54] In light of Carlyle's re-evaluation of British and German criticism, Jeffrey's comments corroborate Carlyle's point that British critics can to some extent intimate the essence of poetry, but as yet lack the proper intellectual form to articulate it. The fact that Jeffrey's review extensively quotes *Wilhelm Meister* without actually critically engaging with it exemplifies Carlyle's diagnosis of British periodical criticism as inferior and inarticulate. If Jeffrey's review mainly consists of a long list of extensive quotations, it fails to acknowledge that 'it is not in parts, but in whole poems, that the spirit of a true poet is to be seen'.[55] This critical impotence derives from the lack of a proper intellectual form firmly based in philosophical argument. Much as Goethe's criticism occurs in the mode of poetry and is philosophically

---

[50] Ibid. pp. 349, 348. For critical analyses of Carlyle's idiosyncratic use of Kantian terminology, see Charles F. Harrold, *Carlyle and German Thought: 1819–1834* (Hamden, CT and London: Archon Books, 1963) and René Wellek, *Immanuel Kant in England 1793–1838* (Princeton, NJ: Princeton University Press, 1931).

[51] Carlyle, 'The State of German Literature', pp. 323, 324, 327.

[52] Ibid. pp. 345–6.

[53] Ibid. p. 332.

[54] Jeffrey, '*Wilhelm Meister's Apprenticeship*', p. 434.

[55] Carlyle, 'The State of German Literature', p. 334.

grounded, so Jeffrey's review is incapable of engaging in proper criticism because of the lack of such a philosophical ground. By transgressing generic boundaries, Goethe delivers the intellectual form that is projected in Carlyle's self-critical performance of the genre of the periodical review, which ultimately professes its own critical impotence and ends by acknowledging that it 'can . . . only name such men as Tieck, Richter, Herder, Schiller, and, above all, Goethe'.[56] The performative critique of periodical criticism crystallises into the essay's undoing of its own form and its referring away from itself to the literary text that delivers a new critical mode.

A similar performative critique of periodical criticism occurs in 'Signs of the Times', published two years after 'The State of German Literature' in the *Edinburgh Review*. In line with 'the general fashion of Intellect in this era', Carlyle argues, poetry is praised 'not as "true," but as "strong"' and 'our highest praise is that it has "affected" us, has "terrified" us'.[57] Discussions of poetry are based on 'theories of its rise, height, decline and fall' and on '"Theories of Taste"' in which 'the deep, infinite, unspeakable Love of Wisdom and Beauty, which dwells in all men, is "explained," made mechanically visible, from "Association" and the like'.[58] As will be the case in 'Characteristics', this critique of criticism is part of a broader cultural critique of 'the Mechanical Age', which 'with its whole undivided might, forwards, teaches and practices the great art of adapting means to ends'.[59] Yet, in 'Signs of the Times' periodical culture is not just affected by Mechanistic ideology, but emerges as one of the driving forces behind it. When the essay opens with a critique of the propensity of 'vaticination' and the way in which 'fatidical fury' spreads through society with unseen speed by means of 'the noble omnipotence of Sympathy', it is through 'all of periodical or perennial publications [that] the most lugubrious predictions are sent forth'.[60] Periodicals are a constituent part of the diseased social body and to 'discern truly the signs of our own time' Carlyle's essay purports to 'look calmly around us . . . on the perplexed scene where we stand' so that 'some of its distinctive characters, and deeper tendencies, more clearly reveal themselves'.[61] To the extent that this privileged vantage point from which to survey 'the rage of prophecy' is defined by the very

---

[56] Ibid. p. 334.
[57] [Thomas Carlyle], 'ART. VII.-1. Anticipation; Or, an Hundred Years Hence', *The Edinburgh Review*, 49.98 (June 1829), 439–59 (pp. 453, 456).
[58] Ibid. p. 454.
[59] Ibid. p. 442.
[60] Ibid. pp. 439, 440, 441.
[61] Ibid. p. 441.

medium that the essay aspires to criticise, this intellectual position is not simply given and has to be created by the essay against its own inevitable participation in the industrial periodical culture it critiques.[62] Like 'Characteristics', the essay shows an acute awareness of this ambivalent position:

> Mark, too, how every machine must have its moving power, in some of the great currents of society; every little sect among us, Unitarians, Utilitarians, Anabaptists, Phrenologists, must have its Periodical, its monthly or quarterly Magazine;— hanging out, like its windmill, into the *popularis aura*, to grind meal for the society.[63]

'Signs of the Times' performs this ambivalence on different levels. Its title clearly inscribes the essay in the periodical culture of its time: probably referring to Matthew 16:3 ('O ye hypocrites, ye can discern the face of the sky; but can ye not discern the signs of the times?'), it clearly resonates with Hazlitt's essays on 'The Spirit of the Age' (published in the *New Monthly* in 1824 and republished in book form a year later), and with other essays published in 1829 (such as 'The State and Prospects of the Country', 'The Present Times' and 'The Condition of the Empire', appearing earlier in 1829 in the *Quarterly Review*, the *New Monthly* and *Blackwood's*, respectively). However, the essay also critiques this periodical context. In the first place, it quite overtly counters the ideological outline of the *Edinburgh Review*, with its criticism of political economists, Enlightenment philosophers (most notably Locke, Hume and Smith) and of 'the general fashion of Intellect in this era', which has become 'nearly synonymous with Logic, or the mere power of arranging and communicating'.[64] Secondly, 'Signs of the Times' distinguishes itself from contemporaneous socio-political commentary in periodicals because of its 'avoidance of political partisanship'.[65] This avoidance not only contrasts with essays in rival periodicals, but also with those published in the *Edinburgh Review*. Most significantly, the essay contrasts sharply with the opening essay of the same issue, by which it is directly preceded. This opening essay presented an extensive response by Thomas Babington Macaulay to Bentham's reaction to his review of Mill's *Essays on Government* (published in the March issue of the *Edinburgh Review*), and was part of a larger polemical exchange

[62] Ibid. p. 441.
[63] Ibid. p. 443.
[64] Ibid. p. 453.
[65] Wendell V. Harris, 'Interpretive Historicism: "Signs of the Times" and *Culture and Anarchy* in Their Contexts', *Nineteenth-Century Literature*, 44.4 (March 1990), 441–64 (pp. 450–1).

between the *Edinburgh* and the *Westminster*, explicitly staged as one between Whigs and Utilitarians. 'Signs of the Times' dissolves partisanship into principles, as Harris notes, and makes the review-essay 'into that essentially new and especially Victorian genre, the philosophical commentary on culture'.[66] Like 'The State of German Literature', 'Signs of the Times' abandons the reviewing mode, refusing even the most minimal engagement with the three works listed in the heading of the essay's original publication, all published in the same year as the review: the anonymous *Anticipation; or, an Hundred Years Hence*, William Alexander MacKinnon's *On the Rise, Progress, and Present State of Public Opinion* and Edward Irving's *The Last Days: A Discourse on the Evil Character of These Our Times*. Significantly, the heading with the titles of the works allegedly under review was removed in the republication of the essay in the *Critical and Miscellaneous Essays*, erasing the essay's original performative gesture of simultaneously employing and criticising the commodified print culture that fuelled the moral demise of its age.

As Tim Milnes argues, the Romantic essay, as practised by Lamb and Hazlitt, 'exhibit[s] a form of *expressive* liminality' in that it 'offer[s] an image of the self that attempts to blend an inherited discourse of sociability and pragmatic intersubjectivity with aspects of an emerging, albeit untheorized transcendental idealism'.[67] It is the 'profound ambivalence' between the Humean empiricist heritage and an emerging Kantian transcendentalism that 'lends the familiar essays its shape' and forces it to engage in 'the experimental *production* of new intellectual territory'. Milnes's indication that this ambivalence at the heart of the Romantic essay would only dissipate 'once the implications of German idealist aesthetics had finally seeped through nineteenth-century British intellectual culture' allows for a reassessment of Carlyle's essays of the 1820s as critical performances of this transition towards 'a fundamentally Kantian settlement between the self, experience, and the world'.[68] Carlyle's essays mark a definite shift away from the Humean 'empirical performative' based in 'the fictions of social cohesion' towards what can be termed a transcendental performative that gestures towards the recovery of a lost wholeness as an antidote to the moral and social effects of industrialisation. As our close reading of two key essays of the 1820s has demonstrated, this transcendental performative occurred in the form of a complex interaction of Carlyle's essays with their immediate periodical

---

[66] Harris, 'Interpretive Historicism', p. 453.
[67] Milnes, *Testimony of Sense*, p. 19.
[68] Ibid. p. 18.

context, ranging from a sustained critique of the principles of taste and logic underlying periodical criticism to the eventual abandonment of the reviewing mode. The gesture that completes this transition occurs when the essay acknowledges its own impotence and refers outside of itself to the literary text for the recovery of transcendental wholeness. While Carlyle's review essays effect a performative critique of the genre and the periodical culture in which they participate and with which they will ultimately prove incompatible, they anticipate the implosion of the essay form in the final cross-generic performance of the genre in *Sartor Resartus*. The latter will subsequently prepare the ground for Carlyle's turn away from the essay form towards the formats of the book, pamphlet and lecture as vehicles for the prophetic mode of the Victorian Sage. *Sartor* thus marks not only the end of the Romantic period, but also Carlyle's abandonment of the periodical culture of the 1820s and its intellectual forms. At the close of the decade, on 3 November 1829, Carlyle wrote to Goethe, announcing several plans for books ('a separate book on *Luther*', 'a *History of German Literature*') and expressing the desire 'more than ever to be a Writer in a far better sense'. If, as Carlyle laments, he was at that moment 'still but an Essayist', he was announcing a transitional moment, not just in the development of his own career, but in that of a genre.[69]

---

[69] Thomas Carlyle, 'Letter to Goethe, 3 November 1829', in *The Carlyle Letters Online*, available at DOI 10.1215/lt-18291103-TC-G-01 (accessed 17 May 2022).

Index